THE ROYAL DUBLIN SOCIETY, 1815–45

'The Dublin Society [...] an almost unmixed republic.'

Sir William Rowan Hamilton,
writing to William Smith O'Brien,
chairman of the Commons select committee
on the Royal Dublin Society, 20 April 1836.

Maynooth Historical Studies

GENERAL EDITOR, RAYMOND GILLESPIE

Over the last three generations the study of Irish history has been transformed almost out of recognition. The work of scholars such as J.C. Beckett, R. Dudley Edwards, R.B. McDowell, T.W. Moody and D.B. Quinn established scholarly standards within which the study of Irish history could proceed and, with their students, demonstrated in their writing how those standards could be applied. In the main these writings concentrated on the traditional historical themes, dealing with the political and constitutional problems which Ireland encountered in the past. More recently a new generation of scholars have built on these insights but have also looked again at the traditional canon of Irish history. Some have re-examined older problems in the light of fresh evidence or new conceptual models. Others have broadened the range of the debate on the Irish past by insisting on the importance of economic, social, local or cultural factors in shaping the Irish historical experience.

The result of this expansion in historical research has been a dramatic growth in publications dealing with the whole range of Irish history and hence a series of lively debates on the nature of the study of the Irish past. Maynooth Historical Studies is part of that new phenomenon. The series contributes to the debate on the interpretation of the Irish past by presenting the results of new research which either looks again at old problems or casts light into hitherto dark corners of the historical landscape. Both the individual volumes, and the series as a whole, reflect the complexity of understanding the evolution of Irish society and in so doing presents the study of Irish history as the vibrant and challenging discipline that it is.

The Royal Dublin Society
1815–45

KEVIN BRIGHT

FOUR COURTS PRESS

Typeset in 11 pt on 12.5 pt Ehrhardt by
Carrigboy Typesetting Services for
FOUR COURTS PRESS LTD
7 Malpas Street, Dublin 8, Ireland
e-mail: info@four-courts-press.ie
http://www.four-courts-press.ie
and in North America
FOUR COURTS PRESS
c/o ISBS, 920 N.E. 58th Street, Suite 300, Portland, OR 97213.

A catalogue record for this title is available
from the British Library.

ISBN 1-85182-813-3

Printed in Great Britain
by MPG Books, Bodmin, Cornwall.

Contents

Illustrations

CREDITS

CHARTS

TABLES

Abbreviations

For the convenience of author and reader the following abbreviations have been used in the narrative and in the footnotes.

AIS	Agricultural Improvement Society (of Ireland)
BAAS	British Association for the Advancement of Science
CSO	Chief Secretary's Office, Dublin Castle
DDA	Dublin Diocesan Archives
DNB	*Dictionary of national biography*
FTCD	Fellow of Trinity College, Dublin
HC	House of Commons, London
MP	Member of Parliament
NAI	National Archives of Ireland
NLI	National Library of Ireland
RAIS	Royal Agricultural Society of Ireland (after 1841)
RCSI	Royal College of Surgeons, Ireland
RDS	Royal Dublin Society (after 1820)
RDS Proc	annual published proceedings of the Dublin Society and Royal Dublin Society
RHA	Royal Hibernian Academy
RIA	Royal Irish Academy
RN	Royal Navy
TCD	Trinity College, Dublin

Special acknowledgment

I wish to record my special thanks to the Royal Dublin Society, its officers and staff.

My interest in the history of the RDS was sparked thirty years ago when I had the privilege of being frequently in the company of James Meenan and Desmond Clarke, the late editors of the last general history of the society, published in 1981.

My interest deepened when I was appointed Registrar in 1987. In the nature of that office, once described to me by historian R. Dudley Edwards as 'quasi-sacerdotal', I discovered that the RDS inhabited a plane of existence outside the conventional legal and accountancy framework to which my business experience had made me accustomed. Profit was essential for its survival, but accidental to its core activities. Other old philanthropic institutions in Ireland and elsewhere share broad similarities with the RDS, but few others have escaped completely from reliance on the state. The very wide remit given to the society by its founders almost three centuries ago has enabled it to adapt to changing circumstances where more rigorously defined organisations have disappeared or fallen under state control. The RDS remains an independent Irish body where people of widely divergent backgrounds and opinions can work together for the common good, and that is no small thing.

During the 1990s I began to devote a good deal of time to a study of the RDS through its own archives and through other sources. I did so with the active encouragement and support of the council, board, and management of the society. Ten years of work resulted in a doctoral degree through NUI Maynooth and this present book is a modified version of that doctoral thesis submitted in 2003.

When I asked the RDS board for financial help with its publication their reaction was prompt and generous. The fact that the book is professionally produced by an academic publisher, and that it is lavishly illustrated for a work of this kind, is largely due to the generosity of the RDS.

Responsibility for the presentation and accuracy of its contents, and for the opinions expressed, is entirely mine.

Kevin Bright
22 September 2004

Acknowledgments

I wish to acknowledge the assistance given to me in the preparation and publication of this work by NUI Maynooth, the Royal Dublin Society, and Four Courts Press.

The modern history department of NUI Maynooth allowed me to revive a dormant interest in history studies through its MA course in local history and to apply the knowledge gained to the completion of a doctoral degree in 2003. I am particularly grateful to Professor Vincent Comerford, Professor Jacqueline Hill, and Dr Raymond Gillespie for the high standards they set, and for their professional guidance so generously given. Having spent many hours researching in the Russell Library, I also acknowledge the patience and generosity of Penny Woods and her staff.

In expressing my thanks to the Royal Dublin Society I hardly know where to begin. I have enjoyed the rare privilege of free and unrestricted access to the Society's archives. The officers and executives of the Society, named or not, my friends and colleagues, have been supportive in every way. In no particular order, I would like to express a special thanks to Liam Connellan (former president), Michael Jacob (president), Dr Austin Mescal (vice-president), Matt Dempsey (chairman) and the members of the Board of Management for voting a generous RDS grant towards the cost of publication. I would also like to thank Shane Cleary (chief executive 1992–2004), and Eileen Byrne (my successor as registrar in 1999) for their constant support. When my word processor expired with 'blue death' in 2002 Shane's instant offer of help lifted my spirits, as did the expertise and diligence of IT manager Brian Reid. Having spent so much time researching in the RDS library and archive I wish to pay a particular tribute to the help given to me by Mary Kelleher and Gerard Whelan. For help and encouragement given at many points over the years I wish to thank R.C. Lewis-Crosby, Dr F.J. O'Reilly, Professor Dervilla Donnelly, the late Sean Tinney, Colonel Bill Ringrose, Dr Chris Moriarty, the late Dr James White, Denis Purdon, Gerry McAuliffe, Pat Hanly, and Brooke Beales.

I thank also Michael Adams and Martin Fanning of Four Courts Press, and for their help with illustrations Mary McFeely of the National Gallery of Ireland and Joanna Finegan of the National Library of Ireland.

Finally, and for a myriad of reasons, I wish to thank my beloved wife Judy.

Kevin Bright

CHAPTER ONE

Introduction

The Royal Dublin Society is popularly perceived nowadays as a venue for mass-audience events, and as the organizer of a prestigious international horse show. Its long, low, front facade on Merrion Road, in the heart of Dublin's richest inner suburb, gives it an aura of understated gentility. The activities that provide its *raison d'être*, supports for Irish art, science, agriculture and industry, are low-key and often not widely known. There is an air of history about the Ballsbridge premises although, in fact, they have served as the Society's headquarters for the relatively short period of eighty years. The Society, founded in 1731, has sojourned at different times in rooms in Trinity College and in the old Parliament House on College Green, in the original Hawkins House, and in Leinster House for over a century. Now approaching the completion of its third century in existence, it is independent although it was at one time an arm of the state.

The sub-title of this work, 'An almost unmixed republic', is taken from an expression used by Sir William Rowan Hamilton to describe the government of the Royal Dublin Society in 1836.[1] Hamilton's phrase was descriptive of the organization of the RDS at that time; largely an unstructured democracy, controlled by its membership assembled in general meetings. This squat pyramidal form of government was both its strength and its weakness. It had the advantage of transparency in its deliberations, and a broad-based consensus in its decisions. However, its decision-making process was cumbersome and slow, even in routine matters, and the need to obtain a wide consensus encouraged it towards a conservative approach in policy making. Its search for consensus caused it sometimes to be, in the words of Sir Dominic Corrigan, 'a great popular society, and therefore in its very constitution more likely to be led by prejudices than by calm consideration'.[2] Corrigan was giving evidence to a parliamentary committee of inquiry, on the eve of a major constitutional change in the society that would transfer its government from the general meeting to an elected and representative council. His observation was almost certainly prompted by the society's earlier confrontations with the state on issues of control, which took their most dramatic forms during the period 1815–45.

The year 1815 has a wide resonance as the year of Waterloo and the end of the Napoleonic wars. It is one of those years to which contemporaries attached

1 *Report from the select committee on the Royal Dublin Society*, appendix xii, HC, 1836 (445), xli.
2 *Report from the select committee on scientific institutions (Dublin)*, p. 41, HC, 1864 (495).

a 'before' and 'after' significance. This book will argue its importance for the RDS as a decisive point in that body's fortunes. The year was marked for the society by the transfer of its headquarters to Leinster House. It was also memorable for an exceptionally large influx of new members, the beginnings of internal reforms, and of serious financial problems. Likewise, 1845 was another watershed year, for Ireland in general since it marked the commencement of a long and devastating potato famine. For the RDS it marked a temporary end to a long period of dissension with the state. The principal argument of this work is that the relationship between the state and the RDS endangered the latter's independence and threatened it ultimately with extinction, and that in asserting its independence the society brought upon itself a largely unfair imputation of sectarian bigotry. A sub-theme is the significant contribution that the RDS made during this period in the development of national educational and cultural institutions.

The book will examine, *inter alia*, the relationship between the society and the state, the extraordinary scope of the society's activities, and its tentative moves towards ultimate financial independence. Particular attention will be given in chapter five to the subject of politics and religion as they affected the society's membership. The charter of 1750 empowered the Dublin Society to elect new members and to adopt by-laws setting out procedures for such elections. No specific restrictions of creed, politics, or nationality, were set down. As the legal treatment of catholics and dissenters in Ireland relaxed from the 1770s onwards, individual members of those communities began to appear in the membership lists. An example was Thomas Braughall, a Dublin catholic merchant, who was elected in 1777, and held the office of joint honorary secretary of the society in 1792–8, at a time when he was also a prominent member of the Catholic Committee. By contemporary standards, when the confessional state still retained much vitality in Europe, the early nineteenth century RDS could claim to be a relatively non-sectarian and non-political body. It had a modest, but growing, catholic component, and its mainly protestant membership tended towards liberal views. However, its archaic form of government left it vulnerable on occasion to transient political passions. The accusation of sectarian bigotry, leveled against the RDS by some contemporaries, was largely unfair. The book will demonstrate that in many respects the society, by early nineteenth-century standards, was remarkable for its inclusive and neutralist approach in matters of religion and politics.

The national significance of the RDS in the early nineteenth century lay in its almost unique role as a provider of educational services and practical supports, directed specifically towards the needs of Irish industry and agriculture at that time. In the early years following its foundation in 1731 the society's efforts were concentrated largely on practical experiments in agriculture, the disbursement of privately funded incentive premiums, and the development of training schools for architects, surveyors, artists and artisans. Beginning in 1761, the Irish parliament took advantage of the expertise of the society to provide a conduit for state development grants to agriculture and industry.[3] Inevitably state support had a distorting effect on the society's development and a great deal of administrative time was taken up with the premium system. The business of premium distribution tended to dominate the society's affairs in the late eighteenth century. By the time of the dissolution of the Irish parliament in 1800 the society, with parliamentary encouragement, was disengaging from the role of premium dispenser and resuming its earlier role as a research and educational establishment. Its eighteenth-century heritage was represented largely by the drawing schools (founded 1750), a museum of natural history and geology (founded 1792), and the botanic garden at Glasnevin (founded 1795). Between 1795 and 1800 professors of botany, chemistry and mineralogy, and veterinary science, were appointed by the society for the purposes of conducting practical experiments and giving public lectures. In a last great gesture of support the Irish parliament granted £15,000 to the society in 1800 (including £3,000 to conduct county statistical surveys), and secured in the terms of the act of union a general commitment to continue premiums for Irish agriculture and manufactures for twenty years. In the same context the Irish parliament, in 1800, relieved the society of much of its earlier involvement in the development of Irish agriculture, by establishing a separate Farming Society of Ireland to undertake those responsibilities.[4]

By 1815, the society's involvement in agricultural development (a core object of its founders), was reduced to experimentation in the botanic garden. In a bold move, considered foolhardy by some because of the financial commitment it represented, the society in that year transferred its headquarters to Leinster House. The purpose of the move was to consolidate its ongoing activities on a single spacious campus, with room for expansion.[5] What might have been a period of growth instead became a period of struggle for survival. Battered by the exigencies of changing government policy, fiscal and political, the society was yet dependent on the largesse of the United Kingdom parliament and obliged to accept increasing state intervention in its affairs. The thirty-year period 1815–45 saw its fortunes reach a nadir. It suffered a chronic shortage of cash resources, forcing it to drop or curtail many of its development programs. It was drip-fed diminishing annual

---

3 *Proceedings of the Royal Dublin Society*, lvi, 27 Jan. 1820. (Hereafter referred to as *RDS Proc.* The proceedings, essentially the minutes of meetings, were first printed in 1764 and have continued in an unbroken series to the present day. Special appendices, reports, catalogues and membership lists were added during the course of the nineteenth century. The pagination system is complex and discontinuous, with sub-sets for volumes, years, and inserts. In practice references are most easily traced by volume number and meeting date, which gives a consistent chronological order.) 4 *RDS Proc.*, lvi, appendix, 'The report of the committee appointed to inquire into the state of the Dublin Society', 2 Dec. 1819. 5 Leinster House was the headquarters of the RDS from June 1815 to November 1924.

grants by a generally unsympathetic government. It resented its dependence on the state, and most especially the opportunities this gave to successive governments to dictate terms for membership, a function under its constitution that the society had theretofore jealously guarded. The cumulative effect of aid cuts and government interference reached a climax in 1835. A crisis arose in that year when a considerable element of the RDS membership concluded, rightly or wrongly, that Dublin Castle was foisting upon the society a candidacy for membership which was in reality a test of loyalty to the newly installed Whig government. The candidate in question was the catholic archbishop of Dublin, and his rejection (see chapter five) produced charges of sectarianism against the society, and a parliamentary inquiry which recommended that the government of the RDS be transferred to an executive council. Changes were introduced, but failed to satisfy the government, which, on a flimsy pretext, withdrew the society's annual grant in 1841. The grant was restored in 1842, after what amounted to an abject surrender by the society. Capital grants were also made available to the society at that time, and were mostly applied to the building of the central glass house range in the botanic garden. By 1845 the RDS had reached an uneasy accommodation with the government, and had reinforced its credentials as a unique national economic development institution.

During the early years of the nineteenth century the Dublin Society had developed a role in science and art without excessively centralized direction, and as the society itself considered best suited to local Irish conditions.[6] The society had involved itself significantly in applied science, particularly in mineralogy where its initiatives produced the earliest Irish regional geological surveys.[7] At the same time it had extended and reorganized the work of the drawing schools and the botanic garden, and published twenty-one county statistical surveys. Due in part to the generosity of its members, it had developed a museum collection of national importance, the natural history section being particularly strong. It had no major rivals in this work, such local, professional, or specialist societies as existed were, as often as not, its collaborators. The Royal Irish Academy was not a direct rival, and both bodies had a considerable overlap in membership. The same could also be said about the Royal Zoological Society. However, a new rival for the loyalties of agriculturists did appear in 1841, and its relationship with the RDS forms part of the subject matter of chapters six and seven.

General historians of this period have had very little to say about the Royal Dublin Society. The fifth volume of *A new history of Ireland*[8] gives five brief mentions to the society. Cormac Ó Gráda and T.W. Freeman[9] both list the

6 *RDS Proc.*, lvi, report, 2 Dec. 1819.   7 G.L. Herries Davies and R.C. Mollan (eds), *Richard Griffith, 1784–1878* (Dublin, 1980), p. 125. [Hereafter Davies and Mollan, *Richard Griffith*.] 8 W.E. Vaughan (ed.), *A new history of Ireland*, v, *Ireland under the union, 1801–70* (Oxford, 1989). 9 Ibid., the references are on pp. 144, 150, 263, 394–5, 547.

society's county surveys as useful sources for information on the economics and demographics of early nineteenth-century Ireland. The former also mentions the influential role on perceptions of Irish economic potential played by Robert Kane's 1843–4 RDS lectures on Irish industrial resources. R.B. McDowell gives credit to the society for its practical assistance to the Irish bogs commissioners 1809–14.[10] R.V. Comerford pays tribute to the role of the RDS agricultural and industrial exhibitions of the 1830s and 1840s in stimulating the development of the commercial exhibition medium both in Ireland and abroad. Comerford's comments are as close as any of the contributors to *A new history of Ireland* get to an evaluation of RDS activities, 1815–45. In other historical works, D. George Boyce[11] also points to the importance of the RDS county surveys (most of which were published 1801–12) as an important source of information on the Irish rural poor. Roy Foster[12] treats the society as an eighteenth-century expression of the experimental and improving strand in Anglo-Irish culture. He stresses the pragmatic and practical nature of the society's approach to economic problems, and the influence that its schools exerted on the evolution of a distinctive style of Irish architecture and design. He observes that the increasing reliance of the RDS on state subsidies tended to discourage its innovatory instincts.

In broad terms, present-day general histories of Ireland treat the society's record kindly to the extent that they mention it at all. With the exception of R.V. Comerford, the historians referred to above deal with the history of the RDS as being worthy of note primarily for its eighteenth-century achievements. This study is an attempt to explain the difficulties experienced by the society in maintaining, let alone building on, those achievements during the period 1815–45, and asserts that despite these difficulties the society's innovatory tradition was continued. Before 1815 the society could be said to have enjoyed the confidence and experienced the generosity of the state. By 1845 any remaining trust which either party had in the other looked severely attenuated, and the process was already in train whereby the state would absorb the society's national institutions.[13] This book examines what happened during the intervening period, the key issues being the relationship between the RDS and the government, the scope and the changing nature of the society's activities during this period, and the circumstances and consequences of the rejection of Archbishop Murray.

One consequence of the Murray affair has been an apparent tendency for later historians of the society to glissade over the period as a dark zone, best avoided. In fairness it must be pointed out that the historians in question were covering periods of 180–250 years of which the period 1815–45 formed at most a sixth. However, granted the need for compression, there is also an appearance

---

10 49 Geo. III, c. 102 (15 June 1809). 11 D. George Boyce, *Nineteenth-century Ireland: the search for stability* (Dublin, 1990), p. 70. 12 R.F. Foster, *Modern Ireland, 1600–1972* (London, 1988), pp. 184–5, 191, 603. 13 The RDS museum, art school, library, and botanic garden, all passed into state control during 1877–91 under the terms of 40 & 41 Vict., c. 234 (14 Aug. 1877).

of wishing to avoid old controversies. Meenan and Clarke[14] devoted four pages to the administrative history of the society 1815–45, concluding that it had lost its sense of purpose during the post-union period, and had become inward looking as a result of increased public scrutiny and declining income. Berry[15] gave a chronological account of events in the society's general history 1815–36, a chapter relying almost exclusively on the report of the parliamentary committee to cover the period 1836–8, and a very brief chronological narrative dealing with the events of 1839–45. Terence de Vere White[16] gave a more thorough account of the Murray affair and its aftermath, concluding that its origins lay in the political tensions and religious antipathies of the time. These three accounts are generally reliable in their scholarship (de Vere White's account contains some minor chronological inaccuracies). However, they give little specific attention to the parlous state of the society's finances, the development of the museum, and of the exhibitions, and the impact of the British Association for the Advancement of Science (BAAS) conference (discussed in chapter four, below) on the role of science in the RDS. Neither do these accounts place much emphasis on the changing composition of the membership, nor the part played by the society's obsolescent administrative structure in aggravating the growing mistrust between the society and the government. This work is intended to fill in some of these gaps, and to present a more comprehensive assessment of the major events of the period.

A key event was the rejection for membership of Archbishop Murray in November 1835. Widespread condemnations in press and parliament ensued and the government had little option but to conduct a public investigation into the affairs of what was a largely publicly funded body. A parliamentary committee of inquiry, chaired by William Smith O'Brien, MP, interviewed witnesses and presented a report in 1836.[17] The report generally endorsed the work of the RDS and recommended an increase in funding to develop the society's museum and expand its scientific lecture program. However, it criticized the RDS's system of organization and government and recommended the establishment of an executive council to deal with the routine business of the society. The Murray affair, and the recommendations of the O'Brien committee, prompted internal debate in the RDS. The doubtful legality of delegating full executive powers from the general meeting of members to an executive council was seen as a serious obstacle and was not attempted until 1838.[18] The doubters had law on their side – until the society's charter was amended in 1865 ultimate executive authority remained legally with the general meeting. The RDS also showed a

14 James Meenan and Desmond Clarke (eds), *The Royal Dublin Society, 1731–1981* (Dublin, 1981), pp. 30–4.   15 Henry Fitzpatrick Berry, *A history of the Royal Dublin Society* (London, 1915), chapters 15–18.   16 Terence de Vere White, *The story of the Royal Dublin Society* (Tralee, 1955), chapters 9–10, 12–13.   17 *Report from the select committee on the Royal Dublin Society; together with the minutes of evidence and appendix*, H. C., 1836 (445), xli. (Hereafter, *Report on the Royal Dublin Society*, HC, 1836.)   18 *RDS Proc.*, lxxiii–lxxiv, reports of special committee, 3 Nov. 1836, and 2, 16 Nov. 1837.

lack of enthusiasm when the state moved in 1840 to amalgamate the numerous scientific societies in Dublin, under the aegis of the RDS as an umbrella body. Dublin Castle decided that the RDS should split into a scientific section and a separate agricultural section.[19] The society resisted strongly and Lord Morpeth, chief secretary, precipitated a major crisis when he called upon it to discontinue taking newspapers for the members' reading room in line with a recommendation of the parliamentary committee report of 1836.[20] The society's defence of its newspaper room and refusal to abolish it[21] resulted in the withdrawal of the parliamentary grant for 1841. The grant was restored at the end of 1841 following a complete capitulation by the society on the newspaper issue.[22]

There were lessons for both the RDS and the government in the events of this era. For the RDS it had become clear that reliance on state support brought with it a government right to intervene in its internal affairs. The price of independence was at that time too great to contemplate, but the threat posed to the integrity of the society in the early 1840s could not be ignored. By 1844 the RDS was beginning to recover from the poor public image created by the Murray affair nine years earlier, and had found favour with the Young Irelanders even before the waning of O'Connell's influence.[23] The state, as it became more and more directly involved with education in Ireland, experienced growing doubts about the wisdom of committing publicly funded practical science and art education to an uncontrollable private institution. By 1849 it had already effected a partial take-over of the art schools.[24] In this seminal period the RDS was forced to address and re-evaluate its function repeatedly. The deterioration in its relationship with the state adumbrated the gradual acquisition by the latter of the society's educational institutions, which was completed between 1849 and 1891. The period also witnessed a new departure for the RDS as it entered the world of exhibitions; its route to eventual financial independence.[25]

Events in Ireland in the aftermath of the act of union shaped and influenced RDS policies on economic development. The decline of traditional handicraft industries in Dublin, the poor condition of agriculture after 1815, widespread poverty and disease, were all reflected to some degree in the evolving prescriptions of the RDS. Sectarian tensions, and political and social movements, appeared to threaten the society's ability to retain public confidence. For the general history of Ireland during this period I have relied to a great extent on the fifth volume of *A new history of Ireland*, and on recent works by D. George Boyce,[26] K.T.

---

19 *RDS Proc.*, lxxvii, report from the council 17 Dec. 1840, printed in minutes of extraordinary meeting held 14 Jan. 1841.   **20** *RDS Proc.*, lxxvii, 25 Jan. 1841.   **21** Ibid., minutes of extraordinary meeting, 11 Feb. 1841.   **22** Ibid., 18, 25 Nov. 1841.   **23** Ibid., p. 110.   **24** John Turpin, *A school of art in Dublin since the eighteenth century: a history of the National College of Art and Design* (Dublin, 1995), pp. 141–7. (Hereafter Turpin, *A school of art in Dublin*).   **25** Kevin Bright, 'The RDS, the museum act, and the horse show, 1835–1915', unpublished M.A. thesis St Patrick's College Maynooth, (1995), tables 6, 7, 11.   **26** Op. cit.

Hoppen,[27] Gearóid Ó Tuathaigh,[28] and Roy Foster.[29] Since Daniel O'Connell was the dominant Irish political figure of the period I have also made much use of the O'Connell biographies by Fergus O'Ferrall[30] and Oliver MacDonagh.[31] For an understanding of the forces for change operating in the wider context of the British administration at this period, I have relied again on MacDonagh[32] and on Sir Norman Chester's analysis of the nineteenth-century state administration.[33]

Turning to the work of the society itself, most histories of eighteenth-century Ireland make some mention of the Dublin Society, usually as an agent used for economic development by the independent Irish parliament, or as an example of 'Enlightenment' thinking amongst the Anglo-Irish establishment.[34] Much less attention has been given to the RDS in the nineteenth century, perhaps because growing state intervention in the educational system, and declining subsidies to the society, made its semi-private efforts appear modest by comparison. Aspects of the RDS nineteenth century activities have been looked at, although generally not in great depth, in articles by modern scholars on the history of science in Ireland. Richard Jarrell propounded the theory that the society was a victim of a bureaucratic imperialism practiced by the department of science and art,[35] the end result of which was the loss of all its educational establishments in 1877. Only three full-length studies have been published on aspects of the society's early-nineteenth-century programs, and they deal with the art schools,[36] the botanic garden,[37] and Richard Griffith's pioneering work in mineralogy.[38] There are no in-depth studies of what were to become the National Library, the National Museum, and the Natural History Museum, or of the development of public lectures and exhibitions as a means of promoting indigenous commerce, agriculture, and science education.

A recent major study of Irish science history, edited by John Wilson Foster,[39] attempts to make up some of the deficiencies in this area by placing natural history studies in the context of Irish cultural and social history. Many of the articles contained in it acknowledge the role played by the RDS in this field. Patrick Wyse Jackson, James P. O'Connor, and Helena Chesney stress the

27 K.T. Hoppen, *Ireland since 1800: conflict and conformity* (2nd ed., London, 1999).   28 Gearóid Ó Tuathaigh, *Ireland before the famine, 1798-1848* (Dublin, 1990).   29 R.F. Foster, *Modern Ireland, 1600-1972* (London, 1988).   30 Fergus O'Ferrall, *Catholic emancipation: Daniel O'Connell and the birth of Irish democracy, 1820-30* (London, 1985).   31 Oliver MacDonagh, *The emancipist: Daniel O'Connell, 1830-1847* (Dublin, 1989).   32 Oliver MacDonagh, *Early Victorian government, 1830-1870* (London, 1977).   33 Sir Norman Chester, *The English administrative system, 1780-1870* (Oxford, 1981).   34 Foster, *Modern Ireland*, pp. 184-5; Maurice Craig, *Dublin, 1660-1860* (rev. ed., London, 1992), pp. 121-2, and C.D.A. Leighton, *Catholicism in a protestant kingdom: a study of the Irish ancien regime* (Dublin, 1994), pp. 114-15.   35 R.A. Jarrell, 'The department of science and art and control of Irish science, 1853-1905', in *Irish Historical Studies*, xxiii, 1983, pp. 330-47.   36 Turpin, op. cit.   37 E.C. Nelson and E.M. McCracken, *The brightest jewel: a history of the National Botanic Gardens, Glasnevin* (Dublin, 1987).   38 Davies and Mollan, *Richard Griffith*.   39 John Wilson Foster (ed.), *Nature in Ireland: a scientific and cultural history* (Dublin, 1997).

importance of the society's acquisition of the Leskean collection in 1792, which laid a world-class foundation for Irish studies in geology, conchology, and entomology. Chesney[40] remarks that the RDS took an innovative approach to the promotion of science and achieved astonishing success in this area. Its unofficial geological surveys were of a high standard. However, Chesney argues, its spending on science was viewed by the government as out of proportion and out of control, and so it fell victim to eventual bureaucratic take-over. Donal Synnott,[41] in his article on botany in Ireland, pays tribute to the early work of RDS officials in the botanic garden, and of its leading botanist members, especially Dr Thomas Taylor and Dr William Henry Harvey.[42] John Wilson Foster, writing on science and nationality, treats the RDS as embodying a perceived association between science and protestantism in nineteenth-century Ireland.

A comprehensive account of the RDS art schools is provided in John Turpin's *A school of art in Dublin since the eighteenth century*,[43] a history of the origin and development of the National College of Art and Design. Turpin describes the RDS schools as forming part of the general growth in art education that occurred throughout Europe in the eighteenth century. The society's schools were disadvantaged, he concludes, by a cumbersome administration which treated the masters as academic servants, allowed mediocre appointments instead of recruiting the most talented masters, and did not delegate authority. Nevertheless, Turpin notes that the society's focus on commercial art prefigured later British policies on industrial design education. The free tuition approach was commendable in Irish circumstances and had a beneficial impact on Irish architecture, draughtsmanship, and manufacturing industry. He suggests that the society failed to make new political alliances or to adjust to the political realities of post-union Ireland. Consequently it became isolated from developments at Westminster and from emerging nationalist politics at home. Turpin argues that the government followed a covert policy of reducing the society's effectiveness by reducing its grants so that it had no option but to accept centrally imposed change in its educational institutions.

Three general histories of the Royal Dublin Society have been published in the twentieth century. The first was Henry F. Berry's *A history of the Royal Dublin Society* (London, 1915), financed by Edward Guinness, Lord Ardilaun, who was president of the society from 1897 to 1913. Perhaps because of the times and the circumstances in which he wrote, Berry's work is reticent in

40 Helena Chesney, 'Enlightenment and education', in John Wilson Foster (ed.), *Nature in Ireland: a scientific and cultural history* (Dublin, 1997), hereafter Foster, *Nature in Ireland*. 41 Donal Synnott, 'Botany in Ireland', in Foster, *Nature in Ireland*. 42 Thomas Taylor (d.1848), MD, made a significant contribution to the study of Irish mosses. He was a member of the Dublin Society's botany committee, 1814–20. William Henry Harvey (1811–66), an expert on algae, was elected RDS professor of botany in 1848. (Sources: *RDS Proc.*, var. dates; DNB.) 43 John Turpin, *A school of art in Dublin since the eighteenth century: a history of the National College of Art and Design* (Dublin, 1995).

dealing with the events of the 1830s. He gives the barest details of the Archbishop Murray episode in 1835, and relies heavily on the 1836 report of the parliamentary select committee to explain the internal debate going on at that time and subsequently. Berry notes an increase in membership following the revival of the RDS interest in agriculture, but does so without comment. His is a sober, reportorial account of the period, with little or no analysis, and it appears as if he was relieved to move the narrative on to safer issues.

Forty years were to pass before Terence de Vere White published *The story of the Royal Dublin Society* (Tralee, 1955). This is a short, pithy, account that does not attempt to supersede Berry's history, but does add more up-to-date material and analysis on the 1830s. White had the advantage of access to the William Smith O'Brien papers in the National Library of Ireland, which throw additional light on the background activities of the RDS agricultural lobby in pushing for constitutional changes. He also concluded that the Irish administration had decided to seek reforms in the RDS even before the Murray affair provided them with a pretext. De Vere White stressed the argument made by RDS supporter Thomas Davis, that the society's organisational structure, and the scope of its objects, seemed too diffuse to nineteenth-century observers. On the issue of government control, de Vere White viewed this as strikingly exemplified by the reading room crisis of 1840–1 when the government suppressed the taking of newspapers by removing the annual grant. He viewed this incident as part of a government pattern of long-term reforms intended to woo the support of the catholic majority of the Irish population.

As previously mentioned, the most recent general history of the RDS is *The Royal Dublin Society, 1731–1981*, edited by James Meenan and Desmond Clarke, and published in 1981. It consists of a long introduction providing a general history, supplemented by fourteen thematic articles by other contributors. James Meenan, an economic historian, was president of the society 1980–3, and Desmond Clarke was its former librarian, and an historical biographer and short story writer. Meenan and Clarke concluded that the RDS lost its sense of purpose, owing to a lack of leadership, in the 1830s. The Westminster government had no interest in the society, and its post-union parsimony resulted in the RDS turning in on itself and becoming unsure of its role. Government interference in the society's affairs after 1836 was seen, by Meenan and Clarke, as carrying political undertones. Chief Secretary Morpeth's inept attempt to partition the society in 1840 was abandoned when his own commission of inquiry recommended it be given an expanded role.[44] These arguments will be considered more fully below.

At the end of 1799 the Dublin Society had fewer than 300 members. Thirty years later membership had more than doubled, and by 1845 it was over 700.

44 *RDS Proc.*, lxxvii, commissioners' report, 3 June 1841.

Three great influxes occurred in 1800–1, 1815, and 1833–5. They produced a perceptible shift in the social composition of the membership, which will be examined in later chapters. After declining for a decade membership numbers began to increase significantly from 1833. It is reasonable to conclude that the new wave of members was at least partly encouraged by an accession of wealthy landowners such as the marquis of Downshire, and James Naper of Lough Crew. Both men were formerly active in the defunct Farming Society[45] and determined to revive the direct involvement of the RDS in agricultural development.[46] The political and religious tensions seething in Dublin in 1835 affected the RDS, and its studied neutrality on such matters collapsed ignominiously with the Murray affair, and is the subject of chapter five. The intake of members plummeted in 1836–7, and revived in 1838–9, only to fall dramatically again in 1840–2. Following the settlement with government in 1842 applications for membership again rose in 1843–4 and thereafter.

The paid officials of the RDS played a role in the shaping of its activities. With few exceptions the society adhered to a policy of appointing well-qualified candidates to fill new offices and vacancies. All senior officials, from head gardener to assistant secretary, were elected to office in the first instance, and obliged to undergo re-election annually thereafter at the November general meeting. There is no instance during 1800–50 of a senior official being dismissed, although the head gardener at the botanic garden almost achieved this distinction over the loss of a Norfolk Island pine in a severe frost.[47] Canvassing for office, especially in the early nineteenth century, was almost impossible to suppress. Punitive resolutions were passed from time to time forbidding touting for support, but invariably the largest attendance at general meetings occurred whenever a senior post had to be filled.[48] There is little overt evidence of nepotism, except perhaps in the case of Thomas Lysaght, elected 'register' (registrar) and law agent in 1808.[49] Lysaght was a son-in-law of RDS vice-president General Vallancey,[50] and was unable to give adequate time to the offices he held during 1808–19, which suffered as a result.[51] Some father-to-son successions in the art schools also gave rise to allegations of nepotism.[52] Attempts to inject an element of open competition into the selection of new appointees, during the

---

45 The Farming Society of Ireland was established in 1800 under the patronage of the Irish parliament which provided it with an annual grant of £5,000. It coordinated the running of local agricultural shows and itself ran two annual shows at Smithfield, Dublin, and Ballinasloe, Co. Galway. It was dissolved in 1828 on the withdrawal by parliament of its annual grant.   46 *RDS Proc.*, lxvi, marquis of Downshire's letter, 1 Apr. 1830.   47 *RDS Proc.*, lvi, censuring of John Underwood, 4, 11 May 1820.   48 *RDS Proc.*, lxvi, election of assistant secretary, 12 Nov. 1829. The attendance of 312 was over half the total membership.   49 The custodian of the register of members was described as 'the register' 1731–1853.   50 Monica Nevin, 'General Charles Vallancey, 1725–1812', in *Journal of the Royal Society of Antiquaries of Ireland*, cxxiii, 1993. 51 *RDS Proc*, liii, economy committee reports, 28 Nov. 1816, 26 June 1817.   52 Turpin, *A school of art in Dublin*, pp. 90–1.

first half of the nineteenth century, were only partially successful. Probationary periods were imposed on some officials, and the concept of competitive trials for lecturers was established in 1834, at the suggestion of Robert Kane, then a candidate for the post of lecturer in natural philosophy.[53] Positions in the RDS were sought after not only as offering a secure livelihood or a supplementary income, but as a stepping stone along a career path. Engineer Richard Griffith, and scientist Robert Kane, both came to public notice through their work for the RDS and subsequently moved on to distinguished careers in the public service.

The period 1815-45 was seminal in the history of the Royal Dublin Society. For over fifty years the society had acted as an agent of government economic and educational policy and had become accustomed to a high level of dependence on state grants. The beginning of the end of that dependency was signaled in the early 1830s, although it was to take a further fifty years before the process of disengagement would be completed. Comparatively little attention has been given to the process of RDS corporate decision making during this period, although some of its deficiencies have been commented on by de Vere White, and John Turpin. The apparent unity of the membership when faced with government *diktats* conceals the differences in opinions that emerged in their internal debates. The charges of elitism, and of sectarianism, were deeply embarrassing to the society in its relations with the wider community, especially as they were at times not altogether without substance. At this distance in time these issues deserve re-mapping, as earlier accounts tend to gloss over them impressionistically. The details of the Murray affair demonstrate the complexities of members' attitudes, and are worthy of deeper study. The RDS as 'almost unmixed republic' (see page 13), was a long-established Irish institution with its own constitution and rules, and showed a surprising lack of subservience towards government when its interests were challenged. With this in mind, an aim of this study is to bring the RDS membership, and equally the operations of the general meetings into sharper focus. This will facilitate a critical review of the 'absence of leadership' argument advanced by Meenan and Clarke. The society's immediate problem was its over-dependence on state support, and the unwieldy nature of its governing body, with a conservative wing reluctant to change, and a liberal wing anxious for internal reforms and new directions. Events were to prove the liberals more in tune with external realities; reforms and new directions were not as impracticable as the conservatives had supposed.

The underlying research for this study includes an analytical profile of the more than 1,700 members whose contributions helped to shape RDS policies in the first half of the nineteenth-century. Earlier histories tend to focus unduly on the relationship between the society and the government, consigning the

53 *RDS Proc.*, lxx, minutes, 30 Jan. 1834.

members to a minor role as transient players. This is to understate the social nature of the society, which cannot be understood without due regard to the part played in its workings by its individual components. From the second half of the eighteenth-century, lists of RDS members were published annually in Watson Stewart's section of the *Treble Almanack* and are the most accessible sources of such information until the practice was discontinued in 1829. No annual lists were published thereafter until the RDS commenced publishing an in-house list in 1845, and therefore a gap exists in the records for the period 1830–44.[54] To fill in the missing data it was necessary to trawl through sixteen years of board minutes, contained in volumes lxvi–lxxxi of the *Proceedings of the Royal Dublin Society* covering the period 1829–44. This work was supplemented by research in reference sources such as *Burke's peerage, baronetage and landed gentry*, the *Dictionary of national biography*, and family, institutional, and contemporary histories and records. The result is a data base on over 1,700 members, continued up to 31 December 1849 to give a full listing for the first half of the nineteenth century. Much of the information yielded is contained in the text, charts, and appendices to this study.

The RDS published annually, bound sets of the printed minutes of board meetings, containing also reports and appendices, and titled *Proceedings of the Royal Dublin Society*. The volumes li–lxxxii provide the principal primary source material for the period 1815–45. Also bound into the *Proceedings* are the printed minutes of the executive council from 1842. Earlier council minutes are available in a bound manuscript volume in the RDS archives, covering the period 1838 to 1844. Manuscript minute books of the standing committees are also held in the RDS archives, most dating from the reform of the standing committees in 1816. Supplementary manuscript records are sparse, but some rough minute books and miscellaneous documents exist, not at present sorted or calendared. Berry, and Meenan and Clarke, consulted the Proceedings, although rarely giving specific references. Turpin used the Proceedings as a principal primary source for his history of the art school, citing them simply as 'Proceedings'.

Contemporary newspapers are a useful source of background information on perceptions of the RDS during the period, and on events such as the Murray affair and the BAAS conference. The *Freeman's Journal* is especially helpful, as it was largely out of sympathy with the RDS in the 1830s, and remained so until Lord Morpeth's attempt to partition the society in the early 1840s. Because it was generally supportive of O'Connell, and of the Whig administration of 1835–41, the *Freeman's Journal* cannot be accused of undue partiality towards the RDS.

Other archives have provided a small amount of supplementary information. There is some relevant material to be found in the miscellaneous Murray Papers

---

54 A single list in galley proof form survives for 1839. An 1802 list published by the society was printed in *RDS Trans.*, iii, 1802–3.

held in the Dublin Diocesan Archives. Another minor source is the Chief Secretary's Office, registered papers, in the National Archives of Ireland. On the whole, they add little to the detail of the on-going arguments between the government and the society, but are occasionally useful to an understanding of the pressures to which the government was itself subject. The most relevant communications between the RDS, the treasury, and Dublin Castle, were for the most part published in the contemporary *RDS Proceedings*. Useful information and insights into the government of the society, and into the opinions of its more conservative members, can be found in the O'Brien Papers in the National Library, and in the Haliday collection of pamphlets in the Royal Irish Academy. The most comprehensive source of primary research material on the RDS, 1815–45 is the RDS archive housed in the society's headquarters in Ballsbridge, Dublin.

CHAPTER TWO

'The child of the Irish parliament', 1815–28

The Dublin Society at the beginning of 1815 had a membership of about 650. It was in the process of moving its headquarters from a house in Hawkins Street, to the former residence of the dukes of Leinster, in Kildare Street. Used as a channel for the economic development policies of the Irish parliament since 1761, it remained well funded under the terms of the act of union with Britain, being in receipt of an annual grant from Westminster of £10,000. The society was in a position to expand the range of services it offered to the public through its botanic garden, art school, veterinary school, geological service, and science laboratory. Dublin Castle had recently made use of the society's facilities and personnel to compile a major report on Irish bog-lands. However, the closeness, and congruence of purpose, that had developed between the society and the Irish parliament ended with the transfer of government to London. The society could no longer rely on the personal influence of its leading members to obtain the parliamentary support necessary to implement its growth plans. In the United Kingdom context it had become a provincial supplicant for state subsidies, in competition with metropolitan-based institutions such as the British Museum.

In this chapter the impact of the changed relationship between the state and the Dublin Society will be examined.

I

In 1819 the Dublin Society was called upon by the government to give an account of its stewardship of its annual parliamentary grant of £10,000. Why the government should choose this time to scrutinize the society's work can be partly accounted for by the pending expiration in 1820 of its commitment to pay an annual subsidy, and partly because of pressures to reduce exchequer spending.

The United Kingdom of Great Britain and Ireland emerged after 1815 as an unchallenged world maritime power based on the world's greatest industrial base, the world's largest navy, and a growing colonial empire.[1] The role of

---

1 Paul Kennedy, *The rise and fall of British naval mastery* (London, 1976), pp. 149–56.

27

central government was narrowly defined; overseeing defence and internal security, foreign relations, and the raising of taxes. There was little effective demand for government intervention in social and economic affairs, and a predominant *laissez faire* attitude inhibited official initiatives, although reform of public services, and the systematic collection of information on population and natural resources had begun.[2] In Ireland government spending on education, health, and economic development was limited to the support of a score or so of public and semi-private institutions. Amongst the miscellaneous items of government spending was the grant-aiding of the Dublin Society, committed to the care of the united parliament by the late Irish parliament, under the seventh article of the act of union.[3] For the first twenty years of the union the grant to the society was fixed at £10,000 per annum. This arrangement, however, was not guaranteed beyond twenty years and it was arguable beyond that point that any further grants given would be solely at the discretion of parliament. The seventh article did not mention any institution by name and simply stated that premiums for agriculture, manufactures, and other purposes would be continued in Ireland for twenty years.[4] Towards the end of 1819 the government reviewed this expenditure. Following a long period (1793–1815) of almost constant war, the treasury had been exhausted and the national debt had reached £900 million. Interest and charges accounted for a third of government expenditure in 1815 and two-thirds by 1818 (following the abolition of income tax in 1816).[5]

The reduction of government expenditure became an increasingly popular political objective in the aftermath of the Napoleonic wars. As early as 1816 Charles Grey (later Earl Grey) formulated a four point policy for a putative whig government not realized until the 1830s, the first target of which was the curtailment of government spending.[6] The post-war desire to restrain government spending transcended partisan politics. While its driving force was middle-class liberalism in pursuit of the Benthamite principle of utility, and the lifting of restrictions on commerce, all chancellors of the exchequer from the 1820s onwards applied a policy of government thrift and treated demands for new spending as anathema.[7] The treasuries of Great Britain and Ireland were amalgamated in 1817. Centralized treasury control was extended over Irish institutions and an attack was launched on activities deemed wasteful.[8] This tightening of financial control was not aimed exclusively at Ireland. Curtailment of government expenditure, the abolition of sinecures, and standardisation and accountability

2 M.S. Anderson, *The ascendancy of Europe, 1815–1914* (2nd ed., London, 1985), pp. 68–71. 3 *RDS Proc.*, lxxix, draft memorial to treasury, 26 Jan. 1843.   4 *The Irish statutes 1310–1800* (H.M.S.O. 1885; reprinted 1995), 40 Geo. III, c. 38 (July 1800).   5 R.K. Webb, *Modern England: from the eighteenth century to the present* (London, 1980) pp. 157–9. Hereafter, Webb, *Modern England*.   6 Eric J. Evans, *The great reform act of 1832* (2nd ed., London, 1994), p. 37. Grey's program also required the liberalization of foreign policy, catholic relief, and parliamentary reform. 7 Oliver MacDonagh, *Early Victorian government, 1830–1870* (London, 1977), pp. 12–18.   8 Oliver MacDonagh, 'Politics, 1830–45', p. 205, in Vaughan (ed.), *A new history of Ireland*, v.

in receipts and expenditures, were widely endorsed. They led to reviews of every aspect of administration, and to the evolution of the treasury as the principal agency of government for exercising centralized financial control.[9]

The first sign of the application of this philosophy to the affairs of the Dublin Society came in 1819. In that year parliament ordered the Dublin Society, the Linen Board, the Farming Society of Ireland, and other charitable and educational institutions supported out of the public purse to submit accounts of salaries, pensions, and capital spending for the decade 1809–18.[10]

Having complied with this order, the Dublin Society followed up with a public statement of its objects, which it saw as 'essentially connected with the interests and improvement of Ireland'.[11] A special committee of the society was appointed on the same occasion to review and make recommendations on its current programs. Chief Secretary Charles Grant, in a letter dated 23 August 1819, advised that the government intended to inquire into the expenditure of the society's annual grant, and that Lord Lieutenant Talbot wished to have an account of its income and expenditure from the inception of the Irish parliament's grant schemes.[12] It was not until weekly board meetings of the society were resumed in November, after the long summer recess, that Grant's letter received attention. Under its 1750 charter of incorporation the society's governing body was its ordinary membership assembled in general meeting on about thirty occasions during the year. A recess (coinciding broadly with the academic, judicial, and parliamentary break) was customarily taken from late July to early November. During the annual session meetings were held weekly, every Thursday. In the period 1800–38 it was the practice to describe these weekly meetings as board meetings. In response to Dublin Castle's request, a draft report on the state of the society was discussed at the general meeting on 9 December 1819. It was amended by the insertion of a statement on the society's contribution to Irish forestry.[13] A further insertion was proposed, critical of some economic results of the act of union. A perceived disbenefit of union was 'The transfer of so much of the wealth and opulence of this country to Great Britain, [and] the loss of a great portion of her [Ireland's] resident nobility and gentry in consequence of the Union'.[14]

A week later the final report with amendments was adopted by the society. Its signatories were Peter Digges Latouche, Henry Joy, John Boyd,[15] the Reverend John Pomeroy, James Mahon, N.P. Leader and Henry Grattan, junior. The latter two were reform-minded political aspirants, allied to whig interests. Grattan, whose famous father was then still alive, was the leading critic of the dissolution

9 Sir Norman Chester, *The English administrative system, 1780–1870* (Oxford, 1981), pp. 98–105. 10 *RDS Proc.*, lv, minutes, 22 Apr. 1819.   11 Ibid., 15 July 1819.   12 *RDS Proc.*, lvi, minutes, 4 Nov. 1819.   13 Ibid. During 1766–1806 trees planted under the Dublin Society premium scheme amounted to more than fifty-five million.   14 Ibid., 9 Dec. 1819.   15 John Boyd (1769–1836), Ballymacool House, Letterkenny, Co. Donegal, was an honorary secretary of the society, 1817–28, and a vice-president, 1828–36. (Sources: King's Inns admission papers; *RDS Proc.*, var. dates.)

of the Irish parliament. The Reverend Pomeroy was dean of St Patrick's cathedral; P.D. Latouche was a member of the banking family, and Joy, Boyd, and Mahon, were all practicing barristers. Henry Joy had been an opponent of the act of union, but was subsequently a supporter of the government.[16]

The report proper gave an extensive synopsis of the work of the society since its foundation over eighty-eight years previously. Assistance had been given to Irish agriculture by publishing papers and tracts, administering incentive premiums, improving stockbreeding, manufacturing agricultural implements, promoting horticulture and improving meadow grasses.

These functions had largely been transferred to the Farming Society of Ireland on its foundation in 1800. Latterly, the society

> have turned their attention to the means of affording instruction not only in agriculture, but in such useful arts as are accommodated to the peculiar situation of the country, and in some degree to make amends for the injury sustained by the absence from Ireland of individuals whose talents, taste, wealth, and influence would be most likely to cultivate and promote the native genius of their countrymen.[17]

The means adopted to achieve this result were described as lectures and schools, free to the public, and for which the society employed six professors in 1819. In its chemical laboratory, the society undertook soil and mineral analyses, and also supplied a chemical testing service to the Linen Board and to Irish manufacturers. In support of mineralogy, the society had founded a geological museum in 1792. The value of the museum was augmented in a practical way by the appointment of Richard Griffith as mining engineer in 1812. His reports were the basis for the development of coal, copper, and lead mining in south Leinster. They also indicated the pressing need for a trigonometrical survey of Ireland, and the society's ambition was to assist Griffith in the preparation of a geological survey of the country. A further ambition was to establish a mining school, a project started under the aegis of the late Dr Richard Kirwan[18] and placed in abeyance for lack of funds.

The professor of natural philosophy provided lecture courses in physics and its application to practical mechanics and manufacturing. The veterinary professor provided two courses of annual lectures, mainly on the care and treatment of horses. (See appendix VI for a list of paid officials 1815–45). The society boasted that

16 F. Elrington Ball, *The judges in Ireland, 1221–1921*, ii (Dublin, 1926). 17 *RDS Proc.*, lvi, committee report, 16 Dec. 1819. 18 Richard Kirwan (1733–1812), FRS, PRIA, was instrumental in obtaining the Leskean geological collection for the society. He also urged the society in 1802 to lobby the government for the creation of an Irish mining board. (Sources: *RDS Proc.*, var. dates; *DNB*).

there is not any branch of useful domestic knowledge in which so very
rapid and evident a reformation has taken place as in the shoeing of
horses, the system of which, in Dublin, some years since, produced
lameness and misery to hundreds of that most valuable animal, and which,
as now practised, is not inferior to that of any city in Europe.[19]

The botanic garden, occupying twenty-seven acres in Glasnevin, had been
established in 1793–5. Free botanical lecture courses were given in the spring
and summer, directed towards the applications of botany in medicine, manufacturing, and agriculture. During 1818–19 it was reported that 11,943 persons had
visited the garden; 4,979 attended the lectures, and 2,266 had been supplied with
medicinal herbs on request. Six gardening students were regularly under
instruction, and experiments were conducted in horticulture, forestry, and
pharmaceutical plant growing. It was presumed that 'much of the present
excellence of the Medical schools in this city may be attributed to the lectures
and to the facilities afforded at the Botanic garden of the Society'.[20]

The society also ran four schools in the ornamental and applied arts – figure
drawing, landscape, architecture, and sculpture. Instruction was free, and average
attendance at the combined schools was over 200 pupils. The courses were of
particular relevance to architects, sculptors, engravers, glasscutters, porcelain
makers, cabinetmakers, surveyors, and engineers. The fine arts committee super-
vized the schools and could supply details of student numbers and distinguished
alumni.[21]

A library and a museum served as ancillary resources to the professorships.
The library was 'peculiarly rich, and very complete' in botanical and scientific
works, 'and many of them are not to be procured in any other Library in
Ireland'. The museum contained collections in geology, zoology, natural history,
art, and antiquities. The society planned to build an exhibition room extension
that could be used to exhibit works of art.[22]

Attached to the report were accounts for 1818 and a summary of receipts and
payments for the period 1784–1819. Robert Shaw, MP for Dublin, and a vice-
president of the society, was requested to take 300 copies of the report to
England and have them distributed to members of parliament.[23] The report and
attachments, together with a covering letter from Henry Joy and John Boyd,
honorary secretaries, were sent to Chief Secretary Grant on 27 January 1820.
The covering letter contained additional observations and comments that give
an insight into how the society viewed its relationship with the late Irish
parliament. Occasional *ad hoc* grants had been made to the society between 1761
and 1784, the first[24] being a grant of £2,000 in 1761.

19 *RDS Proc.*, lvi, report, 16 Dec. 1819. 20 Ibid. 21 Ibid. 22 Ibid. 23 Ibid., minutes, 20 Jan.
1820. 24 *RDS Proc.*, lxxix, letter to treasury, 9 Feb. 1843.

> At that period it was found necessary to sustain the manufactures and to encourage the trade of Ireland by considerable bounties; and the distribution of those bounties was uniformly confided to the zeal and the judgement of the Dublin Society.[25]

The task being, it was thought, largely accomplished by 1784 the Irish parliament had then encouraged the society to direct its efforts towards practical and scientific education, and had provided annual grants for current operations, and capital grants for new projects in mineralogy, botany, and chemistry.

> At this period the affairs of the Society were principally under the management of the Speaker[26] of the Irish House of Commons, and other distinguished and patriotic members of the Legislature ... the Society was moulded by the very hand of the Legislature into that form which it has hitherto retained.

One of the last acts of the Irish parliament was to vote £15,000 for the purposes of the society, and to make arrangements under the union legislation for the continuance of an annual grant,

> thus evincing, to the latest hour of its existence, its sense of the value of this Society, and committing, with its dying breath, its favourite Institution to the protection of that body, to which it was about to transfer the superintendence of the interests of Ireland ... in disseminating scientific knowledge we are obeying the last commands of the Irish legislature, and following, as it were, the dying injunctions of the parent of the institution.[27]

The language was emotive, and displayed a good deal of institutional angst. The immediate reply from Chief Secretary Grant, dated 27 March 1820, brought no comfort.

> I am directed by His Excellency to acquaint you, that, with every respect for your services, and the importance of the objects to which the zeal and attention of your Institution has been directed, His Excellency regrets to say, that, on a full consideration of the exigencies of the country, he cannot recommend to Parliament a sum exceeding Eight Thousand Pounds British to be voted for the present year.[28]

A separate Irish exchange rate continued in force until 1825 with a conversion ratio of £108 6s. 8d. Irish to £100 British.[29] The grant for 1820–1 would

---

25 *RDS Proc.*, lvi, minutes, 27 Jan. 1820.   26 John Foster (1740–1828), 1st Baron Oriel, was speaker of the Irish house of commons, 1785–1800, and a vice-president of the RDS 1775–1828.   27 *RDS Proc.*, lvi, letter to chief secretary, 27 Jan. 1820.   28 Ibid., minutes, 13 Apr. 1820.   29 L.M. Cullen, *An economic history of Ireland since 1660* (2nd ed., London, 1987), p. 107. Hereafter

therefore have converted to approximately £8,667 Irish compared with £10,000 Irish for the previous year, a drop of thirteen per cent. The residual functions of the viceroy after the act of union included the auditing of the Irish civil establishment. Talbot was an inept administrator, his main interest being in livestock breeding, and the burden of government business fell to Chief Secretary Charles Grant, a complete political opposite.[30] Perhaps misreading the tensions that existed between the conservative Talbot and the reform minded Grant,[31] the society, in May 1820, appointed a small committee to 'induce' Grant to maintain the payment at its former level.[32] Its efforts were ineffectual. The dilemma faced by the society was that fifty-nine years of state patronage had almost completely eroded its financial independence, and the changes consequent upon the act of union had severely diminished its ability to influence government policy on Irish economic development.

George III died in January 1820 and the society invited his successor, George IV, to become its patron. When the king agreed, by letter[33] of 16 June 1820, the society expressed its gratitude by changing its title.

> Resolved unanimously,
> That in consequence of the above gracious communication from his Majesty, this Society do from henceforward assume the title of THE ROYAL DUBLIN SOCIETY.[34]

This decision cannot have been influenced by the as yet unplanned royal visit in August 1821. Nor can it have been prompted, as was implied by Berry,[35] by the novelty of royal patronage. George IV was the third, not the first, of the society's royal patrons, as was made clear in the society's address on the accession of Queen Victoria.[36] The most likely explanation is that the society hoped to secure from this gesture a measure of royal protection in its dealings with the government. The meeting on 29 June was chaired by Lord Frankfort de Montmorency, and twenty-five other members were present, a fairly modest attendance. Amongst those present was Archibald Hamilton Rowan, there to report on negotiations between the society and the Dublin manufacturers on wage rates in the silk trade. What the thoughts of the former United Irishman were can only be matter for speculation. Writing to Sir Charles Morgan[37] after George IV's royal visit he said 'until I saw George the Fourth, I never met a person who in features, contour, and general mien out-did their caricature'. As a means for increasing or even maintaining state support the society's gesture

Cullen, *An economic history of Ireland*.   30 Edward Brynn, *Crown and castle: British rule in Ireland, 1800–1830* (Dublin, 1978), index.   31 Ibid., pp. 52–4.   32 *RDS Proc.*, lvi, minutes, 4 May 1820. 33 Ibid., minutes, 29 June 1820.   34 Ibid.   35 Berry, *A history of the Royal Dublin Society*, p. 241. 36 *RDS Proc.*, lxxiv, minutes, 14 Dec. 1837.   37 Lady Sidney Morgan, *Memoirs*, ii (London, 1862), A.H. Rowan to Sir Charles Morgan, 14 Sept. 1821.

proved valueless.[38] William Gregory,[39] under secretary, wrote to the society on 22 February 1821 to say that Grant could not recommend parliament to pay more than £7,000 British for the 1821–2 session. This converted to £7,600 Irish and represented a drop of twenty-four per cent since 1819.[40] Charles Grant was replaced by Henry Goulburn in December 1821 and the new chief secretary advised the society by letter of 29 January 1822 that there would be no change in the annual grant,[41] which remained at £7,000 British (£7,600 Irish) for the rest of the decade.

The Irish parliament had not been quite as generous to the society during 1784–1800 as the nostalgic rhetoric of that body suggested. However, its payments were comparatively timely, appropriate, and flexible, and its votes for new capital acquisitions such as the museum and the botanic garden were treated separately as one-off items. For most of the fifteen-year period 1784–99 the annual operating grant was £5,335. In the final nineteen months of its existence the Irish parliament positioned the Dublin Society to virtually double its demands on the imperial exchequer, at the same time increasing the society's responsibilities in scientific education and charging it with carrying out a statistical survey of the country. These new duties were offset to some extent by transferring most of the society's agricultural functions to the newly created Farming Society of Ireland. The danger in all this for the society was that ninety per cent of its income was state dependent. The remaining ten per cent depended largely on the erratic flow of members' subscriptions, which will be addressed later in this chapter. A further danger lay in the massive depletion of the society's cash reserves as it embarked on major building programs in its Hawkins Street premises in the late eighteenth century. Without guaranteed state support the society could not carry on its day-to-day operations.

II

Part of the society's financial predicament in 1819 was a result of the high spending in which it had indulged using the guaranteed subsidies negotiated for it by the Irish parliament. The culmination of this spending spree was reached in 1815 with the acquisition of Leinster House. During the eighteen-year period 1801–18 inclusive the society's income averaged £11,111 per annum and its expenditure averaged £11,254. By early 1819 its net cash reserves were depleted to a little over £1,000 and its dependency on state funding remained at about ninety per cent. Receipts from non-government sources averaged £1,100 per annum and consisted mostly of members' annual subscriptions and life

38 A conclusion also reached by Turpin, *A school of art in Dublin*, pp. 76–8.   39 William Gregory (1762–1840), under secretary 1812–30. (Source: Brynn, *Crown and castle*.)   40 *RDS Proc.*, lvii, minutes, 1 Mar. 1821.   41 *RDS Proc.*, lviii, minutes, 31 Jan. 1822.

composition payments. On two occasions, in 1809–10 and in 1815, private receipts exceeded the average by a significant margin. The first was due to the unexpectedly large proceeds from running a series of guest lecture courses given by the prominent scientist Edmund Davy (not to be confused with his cousin of the same name who appears later in the narrative). The second was the result of a major influx of new members following the acquisition of Leinster House as the society's headquarters.

John Claudius Beresford,[42] lord mayor of Dublin, proposed on 3 November 1814 that the society should sell its Hawkins Street premises and use the proceeds to purchase Leinster House as a headquarters.[43] A committee was appointed to consider this proposal, consisting of the lord mayor, the Reverend John Pomeroy, Henry Arabin, John Giffard (who chaired the meeting on 3 November), P. Digges Latouche, Dr William Harty, and N.P. Leader.[44] Beresford reported on 8 December 1814 that the Duke of Leinster was willing to sell for an outright payment of £20,000, or a lease payment of £10,000 plus an annual rent of £600. He recommended the latter arrangement, since the grounds were not essential to the society's purposes and could, he suggested, be set for an amount equal to the annual rent. Dr William Harty wanted the entire business referred to the economy committee for evaluation, but the membership liked Beresford's scheme and voted to proceed with it immediately.[45] An agreement was reached with the duke, by 19 January 1815, for a deposit payment of £5,000. In the course of drawing up deeds it was discovered that the Molesworth family retained residual head rents on the plot of ground running from Leinster House to the house of Archibald Hamilton Rowan at 5 South Leinster Street, and that these rights could be purchased for £1,000. John Campbell, a member present,[46] offered a £1,000 interest-free loan for this purpose, repayable over three years, and this was accepted.[47]

Two architects, Francis Johnston, and James Gandon, junior (not the elder Gandon, as is often supposed), and one builder, Alderman Charles Thorp (or Thorpe),[48] were appointed a committee to advise on the preparation and allocation of rooms in Leinster House.[49] They recommended that the library be

---

42 John Claudius Beresford (1766–1846), third son of revenue commissioner John Beresford, was lord mayor of Dublin 1814–15. A leading orangeman, he was also a member of the Dublin Society from 1800, and an occasional attender at general meetings. During his mayoralty he proposed or seconded eleven candidates for membership of the society, mostly associates in Dublin Corporation. (Sources: *RDS Proc.*, var. dates; K. Haddick-Flynn, *Orangeism: the making of a tradition* (Dublin, 1999).)   43 *RDS Proc.*, li, minutes, 3 Nov. 1814.   44 Ibid., 17 Nov. 1814.   45 Ibid., 8 Dec. 1814. 46 John Campbell, Eccles Street, was elected a member of the Dublin Society in 1807, and deleted from the membership list in 1822. He was a member of the economy committee, 1810–21. (Source: *RDS Proc.*, var. dates.)   47 *RDS Proc.*, li, minutes, 19 Jan. 1815.   48 Charles Thorp, lord mayor of Dublin 1800–1, was a member of the society 1801–19. His firm carried out extensive refurbishment work on the theatre in Hawkins Street in 1814. (Source: *RDS Proc.*, var. dates; *Thom's* Dublin directory, 1952, list of lord mayors.)   49 *RDS Proc.*, li, minutes, 2 Feb. 1815.

housed in the first floor gallery, the museum in six smaller rooms adjoining, and that the ground floor be used for offices and committee rooms, except for the ballroom, which could be converted to an art gallery. No provision was made for re-housing the art schools or the laboratory.[50] On 2 March 1815 Thomas Nowlan[51] presented a draft petition for parliamentary permission to enable the society to sell the Hawkins Street premises. On the same occasion the committee was asked to prepare a plan for the accommodation of all departments, including the laboratory and the art schools, in Leinster House.[52] They reported back on 4 May 1815 that new buildings would be required in Kildare Street to accommodate the laboratory, lecture theatre, art schools and galleries. In the meantime those activities should all remain in Hawkins Street, and negotiations should be entered into with Lord Fitzwilliam for a lease of the lawn from the rere of Leinster House to Merrion Square. At the same meeting James Mahon[53] challenged the legality (under the terms of the charter) of the society's taking lands with a rental value of over £1,000 per annum, as might be the case if the lawn was leased.[54] However strong Mahon's reservations, they were over-ruled at the next meeting, where he found himself in a minority of one.[55] The last board meeting held in the Hawkins Street premises took place on 25 May 1815, and the first in Leinster House on 1 June, chaired by Lord Frankfort[56] and attended by 151 other members.[57] Richard Verschoyle,[58] acting for Lord Fitzwilliam, agreed to negotiate a lease of Leinster lawn to the society.[59] By mid-1816 the society had expended £3,145 on additional building work in Kildare Street, a further £2,745 on repairs and alterations, and £524 on furniture.[60]

Meanwhile, no potential buyer had expressed an interest in purchasing the Hawkins Street premises. The main building was held under a lease from the Hawkins family for a rent of ten guineas per annum. The ancillary buildings and areas were held under a perpetual lease from the Commissioners of Wide Streets, vested in Trinity College, and subject to a rent of £600 per annum.[61] Late in 1816 a proposal was received from W.C. Hogan[62] to purchase the theatre

50 Ibid., 9 Feb. 1815. 51 Thomas Nowlan, attorney, was a member of the library committee, 1813–17. (Source: *RDS Proc.*, var. dates.) 52 *RDS Proc.*, li, minutes, 2 Mar. 1815. 53 James Mahon, barrister, was a member of the library committee, 1815–22. (Source: *RDS Proc.*, var. dates.) 54 *RDS Proc*, li, minutes, 4 May 1815. 55 Ibid., 11 May 1815. 56 Lodge Evans Morris (1747–1822), was a member of the Irish parliament, 1768–1800, and a vice-president of the Dublin Society, 1776–1822. A whig, he switched allegiance to the government on being appointed a treasury commissioner in 1795. He was elevated to the peerage in 1800 as Baron Frankfort, and promoted Viscount Frankfort de Montmorency in 1816. (Source: *RDS Proc*, var. dates; *Burke's Peerage*, and G.C. Bolton, *The passing of the Irish act of union: a study in parliamentary politics* (Oxford, 1966), index.) 57 *RDS Proc.*, li, minutes, 24 May, 1 June 1815. 58 Richard Verschoyle was joint agent with his wife, Barbara Fagan, to the Fitzwilliam estate. He was a member of the Dublin Society, 1801–27. (Sources: *RDS Proc.*, var. dates; *Burke's landed gentry*, var. dates.) 59 *RDS Proc.*, li, minutes, 15 June 1815. 60 *RDS Proc.*, lii, minutes, 30 May 1816. 61 Ibid., house committee report, 23 Nov. 1815. 62 William Caldwell Hogan, attorney, York Street, was elected a member of the society on 6 Apr. 1815. He was a founder of the Hibernian Church

and museum in Hawkins Street for £700 and a yearly rent of £59 10s. 0d.[63] In February 1817 Hogan's offer was rejected.[64] At the same time on-going discussions with the Farming Society about joint use of the Hawkins Street premises for agricultural purposes were deferred for twelve months. Richard Darling[65] proposed that the society's involvement with agriculture should be altogether abandoned.

> that the chartered purposes of this Society, to wit, the promotion of husbandry and other useful arts have, as far as practicable by this Society, been attained; and that henceforward it is expedient, that the views of this Society be directed to the higher branches of science and the cultivation of the Fine Arts.

This move was too precipitate for John Smith Furlong,[66] who successfully opposed such a radical change in policy, and counter-proposed that the society should appoint a professor of agriculture.[67]

More than two years had passed and no progress had been made on the disposal of Hawkins Street or on the passage of a bill through parliament thought necessary to effect the sale. Thomas Lysaght, the society's law agent and registrar, was blamed for the delays; and he in turn blamed Thomas Nowlan who had, Lysaght insinuated, changed his mind on the need for a formal act of parliament. The process for arranging the sale of the Hawkins Street premises had to be re-started, and meanwhile there were no worthwhile offers on the table.[68] Ten months later the sub-committee supervising the sale arrangements concluded that it would not be necessary to obtain an act of parliament.

> We are of opinion, that the power of alienating the property of the Society belongs to that body, as an incident to its corporate capacity, and that an act of Parliament is unnecessary to give validity to such alienation. We also conceive it to be unnecessary to take the opinion of counsel on this subject.[69]

A further year passed, and Thomas Lysaght was dead, when a promising offer was received, this time from the Guild of Merchants, bidding £900 for the laboratory buildings. However, the guild failed to follow through with a firm

---

Missionary Society and a committee member of the Hibernian Bible Society. (Sources: *RDS Proc.*, li; F.E. Bland, *How the Church Missionary Society came to Ireland* (Dublin, 1935).) **63** *RDS Proc.*, lii, minutes, 17 Oct. 1816. **64** *RDS Proc.*, liii, minutes, 13 Feb. 1817. **65** Richard Darling, merchant, Townsend Street, was treasurer of Dublin Chamber of Commerce. He was a member of the Dublin Society, 1807–22, and a member of the economy committee, 1816–20. (Sources: *RDS Proc.*, var. dates; *Treble Almanack*, var. dates.) **66** John Smith Furlong, barrister, Leeson Street, was a member of the society, 1800–46, and a member of the botany and agriculture committee at various times between 1809 and 1820. He sponsored Daniel O'Connell for membership in 1811. (Sources: *RDS Proc.*, var. dates.) **67** *RDS Proc.*, liii, minutes, 27 Feb. 1817. **68** Ibid., 17 July 1817. **69** *RDS Proc.*, liv, minutes, 9 Apr. 1818.

offer and withdrew from negotiations on 22 July 1819. Meanwhile, on 10 June 1819, the Mendicity Institution offered a one-year tenancy of part of the premises for a rent of £300, which the society accepted subject to notice to quit on demand.[70] Such notice was served on 8 August 1820, following an offer received from Henry Harris, the newly appointed patentee of the Theatre Royal, on 4 July. Harris wrote that he could not afford to pay any purchase money for Hawkins Street, taking into account its high ground rent, and the costs of converting the premises into a theatre. However, he was willing to take over the place and so relieve the society of its rent and maintenance burden. The sub-committee agreed to accept Harris' offer. A deed of assignment was prepared and sealed and Harris was given possession of the Hawkins Street premises on 8 August 1820.[71]

However, the society's problems with Hawkins Street were by no means over. Harris refused to pay any share of the legal cost of conveyancing.[72] The Mendicity Institution, removed to Copper Alley, complained that the society had agreed to give it a first refusal on the sale of Hawkins Street, and that they had suffered a loss of public interest on their abrupt removal to less salubrious surroundings.[73] Worse news was to come in June 1821 when the representatives of Thomas Magee and Anthony Mealy demanded payment of £40 arrears of rent, with a further ten years to run. This was for the site of a demolished house in Townsend Street, 'nearly where the present entrance gate to the Theatre is placed'. Harris had not been notified of these ground rents and could not be held liable for payment.[74] Bucknall McCarthy,[75] assistant secretary, and P.T. Wilson,[76] Lysaght's successor as registrar, were in the habit of signing drafts for these payments but had completely overlooked their significance.[77]

Within a few years of the act of union an almost complete transformation of the Dublin social scene had taken place, one of the effects of which was the depression of property values, especially after the end of the Napoleonic wars in 1815. In 1800, before the union, 271 Irish peers, and 300 members of the Irish commons had residences in Dublin. By 1821 those numbers had fallen to forty-seven peers and baronets, and five MPs.[78] The Royal Dublin Society was unlucky in its timing of the sale of Hawkins Street. Most of the its activities had been transferred to Kildare Street by the end of 1817, but the continuing cost of the upkeep of Hawkins Street brought an unexpected expenditure of over

70 RDS Proc., lv, minutes, March-April, and June-July 1819.   71 RDS Proc., lvi, extraordinary meeting, 31 Aug. 1820.   72 RDS Proc., lvii, minutes, 29 Mar. 1821.   73 Ibid., minutes, 17 May 1821.   74 Ibid., 7, 14 June 1821.   75 Bucknall McCarthy (1774–1829), barrister, was assistant secretary to the society 1808–29. (Sources: RDS Proc., var. dates; King's Inns admission papers.) 76 Peter Theodore Wilson (1780–1853), half-pay captain of Royal Marines, was appointed housekeeper to the society on 9 July 1807. Following Lysaght's death, Wilson was elected registrar on 29 Apr. 1819. He died in office on 10 July 1853. (Sources: RDS Proc., var. dates; correspondence with Wilson's great-grand-niece, Mrs Valerie Burn, Cumbria, 1998–2002.)   77 RDS Proc., lvii, minutes, 12 July 1821.   78 Constantia Maxwell, Dublin under the Georges, 1714–1830 (rev. ed., London, 1956), p. 261.

£2,000 during 1818–20. Added to this, there was a continuing liability for ground rent, on premises that had been practically given away.

An analysis (appendix IX) of the society's payments during 1818–21 reveals the financial problems to which it was exposed. Fifty per cent of all spending was on salaries, wages, and associated labour costs. Over thirty per cent of spending, excluding salaries and wages, was related to the running costs of Leinster House, the botanic garden, and the geology program. The protracted ownership of the Hawkins Street premises absorbed a further seven per cent of all spending during the period. This left thirteen per cent, about £1,100 per annum, available for running the art school, library, and museum.

III

How did the society tackle the problem of maintaining its core functions on a reduced income stream? Faced with grant reductions of twenty-four per cent it had little option but to increase its private income or reduce its spending. With hardly any hope of substantially improving its income in the short term, all its efforts were concentrated on achieving cost reductions. Here it came up against the ineluctable fact that almost three-quarters of its spending was of a fixed or semi-fixed nature, being applied to payroll, rents, taxes, and insurance. Waiting for an up-turn in the property market was a luxury that had to be foregone, and getting rid of Hawkins Street assumed an urgency which led to those premises being given away. Even that drastic measure still left a further sixteen per cent or thereabouts in cost reductions to be found. The stark reality was that cost reductions could only be achieved by tight control of discretionary spending in the short-term and by a run-down of services over the longer term. The question as to which services to cut was to occupy the society's attention for the remainder of the decade.

Added to this dilemma was the knowledge that the drawing schools had been re-housed on a temporary, and unsatisfactory basis, in the stable lofts and coach houses of Leinster House since 1818.[79] They were remote from the main building, cold and damp, and inadequately lighted.[80] The running costs of the schools were relatively low, a little over £500 per annum, given that the masters had not had an increase of salary since 1800, but capital investment in the fabric of the schools was a matter of necessity. Plans for new purpose designed buildings, at an estimated cost of £2,000 were prepared by Henry Aaron Baker[81] in 1823.[82] In November 1823 the society decided to proceed with a building program for the school and

---

79 Turpin, *A school of art in Dublin*, p. 121. 80 *RDS Proc.*, lix, report, 12 Dec. 1822. 81 Henry Aaron Baker was appointed to succeed Thomas Ivory as master of the society's architecture school in 1786, and held this post until his death in 1836. (Source: *RDS Proc.*, var. dates.) 82 *RDS Proc.*, lix, minutes, 27 Feb. 1823.

gallery, to be financed from private fund raising, and from a timely legacy of
£1,000.[83] Work commenced[84] in December 1824, construction taking a little over
two years, and H.A. Baker reported that the new school building and exhibition
gallery was completed and ready for occupation in March 1827.[85] This building
was the headquarters of the National College of Art and Design until 1980.[86]
The RDS needed a new gallery as much as it needed a new school, having
acquired casts of the Elgin marbles in 1816–17. The result was that Baker produced a top-lit gallery, the most spacious in Dublin until the opening of the
National Gallery in 1864 and confined the school to the badly lit basement. The
students were allowed use of the gallery for sketching and for their own exhibitions, but instruction continued to take place in poor lighting conditions. A
second major acquisition was obtained for the gallery in 1828, when Colonel
Stannus, former East India Company resident in Iran, donated a collection of
casts from the ruins of Persepolis. All these acquisitions were welcomed since
the RDS approach to training in art and design was rooted in the humanist neo-
classical tradition and stressed the learning value of drawing from the antique
and from live models. This philosophy was eventually to bring it into a doctrinal
conflict with the utilitarian views of the Board of Trade.[87] The issue will be
touched on again in chapter eight.

The botanic garden accounted for about a sixth of the society's annual
spending. Its operations were labour intensive, employing a head gardener, two
under gardeners, a housemaid, twelve labourers, and six apprentices, on a full-time
basis. In addition Dr Walter Wade was retained as professor of botany, and
delivered an annual course of public lectures. In 1820 the botany committee
recommended the discontinuance of the apprenticeship scheme and a reduction of
the number of labourers to ten, to reduce costs. Dr Wade vigorously opposed this
suggestion, and the matter was deferred for the time being.[88] The committee
returned to this subject in 1821, recommending that the grounds staff in the
garden be allowed to reduce by natural wastage from eighteen to twelve, eventually
to consist of four labourers and eight apprentices. Further, they recommended that
the post of head gardener be discontinued after John Underwood's retirement.[89]

Underwood, a Scotsman, had been employed as head gardener since 1798.[90]
He incurred the displeasure of the botany committee when a highly prized
Norfolk Island pine was damaged by an exceptionally severe frost on the night
of 24–25 November 1819. A contract to erect a shelter house around the plant
had been scheduled for completion on 24 September but not actually completed

83 *RDS Proc.*, lx, minutes, 27 Nov. 1823.   84 *RDS Proc.*, lxi, minutes, 18 Nov., 9 Dec. 1824.
85 *RDS Proc.*, lxiii, minutes, 1 Mar. 1827.   86 Turpin, *A school of art in Dublin*, p. 105.   87 Ibid.,
pp. 121–33.   88 *RDS Proc.*, lvi, minutes, 5 May 1820.   89 *RDS Proc.*, lvii, minutes, 11 Jan. 1821.
90 *Report of the select committee on the Royal Dublin Society*, 1836; in evidence Dr William Harty
described Underwood as a 'rough Scotsman', 'fond of a glass of whisky in the morning', but a
competent head gardener.

until 4 December. At the board meeting on 4 May 1820 A.C. Macartney[91] moved to dismiss Underwood, who lived on the Glasnevin premises with his wife and seven young children. A committee was appointed to investigate the incident and their report exonerated Underwood and blamed the building contractor, James Carpenter. Underwood kept his job but was called before the board and severely reprimanded for failing to take steps to protect the plant.[92] The first real opportunity to cut payroll costs in Glasnevin occurred with the death of under gardener John Mackie in May 1821. He had become ill due, it was supposed, to 'the damp and unwholesome situation of his bed-room at the garden' and died leaving a widow and six children. The vacancy was never filled, saving £68 per annum.[93]

For several years the board also resisted payment of ecclesiastical tithes on the garden. Archdeacon Ryan presented a bill for £5 13s. 9d. tithe for 1819 and the board responded by passing a resolution

> That a letter be written to Archdeacon Ryan, informing him that the Society are ignorant upon what foundation he grounds his right to tithe; yet, if he will submit it to the Board, it shall be taken into immediate consideration.

The botany committee reported that there was no tithe-able produce in the garden, and Archdeacon Ryan was so advised.[94] This was somewhat disingenuous, as the same committee had reported in 1813 that several tons of hay was cropped annually and that therefore payment of tithe was reasonable.[95] The following year Archdeacon Ryan's successor wrote requesting a composition payment.[96] The economy committee reported that the only construction they could place on the Reverend J. Smyth's letter was that a meadow of about 1½ acres had been mowed that summer and the produce sold for £8. However, by the narrow margin of one vote, the society agreed to pay a £5 commutation fee to the incumbent of Glasnevin.[97] The issue was raised again in 1824, when Underwood reported that the only tithe-able item raised in the garden was six loads of hay.[98] When the society agreed nevertheless to pay a composition fee John Burne[99] attempted unsuccessfully to have its resolution rescinded, and failing that to have the society's liability for tithe assessed exactly.[100] Burne did not pursue his motion any further[101] but within two years it was again taken up,

91 Arthur Chichester Macartney, K.C., was a member of the society, 1810–27, and a member of the library committee, 1816–27. [Source: RDS Proc., var. dates.]   92 RDS Proc., lvi, minutes, May 1820.   93 RDS Proc., lvii, minutes, 12 April, 31 May 1821.   94 RDS Proc., lvi, minutes, June–July 1820.   95 RDS Proc., xlix, botany committee report, 25 Mar. 1813.   96 RDS Proc., lix, minutes, 26 Nov. 1822.   97 Ibid., 8, 19 Dec. 1822.   98 RDS Proc., lx, minutes, 19 Feb. 1824.   99 John Burne, K.C., Merrion Square, was a member of the society 1815–27. He gathered considerable support within the society to oppose the payment of tithes from the botanic garden, 1822–4. (Source: RDS Proc., var. dates.)   100 RDS Proc., lx, minutes, 4 Mar. 1824.   101 Ibid., 11 Mar. 1824.

this time by John Boyd[102] and the demands of the rector of Glasnevin were once more challenged. However, having set a precedent for payment, the society continued to comply.[103]

Meanwhile the fabric of the early buildings in Glasnevin was wearing badly and there were no funds available for major reconstruction work. The botany committee reported on the dilapidated state of the professor's house and lecture room in 1821,[104] which was exacerbated by storm damage in 1823.[105] These problems, though potentially serious, were not immediately pressing, and the botany committee was more concerned with the delays caused by the society's cumbersome decision-making process, which required the authorization of a general meeting for routine expenditures on painting and glazing. The committee was also concerned at the lack of a discretionary fund for purchasing plants to complete collections, leaving them in a lop-sided dependence on gratuitous donations.[106] During the ensuing year (1823–4) the major donations received included Brazilian seeds from Alderman Matthew West, seeds from Mauritius presented by Sir George Lowry Cole, and from Lord Mountnorris in Calcutta.[107] Lord Oriel, who had a famous arboretum in Collon, Co. Louth, donated 160 varieties of trees and shrubs.[108] Walter Synnot (1773–1851), from Ballickmoyler, Co. Antrim, a captain in the 66th foot regiment, sent a very large collection of new and rare bulbs from the Cape of Good Hope.[109]

Despite procedural and financial difficulties, the botanic garden, in its first quarter century of existence, had established a baseline for Irish botany and its relevance to agriculture, medicine, and decorative planting.[110] Credit for this achievement was due not only to the committee but to the research work carried out by the first professor, Dr Walter Wade, who died in 1825, and to the work of John Underwood, head gardener, and John White, under gardener. Wade's *Catalogus systematicus plantarum indigenarum in Comitatu Dublinensi inventarum*, published in 1794, was the first such work in Ireland arranged under the Linnaean system. During his years with the society he published four major works on Irish flora, rare plants and grasses, and a substantial tome on sallows, willows, and osiers.[111] John White, under gardener, 1800–35, made perhaps an even more significant contribution with his *An essay on the indigenous grasses of Ireland*, published by the Dublin Society in 1808; the first ever attempt to reconcile the Linnaean classification with the colloquial English, and Gaelic, names of grasses.[112]

102 *RDS Proc.*, lxii, minutes, 9 Feb. 1826.   103 *RDS Proc.*, lxiii, economy committee report, 7 Dec. 1826.   104 *RDS Proc.*, lvii, botany committee report, 8 Feb. 1821.   105 *RDS Proc.*, lix, minutes, 3 Apr. 1823.   106 *RDS Proc.*, lx, botany committee report, 11 Mar. 1824.   107 Ibid., 4 Dec. 1823, 18 Mar., 1 Apr. 1824.   108 *RDS Proc.*, lx, minutes, 16 Dec. 1824.   109 John Wilson Foster (ed.), *Nature in Ireland: a scientific and cultural history* (Dublin, 1997), p. 318. Hereafter, Foster, *Nature in Ireland*.   110 Donal Synnott, 'Botany in Ireland', in Foster, *Nature in Ireland*, pp. 169–70.   111 David Cabot, 'Essential texts in Irish natural history', in Foster, *Nature in Ireland*, p. 483.   112 Sean Lysaght, 'Contrasting natures: the issue of names', in Foster, *Nature in Ireland*, p. 450.

The chemistry and mineralogy department absorbed approximately a sixth of the society's annual spending during 1819–21. Two professors, William Higgins[113] and Charles von Giesecke, and the mining engineer Richard Griffith accounted between them for £900 in annual salaries. Of these three, the youngest and most productive was Richard Griffith, although by 1822 he had already completed his best work for the society and was increasingly engaged in road building and other public projects commissioned by the government.[114] Griffith had powerful supporters, such as George Knox,[115] but his long absences from Dublin and delays in producing reports resulted in frequent debates on the merits of retaining him in office.[116] Dr Anthony Meyler[117] moved to terminate Griffith's employment from 1 November 1827.[118] However, by that date Griffith had announced his intention of preparing a comprehensive geological map of Ireland, based on the Ordnance Survey work, and that coupled with his reports on surveys of the north-western counties and of the Leinster coal mines silenced his critics for the time being.[119] He came under renewed attack in 1828[120] and ended that year defending his work and his emoluments.[121]

Ever since his appointment as mining engineer in 1812 Griffith's work for the society had occupied only half his time. His employment as government roads engineer in the southwest meant that for most of the period 1822–8 he resided in Mallow, Co. Cork. He moved back to Dublin and lived at 2 Fitzwilliam Place from 1828 to 1878, but his six-year absence from the capital and the extent of his unfinished work for the society made him vulnerable to attack.[122] The RDS supported his geological mapping project. In order to commence this work Griffith was dependent on the prior completion of an accurate Ordnance Survey base map. In the meantime he was dilatory in producing reports on the Connacht coal district, surveyed 1817–19, and the Ulster and Munster coal districts, the latter of which he never completed. In 1827 the government appointed him first

113 William Higgins, FRS, MRIA, born in Collooney, Co. Sligo, in 1763, was educated at Oxford, and published in 1789 a work on phlogiston theory in which he supported the findings of Lavoisier and refuted the theories of Richard Kirwan. He was appointed professor of chemistry to the Dublin Society in 1795, and held that post until his death in 1825. (Sources: *RDS Proc.*, var. dates; Denis Crowley, 'Chemistry', in Meenan and Clarke, *The Royal Dublin Society, 1731–1981*.) 114 *RDS Proc.*, lviii, minutes, 28 June 1822. 115 George Knox, DCL, FRS, MRIA, was the second son of Viscount Northland. He was a member of the RDS, 1800–27, and a vice-president 1820–7. He had a keen interest in geology and in mining exploration, and used his position as vice-president to support the work of Griffith and of Giesecke. (Source: *RDS Proc.*, var. dates.) 116 *RDS Proc.*, lxii–lxiii, minutes, 22 June 1826, 1 Mar. 1827. 117 Anthony Meyler, MD, was a member of the society 1810–48, and served on the library committee, 1824–8. He studied hypocaustic, or warm air, central heating systems in England, and installed heating systems in Swift's Hospital, 1822–3, and Leinster House, 1824–5. Meyler was also active in promoting free science and public health lectures at the RDS. In 1825 he applied unsuccessfully for the post of RDS professor of chemistry, refusing to supply references, and relying on the testament of his work on the central-heating system. (Source: *RDS Proc.*, var. dates.) 118 *RDS Proc.*, lxiii, minutes, 24 May 1827. 119 *RDS Proc.*, lxiv, minutes, 1, 8 Nov. 1827. 120 Ibid., May 1828. 121 *RDS Proc.*, lxv, minutes, 18 Dec. 1828. 122 Davies and Mollan, *Richard Griffith*, pp. 10–13.

commissioner of the general survey and valuation of rateable property, but he could not commence that task either until the six-inch ordnance survey sheets began to be published in 1829.[123]

The society's professor of mineralogy during the years 1813–33 was the colourful Sir Charles Lewis von Giesecke (real name Karl Ludwig Metzler).[124] Von Giesecke studied mineralogy at Gottingen and was commissioned by the Danish court in 1806 to undertake a geological expedition to Greenland. Marooned in 1807 by the naval war between the United Kingdom and France, he learned survival skills from the Inuit people and eventually reached Scotland, destitute, in 1813. His Greenland journal (frequently republished in Denmark), contained a unique record of Inuit place names.[125] In Edinburgh he met John Leslie Foster[126] who encouraged him to apply for the vacant professorship in the Dublin Society and he was elected to that post on 2 December 1813. His most remarkable contribution to the society's geological resource was the gift of his Greenland collection in 1816. The following year, with the permission of the board, he departed on a tour of Europe which took him through Denmark, Germany, Austria and Italy, returning to Dublin in July 1819 with cases of geological specimens, a Danish knighthood, and an exchange arrangement with the Viennese museum. Thereafter he spent his time arranging the RDS geological collections, lecturing, and carrying out regional surveys as directed by the society. His fieldwork bore little comparison in its utility with the earlier work of Griffith, until, in 1826, he was asked to add Irish ornithology and entomology to his specimen collecting. Von Giesecke rapidly laid the foundation for a museum collection of Irish land and water birds, and greatly augmented the Irish insect collection.

During these years the society provided a forum for discussion, debate, and study of Irish mineralogy and geology.[127] Richard Griffith was credited with surveying fifteen per cent of the total of Irish bogland (including the Bog of Allen, between 1809 and 1813).[128] The society was responsible for creating the first Irish entomology collection, catalogued at 2,500 insect species in 1813, expanded to 11,000 species by 1820, and further augmented by Von Giesecke from 1826.[129] The society also provided free chemical analyses to Irish industry and agriculture for example, testing a glaze-detecting fluid for the Linen Board,

123 Ibid., pp. 130–7.   124 White, *The story of the Royal Dublin Society*, pp. 85–91; obituary, *Dublin University Magazine*, v, 1835.   125 G.F. Mitchell, 'Mineralogy and geology', in Meenan and Clarke, *The Royal Dublin Society, 1731–1981*, p. 161.   126 John Leslie Foster (1781–1842), BA, BL, LLD, MRIA, FRS, was the eldest son of the bishop of Clogher, and a nephew and namesake of Baron Oriel. Foster was a vice-president of the RDS, 1813–42. He was an MP for Co. Louth in the protestant conservative interest 1824–30. (Sources: *RDS Proc.*, var. dates; Ball, *Judges in Ireland*, and Walker, *Parliamentary elections*.)   127 Patrick Wyse Jackson, 'Fluctuations in fortune: three hundred years of Irish geology', in Foster, *Nature in Ireland*, p. 94.   128 Peter Foss and Catherine O'Connell, 'Bogland: study and utilization', in Foster, *Nature in Ireland*, p. 118.   129 James P. O'Connor, 'Insects and entomology', in Foster, *Nature in Ireland*, p. 224.

and a coffee substitute manufactured by George Dawson, in 1823.[130] Samuel Wharmby, appointed assistant to William Higgins in 1805, carried out many of the routine testing procedures. Paid an annual salary of £40 he sought an increase to £100 in 1812 which was endorsed by the chemistry committee but opposed by the economy committee on the grounds that it would upset existing salary relativities.[131] To overcome this problem he was paid a 'gratuity' of £60 voted each year from 1813 onwards.[132] Wharmby fell a victim to the policy of retrenchment pursued from 1821 and almost lost his gratuity in 1823.[133] He died shortly afterwards[134] and the gratuity problem was overcome for his successor, Edward B. Stephens, by paying him a 'consolidated' salary of £100 per annum.[135]

Geology, then known as mineralogy, was a new science at the end of the eighteenth century, and the society's systematic involvement in Irish geology began with the appointment of an itinerant mineralogist, Donald Stewart,[136] in 1786. This interest was given an added fillip when Dr Richard Kirwan acquired the Leskean geological collection for the society in 1792 at a cost of £1,350. Nathaniel Gottfried Leske (died 1787) was professor of natural history at Marburg. A pupil of A.G. Werner's, he built up a collection of minerals classified on Wernerian principles, that is, based on their external forms.[137] In the 1790s and early 1800s the society believed that the location of mineral resources, especially coal in workable quantities, would stimulate an industrial revolution in Ireland comparable to that which had been taking place in Britain from the 1760s.[138] In pursuit of this goal Richard Griffith was commissioned to survey the Leinster coal fields in 1809, the first such geological survey undertaken in Ireland.[139] His success in identifying commercial coal seams encouraged a degree of expectations about Irish mineral prospects that were overly optimistic.

Up to the 1790s the society had little formal connection with contemporary science.[140] However, by the early nineteenth century it was poised to enter the emerging system of adult science education, prompted by the requirements of manufacturers and artisans.[141] In 1824 the society appointed a committee to consider how its lecture courses could be made more useful to a working class audience. Dr Anthony Meyler presented the report, recommending that evening lectures be provided for artisans on natural science, chemistry and physics. The committees of natural philosophy, chemistry, and fine arts, were empowered jointly to make arrangements and prepare a syllabus for circulation to tradesmen and manufacturers.[142] As the lecture courses got under way the society decided

130 *RDS Proc.*, lix, minutes, March–May 1823.   131 *RDS Proc.*, xlviii, minutes, 9 Apr., 11 June 1812.   132 *RDS Proc.*, xlix, minutes, 15 July 1813.   133 *RDS Proc.*, lix, minutes, 26 June, 3 July 1823.   134 *RDS Proc.*, lx, minutes, 15 Jan. 1824.   135 Ibid., 22 Jan., 22 June 1824.   136 Stewart was employed on field work until his death in 1811. (Source: *RDS Proc.*, var. dates.)   137 G.F. Mitchell, 'Mineralogy and geology', in Meenan and Clarke, *The Royal Dublin Society, 1731–1981*, p. 159.   138 Davies and Mollan, *Richard Griffith*, p. 123.   139 Ibid., p. 5.   140 Denis Crowley, 'Chemistry', in Meenan and Clarke, *The Royal Dublin Society, 1731–1981*, p. 167.   141 Ibid., G. F. Mitchell, 'Mineralogy and geology', p. 160.   142 *RDS Proc.*, lx, minutes, 15 Jan., 18, 25 Mar. 1824.

to enhance their scope by inviting guest lecturers on specialist topics, the first
being the Reverend Dionysius Lardner, FTCD, who lectured on steam engines
in 1826 and 1827.[143] Further refinements were adopted in 1828, including
holding the lectures at a slightly later time to facilitate artisans, and pasting up
handbills around the city instead of advertising in the newspapers.[144]

Paralleling the movement towards popular science lectures at this period, the
RDS was also evolving its museum towards becoming a comprehensive national
museum. As with the botanic garden, the museum suffered from the lack of an
acquisitions fund and compensated in the same way by accepting gifts from
members and from the general public. The resumption of world trade after
1815, the growth of commerce and of the British empire, expanded the scope of
the RDS museum to global proportions in natural history, geology, antiquities
and ethnography. During 1820–6 private donations of artefacts and specimens
from the Indian sub-continent, North America, Africa, Australasia and the far
east were received. Von Giesecke reported the donation of an Egyptian mummy,
in good state of preservation, the gift of Sir Frederick Henniker in 1824.[145] The
first of several tattooed Maori heads was received in 1826.[146]

A poignant acquisition was the West African collection of Surgeon O'Beirne,
received in 1825. Bryan O'Beirne, surgeon with the 2nd West India regiment,
had been stationed for several years in Sierra Leone, and had taken part in anti-
slavery expeditions to inland areas. His brother wrote

> His mission to Teembo not only wonderfully encreased [*sic*] the gold and
> ivory trade, but, by giving employment, and augmenting the intercourse
> between the Foulah kingdom and the Colony, destroyed the trade in slaves to
> the coast. His exertions in the cause of his country and of humanity, and the
> fatigue he underwent in the last battle against the Ashantees, destroyed his
> health; – he died in London, on the 6th instant. [6 Dec. 1824][147]

O'Beirne also made tentative explorations of the Niger region. His collection of
forty-six items included specimens of regional fauna, and tools and ornaments
of the Mandinka and Bambara peoples.[148]

Perhaps the most important museum acquisition of the 1820s was a full skeleton of *megaloceros giganteus*, the extinct giant Irish deer. Archdeacon William
Maunsell of Limerick invited the society to select remains from a large burial pit
discovered on his lands in 1824.[149] Surgeon John Hart[150] agreed to make the trip

143 *RDS Proc.*, lxii–lxiii, minutes, 6 Apr. 1826, 5 Apr. 1827.   144 *RDS Proc.*, lxiv, report, 28 Feb. 1828.
145 *RDS Proc.*, lx, natural philosophy committee report, 19 Feb. 1824.   146 *RDS Proc.*, lxii, minutes,
16 Mar. 1826. (In 1988 the RDS council formally resolved that all Maori remains acquired by the
National Museum while under the society's control should be transferred to the Maori shrine in
Wellington, New Zealand.)   147 *RDS Proc.*, lxi, minutes, 20 Jan. 1825.   148 Ibid., 14 July 1825, from
a catalogue prepared at Fort Thornton, Sierra Leone, 11 Mar. 1824.   149 *RDS Proc.*, lx, minutes,
22 Apr., 3 June 1824.   150 John Hart (c.1797–1872), MD, FRCSI, studied under Cuvier in Paris.

to Limerick and returned by canal boat with an almost complete set of fossil bones, in April 1825.[151] J.R. Corballis[152] reported in June that the apartments allocated to the museum were inadequate to the task of providing an appropriate setting for the burgeoning collection. The committee was unable to find a suitable location to display the Etruscan vase collection bequeathed by George La Touche in 1824. 'Nor is it in this instance alone that your Committee have been, from the same cause, embarrassed ... the Fossil Elk, for example, has been left since its construction in a situation totally unsuited to Its size and magnificence'.[153] Such complaints were to echo on down to the late twentieth century. Despite pressures of space the society continued to accept donations for the museum and used field trips to fill in gaps in the Irish natural history collection.[154]

In most aspects of its core activities the reduction in the annual grant forced the society to apply a policy of economy and contraction. When Thomas Peall died in 1825 the veterinary professorship was allowed to lapse. Peall had given up a veterinary practice in Bristol to take up the post of veterinary lecturer to the society on 1 December 1800. In 1807 he was appointed a veterinary surgeon in the royal artillery but continued to give an annual course of public lectures for the society.[155] His absence on army duties led to a winding-down of the society's veterinary service and in 1810 Peall's allowances were withdrawn and his assistant, George Watts, was discharged.[156] As the Napoleonic wars drew to a close Peall resumed his duties as veterinary professor and asked the society to support his application for a veterinary post on the Irish establishment, to supplement his income. When this was not forthcoming he asked for, and was given, direct salary increases, wistfully pleading that he had 'every reason to think the Society's recommendation would have procured him promotion, but for the result of the battle of Waterloo'.[157] Peall's lecture courses were developed to cover farm animal dietetics and diseases, and stable management.[158] At the time of his death there were only four veterinarians practicing in Dublin, one of them being Peall's former assistant George Watts.[159] By not replacing Peall the society could effect savings of £260 per annum, and that was the path it reluctantly chose despite affirmations of support in principle for a continuance of the veterinary service.[160]

Elected a member of the RDS in 1825, he use his anatomical skills to reconstruct a skeleton of *megaloceros giganteus*, and published a monograph on his work. (Sources: *RDS Proc.*, var. dates; Foster, *Nature in Ireland*.) **151** *RDS Proc.*, lxi, minutes, 14, 28 Apr. 1825. **152** John Richard Corballis (1796–1879), LLD, QC, JP, and Papal knight, of Rosemount, Roebuck, was a prominent Dublin catholic barrister. He was a member of the RDS 1821–79, and served on the natural philosophy committee, 1822–8. (Sources: *RDS Proc.*, var. dates; Burke, *Irish family records*.) **153** *RDS Proc.*, lxi, natural philosophy committee report, 2 June 1825. **154** *RDS Proc.*, lxii, minutes, 29 June 1826. **155** *RDS Proc.*, xliii, minutes, 9 Apr. 1807. **156** *RDS Proc.*, xlvi, economy committee report, 15 Feb. 1810. **157** *RDS Proc.*, liv, memorial of Thomas Peall, 11 June 1818. **158** *RDS Proc.*, lx, minutes, 1 Apr. 1824. **159** *RDS Proc.*, lxi, minutes, 14 July 1825. See also Hugh Leonard, 'A reflection on the Irish horse', in RDS horse show programme (2000). George Watts (1772–1859), became a horse breeder of international repute. **160** Ibid., minutes, February, and May–June, 1826.

In early 1817 the society held discussions with the Farming Society of Ireland on the potential use of the Hawkins Street premises for joint agricultural purposes. These discussions were at first deferred in 1818, and then discontinued. Richard Darling (see p. 37) put forward a motion in effect stating that the society had no further function in agricultural development. This attempt at the dumping of a cherished object was opposed to the extent of passing (by a narrow margin) a meaningless counter resolution to appoint a professor of agriculture provided no additional expense was thereby incurred. The episode demonstrated the extent to which the society had distanced itself from a direct involvement in practical agriculture after 1800. After 1816, when the separate agriculture committee was discontinued, occasional agricultural topics were dealt with by ad hoc committees, or by a section of the botany committee. Darling's motion was pragmatically grounded and the society's interest in agriculture remained peripheral throughout the 1820s. Attempts to find a food substitute for the potato in laboratory trials,[161] and to raise funds for famine relief in 1822, proved ineffectual. A scheme to promote hemp cultivation[162] to create employment on and off-farm, and to provide an import substitute for ships netting and cordage, was examined but found economically unattractive. Edward Houghton[163] reported that a better return could be obtained by improving tillage methods, or growing timber, and he was censured for a slightly subversive comment on the tithe laws.[164]

During 1823–4 the society championed the Reverend William Hickey's agricultural school in Bannow, Co. Wexford, and tried to enlist government support for similar projects nationwide.[165] John Classon, a merchant with interests in Smithfield market, revived the subject of agricultural schools in 1827, but no funds were available to pursue his idea of establishing a model farm school in Co. Dublin.[166] At a meeting chaired by Sir Robert Shaw in 1828 a resolution was passed requesting the botany committee 'to report on the expediency of establishing a Professorship of Practical Agriculture, and on the means of rendering the Botanic Garden subservient to this purpose, as well as to the advancement of vegetable physiology'.[167] This may have been little more than a gesture, prompted by the winding up of the Farming Society of Ireland, but it did put down a marker for a future return to agricultural development. Reduced to a peripheral role in agriculture by the establishment of the Farming Society in 1800, the RDS provided occasional support to agriculture-related businesses such as the merino wool factory in Stoneyford, Co. Kilkenny. When the Farming Society collapsed in 1828 its government grant of £5,000 per annum was not transferred to the RDS, leaving that body in no position to step

---

161 RDS Proc., lviii, reports on potato starch, May 1822.   162 Ibid., appendix, 20 June 1822.
163 Edward Houghton, barrister, was a member of the society, 1801–33. He served on the botany committee, 1806–28. [Sources: RDS Proc., Treble Almanack, var. dates.]   164 RDS Proc., lviii, reports and minutes, June-July 1822.   165 RDS Proc., lx, memorial to lord lieutenant, 1 Apr. 1824.

into the breach.[168] R.A. Jarrell has suggested that the strength of RDS commitment to early nineteenth-century agriculture rested on its faith in the efficacy of eighteenth-century science. Under resourced and overly optimistic, its efforts to improve Irish agriculture by scientific means at this period were largely a failure.[169]

Also a failure, if not for the same reasons, were the society's attempts to stimulate the flagging fortunes of Irish cottage industries in the 1820s. Constantia Maxwell[170] accused the RDS of increasing the economic difficulties of the Dublin cloth trade by linking weavers wage rates directly to London rates set under the Spitalfields act of 1780. In fact, the society used Coventry rates, not London rates, as the benchmark for setting Dublin rates in 1816–17.[171] Even earlier, the society had impressed on the silk winders the necessity to keep wage rates within 'reasonable bounds' in order to avoid 'inviting foreign competition'.[172]

Aided by a parliamentary grant of £3,200, the society had opened a silk warehouse in Parliament Street in 1765. Its object was to provide a central wholesale, retail and promotional outlet for the weavers and manufacturers of the Dublin Liberties and it operated under the direct management of the society 1765–86, after which it was supervised by a committee of the manufacturers. The manufacturers used the warehouse to cut out the mercer and draper interest in the silk trade. These wholesaler middlemen responded by importing cheaper foreign products to supply their own outlets. In 1780 the Irish parliament passed an act appointing the Dublin Society as regulator of silk weavers wages and piecework rates in the Dublin area.[173] The society's interventions in the labour market in 1796, 1808, 1813, and 1817–18 seems mainly to have been prompted by petitions from the operatives against what were seen as oppressive practices by the manufacturers. An example occurred in 1820 when the manufacturers devised a scheme to create a new class of apprentices who, contrary to custom, were not provided with bed and board. To counteract this, the RDS ordered that apprentices engaged under this scheme must be deemed journeymen and paid accordingly. In a step curiously foreshadowing late-twentieth century Irish practice, the society also ordered an end to gender discrimination in matters of pay.

> And whereas several females have been always, and are still employed in this manufacture, and that doubts have arisen whether they are entitled to

166 RDS Proc., lxiii, minutes, 28 June 1827.   167 RDS Proc., lxiv, minutes, 26 June 1828. 168 Simon Curran, 'The society's role in agriculture since 1800', in Meenan and Clarke, The Royal Dublin Society, 1731–1981, pp. 88–90.   169 R.A. Jarrell, 'Some aspects of the evolution of agricultural and technical education in nineteenth-century Ireland', in Bowler and Whyte, Science and society in Ireland, pp. 104, 113.   170 Maxwell, Dublin under the Georges, p. 276.   171 RDS Proc., liii, minutes and appendices, 30 Jan., 13 Mar. 1817.   172 RDS Proc., xlix, trade and manufactures committee report, 18 Feb. 1813.   173 Berry, History of the Royal Dublin Society, pp. 198–203.

the same rate of wages for the work they perform, as has been ordered for journeymen, we do hereby direct, that the same rates shall be paid to such women, as are directed by this Society to be paid to journeymen.[174]

The society also encouraged raw silk production by the use of growing trials and premiums. It could reasonably claim a role in the development of Dublin's most successful cloth product, poplin (earlier called tabinet), a silk and wool mix with a silk warp and a wool weft.[175] The appreciation of the broad silk operatives for the society's efforts on their behalf was expressed in an address to Archibald Hamilton Rowan in 1823.[176]

Wool production and weaving also attracted the attention of the society. Irish textile production ran against the trend of other European countries by concentrating facilities in the capital, rather than in provincial centres. Production expanded up to the 1770s, but was in decline by the 1790s.[177] During the period 1783–1818 exports of worsted woollen yarn from Ireland fell from 779,604 lbs to 28,616 lbs. In the same period, imports of the product grew from 1,583 lbs to 879,526 lbs valued at over £300,000. Although the raw material (wool) was abundantly available in Ireland, and costs of entry to the industry were relatively low, by 1820 there were only two factories in Ireland engaged in the manufacture of worsted yarn. The firm of Coyle and Kirby of Linen Hall Street, was one of the two worsted yarn manufacturers. They put it that 'by a strange anomaly it appears, that silk, the produce of a foreign country, furnishes employment to the labouring poor of Dublin, while wool, the produce of the soil, gives in this branch of manufacture but little employment to the poor of Ireland'. By an even greater irony, or so it appeared to the RDS, imported woollen yarn was used in the production of tabinets (poplin), an almost exclusively Dublin manufacture.[178] Willing to help revive the industry, the society was nevertheless not satisfied that traditional hand spinning methods could compete with machinery, and decided to conduct comparative trials.[179] Experiments using traditional spinning wheels proved them not as economical as machine production. Nevertheless the select committee appointed to report on the woollen manufacture recommended that the society pursue a policy of encouraging new investment, address the shortage of experienced dyers in Dublin, and promote public support for Irish woollen products. Additionally the select committee recommended that the society put up funds to form a joint manufactory with the Farming Society and the Mendicity Institution.[180] However, the reduction in government grants to

174 RDS Proc., lvi, report of committee on the silk manufacture, 29 June 1820.   175 Muriel Gahan, 'The development of crafts', in Meenan and Clarke, The Royal Dublin Society, 1731–1981, pp. 243–4.   176 William H. Drummond (ed.), The autobiography of Archibald Hamilton Rowan (Dublin, 1840), p. 386.   177 L.M. Cullen, Princes and pirates: the Dublin Chamber of Commerce, 1783–1983 (Dublin, 1983), pp. 18–19. Hereafter Cullen, Princes and pirates.   178 RDS Proc., lvi, report of the committee on the manufacture of worsted yarn, 10 Feb. 1820.   179 Ibid., 9 Mar. 1820. 180 RDS Proc., lvii, report, 11 Jan. 1821.

the society placed this ambition out of reach. The hand-weaving industry depended on a high measure of tariff protection, and entered an irreversible decline after 1826 when silk imports from France and Italy were freely admitted[181] and the economies of specialized factory production made manual production uncompetitive.[182] Weavers' wages fell in real terms in the early nineteenth century as cotton weaving on an industrial scale drove down the cost of clothing and seriously affected the competitiveness of the small workshops. The removal of internal tariff barriers in 1824 made the dumping of English surpluses on the Irish market more profitable. The economic recession of 1826 and the availability of cheap imports precipitated the complete and final collapse of Dublin handloom weaving, except in the sophisticated silk and tabinet trade which survived on a reduced scale into the 1830s.[183]

Greater success attended the society's support for the development of an Irish straw-hat industry. Demand for this fashionable headgear was largely met by imports from Italy. An earlier interest in supplying the demand from local cottage industries was revived in 1820 when Isaac Weld,[184] recently resident in Italy, presented samples of Tuscan straw used in the manufacture of Leghorn hats.[185] However, three years were to elapse before a formal scheme was considered and adopted to offer premiums for Irish straw-hat manufacture in the Leghorn style.[186] Early efforts were encouraging, particularly the discovery that a workable straw could be obtained from the commonly available wild grass known as 'trawnyeen'.[187] Interest in the premium scheme rapidly diffused in the Leinster counties and parcels of straw hats of marketable quality were submitted to the society in 1824.[188] Grass growing trials were conducted in the botanic garden in 1824–5. Isaac Weld reported

> Several of our native grasses are applicable to the purpose; but probably the best one, as being the toughest, and having a fine gloss, is the Cynosurus Cristatus, or crested dog's tail grass, known also by various common names, as trawn-yeen, windle straw, &c. It abounds in most meadows and pastures, on banks of ditches and road sides.[189]

At the end of 1825 the committee reported that interest in the premium scheme had extended into Ulster, the Irish product was capable of competing with the

181 Mary Campion, 'An old Dublin industry – poplin', in *Dublin Historical Record*, xviii (1962). 182 Cullen, *An economic history of Ireland*, pp. 105–8.   183 David O'Toole, 'The employment crisis of 1826', in David Dickson (ed.), *The gorgeous mask: Dublin 1700–1850* (Dublin, 1987), pp. 157–70. Hereafter Dickson, *The gorgeous mask*.   184 Isaac Weld (1774–1856), Ravenswell, Bray, travelled extensively in North America, 1794–5, and in Europe, 1815–18. He was elected a member of the Dublin Society in 1800, served on the fine arts committee, 1823–8, as an honorary secretary, 1828–49, and as a vice-president, 1849–56. (Source: RDS *Proc.*, var. dates.)   185 RDS *Proc.*, lvi, minutes, 27 Apr. 1820.   186 RDS *Proc.*, lix, minutes, 3, 10 July 1823.   187 RDS *Proc.*, lx, report of the straw plait committee, 20 Nov. 1823.   188 RDS *Proc.*, lxi, report, 9 Dec. 1824.   189 Ibid.,

best imports, and rye straw had proven superior as a raw material to the 'hard and wiry' trawnyeen.[190] Satisfied that the introduction of a new industry had been successfully achieved, the society decided to concentrate on the encouragement of volume production and sales.[191] Two factories had been privately established, at Dunboyne, Co. Meath, and at Galtrim, Co. Galway.[192] Annual displays of product were arranged in Leinster House, but the hoped for mass market never materialized. In 1828, disappointed by the failure to replace imports at the lower priced end of the market, the society discontinued its supports.[193]

The micro-economy of the RDS during the 1820s, and its capacity to pursue its objects, was constrained by the necessity of adapting to a considerably reduced annual income. Projects launched or continued confidently in the early years of the century were placed in abeyance or allowed to wind down. This was notably the case for agricultural premiums, the veterinary service, county statistical surveys,[194] scientific publications, and supports for manufacturing. Retrenchment was applied at every opportunity and the death of a paid officer usually signaled a reassessment, or even discontinuance of entire programs. Thomas Peall (veterinarian) and the Reverend Dr John Lanigan (translator, and publications editor) died in 1825 and 1828 respectively and their posts were never filled. Compassion towards the ailing Lanigan, whose health had broken down in 1814, had given rise to a tacit conspiracy within the society to maintain the fiction that he continued to provide an essential service, although he was incapable of any work after 1824. It is a tribute to the character of Lanigan, and to the then-membership of the RDS, that a catholic theologian should inspire such loyal support from largely protestant friends. This was a matter of some pride to the society, and will be discussed further in chapter five.

IV

Attempts by the society to produce a stable flow of income from membership were never very successful in the early nineteenth century. The main problem was the difficulty experienced in collecting annual subscriptions. Resistance to paying annual renewals, due by 31 March each year, presented a recurring problem, against which neither threats nor blandishments were wholly effective. An act of the Irish parliament in 1794 made members' subscriptions an enforceable debt[195] but recovery through the courts was not simple in practice. A resolution passed in 1802 threatened to publish the names of members in

---

appendix A, 14 July 1825.   **190** *RDS Proc.*, lxii, report, 8 Dec. 1825.   **191** *RDS Proc.*, lxiii, minutes, 17, 24 May 1827.   **192** Muriel Gahan, 'The development of crafts', in Meenan and Clarke, *The Royal Dublin Society, 1731–1981*, p. 251.   **193** *RDS Proc.*, lxiv, minutes, 24 Apr., 29 May, 3 July 1828.   **194** Only two county statistical surveys were completed and published after 1820.   **195** 33 Geo. III, cap. 14 (1794).

arrears,[196] but was not followed through and by the end of 1803 cumulative arrears were reported as £2,836 18s. 6d., equivalent to two-to-three years total annual subscriptions.[197] Legal proceedings against members in arrears were started at the end of 1802, but very little change was reported during the next four years and on 13 November 1806 Thomas Lysaght, the society's law agent, was ordered to proceed with greater rigour against defaulters.[198] However, the society's resolve wavered under a barrage of individual protests, and all pending proceedings were discontinued on 19 March 1807. Mistakes had been made, such as occasioned Walter Lambert of Clare-Galway to produce proof that he had been a life member since 1796.[199] In less clear-cut circumstances Richard Ball of Three Castles, and Charles Blake of Lehinch were allowed to compound for life membership, and a sheriff's writ against Colonel Stewart (Co. Tyrone) was withdrawn.[200] Proceedings against defaulters were resumed on 30 April 1807, but arrears remained stubbornly high and on 6 June 1811 the society resolved that all future elections should be for life membership only. Life members made a single payment on election, and it was reasoned that the gradual disappearance of annual memberships would eliminate the difficulties experienced in collecting annual subscriptions. The Dublin Society was not alone in experiencing loss of members and increasing arrears of subscriptions at this time. Membership of the Royal Irish Academy declined from 211 in 1800 to 161 in 1813, while arrears of subscriptions grew from £1,300 to £3,000 during the same period.[201]

In 1800 annual membership of the society cost two guineas per annum, and life membership twenty guineas. An admission fee (fine) of five guineas was also levied on new members. The annual subscription was raised to three guineas in 1801 the life composition fee remaining unchanged at twenty guineas.[202] The life membership fee was raised to thirty guineas in 1811, no more annual members were admitted after 6 June, and life composition was offered to current annual members for fifteen guineas.[203] The effect of this decision was to reduce significantly the problem of arrears over the next decade[204] (although it remained a problem as late as November 1822) and to intensify the volume of cash flow as applications for membership increased during 1811–15. In the euphoria of the move to Leinster House life membership was increased to fifty guineas at the first meeting held there.[205] As time went on, however, it became clear that the resulting initial surge in cash flow was unsustainable as the very high entry cost

---

196 *RDS Proc.*, xxxviii, minutes, 13 May 1802.   197 *RDS Proc.*, xl, minutes, 10 Nov. 1803. 198 *RDS Proc.*, xliii, minutes, 13 Nov. 1806.   199 *RDS Proc.*, xli, minutes, 8 Nov. 1804.   200 *RDS Proc.*, xliii, minutes, 18 Dec. 1806, 19 Mar., 9 Apr. 1807.   201 T. Ó Raifeartaigh (ed.), *The Royal Irish Academy, 1785–1985* (Dublin, 1985), p. 22. Hereafter Ó Raifeartaigh, *The Royal Irish Academy.* 202 *RDS Proc.*, xxxviii, minutes, 12 Nov. 1801.   203 *RDS Proc.*, xlvii, minutes, 7, 14 Mar., 6 June 1811.   204 *RDS Proc.*, liv, instructions to proceed against defaulters were renewed on 4 June 1818. 205 *RDS Proc.*, li, minutes, 1 June 1815.

placed membership beyond the reach of all but a small pool of wealthy applicants. In 1815 some 133 new members were elected, but only nineteen during
the ensuing four-year period 1816–19. As early as 1817 Lord Frankfort attempted
to have the life subscription reduced back to thirty guineas. He had little
support, and subsequent attempts by others in 1818 to reduce the subscription
to thirty-five or to forty guineas also failed.[206] Three years later, following a year
in which only one new member was elected, the general meeting agreed by a
majority of thirty-eight to twenty-nine to revert to the thirty guineas life
subscription.[207] Appendix I demonstrates the pattern of losses and gains in
membership during 1800–49. Between 1800 and 1815 there were only two years,
1804 and 1805, in which losses exceeded gains. After 1815 (under the fifty
guineas regime) it became the normal pattern, only stabilized briefly in 1821
with the royal visit and the reduction of life subscriptions to thirty guineas.
After 1821 natural mortality became a significant factor and the 79 members
admitted during 1822–8 were more than off set by the 161 deleted through
death or resignation during the same period. By 1829 the society faced the
prospect of a steadily declining membership, as the clusters of new members
elected fifteen to thirty years earlier began to disappear and were not replaced.

To secure election an applicant was required to deposit all fees in advance,
secure the sponsorship of two current members, and the endorsement of at least
two-thirds of the members present and voting at a general meeting presided
over by a vice-president. In practice some soundings and canvassing of support
were made in advance, usually by the principal sponsor. Rejection of candidates
was rare, and will be dealt with in chapter five. Once elected, a member was
entitled to attend and vote at the weekly board meetings, go forward for election
to an honorary office or a standing committee, or be appointed to a sub-committee. Participation rates, including attendance at general meetings, varied over
time but rarely exceeded forty per cent of the total membership. During the
thirty-year period 1800–29 the highest attendance at general meetings occurred
in 1808, 1819, and 1829; attendance frequently dipped to less than ten per cent
of total membership in 1804–6, 1810, 1818, and 1823.[208] (See appendix II for an
analysis of attendance at general meetings, 1800–39.)

The seven vice-presidents were declared ex-officio members of every committee in 1802, and the two honorary secretaries were included in this arrangement
from 1821. Prior to 1812 only the economy, fine arts, botany, and chemistry
committees could be classified as standing committees, holding regular meetings,
and supervising specific functions. Other committees were appointed or convened from time to time to deal with or report on specific issues. (See appendices
IX, X, and XI, for a list of vice-presidents and honorary secretaries, 1815–45,
standing committees and their functions, 1815–45, and standing committee

206 RDS Proc., liv, minutes, 4 June 1818. 207 RDS Proc., lvii, minutes, 1 Mar. 1821.
208 Author's database.

members, 1815–45.) The economy committee had been established in 1803 during a cash flow crisis solved temporarily by accepting interest-free loans from Newcomen's bank. Its first recommendation was a total re-organisation of the method of presenting the society's accounts.[209] The *ad hoc* library committee was constituted a standing committee on 5 March 1812 and shortly thereafter a review was conducted of the entire committee system. The recommendations, in themselves a clear indicator of the problems encountered, were that the numbers on committees should be capped, all attendance should be recorded, all vacancies should be filled by annual ballot, and all committees should present annual reports. In a further step to stimulate attendance it was recommended that any committee member attending less than a third of the meetings convened in the twelve months preceding the annual ballot should retire from office.[210] These recommendations were approved by the society on 2 July 1812, however, not having been embedded in the by-laws, they were successfully challenged in 1815. Henry Hamilton, Thomas Walker, and Sir William Cusack Smith were removed from the fine arts committee, having failed to attend any meetings during 1814. Walker and Smith, both busy members of the judiciary, accepted the decision of the general meeting. Hamilton[211] was a former chairman of the committee and had played an important role in reforming the management of the drawing schools in 1809. He successfully challenged his removal from the committee, on the grounds that there was no by-law of the society requiring committee members to attend meetings, and was reinstated.[212]

A review committee was again appointed in 1816, under the chairmanship of Lord Kilmaine.[213] He reported the causes of poor attendance as the indefinite terms of office, multiple committee memberships, failure to keep minute books, and the absence of a superintending control system for expenditure. Kilmaine recommended that six standing committees be established, each with a membership of fifteen elected by annual ballot, and that no paid official should be eligible for membership of any committee.[214] The six recommended standing committees were fine arts, botany, natural philosophy, chemistry and mineralogy, library, and economy. A seventh, the house committee, was added on 27 June 1816. The new committee regulations were agreed by the general meeting on 28 November 1816. An attempt to revive the trade and manufactures committee was rejected[215] and the

209 *RDS Proc.*, xxxix, reports and appendix, 5 May, 16 June 1803.   **210** *RDS Proc.*, xlviii, report, 2 July 1812.   **211** Henry Hamilton (1760–1844), Ballymacoll, Dunboyne, was a member of the fine arts committee, 1800–20 and of the chemistry and mineralogy committee, 1802–26. He presented drawings of Graeco-Roman architecture to the drawing schools in 1821, and a collection of minerals purchased in Rome to the museum in 1825. (Sources: *RDS Proc.*, *Burke*, var. dates; Turpin, *A school of art in Dublin*.)   **212** *RDS Proc.*, li, minutes, February–April 1815.   **213** James Caulfield Browne (1765–1825), 2nd baron Kilmaine, was a member of the society, 1802–25, and served on the botany committee, 1816–20. (Source: *RDS Proc.*, var. dates.)   **214** *RDS Proc*, lii, Lord Kilmaine's report, 6 June 1816.   **215** *RDS Proc.*, liii, minutes, 6 Mar. 1817.

only significant change made before 1838 was a reduction of committee membership from fifteen to nine, and a prohibition on multiple memberships.[216]

Who were the members of the RDS in the first half of the period, 1815–45? The society had 293 members on 1 January 1800. By 1 January 1815 membership had grown to 651, an increase of 119 per cent, and by 1 January 1816 to 772, a further increase of 19 per cent in a single year. Most of the increase had occurred in two clusters, during 1800–1, and during 1815, and had considerably altered the composition of the membership, as can be seen in appendix V; The composition showed little change between 1816 and 1830, although numbers fell by 23 per cent to 598.

The most evident change (see appendix V) in the early nineteenth century was the decline in the agricultural interest. Landowners fell from thirty-two per cent of the membership in 1800 to twenty-two per cent by 1830, or, aggregating the land based interests of 1800 to include also nobles and politicians, the fall was from sixty per cent down to thirty-five per cent of the total. While part of this change must be attributed to the conscious decision to transfer agricultural development functions to the Farming Society, an unknown but clearly operative factor was the switch in political focus to London following the union. Stalwarts of the eighteenth century society such as John Foster and Isaac Corry were rare visitors to Dublin after 1800. A straightforward defection was that of Richard Martin, MP for Co. Galway, who became a member of the society in 1798 and resigned in 1802 following his election to the Westminster parliament in 1801.[217]

While landowners, nobles and parliamentarians remained the largest single group of members, as early as 1815 they were rapidly being overhauled by the growth of urban-based members, most notably from the legal profession. Of the sixty-nine members elected in 1800 only seven were lawyers. In 1810 twenty-six out of sixty two newly elected members were barristers, attorneys, or members of the judiciary. Thirty-three lawyers (twenty-five per cent of the year's intake) were elected in 1815. An allied group, which also increased in representation, was that of government and municipal officials. In 1800 they were represented by a handful of Dublin Castle administrators such as Under Secretary Edward Cooke. Their numbers in the society were augmented, by 1815, by an influx of minor office holders such as John Hughes, secretary to the barrack board, and Andrew Redmond Prior, accountant general to the post office. The Dublin mercantile class also increased in representation within the society quite significantly. The linen, silk and wool trades had close eighteenth century links to the society, as exemplified by members such as William Cope, Joshua Pim, and Thomas Braughall.

After 1800, brewing and distilling, in the persons of members of the Guinness, Roe, Farrell, Busby, and Sweetman families, gradually surpassed the textile merchants in numbers and influence. Far more numerous than either

---

216 *RDS Proc.*, lvii, minutes, 9 Nov. 1820.   217 A good biography of Martin is, Shevawn Lynam, *Humanity Dick Martin 'King of Connemara', 1754–1834* (London, 1975).

group was the Dublin-based service providers such as wine, tea and tobacco importers, printers and stationers, and small manufacturers. A smaller but no less significant increase occurred in the numbers of higher professionals joining the society. The steady increase in clergy members between 1800 and 1830 on analysis reveals an accession of TCD academics, particularly in the 1820s, when Richard MacDonnell, Joseph Singer, Francis Sadleir, and Charles Wall all became members. The numbers of physicians and surgeons, engineers and architects also increased.

The world of the early-nineteenth-century members was shaped and influenced by the recent past and the issues of the day. In global terms, key factors were the seemingly inexorable progress of scientific discovery in every area of human activity, and the application of its results to economic development. Hence the society's fixation on the discovery of mineral resources, the exploitation of which might trigger an Irish industrial revolution comparable to that taking place in Britain. The application of steam power, especially as a means of propulsion, also caught the society's interest. Richard Griffith reported, in 1814, on the actual use of steam engines to replace horse drawn wagons in the Newcastle collieries.[218] The following year Isaac Weld was a passenger on the first steam boat journey across the Irish Sea.[219]

Early nineteenth-century members, as individuals, were influenced by the political, religious and social ambience in which they lived. Many had direct experience of the 1798 rebellion and its aftermath. A number of members had joined the United Irish movement at an early stage, but left before the rebellion broke out. One such was Dr Walter Wade (professor of botany, and honorary member of the Dublin Society) who was reported to have held a United Irish meeting in the botanic garden in 1797.[220] Some, such as Lord Cloncurry, Thomas Braughall, and John Patten (a brother-in-law of Robert Emmet) had been jailed for suspected complicity in rebel activities, or, like Archibald Hamilton Rowan, and Thomas Wogan Browne,[221] had fled the country for a time. Others such as John Giffard, Ambrose Hardinge Giffard, Lord O'Neill, and Sir William Stamer, had family members killed by the rebels. Members especially in the Ulster counties, such as Lords Downshire, Enniskillen, and O'Neill, took a prominent role in the raising of yeomanry corps in 1797, and many continued to have yeomanry links into the 1830s. Lord Moira, on the other hand, refused to have anything to do with the yeomanry.[222] A number of Dublin members had been actively engaged in the suppression of the rebellion and the apprehension of rebel leaders, the most prominent being town major Henry Charles Sirr.[223]

218 *RDS Proc.*, l, minutes, 27 Jan. 1814.   219 John S. Crone, *A concise dictionary of Irish biography* (Dublin, 1928).   220 Patrick Fagan, 'Infiltration of Dublin freemason lodges by united Irishmen and other republicans', in *Eighteenth-century Ireland*, xiii (1998), pp. 65–85.   221 Des O'Leary, 'Wogan Browne', in Seamus Cullen and Hermann Geisse (eds), *Fugitive warfare: 1798 in north Kildare* (Clane, 1998). Hereafter, Cullen and Geissel, *Fugitive warfare*.   222 Allan Blackstock, *An ascendancy army: the Irish yeomanry, 1796–1834* (Dublin, 1998), index.   223 Henry Sirr, and A.H.

Some, such as Benjamin O'Neal Stratford[224] in Co. Wicklow, may well by their conduct as yeomanry officers have helped if not to foment at least to prolong the rebellion. The majority of members, having a strong stake in the *status quo*, had little sympathy with the objects of the United Irish movement, but could show compassion towards the predicament of the individual. An example was Richard Griffith of Millicent, who as colonel of the Clane yeomanry led a vigorous and bloody counter-attack against local rebel forces in 1798, yet by 1803 was using his influence with government to secure a pardon for Archibald Hamilton Rowan.[225] Likewise the Co. Wicklow landowners and yeomanry officers Morley Saunders and William Hoare Hume acted as intermediaries between 1799 and 1804 to protect the Dwyer family from harassment and secure the peaceful surrender of Michael Dwyer, the last rebel leader in the field.[226] Two prominent members of the Dublin Society in 1798 were killed during the rebellion. The fates of Lord Mountjoy (killed leading the Dublin militia at New Ross), and Beauchamp Bagenal Harvey (executed for leading the Wexford rebels), is indicative of the ironies of civil war and the presence of the full range of contemporary political viewpoints within the Dublin Society.

The issues that preoccupied the thinking of the Irish political classes in the early nineteenth century were the legislative union with Great Britain, and catholic emancipation. Opposition to the union was especially strong in Dublin, whose inhabitants correctly surmised that it would lead to a decline in their city's importance.[227] The freemen of Dublin were almost universally hostile to legislative union, as likely to produce a loss of prosperity and prestige. Dublin lawyers were concerned at the prospect of diminished career opportunities. John Giffard was the embattled champion of union on Dublin Corporation, arguing that it would protect protestant interests, and promote stability and prosperity.[228] The society's members, to the extent that their individual politics are clearly discernible, were split on this issue. The divisions often transcended earlier party allegiances, and mirrored attitudes in Irish politics generally. Of the estimated 293 members of the society on 1 January 1800, forty had taken a public stance for or against the union and a further eight were known to be undecided. Excluding the waverers (all eventually supported the measure), twenty-one Dublin Society members were consistent advocates of union and nineteen were consistent opponents. By comparison, the government estimated the disposition of the Irish parliament in May 1799 as 148 pro-union, ninety-eight against union, and fifty-four undecided.[229]

Rowan, were both elected members of the Dublin Society in 1808. **224** Ruan O'Donnell, *Aftermath: post-rebellion insurgency in Wicklow, 1799–1803* (Dublin, 2000), pp. 4–5. Hereafter, O'Donnell, *Aftermath*. **225** Cullen and Geissel, *Fugitive warfare*, pp. 74–5, 105–11. **226** O'Donnell, *Aftermath*, pp. 127–31, 161–80. **227** Gearoid Ó Tuathaigh, *Ireland before the famine, 1798–1848* (Dublin, 1972), p. 31. Hereafter, Ó Tuathaigh, *Ireland before the famine*. **228** Jacqueline Hill, *From patriots to unionists: Dublin civic politics and Irish protestant patriotism, 1660–1840* (Oxford, 1997), pp. 258–63. Hereafter, Hill, *From patriots to unionists*. **229** Patrick M. Geoghegan, *The Irish act of*

The legislative union between Great Britain and Ireland came into effect on
1 January 1801. Along with it came the serious implication for the stability of
the newly united kingdom that about one quarter of its combined population
were catholics and thereby excluded from full participation in the political life
of the nation. In Ireland the protestant interest continued to hold a monopoly of
office and influence, a situation around which Irish politics revolved for the
ensuing thirty years.[230] In the wider United Kingdom context catholic emancipation became the single greatest domestic issue during the period 1805–29.
Against it were ranged deep-rooted anti-catholic sentiments based on veneration
for the protestant constitution of 1688, the church establishment, and conservative
traditionalism. However, to an increasing extent as the years went by, a majority
of parliamentarians came to regard catholic emancipation as a necessary step for
the peaceful development of the Anglo-Irish union.[231] Henry Grattan argued in
1805 that since the extermination of catholics was unthinkable, and partial
assimilation had not worked, there remained to be tried their complete incorporation into the body politic.[232] This departure did not have an easy acceptance,
since for most Britons protestantism had become a badge of national identity, a
framework for decision making, an interpretation of their history, and a distin-
guishing mark against their enemies.[233]

In Ireland many ultra-protestants, fearing the submergence of their identity
and privileges if full civil rights were extended to the catholic majority, banded
together in the Orange Order, which had become gentrified in the Dublin area
on the establishment of its headquarters in Dawson Street in April 1798. The
impression given by early membership records[234] suggests that orangeism
appealed especially to landed proprietors in the northern counties, elements of
Dublin Corporation and the Castle administration, and a number of minor
gentry in the south-eastern counties. The role of orangeism in the suppression of
the 1798 rebellion, and its dissemination amongst the ruling classes, made it
difficult for many Irish catholics to distinguish between it and the government.[235]

Orange representation within the Dublin Society was relatively modest, given
that over ninety per cent of its members were protestants. The high-point of
orange influence seems to have occurred between 1810 and 1819 when deputy
grand-master John Giffard, J.C. Beresford, and their associates wielded considerable sway over the society's deliberations. The numbers of the society's
members who were also members of the socially prestigious L.O.L. No. 176

union: a study in high politics, 1799–1801 (Dublin, 1999), p. 83.   **230** R.F. Foster, *Modern Ireland,
1600–1972* (London, 1988), pp. 290–1.   **231** Norman Gash (ed.), *The age of Peel: documents of
modern history* (London, 1968), pp. 2–3.   **232** D. George Boyce, *Nineteenth-century Ireland: the
search for stability* (Dublin, 1990), p. 34.   **233** Linda Colley, *Britons: forging the nation, 1707–1837*
(London, 1996), p. 59. Hereafter, Colley, *Britons.*   **234** *The formation of the Orange Order,
1795–1798* (Grand Orange Lodge of Ireland, Belfast, 1994), p. 116, esp. Dublin lodge no. 176.
Hereafter, *The formation of the Orange Order.*   **235** Donal Macartney, *The dawning of democracy:
Ireland, 1800–70* (Dublin, 1987), p. 35. Hereafter, Macartney, *The dawning of democracy.*

peaked at 36 in 1810.[236] Giffard's influence may have been responsible for the rejection of four candidates for membership of the society during this period, a matter that will be examined in more detail in chapter five. Unfortunately for the society names such as John Giffard, Dr Patrick Duigenan, and Sir Richard Musgrave, carried weight beyond their numbers in the public perception of strident anti-catholicism. Jonah Barrington described Musgrave as good sensible company on all issues 'except on the abstract topics of politics, religion, martial law, his wife, the Pope, the Pretender, the Jesuits, Napper Tandy, and the whipping-post'.[237] Giffard in particular was active in the Dublin Society during 1810–19, chairing two board meetings in 1814 and being a member at various times of the library, botany, natural philosophy, chemistry, economy, and house committees. Despite this frenetic activity, and the donations of seeds and plants sent from Ceylon by his son Ambrose Hardinge Giffard, he was never elected to higher office in the society. He was deputy grand master of the Orange Order in Ireland 1806–14 and acting grand master 1814–19. W.J. Fitzpatrick[238] characterized the membership of the RDS at this period as 'Ascendancy and terrorists' (identifying fifteen including Giffard, Sirr, and William Cope), and 'friends of national literature and progress' (nineteen including Lord Cloncurry, Dr Richard Kirwan, and Bagenal Harvey). As partisan and impressionistic as this may have been, his division of the membership into forty-four per cent conservatives and fifty-six per cent 'progressives' is plausible. The desire of government to accommodate Irish catholic requirements in the early nineteenth-century was tempered by the equation of reform with revolution in the minds of many conservatives and by the need to encourage protestant support for the union. Prior to 1815 Dublin Castle often indulged extremist protestant positions, as when in 1812 John Giffard, in the common council of Dublin Corporation, moved a vote of thanks to the duke of Cumberland for his resistance to catholic emancipation. The corporation continued to obstruct the admission of catholics, well into the 1820s. Meanwhile liberal sentiment surged in Britain after 1815, and leading Irish catholics, still effectively excluded from full participation in the political life of the country, lent their support to O'Connell's mass movement.[239]

A substantial shift in Irish politics occurred during 1800–23. An initial readiness on the part of catholics to look favourably on the union was disappointed by the repeated rejection of full civil rights, and led to a reformulation of political views under the leadership of Daniel O'Connell. Under his aegis Irish catholicism merged with nationalism and democracy.[240] Prior to this the supporters of catholic emancipation had shown little ability to muster electoral

236 *The formation of the Orange Order*, p. 116, matched against author's database.   237 Jonah Barrington, *Personal sketches of his own times*, ii (3rd ed., London, 1869), pp. 75, 110. Hereafter, Barrington, *Personal sketches*.   238 W.J. Fitzpatrick, *Irish wits and worthies: including Dr. Lanigan, his life and times* (Dublin, 1873), pp. 105–6. Hereafter, Fitzpatrick, *Irish wits and worthies*.   239 J.R. Hill, 'The politics of privilege: Dublin Corporation and the catholic question, 1792–1823', in *Maynooth Review*, vii, December 1982.   240 Macartney, *The dawning of democracy*, p. 62.

support. The Dublin city MP, Henry Grattan, an emancipationist, had a general personal support based on his historic opposition to the union. His fellow Dublin MP Robert Shaw had disappointed ultra-protestants by taking a conciliatory position on emancipation during 1811–12. When Grattan died in 1820, his parliamentary seat was contested by his son, Henry Grattan junior, and by Thomas Ellis, a chancery court judge, and a strong opponent of the catholic claims. Ellis tapped successfully into atavistic protestant fears and defeated Grattan in an acrimonious campaign, the first to be fought straight-forwardly on the religious issue.[241] Ellis, Robert Shaw, and Henry Grattan junior, were all active members of the Royal Dublin Society.

The visit of George IV and the appointment of the Wellesley administration in 1821 ushered in a period of conciliation under which Irish protestant interests were no longer of primary concern to the government. O'Connell's avowed aim of a union of all Irish interests was in stark contrast to his development of an Irish catholic grievance culture with a tinge of anti-protestantism sufficient to swing many Ulster presbyterians into an alliance with conservative protestantism. By 1826 O'Connell was speaking of a 'catholic nation'. O'Connell organized catholic electoral power, through the Catholic Association founded in 1823. This was so successful that anti-catholic protestants were placed in the bewildering position that Irish catholicism had all the appearance of liberalism and reasonableness at a time when the international catholic church was a by-word for social and political reaction. Liberal protestants were also confounded in that their support for catholic civil rights was not matched in O'Connellite rhetoric with any attempt to distinguish between them and the ultra-protestants.[242] The potential of catholic electoral power was first demonstrated in the 1823 Co. Dublin election.[243] The death of Hans Hamilton, MP for Co. Dublin, led to a contest for the vacant seat between the ultra-protestant Sir Compton Domville and the war hero and liberal protestant Henry White of Luttrellstown. Colonel White defeated Domville with the aid of catholic support engineered by O'Connell. It was the first manifestation of a powerful new force on the Irish electoral scene. Hamilton, and the two protagonists for his seat, were all members of the RDS. Twenty-five members of the RDS held parliamentary seats for Irish constituencies at the end of 1828. To the extent that they may be taken as representative of RDS opinion at that time it is worth noting that seventeen (about two-thirds) were on record as supporting catholic emancipation, and eight were opposed.[244]

In 1827 the long-running war-time administration of Lord Liverpool finally disintegrated. The eighteenth-century movement towards parliamentary reform, which had been stalled by the exigencies of fighting a war against Napoleon and restoring conservative regimes in post-war Europe, began tentative moves forward under the Wellington administration. The first major political reform was the

241 Hill, *From patriots to unionists*, pp. 308–16.   242 Boyce, *Nineteenth-century Ireland*, pp. 34–47.   243 Ibid.   244 Author's database.

repeal of the test act in 1828, enabling protestant dissenters to take seats in parliament without taking the religious oath, and thereby was breached the monopoly of office previously confined to members of the established church.[245] In Ireland Daniel O'Connell tested parliamentary rules to the limit by having himself elected as MP for Co. Clare. Meanwhile the Orange Order, dissolved under the unlawful societies (Ireland) act 1825, was legally revived on 25 September 1828, but overshadowed by the Brunswick clubs formed to absorb its erstwhile membership. At O'Connell's instigation Lord Cloncurry formed 'The Friends of Religious and Civil Liberty' as a counterweight.[246] By the end of 1828 almost 200 Brunswick clubs had been formed, aristocratically led, and having a base in orangeism and the evangelical movement.[247] Even sympathetic protestants had fears of Roman catholicism. Its perceived political and intellectual control of its adherents, and its subordination to a reactionary foreign potentate made it appear more constitutionally dangerous than protestant dissent. However, the relief accorded to dissenters made it less rational to continue resistance to catholic emancipation, especially as O'Connell had pushed the issue beyond mere toleration and made it one of freedom of conscience.[248] The impetus towards reform finally overcame parliamentary and extra-parliamentary objections in early 1829 and catholic emancipation was enacted.

Thomas Wyse published a history of the Catholic Association in which he listed the public offices from which catholics were excluded or poorly represented, and acknowledged the role played in the emancipation campaign by sympathetic Irish protestants. At a meeting convened in the Rotunda rooms in February 1829 a petition was launched and signed by 2,500 prominent Irish protestants in favour of catholic emancipation.[249] Sixty-six of those signatories were current members of the RDS (over ten per cent of the total membership), and included a vice-president, John Henry North, an MP of conservative protestant views. Many earlier ultra-protestant members had mellowed, or become disillusioned, or prudently ended their association with extreme loyalist organisations when that cause fell from government favour. Many liberal protestant members shared in the parliamentary victory of their catholic fellow countrymen.

By 1828 the RDS had managed to cope with the reductions in its annual grant, largely by shedding its veterinary service, and allowing a run-down of its activities in geological exploration and in supports to cottage industries. It had made no further attempt (beyond the committee reforms of 1816) to alter its administrative structure. In the early 1830s, the subject of the next chapter, it would have to face a further reduction in grants, and pressures to re-engage with agricultural development.

245 Gash, The age of Peel, p. 2.   246 Haddick-Flynn, Orangeism, pp. 229–36.   247 Foster, Modern Ireland, p. 304.   248 Fergus O'Ferrall, Catholic emancipation: Daniel O'Connell and the birth of Irish democracy, 1820–30 (Dublin, 1985), pp. 180–1. Hereafter, O'Ferrall, Catholic emancipation. 249 Thomas Wyse, Historical sketch of the late Catholic Association of Ireland, ii (London, 1829), appendices xxxi and xxxv. Hereafter, Wyse, Catholic Association.

CHAPTER THREE

'The step-mother of the child', 1829–33

This chapter examines the immediate impact on the society of further reductions to the annual grant provided by government. Fixed at £10,000 Irish for twenty years in 1800, the grant had been reduced in a series of cuts during 1820–2 to £7,600 Irish. Further reductions in 1829–33 resulted in a further curtailment of programs, beyond that already noted in chapter two. The salaries of paid officials were reduced, and vacancies were allowed to remain unfilled. Membership numbers fell in absolute and real terms, and the society became preoccupied with internal debates on its administration, and future role. The political and religious composition of the RDS membership at this time is also reviewed. Political turmoil and epidemic disease added to the difficulties of maintaining useful public services, but, nevertheless, the society's core activities were continued. By the end of this period the RDS had made tentative moves in the direction of a return to agricultural development, and had experimented with the introduction of agricultural and industrial exhibitions, initiatives that were to lay the foundation for its future financial recovery.

In March 1829 the list of Irish miscellaneous estimates was published and the government announced its intention of reviewing its expenditure on the twelve public and twenty charitable institutions supported out of public funds in Ireland. These last included the Royal Dublin Society, together with the Cork and Belfast institutions, Maynooth seminary, the Royal Irish Academy, eight hospitals, orphanages and asylums, five school organisations, the House of Industry, and the commissioners for charitable donations and bequests.[1] The *Freeman's Journal* gave a conditional welcome to the government's committee of inquiry.

> we trust that this Committee will be cautious in its pursuit of economy, and that while it investigates strictly the nature and extent of the demands presented on the public purse, it will remember that justice, as well as generosity calls for the support of those institutions in Dublin which were promised to be upheld at the Union, and which, but for the Union, would need no grant from an Imperial Legislature.

1 *Estimates of miscellaneous services*, 9 Mar. 1829, House of Commons parliamentary papers, Chadwyck-Healey series, box 13, xvi, pp. 298–340.

Two days later the same newspaper noted that the government had appointed the committee. Its twenty-one members included two RDS vice-presidents, John Leslie Foster and J.H. North. The newspaper also reported that the Society for Discountenancing Vice, and the Kildare Place Society (both of which ran schools), and Maynooth college, had been excluded from the inquiry.[2]

An early casualty of the inquiry was, incidentally, a prominent member of the RDS, Sir Abraham Bradley King (1774–1838), former lord mayor of Dublin, and holder of an official patent as king's stationer in Ireland.[3] King confirmed that money sums in lieu of stationery were paid regularly by him to the butler, cook, confectioner, and other household staff of the vice-regal lodge. He did not clarify whether or not these payments were included in his charges to government, but denied ever claiming commission on them.[4] Sir Abraham lost his patent and the question of compensating him became a protracted parliamentary issue. In August 1831 he was declared a bankrupt.[5] This brought about a temporary union of Irish political opinion since many were sympathetic to King's personal plight and representations were made to Lord Althorp to reconsider his case for compensation.[6] Daniel O'Connell was instrumental in securing a pension for him in 1832.[7]

Meanwhile, government probing into the utility of Irish institutions continued.[8] Lord Francis Leveson Gower, chief secretary, wrote to the RDS on 31 July 1829, drawing the society's attention to the recommendations made in its case by the select committee on Irish miscellaneous estimates. This committee approved of the continuance of parliamentary aid to the society, but recommended that certain steps be taken to improve its private finances. These were, firstly that the society should charge admission fees to its science lectures, and secondly that the purchase of books for the library should be restricted to scientific and related texts. The committee also recommended that annual memberships should again be offered to the public (they were suspended in 1811), and gave their opinion 'that the principle of admission by ballot to a Society mainly supported by the public purse, is objectionable, and should be discontinued'.[9]

The society's reply, formulated by a special committee chaired by vice-president John Leslie Foster, was agreed at a general meeting on 3 December 1829.[10] No problem was seen in implementing the select committee's strictures on the purchase of library books, which in any case accorded with the society's own practices in this regard. The society was willing to experiment with setting admission charges for lectures, but did not anticipate a significant addition to its

2 *Freeman's Journal*, 11, 13 Apr. 1829. 3 Sir A.B. King was a member of the RDS 1802–38. (Source: RDS Proc.,var. dates.) 4 *Freeman's Journal*, 14, 21 July 1829. 5 Ibid., 15 July, 12 Aug. 1831. 6 Ibid., 24 Sept. 1831. 7 Oliver MacDonagh, *The emancipist: Daniel O'Connell, 1830–47* (London, 1989), pp. 69–70. Hereafter, MacDonagh, *The emancipist.* 8 *Freeman's Journal*, 3 Aug. 1829. 9 *RDS Proc.*, lxvi, appendices II and III. 10 Ibid., appendix IV.

revenue from this source, since 'the class of persons in the habit of attending these Lectures [mostly consisted of] students, and young persons, in a walk of life too humble to enable them to pay a sufficient sum to realize such an expectation'. The society argued that during 1828–9 about 3,000 persons had attended the lectures. The society maintained an auditorium for science lectures with 500 seats, conducted an art school with an average student body of 200, and admitted almost 30,000 visitors annually to its museum which had become 'in strictness, the National Museum of Ireland'. On the subject of membership, the society had abandoned annual memberships because of the difficulties of collecting subscriptions from members dispersed around the country or living abroad. It was bound to an election procedure by the terms of its charter, and

> this mode of admission has never operated to the injury of the public. In the course of near thirty years there have not been above four instances of the rejection of a candidate; while the number elected since the year 1800 has been 739.
>
> The Society humbly conceives that the abandonment of all power of rejection (if it were practicable) would be pregnant with consequences highly injurious, if not absolutely destructive of the well-being of the Society, and the proper management and government of its internal affairs.

The society's response was late, and weak, omitted any reference to the botanic garden, and frequently repeated (to the extent of copying entire paragraphs) the arguments made to Chief Secretary Grant in 1820 (see chapter 2).[11] The death of assistant secretary Bucknall McCarthy during the 1829 recess no doubt accounts for some lack of incisiveness in the response. His replacement, Edward Hardman, elected on 12 November 1829, was a cautious elderly man, who was given little time to settle into his office and grasp the situation.[12] Isaac Weld had made a more spirited defence of the society in the pages of the *Freeman's Journal*. Weld rather heatedly responded to criticisms made of the diffuse objects and outmoded structure of the RDS by some of the English newspapers,

> The institutions, or the institutes, [the reference was to the London scientific societies] or by whatever name they may be designated in modern times, are but faint copies, and copies only in part, of the grand whole which is displayed in Dublin, and which, moreover, claims the proud pre-eminence of having started into being under a band of Irish patriots, as early as the first part of the reign of George II.[13]

A deputation of RDS vice-presidents met the chief secretary on 18 February 1830 and, a week later, recommended that a system of charges for admissions to

11 *RDS Proc.*, lvi–lvii.   12 *RDS Proc.*, lxvi, 5, 12 Nov. 1829.   13 *Freeman's Journal*, 7 Sept. 1829.

lectures be introduced. The proposed scale of fees was a half-guinea for the full course of lectures, with ladies to be admitted free of charge. In March 1830 this was revised to ten shillings for gentlemen and five shillings for ladies.[14] Some further cost saving measures were canvassed at the same time. On 12 November 1829, the very day on which Hardman was appointed to the post, Dr Anthony Meyler moved to discontinue his salary, on the grounds that it was improvident to pay two officers – the assistant secretary, and the registrar – to attend meetings and record proceedings. When this motion came up for consideration in March 1830 it was roundly rejected, and the work of the registrar and the assistant secretary, as distinct offices, was endorsed.[15] A motion by Hugh Hamill[16] to amalgamate the work of the chemistry and natural philosophy committees was recommended by a review committee, but not taken any further.[17] By the end of 1830 the government was keen to know if the policy of charging for lecture admissions had been implemented.[18] This was discussed at the next board meeting and the conclusion reached was that the admission charges agreed in March 1830 had been fully implemented and had resulted in severely reduced attendance at the lectures.[19]

In parliament, the Wellington administration ended on 16 November 1830, and was replaced by a government of Whigs and Canningite Tories, under the leadership of Lord Grey, the first Whig government since the 1780s.[20] Hobsbawm speculates that this was probably the only period (certainly prior to 1848) when events in the United Kingdom paralleled and were stimulated to some extent by those taking place in continental Europe. A wave of revolutions brought about the final ousting of the Bourbon monarchy in France (1830), Belgian independence (1830), a major revolt in Russian Poland (1830–1), and the commencement of a long period of civil war between liberals and clericals in the Iberian peninsula. In the United States, popular democracy was emergent and taking power under the presidency of Andrew Jackson. Generally a high point was reached for middle-class democracy, with control of affairs passing from a land-based aristocracy to urban-based professionals, industrialists, bankers, and bureaucrats. In the United Kingdom parallel events culminated in the reform act of 1832.[21] Catholic emancipation, parliamentary reform, and the abolition of African slavery, forced a redefining of the sense of British nationhood. In particular, religious intolerance had become less appropriate in the context of an expanding British empire, and had lost its patriotic credentials given the major

14 RDS Proc., lxvi, minutes, 25 Feb., 18 Mar. 1830.   15 Ibid., minutes, 12 Nov. 1829, 4 Mar. 1830. 16 Hugh Hamill, a catholic merchant from Co. Monaghan, was a member of the society, 1810–35, and served on the botany, library, and later the chemistry, and natural philosophy committees. (Source: RDS Proc., var. dates.)   17 RDS Proc., lxvi, minutes, 25 Feb., 1 Apr. 1830. The two committees would eventually be merged into a single science committee in 1867.   18 RDS Proc., lxvii, minutes, 11 Nov. 1830, letter from Chief Secretary Gregory.   19 Ibid., 16 Dec. 1830. 20 Webb, Modern England, p. 195.   21 Eric Hobsbawm, The age of revolution, 1789–1848 (London, 1962), pp. 139–40. Hereafter, Hobsbawm, The age of revolution.

role played by Irish and British catholics, and European catholic allies, in the war against Napoleon.[22]

Following Daniel O'Connell's success at a by-election in Co. Clare in 1828, Wellington concluded that catholic emancipation was necessary to prevent civil war in Ireland. However, it was only with the greatest difficulty that he managed to persuade the king to withdraw his personal opposition and give his assent to the catholic emancipation bill in 1829.[23] In Ireland, O'Connell's 1828 election victory challenged not only protestant ascendancy, but also the political control hitherto exercised by the great landowners. During the early 1830s Irish political opinion was divided into two broadly opposing groups. A Tory-conservative bloc had begun to emerge as a cohesive faction in opposition to the parliamentary moves towards catholic emancipation. In 1828–9 the proto-tories could count on the support of forty-four Irish peers and baronets, and twenty Irish members of parliament. They were opposed by a loose alliance of Whig-liberals, numerically at least as large. By 1832, following the reform of parliamentary representation, and O'Connell's declared intention to work towards repeal of the act of union, party support became more formalized.[24] The results of the 1832 elections were that forty Whig-liberals (including at least five pledged to repeal of the union), thirty-eight mainstream repealers, and twenty-seven Tory-conservatives were returned for Irish seats.[25] It was clear that no single political platform encompassed the viewpoints of the relatively small, property-based, Irish electorate (made even smaller by the disenfranchisement of the forty-shilling freeholders after 1829). To compound matters further, aspects of the major political platforms sometimes had cross party appeal, such as repeal of the union, free trade or its antithesis protectionism, and reduction of government spending, resulting in some strange realignments. Some of this confusion was reflected amongst RDS members. For example, repeal of the union was temporarily favoured in 1833 by the protestant conservative Trinity academic, Thomas Prior.[26] The anti-emancipationist Alderman Frederick Darley supported the reformer and free trader George Dawson in 1831,[27] and Henry Sirr surprised friend and foe alike by his espousal of parliamentary reform in 1831–2.[28] The old system of parliamentary representation was strongly biased in favour of the major landowners. In the north of England especially, economic change was affecting the size and social composition of electorates, there was a growing distaste for the role of influence and patronage in representation, and a growing interest in democratic ideology. Despite its reluctance to accept change, parliament had become fearful of the possible results of its own intransigence.[29]

22 Colley, *Britons*, pp. 340–7. 23 Christopher Hibbert, *Wellington: a personal history* (London, 1997), pp. 268–74. Hereafter, Hibbert, *Wellington*. 24 R.B. McDowell, *Public opinion and government policy in Ireland, 1801–46* (London, 1957), pp. 106–13. Hereafter, McDowell, *Public opinion*. 25 Ibid., p. 134. 26 Ibid., pp. 106–13. 27 Hill, *From patriots to unionists*, p. 343. 28 Frank Thorpe Porter, *Twenty years recollections of an Irish police magistrate* (9th ed., London, 1880), p. 55. Hereafter, Porter, *Twenty years recollections*. 29 Eric J. Evans, *The great reform act of*

The 1832 reforms brought a reduction in the numbers of RDS members with parliamentary seats. Early in 1829 five RDS members sat in the house of lords as United Kingdom peers, and a further four as Irish representative peers. One RDS member, Quintin Dick, represented an English constituency in the house of commons, and a further twenty-two represented Irish constituencies. Their stated public positions and voting records indicate that, of the total of thirty-one, six could be described as ultra-conservative, thirteen as moderate conservative, and twelve as Whig-liberals.[30] The best known of the RDS Whig MPs was Henry Grattan junior, at that time a representative for Dublin. Towering intellectually amongst Irish Tory MPs was RDS vice-president John Leslie Foster. Foster was secretly consulted by Wellington in 1829 and his views sounded on the details of the catholic emancipation bill. He had recommended raising the electoral property qualification to £10, on the assumption that this would help to curtail O'Connell's power base. In the house of commons Foster supported the catholic emancipation bill, giving as his reasons that while he believed Roman catholicism to be incompatible with the British constitution he was willing to accept emancipation as the price of avoiding civil war in Ireland.[31]

Between 1829 and 1832 one RDS peer, Lord Conyngham, and four RDS members of parliament, Edward Cooper (Sligo), Edmund MacNaghten (Antrim), Thomas Lloyd (Limerick), and J.H. North (Dublin University), died. Nine more retired from politics, and one, the Knight of Kerry, lost his seat. When the first post-reform elections were held in 1832 the numbers of RDS members with seats in parliament had dropped from thirty-one to eighteen (ten peers and eight MPs).[32] Neither Henry White, nor Nicholas Philpot Leader, both Whig-liberals, stood for election in 1832. As K.T. Hoppen has shown,[33] the composition of Irish representation in 1832 (over seventy per cent catholic and protestant proto-liberals) had swung towards liberalism, but was still dominated by landed interests. Although it is notoriously difficult to assign precise party labels in this period of political flux, the limited evidence suggests that a parallel development occurred in the diminished number of RDS parliamentarians. Amongst the ten RDS peers with seats in the house of lords, only Lord Meath, Lord Charlemont, and Lord Dunalley could be classed as liberals. The political outlook of the peers remained largely unchanged, and the remaining seven could be classified as moderate conservatives. However, a profound change had occurred amongst the RDS MPs, with the disappearance of many ageing conservatives through death or retirement. The remaining mix of old and new RDS members of parliament consisted of six Whigs, and two Tories. One of the

1832 (2nd ed. London, 1994), pp. 11–18. Hereafter, Evans, *The great reform act*.   30 Brian M. Walker (ed.), *Parliamentary election results in Ireland, 1801–1922* (Dublin, 1978). Hereafter, Walker, *Parliamentary election results*.   31 O'Ferrall, *Catholic emancipation*, pp. 239–40.   32 Walker, *Parliamentary election results*.   33 K. Theodore Hoppen, *Elections, politics and society in Ireland, 1832–1885* (Oxford, 1984) pp. 264, 336. Hereafter, Hoppen, *Elections, politics and society*.

latter, Sir Robert Bateson, MP for Co. Londonderry, could be described as an ultra-conservative. The other, Viscount Forbes, represented landed interests in Co. Longford for thirty years, 1806–36, and fought stiff electoral battles with the repealers. The Whigs; George Evans, C.A. Walker, Thomas Wallace, Samuel White, Viscount Clements, and Henry Grattan junior, belonged generally to an older generation of land based Whig-liberalism. Constitutional reformers, some were also supporters, with varying degrees of enthusiasm, of the English Whigs, and of O'Connell's repeal movement.[34] During 1831–2 O'Connell placed repeal in abeyance to concentrate on parliamentary reform and the abolition of slavery, throwing his support behind the Whig campaigns in parliament. He pressed, during the reform debates, for reductions in government spending, the abolition of sinecures, positive discrimination in favour of catholics, the full integration of Ireland within the union, and the maintenance of centralized British authority in Dublin.[35] With repeal not an issue, it is likely that the majority of RDS members felt comfortable with the Whig-liberal agenda of O'Connell and his parliamentary allies. Apart from the inevitable exceptions among the holders of public offices, and the members of Brunswick clubs, it did not overtly threaten their personal positions.

The 1832 reform of parliamentary representation act only gradually shifted political power, especially during 1833–49, from aristocrats and landowners towards the urban middle classes.[36] S.J. Connolly points out[37] that of 256 Irish MPs elected between 1801 and 1820 a third were of aristocratic parentage, and two-thirds came from the substantial land owning class. This earlier bias towards the *ancien regime* continued to be reflected, albeit to a diminishing extent, in the composition of RDS membership, and in those members who held seats in parliament, up to the 1830s. The profound changes introduced in 1832 meant for the RDS that its ability to have its claims argued at the heart of government was further reduced. Outside the immediate world of parliamentary politics the composition of RDS membership had also been undergoing change. Although it is not possible to be precise, the evidence of numbers suggests that the main body of RDS members in the early 1830s were supporters of the *status quo*, which at that time fluctuated between the agenda of the Whig-liberals, and that of the Tory moderates. Supporters of extreme protestant conservative politics were a minority. That other minority, catholic members, exceeded forty (about seven per cent of the total) by the end of 1833, almost half having been elected since 1815. The more recent catholic members included such prominent figures in commerce and the professions as J.R. Corballis, Anthony Strong Hussey, Patrick Curtis, and Dr J.F. O'Neill Lentaigne. Catholics were well represented on the society's standing committees, especially chemistry, and natural philosophy. In particular, Hugh Hamill, and John Duffy, both in the textile trade,

34 Walker, *Parliamentary election results*.   35 MacDonagh, *The emancipist*, pp. 46, 61–3.
36 MacDonagh, *Early Victorian government*, p. 5.   37 S.J. Connolly, 'Aftermath and adjustment',

played high profile roles on the above committees, and at the society's general meetings.[38]

To return to the society's relations with the government, the impact of the admission fees introduced in 1830 for the public lecture courses had proved, not unexpectedly, to have a bad effect on attendance. A meeting with the Castle administration was requested by the society early in 1831. The government asked for a postponement, pending the arrival of the newly appointed chief secretary Sir Edward Stanley (later earl of Derby, and not to be confused with the RDS member of the same name), and the society decided to suspend all lectures in the meantime.[39] The new government, faced with a mounting economic crisis, slashed spending, and the society discovered on receiving a copy of the Irish miscellaneous estimates that its annual grant was to be reduced from £7,000 British to £5,500 British. An extraordinary general meeting of members was convened on 26 August 1831. Resolutions were passed pointing out that the liberality of earlier parliaments since 1761 had induced the RDS to extend the scope of its operations. The grant had already been reduced from £10,000 Irish to £7,000 British (a reduction of twenty-four per cent) in 1821 and was barely adequate to sustain current programs. The society viewed itself as occupying a position in Dublin analogous to that of the British Museum in London and 'in some respects more practically useful' than that body. It solicited a parliamentary investigation into its affairs,

> in the confident hope that the Imperial Parliament, uninfluenced by partial or imperfect statements, and forming its opinion of the Dublin Society by examination of its Members or Officers, will not disable the Society from a useful execution of the trust reposed in them, or paralyse their future efforts for the public good, by making any reduction in the grant.[40]

A second extraordinary meeting was held on 9 September, during which the resolutions previously passed were worked up into a petition to the house of commons. This was entrusted for presentation to the solicitor general for Ireland, P.C. Crampton,[41] and it was resolved also that letters be written to the Irish MPs requesting their support.[42] Crampton duly presented the petition, which was supported in the commons by N.P. Leader and Sir Robert Bateson. Against accusations of bias in the election of members, Crampton argued that the RDS balloting system was not used for purposes of exclusion, but to conform to the terms of its charter.[43] A third extraordinary meeting was

pp. 5–6, in Vaughan, *A new history of Ireland*, v.   38 *RDS Proc.*, var. dates, and author's database. 39 *RDS Proc.*, lxvii, minutes, 5 May 1831.   40 Ibid., minutes of extraordinary meeting, 26 Aug. 1831.   41 Philip Cecil Crampton (1783–1862), was appointed solicitor general for Ireland on 23 Dec. 1830, a post which he held until 21 Oct. 1834. He was a member of the RDS 1815–62. (Sources: RDS Proc., var. dates; MacDonagh, *The emancipist*.)   42 *RDS Proc.*, lxvii, minutes of extraordinary meeting, 9 Sept. 1831.   43 *Freeman's Journal*, 3 Oct. 1831.

convened on 12 October 1831, following the belated discovery that the govern-ment had already decided, according to a treasury minute of 31 December 1830, to reduce the RDS grant on the grounds that the scheme to raise funds from lecture admissions had proved a failure. This decision was not directly notified to the society, and only came to its attention on 22 September 1831 by virtue of its publication in the parliamentary reports. The government had decided to make 'local contribution the test of the utility of the Royal Dublin Society, and the condition to be uniformly insisted on, in order to justify the grant of public money'. Surprised by the lack of consultation, the society passed ten resolutions for transmission to government. It argued 'That the Royal Dublin Society was adopted, cherished, and maintained by the Parliament of Ireland, as a National Institution'. If such an institution did not already exist in Ireland it would be in the public interest 'to create one which should embrace all the various objects of this Society's care'. Action taken on the basis of the utility test as set by the treasury 'must lead to the extinction of the Society, as it would do, if applied to the British Museum itself'. The society argued that the lecture fees had been introduced on a trial basis only, and had failed because they were unaffordable to 'students and young persons', and because of public resistance to the notion of paying for a service which had up to that point been available gratuitously.[44] Still awaiting a response from government, the society resolved on 3 November 1831 to carry out a review of its income and expenditure.[45]

Three weeks later Chief Secretary Stanley forwarded an extract from a treasury minute of 11 November, returning to the issue first raised in 1829 of the mode of election of members. The society appointed a deputation to meet with the chief secretary to discuss this and the other topics.[46] Meanwhile, the economy committee prepared a draft budget for 1832, based on the proposed reduction in the annual grant, and concluded that the constraints imposed by this reduction could only be met by reducing the salaries of the professors and other officials.[47] Two further meetings were held before the end of the year, but the members were unable to reach agreement on the draft budget and the issue was deferred until early in 1832.[48] At the first meeting of the new year, on 5 January 1832, the society decided to submit an estimate based on the old grant of £7,000 British. John Boyd gave notice of motions to reduce the life members' composition payment from thirty guineas to twenty guineas, and also to change the ballot requirement for the election of members from a two-thirds majority to a simple majority. Both motions were clearly intended to signal that the society was about to take steps towards compliancy on the membership issue.[49] During January an estimate was prepared and a deputation appointed to travel to London to discuss it with the chief secretary and the treasury lords. The

---

44 *RDS Proc.*, lxvii, minutes of extraordinary meeting, 12 Oct. 1831.   45 *RDS Proc.*, lxviii, minutes, 3 Nov. 1831.   46 Ibid., 8 Dec. 1831.   47 Ibid., 15 Dec. 1831.   48 Ibid., 16, 22 Dec. 1831.
49 Ibid., 5 Jan. 1832.

deputation were to take with them a petition to parliament, and 500 copies of his observations on the state of the RDS in 1831, prepared by honorary secretary Isaac Weld. The petition tackled the imputation of unfairness in the election procedures head-on and argued for the retention of the existing system on the basis that an initial screening process was essential since, once elected, there was no mechanism for the expulsion of a member even for the grossest impropriety.[50]

The treasury responded with a minute of 30 March 1832, reducing the annual grant to £5,300 British and recommending that the RDS admit annual members without election.[51] This swingeing cut of twenty-four per cent in the annual grant, added to earlier cuts since 1820, meant that the society's grant income had been reduced by over forty per cent in the space of twelve years. The government proposed to reduce the Irish miscellaneous estimates over-all by fourteen per cent in 1832, the cuts falling disproportionately on the older institutions as scarce funds were redirected towards the new national education system and to public works.[52]

The society had continued the policy of slimming down its fixed costs, especially salaries and wages, begun following the first grant reductions in 1820–1. Natural wastage, through death, retirement, or resignation, was allowed full play. When Edward Bell Stephens resigned his post as laboratory assistant to join a manufacturing company in England, the chemistry committee recommended that he be not replaced.[53] The posts of veterinary professor, and mining engineer, were allowed to remain vacant from 1825 and 1829 respectively. Irritation with Richard Griffith's long absences and lack of output culminated in the suspension of his salary in June 1829.[54] The following month his salary was restored, when the chemistry and mineralogy committee reported that his time spent on field work and lecture preparations was fully in compliance with his contract.[55] In November, Griffith was re-elected mining engineer, resigning the post within a week to take up the full time position of Irish commissioner of valuations.[56] He commenced the valuation of Ireland, a project that was to take well over twenty years to complete, at Coleraine, on 1 May 1830.[57]

By the beginning of 1831, full time staff employed by the society amounted to thirty-eight, compared with forty-five ten years earlier. Two key vacancies – mining engineer, and veterinary lecturer – remained unfilled. Of the fourteen stipendiary officers, ten at least were aged over fifty (two were in their sixties). Only Samuel Litton, Edmund Davy, and Edward Stephens might be regarded as young enough to seek alternative employment, and the latter, as previously mentioned, migrated to England in June 1831. (Details of professors and

50 Ibid., 12, 16 Jan. 1832, and appendix V.   51 Ibid., 19 Apr. 1832.   52 *Statements of the estimates for miscellaneous services, 26 May 1832*. House of Commons parliamentary papers (Chadwyck-Healey series, 1982, box 17, 1832–3, mf 35.235).   53 *RDS Proc.*, lxvii, minutes, 16, 23 June 1831. 54 *RDS Proc.*, lx, minutes, 18 June 1829.   55 Ibid., 2 July 1829.   56 *RDS Proc.*, lxvi, minutes, 12, 19 Nov. 1829.   57 Davies and Mollan, *Richard Griffith*, p. 17.

stipendiary officers 1815–45, that is, the annually elected paid staff, with offices held, and length of service, are given in appendix VI.)

At the end of 1831 the economy and select committees reported jointly to the society's general meeting on the financial state of the institution. They concluded that 'no permanent reduction of the annual expenditure, so as to bring it within the diminished income of the Society, could be effected, without materially encroaching upon the salaries of the Professors and Officers'. They submitted an estimate for 1832 amounting to £5,660 British.[58] In these straitened circumstances John White, under gardener, was instructed to discontinue his annual field trips to collect Irish botanical specimens.[59] On 6 April 1832, following a close vote carried by twenty in favour and seventeen against, the society reluctantly decided to reduce all salaries by a third.[60] Henry Brocas and James Lynch wrote letters protesting the cuts. Lynch also signed a joint letter, to which the other signatories were Sir Charles Giesecke, Edmund Davy, and Samuel Litton. They urged the society to make a direct appeal to Lord Anglesey, the lord lieutenant, before proceeding with the proposed salary reductions. Lynch pleaded in a separate letter against being deprived 'in my old age, of my principal support, a great and manifest injustice after so many years faithful service'.[61] Brocas, who had been reprimanded for unpunctuality and absenteeism, got no sympathy or support from the fine arts committee.[62]

Sir Charles Giesecke died on 5 March 1833, and his affairs were placed in the hands of his executor, Robert Hutton (a member of the coach building family in Summerhill, Dublin, and later an O'Connellite MP for Dublin city).[63] In the course of sorting out his personal effects a sub-committee, appointed by the RDS for the purpose, reported handing over to the administrator Giesecke's diplomas, personal library, and all unpacked Greenland mineral specimens. They noted 'a third class of articles, about which they feel a diffidence in making any specific report: These articles are, a very curious and valuable collection of Toys, Gems, Jewels, and Minerals, all contained in one cabinet'. However, Town Major Sirr confirmed that these items were, to his knowledge, Giesecke's personal property, and so they were also handed over.[64] The librarian, Frederick Cradock, was placed in temporary charge of the museum. Cradock died within six weeks of his appointment.[65] A fortnight later James Lynch, lecturer in experimental philosophy since 1800, was also dead.[66] In less troubled days Lynch had built a large cut-away model of a steam engine to illustrate his lectures on mechanical engineering.[67] Even given their ages, and the prevalence of infectious disease, it is difficult to avoid concluding that the deaths of these three in such a relatively short period of time was accelerated in some measure by the stress induced by loss of income.

58 *RDS Proc.*, lxviii, report, 15 Dec. 1831.   59 Ibid., minutes, 9 Feb. 1832.   60 Ibid., 6 Apr. 1832.
61 Ibid., 5 July 1832, and appendices I and II.   62 *RDS Proc.*, lxix, fine arts committee report, 1
Nov. 1832.   63 Ibid., minutes, 7 Mar., 4 July 1833.   64 *RDS Proc.*, lxx, minutes, 14, 21 Nov. 1833.

A nadir was reached in 1831 from which it took the RDS much time to recover. Nevertheless, most of its core activities struggled on. Richard Griffith presented his last mineralogical survey (on northeast Ulster) early in 1829. This was supplemented by a report prepared by Giesecke, taking in parts of mid-Ulster, in 1830, and marking the last major geological field survey undertaken by the society.[68] Private donations to the museum continued to arrive, being unaffected by changes in the levels of government support, but creating a classification backlog and increasing the existing problems of accommodation. General Freeman presented a collection of semi-precious stones from Ceylon, in 1829.[69] Geographical exploration, and imperial wars, continued to be a valuable source of ethnographical and natural history artefacts. Captain Studdert, RN, donated a collection of sacred idols and books from Burma, in 1830.[70] In the same year Matthew Moran donated, 'Fourteen beautifully gilt leaves of the sacred Burmese writings, taken out of the great temple at Rangoon', and the duchess of Northumberland presented a geological collection from the Mount Sinai region.[71] General O'Halloran presented in 1832 weapons captured from the Rajah of Gurrakotah in 1818, and Captain Norton of the 34th regiment donated 'A Bomarang, or magic stick, used by the natives of New Holland, partly for incantations, partly as missile'.[72] Also in 1832, James O'Hara, a member, presented 'A remarkable collection of petrefied [sic] shells found near Thibet, in the Glen of the Spitee or Table Land, at an elevation of 15000 feet above the level of the sea'.[73] Matthew Moran was again a benefactor in 1833, donating the head of a Nepali tiger 'discovered in the act of devouring a buffalo, which after having killed, he had dragged to the top of a bank twenty feet high, where he was shot'.[74] Finally, after almost five years, the long-awaited Persepolitan casts, twenty-four in total, arrived in Dublin in April 1833, having been shipped from Persia to London via Bombay.[75]

Public admissions to the museum began to exceed 30,000 per annum in 1830,[76] and reached 38,000 in 1831.[77] However, growth was interrupted in 1832. The great cholera epidemic moving slowly westwards from India since 1826 reached Ireland in 1832. The threat of contagion spurred an interest in hygiene, and the cleansing of public places. All public offices closed on 21 March, observed by royal proclamation as a day of fasting and prayer throughout the United Kingdom. In July 1832 the marquess of Anglesey took his family to Wales, and it was alleged that Daniel O'Connell fled to Bath, to avoid the growing risk of contagion. Factories were closed for the same reason. At least

65 Ibid., 21 Mar., 9 May 1833.   66 Ibid., 23 May 1833.   67 *RDS Proc.*, lxv, minutes, 28 May 1829.
68 *RDS Proc.*, lxv and lxvii, reports, 22 Jan. 1829, and 18 Nov. 1830.   69 *RDS Proc.*, lxv, minutes, 16 July 1829. General Quin John Freeman (*c*.1754–1834) was a member of the society 1800–34. 70 *RDS Proc.*, lxvi, minutes, 22 Apr. 1830.   71 *RDS Proc.*, lxvii, minutes, 25 Nov., 9 Dec. 1830. 72 *RDS Proc.*, lxviii, minutes, 5 July 1832.   73 *RDS Proc.*, lxix, minutes, 20 Dec. 1832.   74 Ibid., 7 Mar. 1833.   75 Ibid., 14 Feb., 21 Mar. 1833.   76 *RDS Proc.*, lxvi, report, 22 July 1832.   77 *RDS Proc.*, lxviii, report, 5 Jan. 1832.

20,000 victims died in 1832, and it is probable that this official estimate was seriously understated.[78] In two months, March–April 1832, the cholera epidemic had spread throughout Ireland, its virulent and unfamiliar nature leaving a deep scar on the public memory.[79] The RDS museum was closed to the public in May 1832. At the end of the month Giesecke advised Assistant Secretary Edward Hardman 'that the Museum is thoroughly cleansed and arranged, and fit for the reception of visitors'. Public admissions to the museum were resumed for a few weeks. However, by early July the society resolved 'That on account of the contagious disease now so prevalent in Dublin, the Museum be closed to the public, and that it be referred to the Museum and House Committees to determine when it shall be opened again'.[80] After the deaths of Giesecke and Cradock, Thomas Wall, the museum porter, was temporarily given charge of the museum. He had previously arranged and catalogued the zoological collection under Giesecke's supervision.[81] Appointed in 1825, he had been entrusted by Giesecke on various occasions with responsibilities that allowed him to develop his talents and he effectively managed the entire museum, including the preparation of annual reports, during 1833–6.[82]

As the cholera threat loomed, the RDS directed the resources of its science laboratory towards an assessment of the quick production of chloride of lime, and its application as a disinfectant. Edmund Davy commended its use as a cleansing and deodorizing agent, but warned against the inhalation of chlorine gas and his reports were sent to the Dublin newspapers.[83] This was not the first occasion on which public health information was disseminated by the society in this way. Nine months previously the Dublin newspapers were circulated with a letter written by Davy.

> Last evening I observed in a little child's hand, some white peppermint sugar drops, having bright red spots on them. Suspecting they were coloured with a substance improper for children, I was induced to examine them, and I found that their colouring matter is red lead. Those drops, are, I understand, commonly sold in our streets on slips of paper. As the combinations of lead are known to be poisonous, and the habitual use of peppermint drops containing red lead, may lay the foundation of inveterate diseases in children, such a pernicious application of this pigment, ought, of course, to be made known to the public, and, if possible, prevented.[84]

78 Joseph Robins, *The miasma: epidemic and panic in nineteenth-century Ireland* (Dublin, 1995), pp. 63–9, 79–80, 108. Hereafter, Robins, *The miasma*. MacDonagh, *The emancipist*, p. 85, says O'Connell went to Bath and spoke to audiences on the benefits of the union.   79 Gerard O'Brien, 'State intervention and the medical relief of the Irish poor, 1787–1850', in Elizabeth Malcolm and Greta Jones (eds), *Medicine, disease and the state in Ireland, 1650–1940* (Cork, 1999), pp. 201–3. Hereafter, Malcolm and Jones, *Medicine, disease and the state*.   80 *RDS Proc.*, lxviii, minutes, May–July 1832.   81 Ibid., 31 May 1832.   82 *RDS Proc.*, lxx, 21 Nov. 1833, contains a report by Thomas Wall. 83 *RDS Proc.*, lxviii, Edmund Davy's reports, 8, 15 Mar. 1832.   84 *RDS Proc.*, lxvii, minutes, 2

The society's laboratory also continued its normal function of providing aid to Irish manufacturers. In February 1833 Davy advised the society that he had undertaken comparative trials of Irish manufactured, and imported soaps, at the request of the Dublin Guild of St George (soap and candle makers). The Dublin soap manufacturers were at that time facing stiff price competition from English manufacturers of bar soap, and Davy undertook to analyse the properties of the English product. He concluded that the Irish manufacturers were being disadvantaged by archaic excise duties rather than by any intrinsic merit of their competitors' products.[85] In mid-1833 Davy was granted leave of absence to conduct a course of lectures in Clonmel and Limerick.[86] This marked an important development in the popularisation of science in Ireland, which was to have beneficial repercussions on the society's role in science education for many years to come.

Meanwhile, the issue of free public lectures in Dublin remained contentious. Isaac Weld presented a report in May 1831 advocating a return to the policy of free lectures, especially for artisans and mechanics. The society considered this report on 2 June and concluded that the botany lectures were not specifically mentioned in Lord Leveson Gower's 1829 letter, and could therefore be offered free of charge to the public. At the same time a motion moved by Eccles Cuthbert was adopted, and transmitted to the chief secretary.

> That having, in compliance with the suggestions of the Chief Secretary, tried the experiment of fixing a price for admission to the Lectures of the respective Professors, and having found that experiment totally fail of producing the contemplated effect, it is expedient that the several Lectures be thrown open to the public, as they formerly were, free from all charge of admission, and thus again open the source of useful instruction to all classes of the public, as the Society feels assured it has heretofore done with signal advantage.[87]

Edmund Davy followed up this resolution with a prospectus for chemistry lectures to be offered free to artisans and mechanics. The topics covered were the properties of air and water; the manufacture of industrial chemicals, soaps, salts, paints, and metallic compounds, and the techniques of bleaching, tanning, and dyeing.[88] Government approval for free lectures could not be obtained in 1831, and the society adverted again to this issue in 1833. The honorary secretaries were instructed to communicate with the government, pointing out that after a trial period of two years the policy of charging for admission to lectures had not worked.[89] Once again, this appeal failed to elicit a change in government policy.

June 1831. 85 *RDS Proc.*, lxix, minutes, 28 Feb., 28 Mar. 1833. 86 Ibid., 6 June, 11 July 1833. 87 *RDS Proc.*, lxvii, minutes, 12 May, 2 June 1831. 88 Ibid., 30 June 1831. 89 *RDS Proc.*, lxix, minutes, 31 Jan., 7 Feb. 1833.

The reduction in government funding impacted adversely on all aspects of the society's activities. Turpin argues that the grant reduction made educational development in the arts impossible.[90] Admissions to the art school remained steady, averaging 165 new pupils per annum during the five-year period 1829–33, showing no change on the 1826–7 intake.[91] There can be little doubt that the reduction in pay suffered by the four school masters, from £100 down to £80 per annum, was sufficiently severe to cause at least some of them to seek alternative supplementary employment. However, this may already have been happening before the cuts took effect. The fine arts committee reported in May 1831

> that it appears on examination of the masters' attendance book, that there is a very great neglect on the part of the masters in the Schools in their attendance; and the Committee having in vain endeavoured by every other means to enforce regularity, recommend to the Society to sanction the infliction of pecuniary fines on the masters, for absence from their respective Schools.

On 2 June 1831 Henry Brocas was summoned before the general meeting and reprimanded for habitual unpunctuality and absenteeism, and threatened with dismissal.[92] Brocas was in trouble again in March 1832 for failure to submit monthly returns.[93] At the end of the year the fine arts committee felt compelled to complain that Brocas continued to ignore their instructions, and he was suspended from duties. He retrieved the situation temporarily in January 1833, by apologising to the committee for his earlier neglect. However, he was back before an irate board in April, along with fellow master John Smyth, and both men were formally cautioned for failure to submit quarterly sample drawings.[94]

The gradual collapse of discipline and morale in the art school was matched by events in the botanic garden. In February 1829 the botany committee decided to phase out the apprenticeship scheme and replace apprentices with cheaper 'boy labourers'. This new departure appeared to work satisfactorily at first, but by June 1830 lateness and absenteeism had become a problem, and a formal time-keeping procedure was put in place under the gatekeeper's control. In November the boys sent a letter to the botany committee, complaining that they were not being given the opportunity to improve themselves. Shocked by such temerity, the committee responded that the boys were labourers at weekly wages, not apprentices, and that therefore Underwood had authority to employ them in any capacity useful to the garden. This reply did nothing to improve work

90 Turpin, *A school of art in Dublin*, p. 78.   91 Gitta Willemson, *The Dublin Society drawing schools: students and award winners, 1746–1876* (Dublin, 2000). Hereafter, Willemson, *Students and award winners*.   92 *RDS Proc.*, lxvii, fine arts committee report, 26 May 1831, and minutes of general meeting, 2 June 1831.   93 *RDS Proc.*, lxviii, minutes, 1 Mar. 1832.   94 *RDS Proc.*, lxix, minutes, 20 Dec. 1832, 24 Jan., 4, 25 Apr. 1833.

discipline, and in February 1831 two boys were fined 'for insubordinate conduct when employed at the Society's House; in removing snow, and leaving their work without permission'. A pervasive decline in conduct seems to have smitten the residents and employees at the garden during these years, not helped by the fact that the ageing Underwood and White seemed incapable of imposing managerial authority. The committee reprimanded Mary Coy for failing to keep the basement of the professor's house in a clean condition, and ordered White's son James to be ejected from the premises for unspecified 'outrageous' conduct. Underwood was instructed to call the police if James White attempted to enter the grounds. The garden had been allowed to develop into a small village of over twenty permanent inhabitants by the end of 1833, and ample scope existed for petty complaints, tensions and feuds.[95]

Compared with earlier years the development of the botanic garden for the years 1829–33 seemed almost at a standstill. The botany committee recommended that an investment be made to replace the deteriorating wooden plant houses in Glasnevin with steel-framed houses, and that Samuel Litton, the botany professor, be required to reside for at least part of the year on the premises.[96] Litton reported on the state of the garden at the end of 1830. Its layout was then pretty much as it had been in 1800, with considerable areas devoted to table vegetables, grass and fodder trials, medicinal and industrial herbs. One major new addition was a collection of indigenous Irish plants, and an increase in the numbers of exotic plants and garden flowers, many requiring controlled climatic conditions. The major defects noted by Litton were the lack of secure boundary walls, the poor condition of the hothouses, and the lack of an adequate piped water supply. Litton also advocated the formation of a botanical museum and library.[97] In a further report, in 1831, the botany committee lamented that a rebuilding program could not be undertaken due to shortage of finance, and the best alternative was to implement a phased schedule of repairs to the existing stock of wooden houses.[98] When the water supply problem worsened in the summer of 1832 the committee recommended that John Oldham, a well-known engineer and member of the society, be asked to supervise the installation of a pumped supply to the hothouses.[99] Oldham's solution was a hydraulic ram, commissioned in March 1833, and capable of pumping water from the adjoining river to a reservoir from which the conservatories could be supplied.[100]

95 RDS Archive: Committee of Botany minute book, entries for 16 Feb.,19 Oct 1829; 11 June, 1 Nov. 1830, 7 Feb. 1831, 7 Apr. 1832, 28 Jan. 1833, and 24 Feb. 1834.   96 *RDS Proc.*, lxvi, botany committee report, 26 Nov. 1829.   97 *RDS Proc.*, lxvii, appendix II, report on botanic garden, 24 Nov. 1830.   98 Ibid., select committee report, 16 June 1831.   99 *RDS Proc.*, lxviii, minutes, 7 June 1832. John Oldham (1779–1840) was a member of the society 1827–40. He developed a number of marine steam propulsion systems, and emigrated to London in 1837. In 1812 the Bank of Ireland adopted his design for a bank note numbering machine. [Sources: *RDS Proc.*, var. dates; *DNB*] 100 *RDS Proc.*, lxix, botany committee report, 7 Mar. 1833.

Some tangential activities continued in the grey zone between botany and agriculture. Tobacco growing for the domestic market was investigated in 1829–30 and was the subject of two reports by Edmund Davy.[101] About the same time Isaac Weld presented a report on his experiments on poppy growing and the extraction of opium.[102] At this time Irish agriculture was suffering one of its periodic crises, with local famines and food riots occurring in 1829–31, and a revival of agrarian secret societies all over Leinster in 1832.[103] In 1830 the RDS took an initiative on agricultural development which was to prove of long-term significance. The trigger was a letter from the marquess of Downshire,[104] urging the society to revive its direct involvement in agriculture.[105] As early as 1819, in a letter to Lord Cloncurry, Downshire had described the Farming Society as grossly mismanaged and expressed the opinion that it and the Dublin Society 'require strict inquiry'.[106] By 1830 the Farming Society no longer existed and the RDS had long ceased to have a direct involvement in agricultural development. The society responded to Lord Downshire's letter by inviting him, and another progressive resident landlord, James Naper of Loughcrew, to join a select committee to review the society's services to agriculture.[107] The select committee concluded that local initiatives in agriculture were best left to local associations, but that the RDS could provide a useful national role as a central agency for the diffusion of information on agricultural improvements. For this purpose the select committee recommended the separation of agriculture from botany within the society's administration, and the revival of a separate agriculture committee.[108]

A committee of agriculture and planting was established on 12 May 1830. Its fifteen elected members included Lord Downshire, James Naper, and Lord Cloncurry; and seven other landowners, Sir Samuel O'Malley, George Evans of Portrane, Colonel Palliser, Fenton Hort, John Payne Garnett, George Lucas Nugent, and Colonel Fox of Co. Longford. The remaining five consisted of four long serving members of the society, Dr William Harty (formerly of the botany committee), Robert Bryan, C.S. Hawthorne, John Rorke, and the inevitable barrister (Francis Gore).[109] The new committee wrote to the secretaries of the local agricultural societies throughout Ireland, canvassing for suggestions, and themselves suggesting the establishment in Kildare Street of a repository for

101 RDS Proc., lxvi, reports, 22 Apr., 3 June 1830.   102 Ibid., minutes, 25 Feb. 1830. Weld's paper was ordered to be printed as an appendix, but is not present in the archive copies of RDS Proc., lxvi.   103 Galen Broeker, Rural disorder and police reform in Ireland, 1812–36 (London, 1970), pp. 204–7. Hereafter, Broeker, Rural disorder and police reform.   104 Arthur Blundell Sandys Trumbull Hill (1788–1845) 3rd marquess of Downshire, was a member of the RDS, 1830–45, and a vice-president from 1831. [Source: RDS Proc., var. dates.]   105 RDS Proc., lxvi, minutes,18 Mar. 1830. 106 V.B. Lawless, 2nd baron Cloncurry, Personal recollections of the life and times with extracts from the correspondence, of Valentine Lord Cloncurry (Dublin, 1849), p. 319. Hereafter, Cloncurry, Personal recollections.   107 RDS Proc., lxvi, minutes, 1 Apr. 1830.   108 Ibid., 22 Apr. 1830.   109 Ibid., 12 May 1830.

specimen agricultural produce and implements.[110] This concept was essentially the revival of a permanent agricultural exhibition, or agricultural museum, as operated by the society in the eighteenth century. In a follow up report the committee asked the RDS for funds to convert part of the stable offices in Kildare Street 'as a repository of approved agricultural implements', and recommended experiments on the relative values of sea-weed based manures.[111] However, the agriculture committee had no spending budget under its own control, and depended on the ability of the economy committee to find and make spare funds available to it. In the circumstance of pending grant reductions this was a daunting task.[112] In December 1830 the agriculture committee adopted a new approach, when C.S. Hawthorne[113] gave notice of a motion

> That an exhibition of live stock be held in the yard adjoining this house at such time, and under such arrangements, as the Society may subsequently direct and appoint.[114]

The society agreed in principle 'That an exhibition of Live Stock, with the view of promoting improvement in the breed' should be held on the premises in 1831.[115] In January 1831 dates were set for the exhibition and regulations for exhibitors issued. A show of cattle, sheep, pigs and horses was to take place in Kildare Street on Tuesday, Wednesday and Thursday, 26–8 April 1831. Exhibitors were required to certify the feeds used (distillery wash was prohibited), attend during the exhibition, 'and to prevent confusion, the different lots must be brought to the ground at or before 9 o'clock, on each morning of the show'. The agriculture committee would appoint judges, and a premium list of cash or silver medal prizes was attached to the regulations. While allowing scope for new breeds, there was an expectation that the cattle classes would consist mainly of Leicestershires, Durhams, Holdernesses, Ayrshires and Devons. Sheep were anticipated to be of Leicestershire, or South Down breed; pigs and horses of unclassified breeds. A separate class for Spanish Asses was also included.[116]

In the euphoria of the new departure, an attempt was made to revive the veterinary professorship and establish a veterinary school. However, the requirement that this should be self-financing was a deterrent never overcome.[117] In May 1831 C.S. Hawthorne reported on the results of the first show. Financially it had proved an unexpected success, with expenditure coming in just below the budget of £150 and with the added bonus of £41 in admission receipts. Informal recommendations made by stock exhibitors were discussed, and the

110 Ibid., 3 June 1830.   111 Ibid., 10 June 1830.   112 Ibid., a motion to allocate £500 *per annum* to agriculture was rejected on 29 Apr. 1830.   113 Charles Stewart Hawthorne, former excise commissioner, was a member of the RDS, 1815-34, and an honorary secretary, 1831-4. (Source: *RDS Proc.*, var. dates.)   114 *RDS Proc.*, lxvii, minutes, 2 Dec. 1830.   115 Ibid., 9 Dec. 1830. 116 Ibid., agriculture committee report, 27 Jan. 1831.   117 Ibid., minutes, Feb.-Apr. 1831.

agriculture committee was requested to obtain plans and estimates for the erection of cattle sheds.[118] The first list of prize-winners included breeders such as Robert La Touche of Harristown, A.H.C. Pollock of Mountainstown, William Filgate of Lisrenny, John Farrell of Moynalty, G.L. Nugent of Castlerickard, and William Sherrard of Dunleer. All the aforementioned would continue to play a significant role in cattle breeding, and in the evolution of the show.[119] At Hawthorne's instigation a gold medal essay scheme was added to the show features, initially on the topic of farm labourers' cottages, and later extended to include essays on the condition of agriculture in those areas of Connacht affected by famine in 1831.[120]

At the end of 1831 the society used the opportunity provided by an inquiry made by A.H.C. Pollock, to serve notice on the government that it would only continue to run the livestock show provided it was supplied by parliament 'with sufficient funds for that purpose, and the general maintenance of the Institution'.[121] This attempt to ward off the grant reduction was unsuccessful, but nevertheless the society decided to continue with its most important innovation for decades. Early in 1832 it was decided to further enhance the show features by offering associated lectures on agricultural chemistry and botany.[122] On 26 January 1832 Hawthorne presented plans for the next show. Dairy cattle from the Channel Islands (at that time known generically as Alderneys),[123] and poultry, were added to the judging classes. The latter move was prompted by interest in the eggs and poultry trade, viewed as a means of supplementing the incomes of small tenant farmers and cottiers. A further significant innovation was to be a display area for new or improved agricultural implements, and vegetables both for the table and as animal fodder.[124] The estimate prepared by the society of expenditure for 1832 (£5,300) included an allowance of £250 specifically for the promotion of agriculture, an increase of £100, mostly reflected in an enlarged prize fund.[125] The judges' results for the 1832 show reveal that most of the 1831 prize-winners competed again in 1832. Additional winners of note included John Gerrard of Co. Meath for Hereford cattle and Lord Cloncurry for a short horned ox. A Miss Graydon won first prize for the best pair of domestic poultry bred in Ireland.[126] In April 1833 C.S. Hawthorne reported on the success of the first two shows and added that the society,

> by their recurrence to first principles, and endeavouring to give a stimulus to the agriculturists, which was evidently the principal motive for granting the Royal Charter to the Dublin Society, they have succeeded in exciting

118 Ibid., agriculture committee report, 26 May 1831.   119 Ibid., appendix IV (prize winners). 120 Ibid., minutes, July 1831.   121 *RDS Proc.*, lxviii, minutes, 17 Nov. 1831.   122 Ibid., 19 Jan., 22 Mar. 1832.   123 P.L. Curran, *Kerry and Dexter cattle and other ancient Irish breeds: a history* (Dublin, 1990), p. 31. Hereafter, Curran, *Kerry and Dexter cattle*.   124 Ibid., agriculture committee report, 26 Jan. 1832.   125 Ibid., appendix V.   126 Ibid., appendix VII (prizewinners list).

an interest, which they have reason to hope will extend itself rapidly through the country, and accomplish the great end which the Society have in view -the improvement of Ireland.[127]

By the end of 1833, with the third show successfully completed, James Naper (elected a vice-president of the society in November 1833), reported on behalf of the agriculture committee. He noted that the committee 'consider the Show itself as fully equal, if not superior, to that of the last year, and the attendance of the Public, and the interest taken by them in its results, greatly increased'. He noted also that a new general agricultural association had been formed to represent exhibitors interests and 'that a number of the Members of this new Agricultural Association are becoming Members of the Royal Dublin Society'. The agriculture committee recommended the erection of a weighing machine in the cattle yard, which they estimated would cost £40, readily defrayed from the show admission receipts. In conclusion, they expressed the view that 'the Exhibition ... of Native Produce and Industry, will still further tend to prove, that Ireland only requires the fostering care of her patriotic and influential resident Proprietors'.[128] In an essay published in 1997 Richard Jarrell argued that the RDS initiative simply paralleled contemporary developments in Britain, catering to large landowners and tenants, and focused on livestock breeding and agricultural shows. He did not suggest an alternative course, but did point out the perennial problems of land tenure,[129] which were not within the capacity of the RDS to resolve. In the interests of balance it is worth pointing out that so far from being imitative the RDS agricultural show preceded that of the Royal Agricultural Society of England by a full decade.[130]

Encouraged by the success of the livestock show, the society launched an exhibition of Irish manufactures in 1833. Its origins lay in the society's long associations with the Dublin textile trade, and in an idea first canvassed by Isaac Weld in 1829. Weld was impressed by the industrial exhibitions held in Paris during the 1820s and saw scope for a similar project in Dublin. At his suggestion a sub-committee was formed, chaired by Richard Griffith (no longer an employee), who reported in March 1829 that the Kildare Street premises had ample space to mount such an exhibition, at an estimated cost of £200.[131] In April the society issued a prospectus for a 'National Exhibition of Manufactures'. The response from Irish industries was disappointing and in June the project was postponed indefinitely.[132] Sir Edward Stanley (the prison inspector and

127 RDS Proc., lxix, agriculture committee report, 4 Apr. 1833.   128 RDS Proc., lxx, agriculture committee report, 21 Nov. 1833.   129 Richard Jarrell, Agricultural and technical education, in Bowler and Whyte, Science and society in Ireland, p. 104.   130 The Royal Agricultural Society of England was incorporated by charter in 1841. The Royal Agricultural Society of Ireland, also incorporated by charter in 1841, based its peripatetic shows on the model provided by the English society, and by the Royal Highland and Agricultural Society of Scotland. See Berry, A history of the Royal Dublin Society, p. 298.   131 RDS Proc., lxv, minutes, 12 Feb., 5 Mar. 1829.   132 Ibid., 2

member of the RDS, not the chief secretary) revived the idea at the end of 1832.[133] At Stanley's behest a sub-committee, the Irish manufactures exhibition committee, was appointed in January 1833, consisting of twenty members, and charged with the evaluation of the practicability of establishing an annual exhibition of manufactures. The sub-committee reported favourably on the scheme in February. The members concluded that it 'would be attended with considerable advantage to the country, by creating an honourable emulation among the artisans, to improve their several manufactures, and by exciting in the nobility and gentry a desire to patronize articles of native production and manufactures'.[134] However, it was not until the end of 1833 that the first basic steps were taken to bring the project to fruition.[135]

Forced by the severe reductions in government funding, the society was obliged to curtail its programs in most areas, to shelve projects of doubtful utility, and to focus its resources on core activities and on innovations which offered some prospect of an immediate return. The last in the series of statistical surveys, that on Co. Roscommon, was published in March 1833.[136] The act empowering the society to set wage rates for silk weavers expired in 1831 and was allowed to lapse without any representation from the RDS for its continuance.[137] External requests for a renewal of the system of premium supports for straw plait manufacture were politely long-fingered.[138] Alternative sources of income actually fell, as the numbers of candidates for membership declined from forty-two during 1825–8 to thirty-three during 1829–32. Total membership fell from 625 listed at the beginning of 1829 to 568 at the beginning of 1833. This latter figure must be treated as provisional. The addition of thirty-three new members between 1829 and the end of 1832 is verifiable by reference to the periodical election lists published in the Proceedings (volumes lxv–lxix). However, the deletion by this author of ninety members during the same period is based on an extrapolation. It has been established that forty-one of the ninety were deceased or lapsed by the end of 1832. The additional forty-nine are a weighted proportion, based on the known deletion of 211 members between 1829 and 1839, and the known dates of death ascertained in 121 cases (fifty-seven per cent).[139]

James Naper's reference to a movement of agriculturists into the society in 1833 was as much an aspiration as an accurate statement of a change in membership composition taking place in that year. During 1833 fifty-four new members were elected, the highest annual intake since 1815, and sufficient to bring total membership once again above the 600 level. As regards agriculturists,

Apr., 25 June 1829. 133 *RDS Proc.*, lxix, minutes, 13 Dec. 1832. 134 Ibid., 31 Jan., 14 Feb. 1833. 135 *RDS Proc.*, lxx, minutes, 19 Dec. 1833. 136 *RDS Proc.*, lxix, minutes, 21 Mar. 1833. 137 *RDS Proc.*, lxvii, minutes, 27 Jan., 3 Feb. 1831. 138 Ibid., 2 June 1831. 139 Account has also been taken by this author of the pattern of personal attendances by members at general meetings. The prolonged absence of a previously regular attender has been taken to indicate that the

none were elected in 1829; five (including Lord Downshire and James Naper) were elected in 1830, and two (William Filgate and Robert La Touche) in 1831. Following the first cattle show, four were elected in 1832, including Dr Robert Collins, at that time Master of the Rotunda hospital, but with farming interests at Ardsallagh in Co. Meath, and later (1840-68) a leading member of the RDS agriculture committee. In 1833 thirteen landowners were elected members, including Robert Clayton Browne of Browne's Hill, James Anthony Corballis of Ratoath Manor, Lord Castlemaine and Lord Talbot. Even taking into account the large influx of new members in 1833, there was a net decrease in membership during 1829-33 that can be estimated at about two per cent.

The change in occupational composition of the membership at selected dates during 1800-34 is shown in appendix V. The landowner element, and the general landed interest amongst the membership, continued its slow decline since the beginning of the nineteenth century, and the professional element, particularly in law and medicine, continued to increase along a broad front. However, an interest in agricultural development per se was widely shared, as successful professionals and businessmen also frequently acquired land. Dr Robert Collins has already been mentioned and to him can be added Dr J.F. O'Neill Lentaigne, who had acquired substantial interests in the Tallaght area[140] (and later in Co. Monaghan). A more classic instance is provided by the Corballis family, three of them being members of the RDS at the end of 1833. Richard Corballis (1769-1847) inherited a successful timber business in Dublin and had interests in insurance and in the Grand Canal Company of Ireland. His brother James Anthony Corballis purchased land in the Ratoath district of Co. Meath in 1813.[141] Richard's son, John Richard Corballis pursued a career in law and politics but on his death was the owner of over 2,000 acres in Co. Meath, close to the Ratoath Manor and demesne of almost 1,000 acres which belonged to his uncle James Anthony.[142] On an even grander scale, Hugh Barton, founder of the Barton and Guestier wine business, purchased Straffan House and an estate of over 5,000 acres in Co. Kildare in the late 1820s.

If the early 1830s saw little change in the overall composition of RDS membership they nevertheless witnessed considerable changes in its leadership cadre, and in its paid officials. The business of the society remained vested in the general meetings, 168 of which were convened between January 1829 and December 1833. Attendance averaged thirty-seven per meeting, with very large attendance occurring only when paid offices were at stake.[143] This occurred most decidedly on 12 November 1829, when Edward Hardman, a member of

membership concerned had lapsed.   140 William Domville Handcock, *The history and antiquities of Tallaght* (2nd ed., Dublin, 1899).   141 Gerard Rice, *Norman Kilcloon, 1171-1700* (Dublin, 2001), mentions a Richard Corballis, a substantial tenant of the Plunkett family in Ratoath barony in the eighteenth century.   142 D. Parkinson, 'The Corballis-Corbally families of Co. Dublin', in *Dublin Historical Record*, xlv (1992), pp. 91-100.   143 *RDS Proc.*, lxv-lxx, figures extracted by the

the house committee, was elected assistant secretary at a salary of £300 per annum to replace the late Bucknall McCarthy. Almost half the membership (312 out of 630) attended that meeting, and 299 members cast their votes. Hardman received thirty per cent of the votes, defeating seven other candidates including Reverend J.P. Griffith, Reverend Richard MacDonnell (later TCD provost), Isaac Weld and Hugh Hamill.[144] Almost five years elapsed before the next extreme high in attendance occurred and once again the occasion was the ballot for a stipendiary office. John Patten[145] was elected librarian in the place of Frederick Cradock on 21 February 1833. About a third of the membership attended the meeting and 213 votes were cast, of which forty-four per cent went to Patten. He defeated four other candidates, including John Anster,[146] a member of the library committee.[147] The election of committee members to paid offices, as in the case of Hardman, caused some disquiet to those moral arbiters Doctors Anthony Meyler and William Harty.[148] However, precedents for such appointments existed, and the perceived risk to the impartiality of paid officials was dealt with by the passage of a standing order prohibiting members who held paid offices in the society from speaking or voting as members at general meetings or committee meetings.[149]

New by-laws and regulations were introduced to tighten up the operation of the committee system, and to meet government criticisms of the membership election system. From 1830, ballot papers for standing committees were ordered to include details of committee members' attendance, and the standing committees were placed under an obligation to nominate candidates in excess of the numbers of vacancies, in order to create annual elections.[150] The first of the new ballot papers revealed that committee members Sir William Stamer, Robert Hutton, Paul L. Patrick, and the Reverend Franc Sadleir, FTCD, attended no meetings in 1830, and (except for Sadleir) none were re-elected. Otherwise changes of committee personnel occurred slowly at first, probably because the near static membership pool of the early 1830s did not provide a sufficient number of fresh members willing to go forward for election to committees. Nevertheless, of the sixty-three members on seven standing committees at the end of 1828, thirty-five (fifty-five per cent) had been replaced by the beginning of 1833. In addition, an eighth standing committee had been established for agriculture.[151] Internal committee housekeeping was further improved after

author from the attendance records.   **144** *RDS Proc.*, lxvi, minutes, 12 Nov. 1829.   **145** Former member of the chemistry committee, and a brother-in-law of Robert Emmet's. (Sources: *RDS Proc.*, var. dates; Leon O Broin, *The unfortunate Mr. Robert Emmet*, Dublin, 1958.)   **146** John Anster (1793–1867), regius professor of civil law at TCD, and translator of Goethe's Faust, was a member of the society's library committee. (Sources: *RDS Proc.*, var. dates; *DNB*, Meenan and Clarke, *The Royal Dublin Society, 1731–1981.*)   **147** *RDS Proc.*, lxix, minutes, 21 Feb. 1833. **148** *RDS Proc.*, lxvi, minutes, 5, 12 Nov. 1829.   **149** Ibid., 19 Nov. 1829.   **150** Ibid., 12 Nov. 1829, 3 June 1830.   **151** *RDS Proc.*, lxix, minutes, 8 Nov. 1832. Multiple membership of committees was allowed, except for members of the economy committee.

Edward Hardman reported on the state of the committee minute books in 1829. Only the fine arts and the chemistry committees' minute books had been kept up to date, the remaining five committees being between one and four years in arrears. Hardman was given permission to employ a clerk to get the minute books up to date.[152]

Consideration was also given to the reintroduction of annual membership. A sub-committee reported on the subject in May 1830, recommending that annual membership be made available for a subscription of three guineas per annum. However, the difficulties of collecting annual subscriptions were still viewed as a major deterrent, and it was decided to defer discussion of the matter until the end of the year. In the meantime the sub-committee recommended that the legal issues surrounding the collection of annual subscriptions be addressed.[153] No further progress was reported at the end of the year, and in June 1831 Dr Isaac D'Olier[154] called for a total review of the membership by-laws.[155] D'Olier's move was supported, and given added impetus, in January 1832 when John Boyd called for a reduction of the life membership fee from thirty guineas to twenty guineas. Boyd also moved for an amendment of by-law 42, to allow the election of members by a simple majority,[156] instead of the two-thirds majority required since that by-law was adopted in 1767.[157] The review sub-committee reported on 1 March 1832 and recommended, inter alia, that the election of members should take place by simple majority vote. A month later they added a recommendation that a new class of 'annual associate' members be created, at an annual fee of three guineas, 'in deference to the wishes of Government'. Associate members were to have restricted rights. The recommendation was that they 'shall not be incorporated Members of the Society; neither shall they have any vote; nor any concern nor interference whatsoever with the management of the property or affairs of the Society; neither shall they be permitted to be present at the Meetings of the Board, or of the Committees of the Society'.[158] Dr Isaac D'Olier presented a comprehensive review of the by-laws to the stated general meeting held on 7 June 1832. Amongst his recommendations were the creation of a new class of associate members (as recommended above), and the dropping of the two-thirds rule for the election of members. The meeting, chaired by Sir Robert Shaw and with thirty other members present, adopted all the changes recommended, subject to their being confirmed by the next stated general meeting in November.[159] The meeting held on 8 November was chaired by Lord Harberton, with thirty-eight other voting members present. The

152 RDS Proc., lxvi, report, 19 Nov. 1829.   153 Ibid., minutes, 12 May, 3 June, 1 July 1830.
154 Isaac Matthew D'Olier, LLD, MRIA, governor of the Bank of Ireland, was a member of the society's botany, and fine arts, committees in the 1830s. (Source: RDS Proc., var. dates; Treble Almanack.)   155 RDS Proc., lxvii, minutes, 2 June 1831.   156 RDS Proc., lxviii, minutes, 3 Nov. 1831, 5 Jan. 1832.   157 RDS Proc., iv, amendments to by-laws, 12 Nov. 1767.   158 RDS Proc., lxviii, minutes, 6 Apr. 1832.   159 Ibid., minutes, 7 June 1832.

changes proposed to the membership rules proved unacceptable to a large number of those attending and the proposal to elect members by a simple majority vote was dropped. The revival of annual membership in the form of associate status was given a rough passage and adopted by a majority of just two votes. It is perhaps of significance that of the thirty-nine members present and voting, nineteen had been present at the meeting on 7 June and twenty had not. However, there is no obvious evidence of an anti-change clique specific to either group and the opposition to reform of the election procedure, which was to have profound implications three years later, must be taken as an accurate reflection of the views of the then active members.[160] It did, of course, point up the difficulty of making changes under government by general meeting.

160 *RDS Proc.*, lxix, minutes, 8 Nov. 1832.

CHAPTER FOUR

Exhibitions and a conference, 1834–5

The deaths of key officials and exchequer parsimony brought the Royal Dublin Society to a point where its continued useful existence was threatened during 1832–3. This chapter examines its attempts at re-defining its role in the ensuing two years. The long predicted influx of agriculturists at last began to manifest itself in 1834, fuelled by the success of the agricultural show. A parallel development occurred in mercantile representation as the manufactures exhibition began to draw support, and there is some evidence of an incipient rivalry between elements in the two groups. Meanwhile, some of the older established departments experienced a revival of their own on the appointment of new and dynamic replacement officials. The change of pace was most marked in the botanic garden and in the science departments. Almost fortuitously the society found itself aligned with the most innovative wing of scientific thought then current. The culmination of this promising period was the society's participation in the first modern international conference held in Dublin, that of the British Association for the Advancement of Science (BAAS), in the summer of 1835.[1]

By mid-1835 the RDS seemed to have climbed out of the trough of the 1820s, and its membership numbers once more exceeded 700. Eighty-four new members were elected in 1834 and an estimated twenty-four were deleted, leaving a net gain of sixty, the greatest accession of new members since 1815. During the first half of 1835 a further fifty-four new members were elected. For the first time in decades the intake of agriculturists exceeded that of every other category, including the still well represented lawyers. There was also a marked increase in the number of medical practitioners elected. The RDS strategy of promoting agriculture and industry through exhibitions, and its commitment to applied science, seemed to have paid dividends and there was an indefinable yet almost tangible change in the calibre of the new members. For the most part they were relatively young and at the most vigorous period of their lives, and the intake of 1834–5 would leave their mark on the RDS in a manner rarely matched by any other year cadre.

1 See, for background information, Jack Morrell and Arnold Thackray, *Gentlemen of science: early years of the British Association for the Advancement of Science* (Oxford, 1981), hereafter, Morrell and Thackray, *Gentlemen of science*.

The politics of the RDS members will be dealt with in more detail in the next chapter. Suffice it to mention at this point that the political sentiments of the members were tempered by the fact that for the most part they were overwhelmingly protestant, and drawn from the wealthiest socio-economic groups. They therefore tended to reflect the political culture and experience of the mercantile and professional classes of protestant Dublin, and of the large landowning magnates. Paralleling the main developments of contemporary British politics, the members were divided broadly into a Whig-liberal wing (probably a slight majority) advocating constitutional and social reforms, and a Tory-conservative wing (a substantial minority). The latter group was opposed, not necessarily to all change, but certainly to what they saw as abrupt or disruptive changes in the *status quo*. Both groups contained extremes of intellectual or emotional protestantism, the most militant of whom were attracted into the anti-catholic Orange Order and its affiliates. Both groups contained elements that believed that the union with Great Britain had failed and should be repealed.[2] The minority of members who had earlier connections with the United Irishman revolutionary republican movement of the 1790s (see pages 33, 59–62), had largely died out by 1835.

Prominent amongst the young generation of liberal landowners was Charles William Hamilton (1802–80), of Hamwood, Dunboyne. Hamilton's family had long connections with the RDS, and with the Carton estate of the dukes of Leinster. Robert Archbold of Castledermot was also a keen agriculturist and, like Hamilton, would later become a member of the RDS agriculture committee, and a regular participant at the livestock exhibitions.[3] The presence of a north Leinster land owning nexus within the society was further strengthened at this time by the election of Lords Kildare, de Robeck, and Killeen, Sir William Somerville, George Taaffe of Smarmore Castle, Edward Lawless of Lyons, and Thomas Lee-Norman of Ardee. Reinforcements from slightly more distant Leinster counties included the Duckett brothers of Co. Carlow, and the Wexford magnates Robert Doyne, Sir Thomas Esmonde, and Lord Carew. There was a distinctly liberal flavour to the politics of this group and four of them were or would later become MPs in the liberal interest (Lord Killeen, Lord Carew, Robert Archbold, and Sir Thomas Esmonde).[4]

Ulster landowners were also well represented in the 1834–5 intake, which included William Willoughby Cole (1807–86) later 3rd earl of Enniskillen, and John Crichton (1802–85) later 3rd earl of Erne. Amongst the other Ulster landowners elected at this time were the Stewart brothers, Alexander Robert (1795–1850) and John Vandaleur (1802–72), of Ards House, Sheephaven, Co. Donegal, and William Humphreys (1798–1872), of Ballyhaise, Co. Cavan.[5]

---

2 See for example Hill, *From patriots to unionists*, esp. pt 3, chaps 11–14, and Cullen, *Princes and pirates*. 3 *RDS Proc.*, var. dates. 4 Walker, *Parliamentary elections*. 5 Ulysses de Burgh, *The landowners of Ireland* (Dublin, 1878), hereafter, de Burgh, *The landowners of Ireland*.

Ulster mercantile interests were represented by new members such as Michael Andrews, linen manufacturer, of Ardoyne, Belfast, but were numerically outweighed by recruitment from the Dublin merchants. Outstanding amongst the latter were the brothers James and William Haughton, Dublin corn and flour merchants. The Haughtons (former quakers, they became unitarians in 1834), were prominent supporters of the abolition of African slavery.[6] Garrett Wall, Thomas Baird, and Thomas Willans, woollen manufacturers, were elected life members in 1834-5. Hibernian Mills, Kilmainham, the Willans family enterprise, specialized in tweeds. Their business was given a major fillip when Lord Anglesey adopted the Irish tweed overcoat as both a fashion and an economic statement in 1829.[7]

Representative of a major influx of scientific and medical members at this period were Robert Ball, Richard Carmichael, Percival Hunt, James Macartney, Sir Henry Marsh, Joseph M. O'Ferrall, and William O'Brien Bellingham. Robert Ball (1802-57) became first secretary of the Dublin zoological society in 1837. Surgeon Richard Carmichael (1776-1849), was the first Irishman to be elected a corresponding member of the French Academy, and co-founded a school of medicine in Dublin which was later amalgamated with the Royal College of Surgeons, Ireland.[8] Percival Hunt (1802-48), son of a Co. Wicklow landowner, was physician to the Jervis Street charitable infirmary.[9] Professor James Macartney (1770-1843), a former United Irish supporter, was professor of anatomy in Trinity College 1813-37. At his urging TCD built a new medical school on campus 1823-5 and began catching up with contemporary developments in medical education. Macartney retained his impatient radical zeal and fell foul of the college authorities for his supposed preaching of atheism and for an assault with an umbrella on the architect of the medical school. From 1832 he was engaged in a running battle with the college board over lecture times, which culminated in his being locked out of his own lecture room in 1835.[10] By comparison with Macartney, Henry Marsh (1790-1860) represented the amiable and affluent face of Dublin medicine in the 1830s and his private practice catered mainly to the wealthy. He was professor of medicine at the RCSI, 1828-32.[11] Joseph Ferrall (1790-1868) and William O'Brien Bellingham (1805-57) were respectively the first and second surgical appointments to the newly opened St Vincent's hospital.[12]

Twenty-five lawyers were elected to life membership of the society in 1834-5. Amongst their number were William Henry Curran, Francis Magan, Michael

6 Samuel Haughton, *Memoir of James Haughton* (Dublin, 1877), hereafter, Haughton, *Memoir*. For information on the abolitionist activities of James Haughton, see also Noel Ignatiev, *How the Irish became white* (London, 1995).   7 *Freeman's Journal*, 1 Apr. 1829.   8 Sir Charles Cameron, *History of the Royal College of Surgeons in Ireland, and of the Irish schools of medicine* (2nd ed, Dublin, 1916). Hereafter, Cameron, *RCSI*.   9 Ibid., see index.   10 See Crone, *A concise dictionary of Irish biography*; Eoin O'Brien, *Conscience and conflict: a biography of Sir Dominic Corrigan, 1802-1880* (Dublin, 1983), pp. 51, 110, Malcolm and Jones, *Medicine, disease and the state*, pp. 85-93, and

O'Loghlen, and Edward O'Brien. W.H. Curran (1789–1858), the son and biographer of the famous advocate, John Philpot Curran, was a close confidant and adviser to Lord Anglesey during the latter's two terms as lord lieutenant.[13] Francis Magan (1772–1841), was a United Irishman who became a paid informant of the government. His efforts led to the discovery and arrest of Lord Edward Fitzgerald in 1798. Magan was appointed a waste-lands commissioner in 1821, and was in receipt of a secret service pension until 1834.[14] Michael O'Loghlen (1789–1842) was one of the first Irish catholics appointed a king's counsel after 1829. An O'Connellite, he was appointed solicitor general 1834–5 and attorney general 1835–6, and served as liberal MP for Dungarvan 1835–7.[15] Edward O'Brien (1806–40) was a younger brother of William Smith O'Brien, MP, and had recently been admitted to the Irish bar at the time of his election as a life member of the RDS. He became ill, probably while engaged in charitable work in Dublin, and died in 1840. He was the author of a posthumously published semi-autobiographical novel, *The lawyer*.[16]

Early deaths were exceptional amongst the privileged social group comprising the membership of the RDS in 1834–5. Fifty-eight members, including nineteen with recent service on committees, are known to have died during 1834–5. Age at death is known in twenty-three instances, and averaged seventy years.[17] Amongst the best known and influential members lost at this time were honorary secretary Charles Stewart Hawthorne, Archibald Hamilton Rowan, and Hugh Hamill, all of whom had given long and dedicated service on committees. Hawthorne's position as an honorary secretary was taken over by Robert Butler Bryan.[18] Between 1833 and 1837 the composition of the society's standing committees altered by forty per cent, with forty-six out of 115 committee members being elected for the first time. Turnover was particularly marked on the committees of fine arts, natural philosophy, and agriculture, all of which experienced a change in membership exceeding fifty per cent.[19]

In the case of the agriculture and planting committee, nine of the original members resigned during 1834, mostly to transfer to other committees, and C.S. Hawthorne died. A further two early members resigned in the course of 1835. The vacancies created were mostly filled with enthusiastic supporters of the agricultural exhibition.[20] The success of the early exhibitions boosted the confidence of the committee and made it attractive to newcomers. The

McDowell and Webb, *Trinity College*, pp. 89, 142–3.   **11** Cameron, RCSI, and DNB.
12 Cameron, RCSI, and Davis Coakley, *Irish masters of medicine* (Dublin, 1992), hereafter, Coakley, *Masters of medicine*.   **13** Donal A. Kerr, *A nation of beggars: priests, people, and politics in famine Ireland, 1846–1852* (Oxford, 1994). Hereafter, Kerr, *A nation of beggars*.   **14** DNB; see also Stella Tillyard, *Citizen lord: Edward Fitzgerald, 1763–1798* (London, 1998), pp. 259–72.   **15** Ball, *Judges in Ireland*, index.   **16** Richard Davis, *Revolutionary imperialist: William Smith O'Brien, 1803–64* (Dublin, 1998). Hereafter, Davis, *Revolutionary imperialist.*   **17** Information derived from author's database.   **18** *RDS Proc.*, lxx, minutes, 17 Apr. 1834.   **19** *RDS Proc.*, var. dates, author's analysis.   **20** Ibid.

patronage of the society was sought and given to several newly launched farming publications, notably the *Irish Farmer's Journal* and the *Irish Farmers and Gardeners Magazine*.[21] Special premiums were offered by the society in 1834 for essays on land management, laying particular stress on a perceived need to improve the living conditions of cottiers and labourers. Medals were offered for the best essays on consolidation of farms, and the development of good pastures. Also on the construction or improvement of labourers' cottages, the quantity of adjoining land required to support a labourer's family, 'and their fitness to promote the comfort and health of the inhabitants; also the rent charged for the same'. Essayists were particularly directed to take account of the Reverend William Hickey's ('Martin Doyle') *Address to the landlords of Ireland*, which was extensively quoted as a guide for the fourth premium. Finally, and probably influenced by the earlier trials conducted by Lord Cloncurry, a premium was offered for a factual account of the cultivation of New Zealand flax (*phormium tenax*) on boggy soils.[22]

Agricultural exports and prices were rising during the 1830s, but over 500,000 landless labourers lived in very insecure and near destitute circumstances.[23] Potatoes accounted for a fifth of total agricultural output at this time.[24] Localized seasonal famines were common events, especially in the western counties where dependence on the potato crop was highest. On the urging of Leland Crosthwaite[25] the society offered prizes during 1834–5 for essays on the potato crop and the 1833 potato famine in Connacht.[26] Eleven essays were received, those judged best being the essays of William G. Andrews of Comber, Co. Down, and Ninian Niven, curator of the society's botanic garden.[27] Andrews wrote that

> Having so completely established the Potato as a leading crop in our agricultural rotations, and as a leading article of food to our population, we had almost forgotten that it was not indigenous, till some alarming symptoms of degeneracy have appeared, in the more early decay of the tubers, and partial failure of the crop; from which many intelligent persons have begun to fear that the Potato might ultimately follow the example of some other naturalized exotics, which have flourished for a time in our climate, and ultimately cease to grow in it.[28]

21 *RDS Proc.*, lxx, minutes, 23, 30 Jan., 6 Mar. 1834.   22 Ibid., appendix II.   23 Cullen, *An economic history of Ireland*, pp. 109–10.   24 Cormac Ó Grada, 'Poverty, population and agriculture', in Vaughan, *A new history of Ireland*, v, p. 122.   25 Leland Crosthwaite, junior, served on the society's botany committee, 1833–52, and on the agriculture committee 1835–7. He was an active supporter of Daniel O'Connell in the 1830s, although not involved in the later repeal movement. [Sources: *RDS Proc.*, var. dates; *Freeman's Journal*, var. dates 1835–6.]   26 *RDS Proc.*, lxx, minutes, 10 July 1834.   27 *RDS Proc.*, lxxi, agriculture committee report, 5 Feb. 1835. 28 Ibid., appendix VII, 1 Nov. 1834.

Andrews made inquiries on potato failures in the Ulster counties of 'Antrim, Down, Derry [sic] and Donegal', and in southeast Scotland. He concluded that a shift in the pattern of planting to late spring, and earlier lifting of the crop, was a contributory factor to crop failure. Where earlier planting in March, and late lifting continued, such as in the vicinity of Strangford Lough, no failure had been experienced. A secondary factor, he believed, was climate variation, noting that the winters of 1831-3 had been very mild in the northeast with few night frosts, and that potatoes did not store well in warm conditions.[29] Niven's essay was much briefer, and concentrated on the empirical testing of four commonly ascribed reasons for potato crop failure, viz. soil exhaustion, fungal infection, poor quality imported seed, and planting during dry and warm weather. From trial plantings in April 1834 he concluded that none of the causes ascribed were solely responsible for the crop failure. As regards fungal infection, he decided this was a consequence and not a cause of crop disease. He did conclude that the planting of cut seed potatoes, or the accidental bruising of whole seed potatoes, could contribute to the onset of disease. He also concluded (with ominous prescience given the later discovery of the pathology of *sp. phytophthora infestans* which caused the great failures of the late 1840s), that 'atmospheric influence' was the remote trigger of potato blight. Like Andrews, he noted the relative mildness of recent winters.[30] Austin Bourke regarded Niven, and particularly his 1834 essay, as the soundest of the early commentaries on potato disease in Ireland.[31]

The fourth and fifth annual cattle shows took place in 1834 and 1835, and the 1835 show was visited by the lord lieutenant, the earl of Haddington, who was escorted by the duke of Leinster. At the show's conclusion the Agricultural Society of Ireland[32] hosted a dinner in Morrison's hotel, Dawson Street, attended by the lord lieutenant and many members of the RDS, including the duke of Leinster, James Naper, Lord Cloncurry, Sir Edward Stanley, Sir John Burke, and Leland Crosthwaite. A toast to the RDS was responded to by John Boyd, vice-president, who caused much laughter by a reference to the reductions in the government grant. Boyd contrasted the treatment given to the society by the Irish parliament and the United Kingdom parliament, and remarked – 'The step-mother of the child has certainly not been as liberal as the parent'.[33]

The committee of agriculture was pleased with the progress of the annual cattle show and the revived premium schemes, but frustrated by lack of funds and the absence of a clear-cut program for future development. The committee expressed its dissatisfaction in a report delivered to the society's general meeting on 19 February 1835. It acknowledged the society's financial difficulties.

---

29 Ibid.   30 Ibid., appendix VIII. See also Mary E. Daly, *The famine in Ireland* (Dundalk, 1986), pp. 52-5.   31 Austin Bourke, *The visitation of god: the potato and the great Irish famine* (Dublin, 1993), pp. 29-32, 157.   32 Precursor of the Royal Agricultural Society of Ireland, founded 1841 and merged with the Royal Dublin Society in 1888.   33 *Freeman's Journal*, 16, 22 Apr. 1835.

When the government withdrew its support from the Farming Society, the country, feeling the want of such an institution, naturally turned to the Royal Dublin Society, as that, which [sic] by reverting to a subject that had formed so important a feature in its original character, could most efficiently provide for that want; but the peculiar circumstances of the difficulty in which the Society was at that time placed, prevented it from acting as vigorously as it had evinced an inclination to do. A heavy debt was still due to the Duke of Leinster, and the grant from government was reduced so suddenly and unexpectedly, as to increase very much the difficulties to which any decrease of income must naturally have subjected it.[34]

The committee suggested that it be put in funds to carry out a four-point program. This was intended to consist of; (1) the collection of national agricultural statistics, and the dissemination of information on best agricultural practices, (2) correspondence with local agricultural societies, (3) the operation of a public agricultural museum [permanent exhibition] of seeds, produce, models, implements, and machinery, and (4) the appointment of a professor of agriculture to superintend the program and deliver lecture courses.

The committee urged the society

> to petition parliament for a fund to be allotted exclusively to the objects described in the resolutions submitted to you, and in making this recommendation, they would beg of the Society to consider that they are not advocating any new principle, or asking for the appropriation, to their use, of any portion of the funds which are now so well allotted in furthering the other objects of this old and valuable Institution, but simply asking for a sanction to the outline thus laid down for their future guidance, and authority for carrying the same into effect according as the future circumstances of this Society may admit of their doing so,[35]

The agriculture committee's report was referred to the general selected committee, a sub-committee of the general meeting 1829–34, which functioned as a standing committee between 1834 and 1838,[36] and consisted of the honorary officers (that is, vice-presidents and honorary secretaries), and elected representatives of each of the standing committees.[37] The primary function of this committee was to advise the general meeting on proposed policy changes and on major issues of the day. It was constituted a standing committee in June 1834, and dissolved in 1838.[38] The general selected committee reported to the general meeting on 12 March 1835. The committee endorsed the re-establishment of an

34 *RDS Proc*, lxxi, agriculture committee report, 19 Feb. 1835.   35 Ibid.   36 RDS Archive: General Selected Committee minute book, 1832–38.   37 *RDS Proc.*, lxx, resolution of general meeting, 20 Feb. 1834.   38 Ibid., 5 June 1834.

agricultural museum, but could not support the appointment of a professor of agriculture 'from the total absence of funds applicable to such object'. Regarding the first and second proposals, the committee considered that these were in part already met and recommended that their expansion be deferred pending further discussions with local societies and cattle breeders.[39]

A shortage of funds for development purposes constantly thwarted the ambitions of the agriculture committee. In an attempt to circumvent this problem, C.W. Hamilton proposed that the subscriptions of associate annual members (a category reluctantly agreed to in November 1832, but not implemented) be applied exclusively to the purposes of that committee. The committee's annual allocation of funds from the society, limited to £150, was 'evidently inadequate to those objects which the Committee contemplate'.[40] Hamilton's proposal was referred to the general selected committee on 9 April 1835. In a report given to the general meeting by Sir Edward Stanley on 16 April, the general selected committee almost out-of-hand rejected Hamilton's proposal, delivering a barely concealed rebuke to Hamilton for raising the idea in the first place.

> after the most mature consideration of the resolution, they are decidedly of opinion, that the proposition therein contained is, on various grounds, objectionable; that your Committee cannot recommend its adoption; and although it may not be necessary, or even expedient, to state all the motives on which they ground this opinion, they feel, at all events, satisfied, that after experience had of the past failure of all annual subscriptions, and the little hopes that exist of any future ones, the resorting to a scheme that would probably prove abortive, could only have the effect of bringing discredit on the proceedings of the Society.[41]

It was clear that the general selected committee viewed Hamilton's proposal as a 'Trojan horse' for reviving annual membership, albeit in a form already agreed to in principle by the general meeting. Apparently undismayed, Hamilton applied himself again to the problem of obtaining additional funds for agriculture in a new and provocative proposal submitted to the general meeting on 28 May 1835. This time he proposed that a new class of 'country' annual membership be created. Members admitted to this category 'must be resident at least fifteen miles from Dublin', and would be asked to pay an annual subscription of £2, the entire of which was to be allocated to the agriculture committee.[42] Hamilton's new proposal was taken to the next stated general meeting, and rejected by forty-one votes to seven.[43] The reluctance of the general body of

---

39 *RDS Proc.*, lxxi, general selected committee report, 12 Mar. 1835. 40 *RDS Proc.*, lxxi, minutes, 2 Apr. 1835. 41 Ibid., general selected committee report, 16 Apr. 1835. 42 Ibid., minutes, 28 May 1835. 43 Ibid. minutes, 4 June 1835.

members to re-introduce annual membership could not have been clearer. Other factors were almost certainly in play, including an aversion to conceding anything to the young and brash Hamilton, and the possible illegality under the charter of splitting subscriptions along sectional lines. There was a distinct hint of proprietary jealousy also on the part of Sir Edward Stanley, who had thrown his own energies behind the equally under-funded manufactures exhibition.

Stanley presented a report from the manufactures committee on 23 January 1834, pursuant to the resolution of the society of 19 December 1833 to hold an exhibition of Irish manufactures. The report concluded that an exhibition could be held in May 1834, using the cattle sheds and the statue gallery in Kildare Street.[44] Manufacturing industry in Dublin, and especially in the textile trade, was experiencing profound change in the 1830s as lack of investment in machinery, specialisation, support industries, and economic infrastructure exposed it to severe competition from the textile centres of northern England. Cloth output in Dublin fell by over fifty per cent between 1822 and 1838, and in the decade 1825-35 imports of cloth more than doubled. From self sufficiency in cloth Ireland moved to import dependency, although a small scale cotton industry survived to the north of Dublin, and a successful linen industry was developed in the Belfast area. Smaller Dublin industries such as glass, pottery, paper and engineering did experience some growth during the 1830s.[45] In this economic climate the RDS convened a public meeting with Irish manufacturers in March 1834. The attendance was disappointingly low, possibly because of an inadvertent clash with the Dublin Chamber of Commerce, which happened to have convened a meeting at the same hour and date.[46] Many of the chamber's key officers, including its president Arthur Guinness II, Hugh Hamill, Edward Croker, Samuel Bewley, and William Willans, were also active members of the RDS.[47]

Nevertheless, the society decided to proceed with a manufactures exhibition, and sufficient support was generated to mount a successful first show in May 1834.[48] Sir Edward Stanley reported 'the unprecedented interest which the public has taken in this great national effort' and pleaded for additional funds and continued patronage for the exhibition.[49] Fifty-two premiums were awarded to exhibitors, including one gold medal for textiles. While most exhibitors were Dublin based, the prize-winners included Peter Canning of Cork (brass fenders), Andrews of Belfast (table linen) and Colston of Kells (lace work). Smyth's of Balbriggan (hosiery) was awarded a small silver medal, and the major textile manufacturers, Willans, Duffy, Fry, and Atkinson, were well represented in the prize list. The range of exhibits also included leather work, furniture, wall paper, clocks, carpets, cutlery, glass, whips, book binding, fire arms, and several items of farm machinery which might have been more appropriately shown at

44 RDS Proc., lxx, manufactures committee report, 23 Jan. 1834.   45 Cullen, An economic history of Ireland, pp. 106-9, 124.   46 Freeman's Journal, 5 Mar. 1834.   47 Cullen, Princes and pirates, index. 48 RDS Proc., lxx, minutes, 22 May 1834.   49 Ibid., manufactures committee report, 29 May 1834.

the cattle show.[50] The society decided to continue support for the manufactures committee and make preparations for a second exhibition.[51]

Sir Edward Stanley reported to the general meeting on 26 June 1834 that existing accommodation in Leinster House was not adequate to properly house the manufactures exhibition, and,

> the most effective and economical mode of obtaining the accommodation required, would be by taking down the present stables, and building on that site a suitable building of about 230 feet long, by 40 feet wide, applicable not only to the exhibition of Manufactures, but to other purposes.

Sir Edward further recommended that architects' plans should be sought for the new building and application made to the government for a construction grant.[52] The society, late in 1834, directed the manufactures committee to obtain plans and estimates for an exhibition building.[53] To deal with the issue of funding Sir Edward Stanley recommended that new members' admission fees, previously applied to reducing the debt on Leinster House, which was almost discharged, should in future be used to pay for the construction of an exhibition hall.[54] In April 1835 Sir Edward requested an allocation of at least £150 (that is, at least the same as the annual allocation to agriculture) to cover the operating costs of the second exhibition of Irish manufactures. He informed the general meeting that exhibitor interest greatly exceeded that for the first show, and asked permission to use additional space in Leinster House to meet the enlarged display requirements.[55]

Public interest in the second exhibition, held in May 1835, exceeded even Sir Edward's sanguine expectations, and it was agreed to extend it by an extra day and to open the show at ten o'clock in the morning instead of at twelve noon to accommodate public demand.[56] According to a report in the Freeman's Journal the 1835 show was attended by an 'immense concourse' of 'all ranks and persuasions'. The lord lieutenant, Lord Mulgrave, visited twice, on each occasion spending over two hours viewing the exhibits.[57] The relative increase in the size of the second show can be gauged from a comparison of the prize lists. Fifty-two prizes were awarded in 1834, and eighty-one in 1835. In the latter year the gold medal top prize was won by Michael Andrews, linen manufacturer, Ardoyne, Belfast, for sheets and double damask table linens. Andrews had set up a damask factory in Belfast in 1810, and was the first manufacturer to introduce the Jacquard loom into Ireland, in 1823.[58] Smyth's of Balbriggan were again represented in 1835 and won a large silver medal for cotton stockings. Two new entrants were later to become internationally known for their sophisticated scientific instruments. They were Yeates of Grafton Street, and Kilkenny-born

50 Ibid., appendix V.   51 Ibid., minutes, 12 June 1834.   52 Ibid., minutes, 26 June, 3 July 1834.
53 RDS Proc., lxxi, minutes, 20 Nov. 1834.   54 Ibid., 19 Mar. 1835.   55 Ibid., manufactures committee report, 16 Apr. 1835.   56 Ibid., minutes, 28 May 1835.   57 Freeman's Journal, 30 May 1835.   58 Conrad Gill, The rise of the Irish linen industry (Oxford, 1925), p. 269, fn 3.

Thomas Grubb who won a large silver medal in 1835 for 'A Cast Iron Billiard Table'. Another interesting newcomer was Philip Dixon Hardy, who exhibited specimens of printing work.[59] Encouraged by the results of the 1835 show, the society decided to allocate £1,200 from its reserves to the building of an exhibition hall, and to ask the government for an equal amount. In agreeing to allocate money from the reserve created by its subscription funds, the society stated that it did so 'under the expectation that Government may be induced to grant a similar sum to enable the Society to accomplish the national object in view'.[60] In the event, this expectation was not well founded.

The museum committee, also starved of funds, attempted to piggyback on the success of the manufactures exhibition. When Sir Edward Stanley first raised the idea of building a stand-alone exhibition hall in 1834 a motion was raised at a general meeting to house the museum in part of the building. This was defeated by fifteen votes to seven.[61] The museum collection was steadily growing and visitor numbers averaged over 25,000 per annum in 1833-4.[62] A continual flow of large donations created increased pressure on the limited display and storage space available. A Kilkenny member, John Robertson, donated 'a valuable collection of foreign birds'.[63] Two large Hindu stone figures ('one of the Brama, and one of the Ganesa'), taken from a temple near Surabaya in Java, were consigned to the society through Surgeon McTernan, RN.[64] The Imperial Brazilian Mining Association, London, presented specimens of Brazilian gold to the society.[65] Samuel Bewley presented the first ever Chinese port clearance document issued to a Dublin-registered ship, following the abolition of the East India Company monopoly. Long seen by British and Irish merchants as an archaic restriction, the East India Company's monopoly of the tea trade had been the subject of public protests in Dublin and other centres in 1834.[66] Displaying a local patriotic pride, Bewley advised the society that his Waterford-built schooner *Hellas*, captained by Dubliner Anthony Scanlan, left Canton on 22 October 1834 and reached Kingstown harbour on 20 February 1835.[67]

Thomas Wall (described as the museum porter but in practice the assistant keeper) continued to manage the museum until the appointment of a replacement for Sir Charles Giesecke in 1834.[68] There was a considerable interest in the vacant post, and applications were received from nine candidates, including Joshua Abell, Dr John Murray of Edinburgh, and Dr Whitley Stokes, professor of physic in TCD.[69] Stokes withdrew his candidacy on the day of the election, and Dr John Scouler, who had no previous connection with the society,

59 *RDS Proc.*, lxxi, appendix XII, 25 July 1835.   60 Ibid., manufactures committee report 2 July 1835, and general meeting minutes 9 July 1835.   61 *RDS Proc.*, lxx, minutes, 3 July 1834. 62 *RDS Proc.*, lxx–lxxi, museum committee reports, 23 Jan. 1834, 18 Dec. 1834.   63 *RDS Proc.*, lxxi, donations to museum, 9 July 1835.   64 *RDS Proc.*, lxx, minutes, 6 Feb., 6 Mar. 1834. 65 RDS Proc., lxxi, minutes, 12 Feb., 19 Mar. 1835.   66 Haughton, *Memoir*, pp. 22–3.   67 *RDS Proc.*, lxxi, Bewley to Hardman, 18 Mar. 1835.   68 Thomas Wall succeeded Richard Glennon as museum porter in 1825. *RDS Proc.*, lxii, minutes, 24 Nov. 1825.   69 *RDS Proc.*, lxx, notice of

was elected RDS professor of mineralogy and geology.[70] Scouler left the post of professor of natural history in the Andersonian University, Glasgow, to take up his new appointment. At the end of his first year in Dublin he reported on the state of the museum. The mineralogy collection was intact, but arranged under the obsolete Wernerian system and should, he recommended, be reclassified under the Berzelian system. He also recommended the organisation of a separate Irish geological and fossil collection, and the reclassification of the zoology and conchology (shells) collections.[71]

Scouler's was the first of three important staff appointments made by the society in 1834. The other two were Ninian Niven, appointed to replace John Underwood as head gardener in the botanic garden, and Robert Kane, appointed to replace James Lynch as lecturer in natural philosophy.

The botany committee had been planning the retirements of Underwood and White for some time, and submitted a report to the society on this subject in April 1834. Underwood retired from the post of head gardener on 6 March 1834 and was given a pension of £50 per annum and permission to reside for his lifetime in the model cottage in the grounds of the botanic garden.[72] He died in August 1834, and his near destitute widow, Mary Underwood, petitioned the society for assistance. Touched by her plight, the botany committee, with support from the bishop of Kildare, vigorously lobbied the society and the government and secured a half pension for Mrs Underwood and the right to continue to occupy the model cottage.[73] At the time of John Underwood's retirement the botany committee recommended that John White be retired as under gardener on a pension of £40 per annum, and that the post of under gardener be abolished.[74] The economy committee recommended that White should be allowed to continue in office for a further year,[75] and he was directed to vacate the gate lodge and given an allowance to secure outside accommodation.[76] White had been accustomed to having residential accommodation in the botanic garden for thirty-five years, and that he probably resented having to leave is implied from an order issued by the committee a week after the order to vacate,

> That the Assistant Secretary do acquaint John White, that his conduct having been represented to them by the Curator [Ninian Niven] as highly unsatisfactory, and unbecoming a person in a subordinate situation, the Committee admonish him against a repetition of that conduct, if he wishes to avoid more severe marks of their displeasure.[77]

meeting, 13 Feb. 1834.   **70** Ibid., minutes, 13 Feb. 1834.   **71** *RDS Proc.*, lxxi, appendix V, 25 July 1835.   **72** *RDS Proc.*, lxx, minutes, 20 Feb., 6 Mar., 17 Apr. 1834.   **73** *RDS Proc.*, lxxi, memorial of Mrs Underwood, 6 Nov. 1834; botany committee report, 20 Nov. 1834. Mrs Underwood continued to receive a half-pension and to reside in the cottage until her death in 1861 (*RDS Proc.*, xcviii, council minutes, 15 May 1862).   **74** *RDS Proc.*, lxx, botany committee report, 17 Apr. 1834.   **75** Ibid., economy committee report, 1 May 1834.   **76** Ibid., minutes, 10 July 1834.   **77** RDS Archive: Committee of Botany minute book 1834–45, 7 July 1834.

John White eventually retired on 1 April 1835, and died on 18 December 1837.[78] With his departure the last connection with the early pioneers of the botanic garden was ended. The treasury refused a pension to his widow but the society did make some provision for her through a subscription fund collected privately from concerned members.[79]

On the same day that Underwood's retirement was announced (6 March 1834), Ninian Niven was elected head gardener in his place. Niven had been head gardener at the chief secretary's lodge in the Phoenix Park.[80] He was a skilled horticulturist and landscape architect and quickly brought a new style of garden management to the society. Within four years (he resigned in 1838) he revived the training schemes for young gardeners, and remodeled the Glasnevin gardens, giving them a layout that remained largely unaltered in the late twentieth century.[81] The botany committee was anxious to establish formal lines of communication with the developing horticultural industry in Britain and in the autumn of 1834

> the Committee dispatched Mr. Nevin [sic] to England and to Scotland, for the purpose of visiting the several botanic establishments, the public nurseries, and the most distinguished private collections, with the double view of procuring a supply, both by purchase and from donations, and of establishing a correspondence with the directors and proprietors of such establishments, whereby an advantageous communication and interchange of plants may hereafter take place[82]

This first expedition took six weeks (4 September–17 October 1834), and over 2,000 miles. Niven visited all the major botanic gardens, including Kew, and the major nurseries, including Dickson's of Chester. He received donations of almost one thousand species, and purchased a further 261.[83] Again on the instructions of the botany committee, Niven made a second tour of England in the period 12–27 February 1835, the highlight of which was a visit to Arley Hall in Staffordshire, seat of Lord Mountnorris.[84] At Arley Hall, Niven was given 'nearly six hundred species of plants, hardy and exotic; many of them rare and expensive'. He also received about five hundred plants, and set up reciprocal arrangements with Wentworth House (Lord Fitzwilliam), Chatsworth (duke of Devonshire), and with the botanic gardens at Sheffield and Liverpool. The result of this brief expedition was the acquisition of over a thousand plants new to the Dublin botanic garden.[85]

78 RDS Proc., lxxi, botany committee report, 19 Mar. 1835. RDS Proc., lxxiv, memorial of Mrs Jane White, 8 Feb. 1838.   79 RDS Proc., lxxiv, minutes, 26 Apr., 14 June 1838.   80 RDS Proc., lxx, botany committee report, 13 Feb. 1834.   81 Phyllis Clinch, 'Botany and the botanic gardens', in Meenan and Clarke, The Royal Dublin Society, 1731–1981, p. 193.   82 RDS Proc., lxxi, botany committee report, 6 Nov. 1834.   83 Ibid., appendix I.   84 Arthur Annesley, 2nd Earl Mountnorris, was a member of the society, 1796–1844. On 29 Jan. 1835 he invited Niven to select plants from his garden at Arley Hall. [Source: RDS Proc., var. dates.]   85 RDS Proc., lxxi, botany committee

The third important staff appointment made in 1834 was that of a lecturer in natural philosophy to replace James Lynch, who had held this post from its inception in 1799 until his death in 1833. Interest in the post was so slight at first (only one candidate presented) that the society decided in January 1834 'to allow further time for persons of science and mechanical knowledge to offer themselves'.[86] A novel development occurred at the end of the month when Robert Kane proposed himself as a candidate and requested permission to deliver a probationary lecture course.[87] Up to this point only Edward Bell Stephens had submitted a formal application. Stephens had the double advantage that he had previously worked between 1824 and 1831, as laboratory assistant under Lynch, and was the son of Edward Stephens, a Dublin soap merchant, well known and active in the society.[88] Robert John Kane (1809–90) was the son of John Kane, a catholic United Irishman who had fled to Paris, studied chemistry, returned to Dublin in the early nineteenth century and set up a profitable chemical works.[89] Robert Kane was educated in Trinity College, where he studied medicine, and developed a broad interest in contemporary scientific issues. In 1832 he was co-founder with Robert Graves of the *Dublin Journal of Medical Science*.[90] At the time of his application to the society he was working as professor of chemistry in the Dublin Apothecaries Hall.[91] The RDS natural philosophy committee accepted Kane's suggestion, agreeing to a course of trial lectures to be given by Stephens, Kane, and a third candidate Matthew O'Brien.[92] The trial lectures were held in March-April 1834 and on 17 April a ballot was held to fill the post of lecturer in natural philosophy. Robert Kane was elected by a clear margin; receiving ninety-eight votes, compared with seventy-one and sixty-nine votes received respectively by Stephens and O'Brien.[93]

At this point it is appropriate to give a separate account of the developing role of science in the mid-nineteenth century, and the growing public respect for its practitioners. For Dubliners, and for the RDS, local pride in scientific achievement reached a pinnacle in the meeting of the recently formed British Association for the Advancement of Science, in Dublin in 1835. Scientific method, as a whole approach to understanding of the physical world, had origins stretching back to antiquity, but did not seriously impact on the popular imagination until the industrial revolution of the late-eighteenth century. The term 'scientist', describing a person skilled in the application of scientific method to the understanding of physical phenomena, was first used in 1833 and gradually replaced the earlier term 'natural philosopher'.[94] The new definition was narrower than its predecessor, more focused on theory, and tending to

report, 5 Mar. 1835.   86 *RDS Proc.*, lxx, minutes, 23 Jan. 1834.   87 Ibid., 30 Jan. 1834. 88 *Report on Royal Dublin Society*, HC, 1836, evidence of Dr William Harty.   89 Foster, *Nature in Ireland*, p. 374.   90 Coakley, *Irish masters of medicine*, p. 93.   91 DNB.   92 *RDS Proc.*, lxx, natural philosophy committee report, 6 Mar. 1834.   93 Ibid., minutes, 17 Apr. 1834.   94 Morrell and

exclude earlier applications grouped broadly as 'mechanical arts'. The communication of scientific information through mathematical notation gradually
assumed a higher status in the new scheme of things and supplanted and subor-
dinated empirical demonstration.[95] Scientific studies had become more specialized,
and the leading scientists tended to come from the metropolitan universities, with
a grounding in physics, chemistry, and mathematics. In Europe Justus von Liebig
transformed the university laboratory from a preparation room into a teaching
device.[96] Increasing literacy and interest in education saw the emergence of a
middle class intelligentsia in the cities and the new scientists, with their well-
publicized findings, offered a knowledge bridge between aspiring middle-class
intellectuals and aristocratic learning.[97]

Even in Ireland, the least prosperous part of the United Kingdom, a notable
increase in the numbers of middle class professionals occurred during the first
third of the nineteenth century, especially in the ranks of lawyers and physicians.[98]
The student population of Dublin University tripled between 1800 and 1830,
most of this increase occurring in the years after 1813.[99] Within the Irish legal
profession, the numbers of bar students and solicitor's apprentices registered at
the King's Inns peaked during the period 1831-40. The lower end of the profession, solicitors and attorneys (the distinction was not abolished until 1877)
developed a social and economic confidence reflected in the establishment of a
representative body, the Law Society of Ireland, on 24 June 1830. Solicitors in
particular, whose bailiwick was the chancery court and the equity side of the
exchequer court, thrived after 1816, when they were given a monopoly of property
conveyancing. The numbers of barristers recorded by the King's Inns increased
by over 150 per cent during the period 1811-40, while the numbers of solicitors
recorded increased by over 100 per cent.[100]

The medical profession in Dublin was much smaller numerically than the
legal profession, and by any yard-stick its structure at this period was complex
and ill-defined.[101] Socially, and academically, physicians regarded themselves as
of higher status than surgeons, and the process of admission as a registered
physician was complicated and expensive in Dublin. It was often by-passed
through the expedient of taking a medical degree in Edinburgh. Irish graduates
accounted for almost thirty per cent of the total of 800 medical graduates from
Edinburgh during the last quarter of the eighteenth century. Dublin lacked a
clinical medical school, making do with special wards in Mercer's hospital.[102]
Nevertheless, from the 1820s new medical schools flourished in Dublin; new

Thackray, *Gentlemen of science*, p. 96.   **95** Ibid., pp. 258–61.   **96** Ibid, pp. 346–7.   **97** Ibid., pp.
16–19.   **98** Oliver MacDonagh, 'Ideas and institutions, 1830–45', in Vaughan, *A new history of
Ireland*, v, p. 193.   **99** R.B. McDowell and D.A. Webb, *Trinity College Dublin, 1592–1952: an
academic history* (Cambridge, 1982), pp. 80–5. Hereafter, McDowell and Webb, *Trinity College
Dublin*.   **100** Daire Hogan, *The legal profession in Ireland, 1789–1922* (Dublin, 1986). The first
president of the Law Society, Josias Dunn, was also an active member of the RDS, 1802–48.
101 McDowell and Webb, *Trinity College Dublin*, p. 140.   **102** J.D.H. Widdess, *A history of the*

hospital's such as St Vincent's (1835) were opened and older hospitals rejuvenated, and the beginnings of modern medical science ushered in the era of 'The Dublin School' as an international centre of excellence.[103] The universities and the medical profession in particular were a source of scientific professionalism, but not in any exclusive sense. Much of the interest and the best work in scientific research and discovery came from military and mercantile sources, and from the leisured classes including the aristocracy.

Within the RDS, the committees of botany, chemistry and mineralogy, and natural philosophy, directed their efforts for the most part towards the application of science to practical solutions for industrial and agricultural problems. It was therefore a use of scientific method focused on empirical experiment, usually in the laboratory or the botanic garden, rather than the development of scientific theory. Throughout the 1830s, the RDS chemistry committee was dominated by, and reflected the interests of, the medical profession, and the mercantile class. The latter was represented mostly by Dublin textile manufacturers such as John Duffy, Hugh Hamill, and William Willans. Their interest in chemistry was practical and concentrated on the development of dyes for cloth production on an industrial scale. By contrast the natural philosophy committee started the 1830s dominated by Trinity College academics, switching in mid-decade to a broader representation, including landowners, lawyers and merchants. The reasons for this shift are not clear but were probably related to the success of the Trinity College theorists, especially W.R. Hamilton, Humphrey Lloyd, and James MacCullagh in the early 1830s, and a consequent growth of interest in pure as opposed to applied science amongst the academics.[104]

As scientists grew in prestige in the universities they became increasingly unhappy with the representative role of the London-based Royal Society. It was dominated by court appointments and no longer seemed to adequately express their interests.[105] It offered no resistance to the government in 1828 when, in the familiar pursuit of financial retrenchment, the Board of Longitude was abolished. The original purpose of the board, to develop an accurate sea-going chronometer for navigation,[106] had long been achieved, but its continued existence was a major source of employment for scientists. At the same time the Scottish Royal Society in Edinburgh had its own difficulties securing government funds.[107]

Discontented scientists corresponded with each other and canvassed the notion of a general meeting of scientists from which it was hoped that widespread benefits would ensue.[108] In Dublin, Bartholomew Lloyd, provost of Trinity College, 1831-7, embarked on a course of educational reforms with the support of new science minded academics such as his son Humphrey, W.R.

Royal College of Physicians of Ireland, 1654-1963 (Edinburgh, 1963), pp. 96-7.   **103** Coakley, *Irish masters of medicine.*   **104** *RDS Proc.*, lxvi-lxxvi, committee membership 1829-40, author's analysis.   **105** Morrell and Thackray, *Gentlemen of science*, pp. 22-9.   **106** Dava Sobel, *Longitude* (London, 1998 ed.).   **107** Morrell and Thackray, *Gentlemen of science*, pp. 42-4.   **108** Ibid., pp. 298-9.

Hamilton, and Richard MacDonnell.[109] The scientists of Cambridge, and some of the Oxford colleges, had close links with their counterparts in Dublin, not least because of their backgrounds in a type of cultured anglicanism, and moderate conservativism opposed to extremist views in politics or religion. They shared also a vision of scientific work as universalist and ideologically neutral.[110] Their appeal, and that of the Edinburgh scientists, for a general meeting of 'friends' and 'cultivators' of science was couched in an inclusive manner and drew support from a broad base of middle class interests, including industrialists, engineers, government officials, and other professionals.[111]

York was chosen as the venue for the first meeting because of its relatively central location and accessibility from Edinburgh, Dublin, and London.[112] Efforts to engender interest depended on the personal lobbying of a few enthusiastic individuals, as there was no supervising structure. Brewster, the secretary of the Scottish Royal Society, was particularly active, but produced neither a program nor a constitution for the conference.[113] Nevertheless, with the help of local York supporters, arrangements were made for an initial meeting during the week commencing 26 September 1831. Over 350 individuals attended, setting a pattern of mixed social and scientific events that would characterise future meetings. The British Association for the Advancement of Science (BAAS) was formally established on 27 September 1831. Bartholomew Lloyd, one of the small coterie of foundation members, expressed the hope that the association would include Dublin as a future venue.[114] The next three meetings were held at Oxford (1832), Cambridge (1833), and Edinburgh (1834). William Rowan Hamilton pressed for a Dublin meeting in 1833 but eventually deferred to the claims of Cambridge. After Cambridge, the claims of Edinburgh and Dublin were prioritized by the association as being more worthy of recognition, on academic and political grounds, than those of the rising commercial cities of Liverpool and Manchester. By a steady circular progression around the centres of learning in the United Kingdom the association hoped to develop interest in science on a national scale and in a cohesive manner.[115]

The rapid increase in attendance (over 1,000 registered by 1833), and the growing length and popularity of the meetings, made it necessary to divide the sessions into sections, each covering a group of subjects. Fringe subjects, such as phrenology, had to be content with separate peripheral sessions.[116] Women were admitted to the general meetings from the outset, although with some reluctance, and with elaborate attempts to control their numbers.[117] From the second meeting at Oxford in 1832, spectacle and pageantry became an integral part of the socialising aspects of BAAS gatherings. Oxford and Cambridge held fireworks displays, outmatched in explosive impact by Edinburgh, which

109 McDowell and Webb, *Trinity College Dublin*, pp. 152–7.   110 Morrell and Thackray, *Gentlemen of science*, pp. 22–9.   111 Ibid.   112 Ibid., p. 63.   113 Ibid., pp. 70–7.   114 Ibid., pp. 88–91.   115 Ibid., pp. 102–9.   116 Ibid., pp. 130–3, 138.   117 Ibid., pp. 152–5.

arranged a detonation in Craigleth quarry designed to bring down 20,000 tons of rocks. Such displays added to the sense of occasion, and to the public image of the power and immediacy of science. However, the pomp and spectacle left the association open to ridicule from some quarters (Charles Dickens described it as 'The Mudfog Association for the Advancement of Everything').[118] In his inaugural speech at York in 1831, Lord Harcourt, first president of the BAAS, avoided any references to potential conflict between science and religion, and made it clear that there could be no place in the association for overt sectarianism. Nevertheless, the inner elite of the association was predominantly made up of liberal anglicans, with a token presence of unitarians and quakers. Rank and file members were drawn from a broader and more representative religious base, but there was a notable absence of jews, catholics, and protestant dissenters from the inner circle. Scriptural evangelicals were dismayed at the platform given by the BAAS to geologists who did not accept the creationist version of the age of the earth, and high church tractarians such as John Henry Newman feared that the association's work would encourage pantheism.[119]

Early in the life of the BAAS a division appeared in the ranks of scientists between those who favoured a traditional empirical approach to the development of scientific theories, and those (mainly Cambridge and Dublin based) who advocated a mathematical and theoretical approach. The cause of the latter faction was greatly advanced by the work of William Rowan Hamilton (1805–65) on physical optics. Hamilton, who was astronomer royal of Ireland and professor of astronomy at TCD, benefited in turn from the influence on Dublin University of the academic reformer Bartholomew Lloyd. Lloyd was a mathematician and natural philosopher, and provost of Trinity College, 1831–7. He introduced French mathematical modeling techniques to the college, and, by 1834, a degree examination (moderatorship) based on the Cambridge mathematical tripos.[120] W.R. Hamilton had developed and applied complex mathematical techniques to the study of optics. In 1832, in a paper read to the Royal Irish Academy, he took this approach to Augustin Fresnel's recently published wave theory of light, and predicted that a single ray of light could be refracted into a cone if passed through a crystal.[121] Humphrey Lloyd, son of the provost, using a crystal of aragonite, verified Hamilton's prediction of internal conical refraction in a laboratory experiment known as 'Lloyd's mirror', and still in use as a teaching aid.[122] Hamilton's deduction of conical refraction neither proved nor disproved Fresnel's wave theory and its real importance to mathematical physics has only been understood in retrospect.[123] Nevertheless, and however dimly understood, there was a widespread contemporary recognition in the early 1830s that the Dublin

118 Ibid., pp. 158–63. 119 Ibid., pp. 228–31. 120 Ibid., pp. 466–80. 121 David Attis, 'The social context of W.R. Hamilton's prediction of conical refraction', in Bowler and Whyte, *Science and society in Ireland*, pp. 19–21. 122 T.E. Nevin, 'Experimental physics', in O Raifeartaigh, *The Royal Irish Academy*, p. 241. 123 Sean O'Donnell, *William Rowan Hamilton: portrait of a prodigy*

scientists had permanently broken a long established assumption of scientific methodology, to the gratification of the Cambridge mathematicians, and the discomfiture of the Scottish empiricists. The result of Hamilton's prediction was that the mathematics-based theoretical approach became the new scientific orthodoxy and the gradualist approach of the empiricists fell out of favour.[124]

The Dublin scientists made a renewed effort to bring the BAAS to their city and lobbied vigorously during the Edinburgh meeting in 1834. From the outset Dublin's scientific community, mostly based in Trinity College, was ranked amongst the top five permanent supporters of the association.[125] Prior to the 1834 meeting the lobbyists approached major institutions in Dublin seeking offers of accommodation. Amongst those approached was the Royal Dublin Society and the society promptly adopted the wooing of the BAAS conference as a 'desirable object'.[126] Dublin's claim for preference was strong, well argued, and rested on the availability of superior accommodation.[127] George Tuthill presented a report to the society on 3 July 1834, urging support for the efforts being made by Trinity College and the Royal Irish Academy and pointing out that the most pressing need of the BAAS would be for meeting rooms for the section meetings.[128] Isaac Weld reported to the RDS in November that he had attended the Edinburgh meeting to add the society's voice to the representations of Trinity College and the Royal Irish Academy, and that the BAAS had agreed to hold the 1835 conference in Dublin.[129] Humphrey Lloyd[130] wrote on 8 December 1834 setting out tentative arrangements for the section meetings. It was hoped that the geological section could be accommodated in the RDS theatre, and the natural history section in the RDS board room. The remaining section meetings would be held in Trinity College and the Royal Irish Academy.[131]

A local committee was appointed, and the Dublin meeting was extensively advertised in the national newspapers, and circulars issued to over 2,500 potentially interested parties.[132] The Dublin committee consisted of fifteen members, of whom five were also members of the RDS, a further three (Humphrey Lloyd, Joseph Portlock, and Mountifort Longfield) would later become members, and one, Samuel Litton, was professor of botany in the RDS botanic garden.[133]

One problem the organizers had to tackle was whether to confine the event to men only, or to admit women visitors. Science was not considered a suitable interest for women in the 1830s but women were present at the York meeting

(Dublin, 1983), pp. 99–105. Fiacre O Cairbre, 'William Rowan Hamilton (1805–1865): Ireland's greatest mathematician', in *Riocht na Midhe*, xi (2000), pp. 124–50.   **124** David Attis, op. cit.   **125** Morrell and Thackray, *Gentlemen of science*, p. 126.   **126** *RDS Proc.*, lxx, minutes, 19 June 1834.   **127** Morrell and Thackray, *Gentlemen of science*, pp. 175–87.   **128** *RDS Proc.*, lxx, report, 3 July 1834.   **129** *RDS Proc.*, lxxi, minutes, 13 Nov. 1834.   **130** Humphrey Lloyd (1800–81) succeeded his father Bartholomew Lloyd as professor of natural philosophy at TCD, 1831. He was later a member of the RDS, 1847–81, and a vice-president, 1858–81. (Sources: *RDS Proc.*, var. dates; Crone, *Dictionary of Irish biography*.)   **131** *RDS Proc.*, lxxi, minutes, 18 Dec. 1834.   **132** Morrell and Thackray, *Gentlemen of science*, pp. 146–9.   **133** Author's database.

and their presence was of considerable significance in projecting science as a public resource. The BAAS attitude towards admitting women to meetings was ambivalent – their presence clearly added to the sense of social occasion, and it would be unchivalrous to turn them away, nevertheless, admitting them in unrestricted numbers might cause over-crowding and inhibit the lecturers in their choice of subjects. The compromise adopted was to confine women to the general meetings and resist, though not very successfully, all attempts to allow them to attend the specialized sectional meetings. The question of admitting women to the evening and section meetings exercised the Dublin organisers, as it had done those at previous venues, and, as on earlier occasions, their presence was confined theoretically to general meetings. The Dublin committee adopted elaborate admission rules, but in the end controlled numbers in all categories by pricing as much as by regulation.[134] By the summer of 1835 the RDS had firmed up accommodation arrangements for the BAAS. The theatre and the nearby assistant secretary's office, the board room and the adjoining conversation room, were allocated to the geology (section C) and natural history (section D) meetings respectively and to ancillary committee work. Visiting members of the BAAS were also to be given access to all departments of the society.[135] A subscription fund was launched to provide a 'Public Entertainment' for the BAAS visitors, in the botanic garden.[136]

The week of 10–16 August 1835 was one of exceptionally fine late-summer weather. The early apprehensions of Bartholomew Lloyd, that visitors would be deterred by the prospect of a sea crossing, proved unfounded. Infrastructure constraints; transport, accommodation, and auditoria capacities, were of far greater significance. Sir John Tobin (1762–1851), lord mayor of Liverpool, offered free passage on his steamship *Sir William Penn* to early travelers. Over one hundred passengers availed of this offer on 7–8 August, including such luminaries as Charles Babbage. On arrival they were met by a reception committee and conveyed to the city on the recently opened Kingstown-Dublin railway. In Dublin they were entertained to a *conversazione* and supper by the King's and Queen's College of Physicians. On the opening day a general meeting was held in the Rotunda rooms, attended by an estimated 2,000 people and the adjoining gardens were illuminated for evening promenaders. The mix of scientific papers and socialising had become an established pattern for the BAAS by 1835 and although the Dublin committee tried to curtail the festive aspects of the conference they were obliged to compromise by dedicating several evenings to *soirees* and entertainments. The organisation of this element of the conference was entrusted to a twenty-five member hospitality committee, which included RDS members Edward Lawless, John Richard Corballis, and Dr Richard Townson Evanson. The zoological society hosted a *dejeuner* for 500 BAAS

134 Morrell and Thackray, *Gentlemen of science*, pp. 148–55.   135 *RDS Proc.*, lxxi, general selected committee report, 25 June 1835.   136 Ibid., minutes of extraordinary meeting, 25 July 1835.

members on Tuesday, 11 August. The following day the RCSI hosted a breakfast for 600,[137] the attendance including the Arctic explorers Ross and Franklin, and the poet Thomas Moore.[138] The zenith of public entertainments was the *fete champetre* given by the Royal Dublin Society for 1,300 visitors in the botanic garden, on Friday, 14 August. Private entertainment provided by individual hosts was also lavish, and Morrell and Thackray single out three prominent members of the RDS as being particularly generous. Isaac Weld gave a dinner at his home near Bray for a group of distinguished guests including W.R. Hamilton and Sir John and Lady Franklin. George Putland entertained over one hundred guests, including Sir John Ross and Sir John Tobin, at his villa, also near Bray. Thomas Hutton organized a botanical and geological field trip to Lambay Island, for twenty-three guests.[139]

The elaborate ticketing arrangements and restrictions on admissions gave rise to much criticism. Late comers were refused tickets, and even press reporters were required to pay a £1 membership fee to gain admission to meetings. Some of the press accused the organizers of political motivations.[140] By the early 1830s the Irish newspapers were reporting much more domestic news than in earlier decades, and were becoming significant influencers of public opinion. In broad terms the Dublin press was divided into two opposing camps, with protestant conservative opinion represented by the *Dublin Evening Mail* (daily circulation 2,900), and liberal and O'Connellite opinion represented by the *Freeman's Journal* (800), *The Pilot* (750), and the *Morning Register* (750).[141] Reporting styles were often polemical, and the O'Connellite press, including the *Freeman's Journal*, made accusations of anti-catholic sentiment on the slightest grounds. The *Freeman's Journal* initially described the BAAS organizers as 'a clique of bitter Orangeists' and attacked the meeting with a peevish 'We are not of the number who attach great importance to the objects, meetings, or reports of the thing called "The British Association"'.[142] Later in the week they mellowed somewhat. The zoo function attracted 6,000 visitors and the press complained of having to queue for two hours at a badly regulated entrance. However, the RCSI fed the reporters well at a breakfast presided over by Alexander Read[143] and 'Unlike that miserable, consumptive, Orange clique, called commonly the College of Physicians – there was no niggardliness, no paltriness, no exclusiveness about the College of Surgeons'.[144] Press praise for the entertainment arrangements peaked with the RDS fete in Glasnevin. The presence of a large number of ladies was welcomed, as was the buffet service that continued all afternoon.

137 Morrell and Thackray, *Gentlemen of science*, pp. 175–87.   138 *Freeman's Journal*, 12 Aug. 1835. 139 Morrell and Thackray, *Gentlemen of science*, pp. 175–87.   140 Ibid.   141 Brian Inglis, *Freedom of the press in Ireland, 1784–1841* (London, 1954), pp. 190, 204, 232–4. Hereafter, Inglis, *Freedom of the press in Ireland*.   142 *Freeman's Journal*, 11 Aug. 1835.   143 Alexander Read (*c*.1786–1870), surgeon to Mercer's hospital 1809–51, was president of the RCSI in 1835, and a member of the RDS chemistry committee 1833–58. (Sources: *RDS Proc.*, var. dates; Cameron, *RCSI*). 144 *Freeman's Journal*, 13 Aug. 1835.

Two military bands played an extensive programme of music, and the layout of the dining marquees ensured that all visitors were adequately looked after. 'It was really a national fete, and was conducted in a manner which reflects infinite credit on the managers.'[145] The fete was also a financial success for the RDS, producing a surplus of almost £96 after meeting direct expenses. An allocation of £50 was given as a charitable donation to the Mendicity Institute, and the balance of £46 set aside for improvements to the botanic garden.[146]

The serious work of the BAAS conference took place at the day-time section meetings, the bulk of which were held in Trinity College and the Royal Dublin Society, and attended by up to 600 members of the association.[147] Sections A and B (TCD) concentrated on mathematics, physics and chemistry. Sections C and D (RDS) on geology and zoology. Section E gave scope for occasional lectures on anatomy and medical science.[148] RDS staff and members featured prominently amongst the lecturers. Edmund Davy lectured in section B, on anti-corrosion paints, and the comparative values of Virginia and Irish grown tobacco. Robert Kane also lectured in section B, on the properties of sulpho-methylates, and chlorides of tin. Richard Griffith lectured in section C, on crystalline rocks, and on his comprehensive geological map of Ireland, still in manuscript form as it was not readied for publication until 1838.[149] In section D, Ninian Niven lectured on the classification of plants, and in section E medical doctors Robert Harrison and Robert Collins lectured respectively on heart disease, and child birth.[150] Harrison's work, *On surgical anatomy of the arteries*, had been published the previous year.[151] On the final conference day Trinity College hosted a dinner for 300 BAAS members in the examination hall. During this function, William Rowan Hamilton was knighted by the lord lieutenant.[152]

These high-profile events helped to popularize science amongst the literate classes, and to make it fashionable at the highest levels of society. Two foreign visitors, the German F. von Raumer, and the French writer Alexis De Tocqueville, commented on the contrast between the squalor of the Dublin poor and the splendour of the institutions and living conditions of the professional and upper classes.[153] However, the general body of scientists, at that period, were not advocates of change in the social order and regarded even statistics and their application to social studies as inappropriate subjects for the BAAS meetings.[154] New subjects and extensions of scientific inquiry often had to endure a long wait before acceptance into the BAAS mainstream, as for example agriculture, which was not admitted into section B until 1843, despite the support of the landed interests.[155] The BAAS was not alone in resisting novel subjects. In a rare display

145 Ibid., 15 Aug. 1835.   146 *RDS Proc.*, lxxii, report, 19 Nov. 1835.   147 Morrell and Thackray, *Gentlemen of science*, p. 133, indicates that approximately fifteen per cent of BAAS members in 1835 were based in Ireland.   148 Ibid., pp. 175–87.   149 Davies and Mollan, *Richard Griffith*, p. 143. 150 *Freeman's Journal*, 11, 13 Aug. 1835.   151 *RDS Proc.*, lxxi, donations to library, 6 Nov. 1834. 152 Morrell and Thackray, *Gentlemen of Science*, pp. 175–87.   153 Ibid.   154 Ibid., pp. 344–7. 155 Ibid. p. 281.

of closed-mindedness, for which it appeared that Sir Edward Stanley could be thanked, the RDS fought shy of the new discipline of political economy. Archbishop Richard Whately had recently endowed a TCD chair in political economy, and when offered a series of lectures on that subject in 1834 the RDS had rejected it on the grounds that, 'they apprehend it would be difficult to keep such a subject clear of political matter'.[156] An earlier generation of RDS members had exhibited no such sensitivities when electing to honorary membership Citizen Goldberg, minister of political economy in the Batavian Republic, for his donation of botanical works to the society in 1802.[157] Richard Whately had been appointed professor of political economy at Oriel College, Oxford, in 1829. Made anglican archbishop of Dublin in 1831, he had early antagonized the Dublin University authorities by his unwelcome and superfluous interventions on the topic of academic reform. TCD reluctantly accepted his 1832 offer to endow a chair of political economy, the conservative elements in the college seeing the new discipline as dangerously left-wing, and fearing it would be used as a political platform to promote the views of Whigs and radicals. In the event Whately's appointees to the chair of political economy in TCD were all of exceptional merit, and included subsequent RDS members Mountifort Longfield, 1832–6, Isaac Butt, 1836–41, and John Elliott Cairnes, 1856–61.[158]

The BAAS meeting gave some stimulus to local pride in Dublin, and was compared by one observer to the royal visit of George IV fourteen years earlier. It was followed up quickly by Philip Dixon Hardy, who published an unofficial but well regarded report of the proceedings in September.[159] The role of science was viewed by its leading Dublin practitioner, Sir W.R. Hamilton, as being above politics and sectarianism and a channel for 'universal philanthropy'.[160] For the Royal Dublin Society, the success of its participation in the conference and the individual performances of its young professors and members (W.R. Hamilton had been elected an honorary member in 1834) reinvigorated its interest in scientific education. An immediate result was the introduction of evening scientific meetings at the RDS in January 1836,[161] the success of which was to become a source of pride and comfort in the grimmer days ahead.

---

156 *RDS Proc.*, lxxi, general selected committee report, 6 Nov. 1834.   157 *RDS Proc.*, xxxviii, minutes, 17 June 1802.   158 D.H. Akenson, *A protestant in purgatory: Richard Whately, archbishop of Dublin* (South Bend, 1981), pp. 68–9, 104–5. Hereafter, Akenson, *A protestant in purgatory.* 159 Morrell and Thackray, *Gentlemen of science*, pp. 175–87.   160 Ibid., pp. 372–3.   161 *RDS Proc.*, lxxii, general selected committee report, 10 Dec. 1835.

CHAPTER FIVE

The black-beaning of Dr Murray

On 26 November 1835, Dr Daniel Murray, Roman Catholic archbishop of Dublin, was rejected for membership of the Royal Dublin Society. The incident raised issues concerning religious and political bias within the society, the effectiveness of its mode of governance, and its relations with the state. To set the scene, this chapter first considers the political climate, the religious tensions, and the government of Ireland in the mid-1830s. It then goes on to examine the rejection episode, the fall-out from it, and the subsequent parliamentary committee of inquiry. Finally, it offers some reflections on the possible reasons for rejection, and on its long-term consequences.

The year 1835 started well for the society, with another successful cattle show in April and a prominent role in the BAAS conference in August. Applications for membership continued at the same high levels as in 1834. However, rising political and religious tensions came to a head in the wider community, and, despite efforts to maintain neutrality in such matters, the RDS failed to avoid being implicated in public controversy. The occasion for this unwelcome development was a well-intentioned arrangement that backfired, resulting in the very public and unexpected rejection for membership of the catholic archbishop of Dublin. The popular and influential archbishop was an unlikely subject for such treatment, which caused an internal crisis in the RDS, a loss of public confidence, and close scrutiny by an unsympathetic government. The principal source of information on the RDS for this period is the report of the parliamentary select committee of inquiry, published in July 1836, and the society's published proceedings (volumes lxxi, lxxii, 1834–5 and 1835–6). A consideration of the political climate in Ireland in the mid-1830s is necessary at this point for an understanding of the tensions prevalent at the time of Archbishop Murray's rejection. In-depth discussions of this period can be found in the *New history of Ireland*, v, and in the works of R.K. Webb, Virginia Crossman, D.H. Akenson, D.G. Boyce, and Oliver MacDonagh.

Following the 1832 reform act, parliament remained the preserve of the wealthy, with MPs required to have a substantial property qualification. The Whigs secured an overwhelming majority of parliamentary seats in the first post-reform election, but the Tories retained a powerful presence. The radicals did not have a coherent program, but frequently formed tactical alliances with the Irish liberal-repealers, a combination more feared by the Tories than by the

Whigs. Party allegiances were usually clear from election pledges and voting patterns, but party discipline was non-existent, and all MPs were effectively independents. The peers were predominantly Tory supporters and provided a formidable obstacle to Whig-liberal measures. Lord Grey's 1830–4 Whig adminis-tration was a coalition of interests and almost fell in May 1834 when its con-servative elements opposed an Irish church reform bill. The conservative element was replaced, but at the price of increased reliance on the radicals, and Grey resigned in July 1834 when the radicals, in support of O'Connell and his Irish MPs, opposed the renewal of an Irish coercion act. Lord Grey's successor, Lord Melbourne, was an old-fashioned moderate liberal. Melbourne had little option but to rely on increased radical support, which quickly unraveled, and he was replaced in December 1834 by a Tory minority government led by Sir Robert Peel. Peel's short-lived administration fell in April 1835, the divisive issue being, once again, an Irish church reform bill. Melbourne returned to office, but found himself even more reliant on the radicals and their O'Connellite allies.[1]

The Whig-liberals tended to split along broadly radical versus moderate lines on the issues of Irish church reform and public order. A reassessment of their Irish policy was essential to preserve party cohesion, the key issue being the best means to accommodate Irish majority aspirations within an integrated United Kingdom. In late 1830 Grey's government re-appointed Lord Anglesey to a second term as Irish lord lieutenant. Anglesey's return to Dublin was greeted by Daniel O'Connell with the launching of a campaign for repeal of the union, parliamentary reform, and the abolition of established church tithes.[2] Even out of office, Anglesey had attempted to dissuade O'Connell from pursuing repeal.[3] Apart from discouraging repeal, Anglesey was anxious to promote extensive and fundamental reforms in Ireland. Encouraged by Lord Cloncurry, he introduced a national education bill in 1831. The act established a national board of education in 1832 providing for the separate religious instruction of children of different denominations. It was generally welcomed by the catholic hierarchy, and gener-ally opposed by the established church and the presbyterians.[4]

On 12 February 1833 Anglesey brought forward to parliament a plan for Irish church reform of such a radical nature that it shocked conservative protestants and delighted O'Connell.[5] The payment of tithes to support a minority church seemed so patently unjust that some measure of reform was clearly indicated. Following the post-war collapse of farm prices, and the outbreak of localized famines in 1821, the withholding of tithes, especially in the southern counties,

---

1 Webb, *Modern England*, pp. 213–17.   2 Virginia Crossman, *Politics, law and order in nineteenth-century Ireland* (Dublin, 1996), pp. 49–51. Hereafter, Crossman, *Politics, law and order*. 3 Marquess of Anglesey, *One-leg: the life and letters of Henry William Paget first marquess of Anglesey, 1768–1854* (London, 1961), p. 243. Hereafter, Anglesey, *One-leg*.   4 Walter Alison Phillips, *History of the Church of Ireland: from the earliest times to the present day*, iii (London, 1933), pp. 309–11. Hereafter, Phillips, *History of the Church of Ireland*.   5 Ibid., pp. 265–70.

became widespread, leading to serious financial difficulties for many parish clergy. By 1823 the Irish administration recognized that state intervention was no longer avoidable.[6] Chief Secretary Goulburn introduced an act to create a commission for the commutation of tithes. This was a system of substituting for tithes the income from designated lands, and met with the general approval of the Church of Ireland bishops. The tithe composition statutes of 1823 and 1824 were a moderate success, and covered about half the parishes of Ireland by 1832.[7] Nevertheless, they did not provide a comprehensive answer to the principle of equity in taxation, and anti-tithe agitation recurred on a massive scale, especially in the southeastern counties, from 1831. The Whigs eventually were obliged to confront the issue of the position of the Irish church in a United Kingdom context, and began to introduce administrative reforms from 1833. Initially they patched over the problem of the withholding of tithes by, in effect, extending loans to those liable for the tax, and later extending loans to the affected clergy.[8]

The Irish church was an instrument of patronage which, despite its endowed wealth, levied tax on a general population of whom almost ninety per cent were not its adherents. The 1833 Irish church bill proposed that tithes be commuted into a land tax, archdioceses reduced in number, and parish cess (tax) for the upkeep of church property replaced by a graduated tax on clerical stipends. Most controversially, it also proposed the appropriation of surplus church revenues to subsidize the national education system. When Grey's coalition fell on these issues in May 1834, it left in its wake apprehensive and suspicious conservatives, and disappointed radicals and O'Connellites.[9] Peel's short-lived administration fell on the same issue in April 1835, having presented an Irish church reform bill very little different to the controversial bill presented by the Whigs in the previous year.[10] Reform of the Church of Ireland had political as well as spiritual implications. In the view of conservative protestants both in England and Ireland, the union of the two national churches and kingdoms in 1801 had to be implicitly weakened by any change in the official status of the Irish church. Protestant fears were reinforced by O'Connell's agitation for repeal and his stated ambition to 'restore' the property of the Church of Ireland to the Irish 'nation'.[11]

O'Connell's launch, on 23 October 1830, of a movement for repeal of the act of union, marked a parting of the ways with many of his Irish protestant supporters, and the abandonment of repeal as a worthwhile object by conservative protestants hitherto of two minds on this issue. In April 1834 O'Connell tested repeal in the house of commons where it was defeated by an overwhelming majority. Despite his claims to represent the Irish 'nation' he could not rely on the support of even a third of Irish MPs, and was forced to recognise that there

6 D.H. Akenson, *The Church of Ireland: ecclesiastical reform and revolution, 1800–1885* (New Haven, 1971), pp. 103–5. Hereafter, Akenson, *The Church of Ireland*.   7 Ibid., pp. 106–9.   8 Ibid., pp. 158–9.   9 Webb, *Modern England*, pp. 230–4.   10 Akenson, *The Church of Ireland*, p. 185. 11 Boyce, *Nineteenth-century Ireland*, pp. 63–4.

was no popular movement for repeal, such as had existed for catholic emancipa-tion.[12] O'Connell's failure to achieve broad support for repeal was compounded by the defeat of the tithe bill in August 1834. From this low point, O'Connell's political fortunes revived following his launch of an anti-tory association, composed of repealers and Irish liberals,[13] on 24 November 1834. A general election took place early in 1835, and the anti-tories took sixty-five out of 105 Irish seats. O'Connell claimed, with some justification, to control sixty 'liberal' MPs, including about thirty-four who could be classified broadly as 'repealers'. Although there was no whip system in 1835, and attempts at head counts are therefore imprecise, the commons also contained about 300 conservatives, and 290 liberals and radicals. In the absence of a centre party of moderate conservatives and liberals, O'Connell held the balance of power. The conservatives, already relying on the votes of forty Irish MPs, could make no deals with him. Many leading liberal-radicals disliked O'Connell's populist approach to political issues, but they needed his support. Through Lord John Russell, who was at pains to give the impression he had taken no initiative in the matter, O'Connell was invited to a pre-sessional meeting of liberal MPs at Lichfield House, Westminster, on 18 February 1835. The resultant 'Lichfield House compact' was an informal arrangement whereby O'Connell undertook to support the liberals and suspend repeal agitation, provided the liberals undertook to address the issues of equal terms for Ireland in parliamentary reforms, reform of the tithe laws, and of municipal representation. A deal was concluded by the end of March and on 9 April O'Connell issued an open letter to the people of Ireland pledging support for Lord Melbourne.[14] On 18 April 1835 Daniel O'Connell and his parliamentary supporters joined the government benches. For a few middle-class Irish catholics power sharing and political equality were becoming a reality.[15]

Into the maelstrom of a bitterly divided Irish society the Melbourne govern-ment sent a determined and unequivocally liberal team to head up the Irish administration in 1835.[16] The new viceroy, Lord Mulgrave, chief secretary Lord Morpeth, and under secretary Thomas Drummond, worked consistently well together. Morpeth was well-informed, well-organized and efficient, and worked closely with the conscientious and hard-working Drummond who took no initia-tives not sanctioned by Mulgrave.[17] The three were exponents of the Whig-liberal philosophy that radical action on reforming the Irish administration was the best means of redressing years of neglect, and building the confidence of the Irish public.[18] Constantine Henry Phipps (1797–1863), 3rd Earl Mulgrave, later

12 Ibid., pp. 65–6.   13 McCartney, *The dawning of democracy*, p. 125.   14 A.H. Graham, 'The Lichfield House compact, 1835', in *Irish Historical Studies*, xii (1960), pp. 209–25. 15 MacDonagh, *The emancipist*, pp. 117–23.   16 For a history of the early liberals see Jonathan Parry, *The rise and fall of Liberal government in Victorian Britain* (New Haven, 1993).   17 M.A.G. Ó Tuathaigh, *Thomas Drummond and the government of Ireland, 1835–41* (Galway, 1977), pp 3–7. Hereafter, Ó Tuathaigh, *Thomas Drummond*.   18 Crossman. *Politics, law and order*, p. 69.

marquess of Normanby, spent four years as Irish lord lieutenant until his appointment as colonial secretary in 1839. Mulgrave's young team was undeterred by the clamour of opposition from placeholders to their reform programs.[19] The new chief secretary, George Howard (1802–64), Viscount Morpeth, later 7th earl of Carlisle,[20] took office in April 1835 and moved quickly to introduce a tithe reform bill in late June. The bill proposed to abolish tithes and tithe composition and to replace them by land rents. Morpeth also proposed to abolish all clerical benefices with less than fifty parishioners, a move that would have effectively eliminated a third of all Church of Ireland parishes. He also proposed to transfer all surplus church revenues to the purposes of the national education system.[21] Thomas Drummond set sail for Ireland on 18 July 1835,[22] and assumed office as under secretary on 21 July.[23] In retrospect, Drummond's brief career (he died in office in 1840 and is buried in Mount Jerome cemetery) was perhaps the most successful under secretaryship of the nineteenth century. He worked in such close harmony with Mulgrave and Morpeth that conspiracy theorists suspected the trio were not free agents but O'Connell's puppets. Conservative suspicions were especially aroused by their choice of appointees to senior legal posts. Three of the six most senior legal appointments made by the Mulgrave administration in 1835–6 went to catholics; O'Loghlen, Woulfe, and Ball, the remainder being protestant liberals, approved or at least not opposed by O'Connell.[24] In 1830s Ireland no public action was immune from the convergence of political and religious identity. The introduction of a municipal reform bill on 31 July 1835, intended to make corporations elective and based on property qualifications only, failed to overcome religious inspired opposition.[25]

Religious tensions in 1830s Ireland were fuelled by the uncertain status of the established church following catholic emancipation. To this was added the curtailment of the public position of the church, by the loss of sees and clerical revenue under the church temporalities act, and the undermining of the financial independence of dioceses and parishes through the growing tithe legislation.[26] Many parish clergy, especially in the south, suffered real financial hardship as the result of the withholding of tithe payments. Their plight took on a somewhat exaggerated significance in the minds of conservative protestants.

> The beggared clergy are surrounded by the malignant authors of their woes. They are living amongst those to whom their fallen state is a subject at once of triumph and of mockery.[27]

19 For a biassed, but possibly not inaccurate comment on reactions in Dublin, see Cloncurry, *Personal recollections*, p. 468. 20 MacDonagh, *The emancipist*, p. 357. 21 Akenson, *The Church of Ireland*, pp. 186–8. 22 John F. M'Lennan, *Memoir of Thomas Drummond* (Edinburgh, 1867), pp. 183–5. Hereafter, M'Lennan, *Memoir of Thomas Drummond*. 23 *Freeman's Journal*, 22 July 1835. 24 Maurice R. O'Connell (ed.), *The correspondence of Daniel O'Connell*, vii (Dublin, 1978–82), 2106, O'Connell to Lord Duncannon, 2 Sept. 1834. Hereafter, O'Connell, *Correspondence*. 25 MacDonagh, *The emancipist*, pp. 131–3. 26 Phillips, *History of the Church of Ireland*, iii, pp. 300–6. 27 *Dublin*

A change in the tone of Irish protestantism in the early nineteenth-century, from a tolerant laxity to the fervour of evangelical revivalism, did not help.[28] Around the same time a millenarian movement took hold amongst some protestant scholars, their readings of biblical revelations and prophecies predicting the second coming of Christ and the overthrow of the papacy. This was matched on the catholic side by 'The prophecies of Pastorini', a folk version of speculations on the book of revelations, published in 1776 by an English Roman Catholic cleric Charles Walmesley. The Irish version predicted a total extermination of Irish protestants in the papal jubilee year of 1825.[29] Rumours of a catholic uprising planned for the end of 1824 caused widespread near panic, especially in isolated protestant communities.[30]

Protestant fears of assimilation or destruction by the catholic majority were very real from 1825 onwards, and led in some quarters to a reduction in social contacts and a growing separateness which could only compound existing misunderstandings. Irish protestants generally, like their co-religionists in Britain, shared a deep atavistic fear of the authoritarian behaviour of the papacy. They noted the anti-liberal policies of the post-Napoleonic popes, as exhibited by Leo XII in his 1823–31 government of the Papal States. His successor Gregory XVI (1831–46) continued this policy, and nurtured ultramontanist views that placed the papacy and a centralized Roman administration in opposition to local church autonomy and to secular liberalism. Nevertheless, Gregory XVI showed a reluctance to condemn radical democracy when it emerged in catholic communities subject to the regimes of other religions. The increasing presence of Irish catholic priest activists in the anti-tithe, repeal, and national education movements, convinced many protestants that these issues were part of a wider agenda for advancing the power of the Roman Catholic church.[31] John Staunton Rochfort, a member of the RDS, summarized the causes of the breakdown in intercommunal relations in the southeast of Ireland in 1832.

> Remotely, I should say, to the general feeling of hostility between the ancient Irish and English, which has been transferred to the two religions, and that excited by various causes; the agitation for emancipation and tithes, and the various things of that kind, and the revolutions of Paris and Belgium.[32]

The interests of the established church collided with Irish catholicism from the 1820s, especially in the spheres of education and patronage.[33] The most

University Magazine, i, 1833, p. 214.   28 Joseph Liechty, 'The popular reformation comes to Ireland', in R.V. Comerford, M. Cullen, J.R. Hill & C. Lennon (eds), Religion,conflict, and co-existence in Ireland (Dublin, 1990), pp. 170–1, 181.   29 Ibid., pp. 63–5.   30 Crossman, Politics, law and order, p. 10.   31 Bowen, The protestant crusade in Ireland, pp. 4–5, 49.   32 Report of select committee on the state of Ireland, HC, 1832, evidence of J. S. Rochfort, 16 June 1832. (Healey-Chadwyck microfiche series.)

successful education initiative of the early nineteenth century was the Kildare Place Society (The society for promoting the education of the poor in Ireland). In its early years the society was a genuinely non-denominational body, and received substantial parliamentary grants from 1816. It came close to becoming a national education system, and its innovations of standard texts, teacher training and regular inspections, were continued by the national education board from 1832. Up to the 1820s the society had the support of most leading catholics, and liberals. However, many catholics were uneasy about the protestant dominated committee and its policy on scripture reading, and Daniel O'Connell resigned on the latter issue in 1819. From 1820 the society began to make grants to proselytizing bodies, and an attempt by Lord Cloncurry in 1822 to have a better religious balance on the managing committee was rejected. The government responded by appointing an education commission in 1824, and its nine reports published over the following three years ultimately led to the dissolution of the Kildare Place Society in 1832.[34]

Other occasions for catholic-protestant conflict followed when attempts by O'Connell in late-1831 to woo orangemen to repeal led to the creation of defensive protestant associations, organized along the lines of the Brunswick clubs.[35] Orangeism, *per se*, reached a peak of strength by November 1834, in mass demonstrations to oppose any diminution in the privileges of the established church.[36] O'Connell's campaigns renewed protestant fears of political popery, and from the 1820s Reverend Henry Cooke emerged as the voice of lower-class anglican and presbyterian opinion in Ulster.[37] Lord Roden's great protestant rally, attended by 60,000 at Hillsborough on 30 October 1834, was addressed by Cooke, who proposed a marriage of all protestant denominations in a unified opposition to O'Connell and repeal.[38] Melbourne's dependence on radical and O'Connellite support in 1835 prompted him to accede to demands for a public inquiry into orangeism. The reports on Irish orangeism, presented on 20 July and 6 August 1835, confirmed that the order in Ireland controlled the yeomanry, had lodges in the army, was virtually immune to the law in Ulster, and was frequently involved in civil disturbances. The presence of lodges in the army gave rise to accusations of a planned *coup d'etat* by the grand master, the duke of Cumberland.[39] The implication of a conspiracy against the future accession to the throne of Princess Victoria was particularly damaging, and led to the dissolution of the grand lodge in April 1836.[40] In Dublin, conservative protestant solidarity was undermined by the presence since 1831, as anglican

33 McDowell, *Public opinion*, pp. 24–5, 33–5.   34 D.H. Akenson, *The Irish education experiment: the national system of education in the nineteenth century* (London, 1970), pp. 86–95. Hereafter, Akenson, *The Irish education experiment*.   35 Hereward Senior, *Orangeism in Ireland and Britain, 1795–1836* (London, 1966), pp. 250–1. Hereafter, Senior, *Orangeism in Ireland and Britain*. 36 Ibid., p. 252.   37 Marianne Elliott, *The catholics of Ulster: a history* (London, 2000), p. 271. 38 Haddick-Flynn, *Orangeism*, pp. 261–2.   39 Senior, *Orangeism in Ireland and Britain*, p. 267. 40 Haddick-Flynn, *Orangeism*, pp. 266–71.

archbishop, of Richard Whately, an intellectual whose religious stance was formed at Oxford in the 1820s, and who distrusted evangelical enthusiasm, and intolerance.[41] Whately was a liberal in politics and in religious and educational matters. He gained further favour with liberals by his advocacy of the study of political economy, and was appointed by Grey's government to succeed Archbishop Magee in September 1831.[42]

Returning to the affairs of the RDS, as with the house of commons political opinion amongst the members of the society appeared almost equally divided between conservatives and liberals, with the latter having a slight preponderance. During 1835 the membership of the RDS, at that time numbering about 700, included six peers, and seventeen MPs, holding seats in parliament. The peers were predictably conservative, with the exceptions of Baron Dunalley, and the earl of Leitrim. Two of the seventeen MPs lost or resigned their seats. The Co. Carlow conservative Thomas Kavanagh, was unseated on petition, and the catholic liberal-repealer Sir Michael O'Loghlen was appointed Irish solicitor general. The remaining fifteen MPs consisted of seven Tory-conservatives, and eight Whig-liberals. The seven conservatives included three hard-liners; J.D. Jackson, Sir William Verner, and Sir Robert Bateson. The first represented Bandon; the latter pair represented Ulster constituencies, and all, especially Verner, were members or supporters of the Orange Order. The eight liberal MPs included two who were at that time O'Connellite repealers, Henry Grattan junior, and Charles A. Wallace. Whig-liberal numbers might have been slightly higher, except that Robert Shapland Carew had resigned his parliamentary seat on his elevation to the Irish peerage as 1st Baron Carew, and Colonel Henry White did not regain a seat until 1837.[43]

By the mid-1830s approximately sixty RDS members were catholics, almost nine per cent of the total. Compared with the position in 1815, this represented almost a doubling of catholic members in absolute and relative terms.[44] However, the membership of the RDS remained overwhelmingly of the established church, and the position of that church in Irish society was determined, more than anything else, by its relationship to the Roman Catholic majority.[45]

At first sight it seems strange that a predominantly liberal RDS should clash with a liberal administration over a liberal archbishop. It is pertinent to ask – what sort of man was Dr Murray, and what were his politics and his reputation at the time of his proposal for membership of the society? Archbishop Daniel Murray, the spiritual leader of Dublin's catholics since 1823, was a notably pious, gentle, and conciliatory man, who avoided public controversy whenever possible. In dialogue with Irish protestants he was known to prefer the use of the term 'beloved fellow Christians'.[46] Contemporaries remarked on the mildness of

41 Akenson, *A protestant in purgatory*, p. 38. 42 Ibid., pp. 66–76. 43 Ibid., biographical notes; Walker, *Parliamentary elections*, and author's database. 44 Author's database. 45 Akenson, *The Church of Ireland*, pp. 71, 142–3. 46 Bowen, *The protestant crusade*, p. 8.

Murray's disposition and government officials found him easy to work with. Pusey described him as an ecumenical prelate, however, a Jesuit contemporary found him evasive. Nevertheless he was not timid, as his positions on the veto question in 1816, and later on national education, amply demonstrated.[47]

Murray played a major part in the revival of Irish catholicism in the early nineteenth century, which saw the investment of about £5,000,000 in the construction or refurbishment of church buildings. In the Dublin archdiocese Murray oversaw, between 1823 and his death in 1852, the acquisition of £1,200,000 worth of property, including the construction of ninety-seven new churches.[48] He encouraged the development of catholic charities, including hospitals and orphanages, as also of religious sodalities, confraternities, and devotions to the recital of the rosary, the stations of the cross, and benediction of the blessed sacrament.[49] He was a major influence in the founding of philanthropic and educational orders of nuns, such as the Sisters of Charity (1815), and the Sisters of Mercy (1828).[50]Archbishop Murray did not confine his charitable work exclusively to the catholic community, and was a trustee of such non-denominational charities and co-operative projects as the society for bettering the condition of the poor, the association for the suppression of street begging, and the Meath Street savings bank.[51] His involvement in these and similar bodies brought him into regular contact with protestants of all shades of opinion, and with protestant members of the RDS. The society for bettering the condition of the poor had forty-six trustees, and twenty-three were also RDS members. The association for the suppression of street begging had seventy-three committee members (including Daniel O'Connell), of whom twenty were RDS members. The Meath Street savings bank had seventeen trustees, of whom eleven were RDS members.[52]

Murray also helped to modernise Irish catholicism, which as a popular religion in the early nineteenth-century, especially in rural areas, was an amalgam of orthodoxy, and the remnants of older beliefs. Pre-christian practices tended to manifest themselves at times, particularly on funereal occasions such as wakes and patterns. The official catholic church spent much effort in replacing old and quasi-superstitious customs with more respectable and orthodox devotions. As the catholic church in Ireland moved towards ultramontanism it sought to adopt best current Roman practice, replacing the plain and relatively unadorned style of earlier Irish catholicism with colourful and clerically controlled liturgies.[53]

47 Donal A. Kerr, *Peel, priests and politics: Sir Robert Peel's administration and the Roman Catholic church in Ireland, 1841–1846* (Oxford, 1982), pp. 16–21. Hereafter, Kerr, *Peel, priests and politics*. 48 K. Theodore Hoppen, *Ireland since 1800: conflict and conformity* (2nd ed., London, 1999), p. 69. Hereafter, Hoppen, *Ireland since 1800*. 49 K. Theodore Hoppen, *Elections, politics, and society in Ireland, 1832–1885* (Oxford, 1984), p. 197. Hereafter, Hoppen, *Elections, politics, and society*. 50 S.J. Connolly (ed.), *The Oxford companion to Irish history* (Oxford, 1998), index. Hereafter, Connolly, *The Oxford companion*. 51 *Treble Almanack*, 1834. 52 Ibid., and author's database. 53 Hoppen, *Ireland since 1800*, pp. 70–3.

Cardinal Cullen is often credited with engineering this revolution in Irish catholic devotional practices from the 1850s, but he was building on foundations put in place by Archbishop Murray from the 1820s.[54] Murray was generally sure-footed in presenting an image of Irish catholicism as rational and non-triumphalist. However, early in his archiepiscopal career, he had adopted a position that aroused protestant fears of catholic spiritual fanaticism. The occasion was his support for the distance faith healing of Prince Alexander von Hohenlohe. Ordained priest in 1815, Hohenlohe, was also born a prince of the Holy Roman Empire. Early in the 1820s he developed a reputation across Europe as a faith healer. Overwhelmed by the demand for his services, he resorted to distance healing by prayer, and several Irish cures were attributed to him. One such was the curing of Mary Stuart, a nun in Ranelagh, in 1823. Murray investigated the Stuart case personally, and then took the unusual step of issuing a pastoral letter in which he attributed her cure directly to divine intervention. In the Stuart case, most catholic doctors, and Daniel O'Connell, accepted the miraculous nature of her recovery. Protestant doctors generally rejected the miraculous and offered a hypochondriacal explanation. At a professional level the dispute was conducted with civility; at the non-professional level it was conducted on partisan religious lines. Murray's pastoral, and a similar pastoral issued by Bishop James Doyle of Kildare and Leighlin, with their inference of divine favouring of the Roman Catholic religion, fuelled the apprehensions of nervous protestants.[55] Also in 1823, and despite his best attempts to avoid being drawn into the public debates raging between protestant evangelicals and catholic militants on doctrinal matters, Murray found himself dragged into a public defence of the Roman Catholic position on the minutiae of the arrangement of the decalogue.[56]

In the civil sphere, Archbishop Murray had a strong commitment to the promotion of universal education. On 16 December 1824 he gave evidence to the government commission on Irish education. He saw no problems with the joint education of children of different religions, provided the sensitivities of catholic children were taken into account, and they were given adequate means for instruction in their own religion. He confirmed this position on behalf of the Roman Catholic hierarchy, in January 1826, even agreeing to the deletion of controversial notes in the children's version of the Douai bible, to avoid giving offence to protestants.[57]

Murray not only approved of mixed education under a national education system, but when the board of education was established in 1832 he agreed to serve on it as an official Roman Catholic representative. Initially he also had the support of the majority of his fellow bishops. The early board meetings were

54 Hoppen, *Elections, politics, and society*, p. 194.   55 Laurence M. Geary, 'Prince Hohenlohe, Signor Pastorini and miraculous healing in early nineteenth-century Ireland', pp. 41–53 in Malcolm and Jones, *Medicine, disease and the state*. 56 Bowen, *The protestant crusade in Ireland*, p. 105. 57 Akenson, *The Irish education experiment*, pp. 95–100.

dominated by Murray, the anglican Archbishop Richard Whately, the catholic A.R. Blake, and the presbyterian James Carlile.[58] Whately, as an outsider, was in a position to take a disinterested view of the problems facing the Church of Ireland and its relations with the wider community.[59] Murray and Whately established a bond of friendship and understanding, sharing the view that children should be educated jointly, and supporting each other consistently. Murray's commitment to the national education scheme prompted him to encourage Edmund Rice to attach six of his christian brothers' schools to the system in 1833–4, an experiment which failed when the brothers' practice of hourly prayer conflicted with the board's rules on religious observance.[60] During the early years of the national education system, catholic reservations about inter-denominational primary schools remained largely muted. Church of Ireland objections were more vociferously expressed, and led to a general withdrawal of support, despite Whately's presence on the board. The presbyterians at first vacillated, but the general synod of July 1835 finally opposed mixed schooling. The Orange Order supported presbyterian opposition to mixed schooling.[61]

In internal church matters, Murray actively encouraged the holding of informal annual meetings of the Irish bishops. These meetings made no authoritative decisions, but their occurrence tended to reinforce episcopal authority against dissident clergy or fractious laity, and also helped to present a joint front in relations with the government. The Congregation of Propaganda in Rome, which had responsibility for Irish catholicism in policy matters, was unhappy with these meetings, fearing they could lead to the development of gallican attitudes of local church autonomy.[62] Murray's pastoral accomplishments were extensive, in church building and parish organisation, the encouragement of religious orders, education, and care for the ill and for orphans. He also supported the development of overseas missions. Politically he was a moderate, opposed to clerical involvement in politics, and to the repeal movement, which he regarded as having the potential to produce widespread disorder.[63] In the opinion of many protestants Dr Daniel Murray represented an accommodating type of catholicism whose other extreme was represented by the intransigent MacHale of Tuam. Archbishop John MacHale epitomized, especially for conservative protestants, an anti-British and anti-protestant attitude emerging amongst elements of the catholic clergy.[64]

Archbishop Murray was persuaded to put his name forward as a candidate for election to membership of the Royal Dublin Society in June 1835. According to William Meagher's biographical notes, he did so as 'a qualifying local condition' to enable him to attend the meetings of the British Association for the Advancement of Science.[65] Murray was proposed for membership on 11 June

58 Akenson, *A protestant in purgatory*, pp. 166, 173.   59 Akenson, *The Church of Ireland*, p. 167. 60 Akenson, *The Irish education experiment*, pp. 131, 204.   61 Ibid., pp. 178–9.   62 Kerr, *Peel, priests and politics*, p. 3.   63 Ibid., pp. 16–21.   64 Bowen, *The protestant crusade in Ireland*, pp. 8–15. 65 William Meagher, *Notices of the life and character of his grace most rev. Daniel Murray, late*

1835[66] by the catholic barrister John Richard Corballis, and seconded by Stephen Creagh Sandes (1778–1842), a senior fellow of TCD, who was appointed anglican bishop of Cashel in 1836.[67] The ballot for Murray, and nine other candidates, was scheduled for 9 July 1835. Seventy-six members were present at the July meeting, including Corballis and Sandes. Lord Cloncurry and his son Edward Lawless were also present, as were a large number of catholic members, presumably keen to support Murray's candidacy. The two honorary secretaries, Weld and Bryan, were present, but no vice-presidents, and the chair was taken by Dr William Harty, a long serving member of the botany and agriculture committees. Since no vice-presidents were present the by-laws did not permit the holding of a membership ballot, and Harty had no option but to defer the ballot to a later meeting.[68]

Unfortunately, between 11 June and 9 July 1835 Archbishop Murray had come into the public eye in a highly prejudicial light. Having been at pains to avoid public religious controversies, he found himself the subject of protestant evangelical attacks in June-July 1835. The occasion was the evangelicals' belief that Murray had approved the controversial theological works of Pierre Dens for the education of catholic seminarians.[69] Irish evangelicals inevitably came into contact with their English counterparts based in Exeter Hall, London, which became a centre both for proselytising missions and for protest meetings.[70] At an Exeter Hall meeting in June 1835, apart from the usual condemnations of popery, Dens' theology, re-published in 1832 and in use in Maynooth seminary, was specifically condemned.[71] Pierre Dens was president of Mechlin Roman Catholic seminary, 1735–55, in the then Austrian Netherlands. He published a fourteen-volume *Theologia ad usum seminariorum et sacrae theologiae alumnorum*, based on the teachings of Thomas Aquinas. It contained a good deal of counter-reformation theological argument. In 1835, the evangelical rector of Harold's Cross, McGhee, pointed out that the eight-volume edition of Dens, then in use in Ireland, contained statements that it was permissible to compel heretics and apostates to return to the Roman Catholic church by physical force. McGhee further claimed that Dens' work, and by implication all its contents, had been approved by the Irish catholic hierarchy since 1808. He also claimed that a synod of the Leinster bishops in 1831 had approved 'secret statutes' authorizing the spread of the anti-protestant arguments of Dens.[72] Since Dens' work appeared to have the sanction of Archbishop Murray as head of the Dublin archdiocese, the anglican bishop of Exeter attacked Murray in a speech to the house of lords, describing him as unfit to be a commissioner of education.[73] Murray argued that

archbishop of Dublin (Dublin, 1853), pp. 69–71. Hereafter, Meagher, *Archbishop Daniel Murray*. 66 *RDS Proc.*, lxxi, minutes, 11 June 1835. 67 Phillips, *A history of the Church of Ireland*, iii, index. 68 *RDS Proc.*, lxxi, minutes, 9 July 1835. 69 *Freeman's Journal*, 6, 9 July 1835. 70 Bowen, *The protestant crusade in Ireland*, pp. 66–7. 71 Hill, *From patriots to unionists*, pp. 366–7. 72 Bowen, *The protestant crusade in Ireland*, pp. 114–16. 73 *Freeman's Journal*, 20 July 1835.

the Irish edition of Dens had been published as a private speculation, but the identification of the publisher as Richard Coyne, official publisher to Maynooth College, did nothing to calm the evangelicals. Murray was accused of casuistry and evasiveness.[74] He felt obliged to write directly to the prime minister, Melbourne, denying that he had directed the publication of Dens' work, and claiming that the offensive sections were regarded in catholic circles as 'obsolete', and not as articles of faith.

> I do not entertain the doctrines thus attributed to me; my solemn oath attests the contrary. Blessed be God! those doctrines are now little more than the record of by-gone intolerance.[75]

Embarrassed by their failure to hold a ballot on 9 July 1835, the RDS general meeting passed a resolution requesting the general selected committee to inquire if 'a more punctual' attendance of vice-presidents could be organized.[76] The best recommendation that committee could come up with was that all vice-presidents should be written to by the assistant secretary, and particularly requested to attend on ballot days. Subsequently the assistant secretary presented a return of the attendances of vice-presidents during the preceding year, from which it was clear that the earl of Meath, J.L. Foster, and Henry Joy, had attended no meetings.[77] The next ballot day was scheduled for 26 November 1835, and fifteen candidates for membership were listed, including Dr Daniel Murray. Sir Robert Shaw, vice-president, chaired the meeting, at which 145 other members were present (about twenty per cent of the membership). Thirteen candidates were elected; brewer Michael Powell's name was apparently withdrawn, and Archbishop Murray was rejected.[78] The details of the voting were never fully disclosed. A two-thirds majority was required for election, and, according to a report in the *Freeman's Journal*, J.R. Corballis stated that the vote was seventy-nine in favour of Murray, and sixty-five against.[79] Almost thirty years later, Dr William Steele confirmed that the majority in favour of Murray was fourteen 'or thereabouts'.[80] Steele was assistant secretary from 1851, and may have had this information directly from Corballis, or from Isaac Weld, an honorary secretary in 1835. Whatever the actual size of the majority in favour of Dr Murray was, it failed to match the two-thirds rule, and the candidate was therefore rejected.

The fall-out from Murray's rejection manifested itself within days, when Lord Cloncurry, who was not present at the meeting, condemned the action in a letter to the *Freeman's Journal*.

74 Bowen, *The protestant crusade in Ireland*, pp. 115–16.   75 Cited in William Meagher, *Archbishop Daniel Murray*.   76 *RDS Proc.*, lxxi, resolution of general meeting, 9 July 1835.   77 *RDS Proc.*, lxxii, minutes, 5 Nov. 1835.   78 Ibid., 26 Nov. 1835.   79 *Freeman's Journal*, 5 Dec. 1835. 80 *Report from the select committee on scientific institutions* (Dublin), HC, 1864 (495), evidence of W.E. Steele, 15 July 1864. Corballis' contemporary statement of 144 votes cast is reasonably close

The malignant vote of Thursday last, by which a wanton insult was attempted to be put upon one of the most amiable and beloved characters in this country , has alarmed those who took leave of decency and all Christian feeling, when they black-beaned Dr Murray ... for now there can be no mistake as to the bigoted motives which actuate a considerable number of the Society's members – no pretence that Orange politics and sectarian rancour have not taken root in Leinster House, to the destruction of the object for which the Dublin Society was founded – and hence the regret which we know to be felt by the stupid bigots who black-beaned the Catholic Archbishop of Dublin.

Cloncurry predicted that the government would withhold the annual grant pending a reform of the system for admitting members, and would attack the secret ballot, an innately democratic principle, on the grounds of its potential as a source of mischief.[81]

The next general meeting took place on 3 December 1835, chaired by Sir Robert Shaw, and with sixty-five other members present. J.R. Corballis attempted to table a motion for insertion in the minutes, which was suppressed by twenty-seven votes to twenty-six. The Reverend E.G. Hudson[82] gave notice of a motion to submit a case to legal counsel to consider whether the second by-law, on the election of members, was in conformity with the charter and with the civil law. Richard Everard[83] gave notice of a motion to rescind the secret ballot and substitute open voting. J.R. Corballis returned to the fray with notice of a motion to disclose the numbers voting for each candidate on 26 November 1835. Dr Anthony Meyler lent his support to Corballis, giving notice of a resolution,

That it is the privilege of every Member to give notice of any motion appertaining to the business of the Society, and that it is an infringement of the rules and an invasion of the rights of the Members, to refuse the insertion of such notice in the Proceedings of the Society, there being nothing objectionable in the terms of the motion itself.[84]

Two days later the *Freeman's Journal* published a report critical of Sir Robert Shaw's handling of the meeting on 3 December. According to this report, Corballis' suppressed motion was to have by-law two temporarily suspended,

to the 146 names recorded in the proceedings, and indicates that there were two abstentions. Therefore, according to Corballis, fifty-five per cent of those voting favoured Murray, a short-fall of sixteen votes under the required two-thirds majority rule. 81 *Freeman's Journal*, 2 Dec. 1835. 82 Reverend Edward Gustavus Hudson (1792–1851), dean of Armagh *in absentia*, was a liberal, and a member of the RDS 1810–51. (Sources: *RDS Proc.*, var. dates; Cornelius Smith and Bernard Share, *Whigs on the Green* (Dublin, 1990), p. 156.) 83 Richard Everard, barrister, Elm Park, Blackrock, was a member of the society, 1821–36. (Source: *RDS Proc.*, var. dates.) 84 *RDS Proc.*, lxxii, minutes, 3 Dec. 1835.

and Dr Murray declared elected a member.[85] If correctly reported, Corballis may well have had precedents in mind, as when by-law 72 was suspended to facilitate the BAAS meeting earlier in 1835. It was certainly the case that by-law two had been suspended from time to time, and amended in 1831,[86] to facilitate the election of an in-coming lord lieutenant to the presidency. But, in fairness to Shaw, there was no precedent for suspending a by-law in order to overturn a vote of the members.

The next general meeting was held on 10 December 1835, again chaired by Sir Robert Shaw, and with 153 other members present. Hudson's motion to have by-law two referred to a legal adviser was defeated by ninety-four votes to forty-six. Corballis withdrew his motion to have the numbers voting for and against each candidate disclosed. Instead, he read to the meeting a letter dated 7 December 1835 which he had received from Dr Murray on the subject of the ballot, and which is worth quoting in full. Murray wrote,

> It is to me a subject of unaffected concern, that I have become most unintentionally a source of disagreement among the Members of the Royal Dublin Society. It has been my object through life to conciliate, not to disunite;- and it could not, of course, fail to be particularly distressing to my feelings to be an occasion of dissension in a body, which, if united, is so well calculated to do extensive good, and the combined efforts of all whose Members are so much wanted for the improvement of the country. As far as I am concerned, all future discussion on the subject of the late Ballot would be entirely useless. The decision come to on that occasion was final. It has disclosed the fact, that my cooperation for the advancement of the purposes of the Society would not, in the opinion of a considerable portion of its Members, be likely to prove beneficial. This is quite sufficient to render it impossible for me to entertain the slightest wish to take a part in the proceedings of that body. As far as regards me, therefore, the renewal of a discussion on that subject could lead to no possible advantage; I would but distract the attention of the Members from the immediate and practically useful objects of the Society.
>
> I need hardly say how deeply I feel indebted to you [Corballis], to Dr. Sandes, and to the numerous other Members of the Society, who evinced towards me a warmth of kindness, which I cannot but consider exceedingly flattering. I pray you to convey to them what you know to be my feeling on the subject, together with my earnest solicitation, that, in the future transactions of the Society, I may be wholly lost sight of; that the recent cause of momentary disagreement may be forgotten; and that the whole body may join in cordial union to promote the great objects of national improvement, for which the Society was established.

85 *Freeman's Journal*, 5 Dec. 1835. 86 *RDS Proc.*, lxvii, minutes, 3 Mar., 2 June 1831.

On the motion of Robert Day,[87] seconded by the earl of Charlemont, Dr Murray's letter was entered on the minutes.[88] It was a masterly statement, which preserved the dignity of Murray's office, but closed the door on rapprochement, and, however unintentionally, left the society exposed to indefinite public opprobrium. It must be said that its immediate effect was to exercise a calming influence on the protagonists and reduce the scope for public controversy. Murray's biographer described it as 'an eternal monument, let us trust, of the irresistible power of Christian forbearance over narrow-mindedness and bigotry', and so it appeared to many of his contemporaries.[89] Dr Stephen Sandes of TCD wrote to Murray on 14 December 1835,

> I beg leave to offer my most respectful thanks for the condescending notice you were pleased to take of me as a Member of the Royal Dublin Society, and were it allowable to an individual so humble as myself to convey to you his estimate of your conduct and your motives I would state my most unqualified admiration of that dignified and Christian feeling which induced you to exert your influence in averting those consequences to which some ill-judging members had exposed the Society.[90]

The Murray affair was in the public domain, and the society could do nothing to stop public comment. As a partially public institution it had for long followed a policy of publishing the minutes of its proceedings, and the defensive reticence it at first displayed by lack of explanations was undermined by the readiness of disgruntled members to take their versions of events to the newspapers. At the last general meeting of 1835, held on 17 December, Doctor William Harty gave notice of a motion

> that in case the very irregular practice of communicating to the public prints, reports of the discussions occurring in the Society, be persevered in, he will, at the next meeting, bring the subject under the notice of the Society, as one of great importance to its best interests.[91]

Early in 1836 the society received a letter from Lord Morpeth, chief secretary, inviting it to send a deputation to discuss its constitution.

> I find that the select committee of the House of Commons on Irish miscellaneous estimates, in 1829, stated that the 'principle of admission by

87 Robert Day (1745–1841), former judge of the common pleas, was a member of the society 1790–1841. He was a moderate protestant conservative, with tolerant views on religion. (Sources: *RDS Proc.*, var. dates; Ball, *The judges in Ireland*, and Ella B. Day, *Mr. Justice Day of Kerry 1745–1841; a discursive memoir* (Exeter, 1938).) 88 *RDS Proc.*, lxxii, minutes, 10 Dec. 1835. 89 Meagher, *Life of Archbishop Daniel Murray*, pp. 69–71. 90 Dublin Diocesan Archives: Archbishop Daniel Murray papers, miscellaneous correspondence, AB3/31/3–4. 91 *RDSProc.*,

ballot in a society mainly supported by the public purse, is objectionable, and ought to be discontinued'. In this opinion the Lords Commissioners of His Majesty's Treasury, in a minute dated the 14th of November, 1831, express their entire concurrence.

I do not affect to conceal that recent occurrences have impressed the government with the necessity of complying without delay with the spirit, at least, of this representation. While the Lord Lieutenant, in common with his predecessors, willingly admits the many services conferred upon the public by the Royal Dublin Society, representations have been made which induce his Excellency to think, that important improvements might be introduced into the mode of transacting its business, and apportioning its income.

Under these circumstances, while his Excellency feels that he could not recommend to his Majesty's government a continuance of the annual vote in the estimates of the ensuing session, without certain modifications in the constitution of the Society, he is still anxious to carry along with him, in any projected remedies, the assent and assistance of the members of the Dublin Society; I am, therefore, directed by his Excellency to suggest, that the Society should be pleased to appoint a committee or deputation for the purpose of conferring with the Chief Secretary, or in his absence with the Under-Secretary, respecting the course which it may be deemed advisable to pursue.[92]

On foot of this invitation, Isaac Weld and James Naper had two preliminary meetings with Thomas Drummond, under-secretary, prior to his formal meeting with the official RDS deputation. Weld said afterwards that he thought he had explained to Drummond that the society could not delegate to the deputation powers to take decisions on its behalf without referring back to the RDS general meeting. Nevertheless, the official meeting with Drummond on 2 February 1836, at which an RDS deputation of seven including three vice-presidents was present, turned out to be a fiasco. On being told that the deputation had no plenary powers and were present simply to hear the government's propositions, Drummond terminated the meeting and told the deputation he would transmit the government's propositions directly to the society.[93] Drummond informed the society, by letter of 3 February 1836, that since 'the deputation, whom I had the honor of meeting yesterday, were not empowered, agreeably to the wish expressed in Lord Morpeth's letter, to offer any opinion or observations on the alteration of the constitution of the Society', Lord Morpeth had decided to refer his propositions in the first instance to the treasury. Drummond's letter was read to the general meeting of the same day, but not

lxxii, minutes, 17 Dec. 1835.   92 NAI: CSO RP 1836, 229/3/612, Morpeth to RDS, 20 Jan. 1836.
93 Report on Royal Dublin Society, 1836, evidence of Isaac Weld, 29 Apr. 1836.

discussed. Most of the meeting was taken up with a discussion of Dr Harty's motion on disclosures to the press. Some rather weak resolutions were passed declaring that a continuance of such disclosures, unless 'done through the medium of regularly recognized reporters', would tend 'ultimately to convert the Society into a debating or political association'.[94]

The government's propositions, fifteen in number, arrived at the RDS on 18 February 1836, in time to be read to the general meeting that afternoon. Proposition I was that simple majority votes should in future decide the election of candidates for membership. Four propositions (IV–VI, and VIII) required a constitutional change, as they recommended that the governing body of the RDS should be an annually elected twenty-three member council. Numbers IX and X proposed the introduction of audited, published annual accounts, divided into public and private sections. Numbers II, III, VII and XI–XIV involved minor changes to existing procedures and by-laws. Number XV, however, while restating an agreed policy that the acquisition of books for the library should be confined to texts appropriate to a literary and scientific institution, added 'there shall be no News-room permitted in the house of the Society'.[95] Taken aback, the meeting supported the printing of an eight-point notice of motion by Dr William Harty, which included a statement that the society's members 'challenge the strictest scrutiny of their proceedings'.[96]

Dr Anthony Meyler was stung by the proposal to abolish the newspaper room. He had not been present at the meeting on 26 November, and had up to that point conducted a fairly restrained personal correspondence with the press on the implications of the Murray affair. Now he launched a vitriolic attack on Lord Mulgrave by a letter published in the *Evening Mail* on 24 February 1836.

> 'There shall be no news-room permitted in the house of the society'. The autocrat of all the Russians would scarcely, from his imperial palace, have put forth so arbitrary a mandate. Verily, my Lord Mulgrave, it has been often said, that the Whigs, when in power, out-Tory even the Tories; but a Whig Lord Lieutenant, under a Radical council, out-Herods even Herod.[97]

The *Freeman's Journal* commented on Dr Meyler's letter,

> No one disputes the utility of the society, under proper management; therefore, the letter is totally uncalled for. But Dr Meyler will scarcely deny its present intolerance. The letter is remarkable, first, as the production of a Catholic, and secondly, as the Mail has been chosen for its publication.[98]

94 *RDS Proc.*, lxxii, minutes, 4 Feb. 1836.   95 Ibid., 18 Feb. 1836.   96 Ibid.   97 *Report on Royal Dublin Society, 1836*, pp. 242–3.   98 *Freeman's Journal*, 28 Jan. 1836.

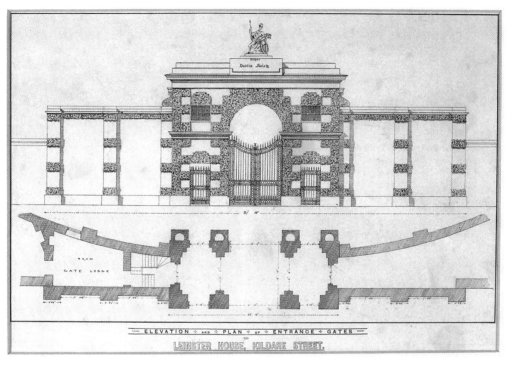

1 Leinster House main gate, architect's drawing, *c.*1820 (*courtesy* Royal Dublin Society). The statue of *Hibernia* was positioned there in 1815.

Ballinasloe Show

Premium in Class

Adjudged to

2 Farming Society prize card, Ballinasloe Show, by Henry Brocas, n.d. The Farming
Society of Ireland took over the agricultural activities of the RDS, 1801–28.

3 Sir Charles Giesecke, RDS mineralogy professor 1813–33.
Portrait by Sir Henry Raeburn, Edinburgh, *c.*1813
(*courtesy* Royal Dublin Society).

4 Thomas Braughall by John Comerford (*courtesy* Royal Dublin Society).
A leading member of the Catholic Committee, Braughall was an
honorary secretary of the RDS, 1792–8.

5 Lord Frankfort de Montmorency, print, 1816 (*courtesy* Royal Dublin Society).
He chaired the first meeting of the RDS in Leinster House, 1 June 1815.

6 *Hibernia* by Edward Smyth, 1799 (photographed 2004), (*courtesy* Royal Dublin Society).
Moved to Leinster House from Hawkins Street in 1815,
and to the arena entrance at Ballsbridge in 1928.

LEINSTER HOUSE SOCIETY'S HEADQUARTERS, 1815-1924.
(*The Irish Volunteers of 1799 drilled on the Lawn.*)

THE PARLIAMENT HOUSE, 1753.
The First Home of the Society.

7 Page from 1931 RDS bicentenary book (*courtesy* Royal Dublin Society),
showing earlier RDS headquarters in Leinster House, 1815–1924 (*top*),
and in the Parliament House, 1732–57 (*bottom*).

8 *Entrance to Dublin Society house*, by Henry Brocas, 1818.
Brocas was RDS drawing schoolmaster, 1800–37.

9 A.H. Rowan by W.H. Holbrooke. A founder of the United Irishmen, Rowan was a member of the RDS natural philosophy committee, 1816–29.

10 Leicestershire sow by Henry Brocas (*courtesy* Royal Dublin Society). Brocas painted many prize animals for the Farming Society of Ireland.

11 Leicester ram, artist unknown, probably by Henry Brocas. Improvement of Irish breeding lines was a livestock objective of the Farming Society.

12 Sir Richard Griffith (1784–1878) by Sir Thomas Farrell, 1880 (*courtesy* Royal Dublin Society). RDS mining engineer, 1812–29, Griffith was later director of the Primary Valuation.

13 Lord Anglesey by Robert William Sievier, 1830 (*courtesy* Royal Dublin Society).
Lord lieutenant of Ireland, 1828–9 and 1830–3, his reform proposals
antagonised conservatives.

14 Trinity College by Henry Brocas, 1829. Under Bartholomew Lloyd, provost, 1831–7, TCD grew in reputation as a centre for scientific research.

15 *View of the Castle Gate and Royal Exchange*, by Henry Brocas, n.d.
Dublin Castle remained the centre of power and patronage
in Ireland after the Act of Union.

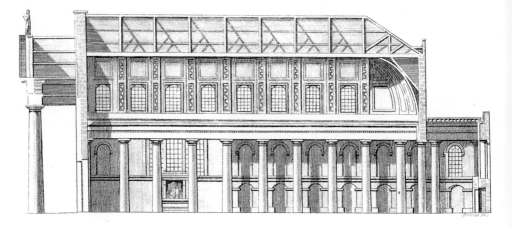

16 St Mary's Roman Catholic Pro-Cathedral, Dublin, by Henry Brocas. Built 1815–25, and formally opened by Archbishop Daniel Murray, 14 November 1825.

Meyler had been born and educated as a Roman Catholic and had practiced that religion for most of his adult life. However, by 1835 he was becoming alienated from catholicism, prompted as much as anything else by an aversion to O'Connell's demagogic behaviour and his alliance with the liberals and a large element of the Irish catholic hierarchy.[99] Terence de Vere White has maintained that Meyler's attack on Mulgrave was the result of the latter's refusal to attend Meyler's lectures on chemistry.[100] This seems unlikely, for while it is true that Meyler was a member of the chemistry committee, he did not lecture on the chemistry syllabus, his own special interest being the engineering and health aspects of heating and ventilation.[101] The *Freeman's Journal* recognized Meyler's technical interest when it wrote of the RDS that it 'would run learned doctors at his lordship [Mulgrave], who would envelope him in a smoke which would defy all powers of ventilation'.[102] Meyler wrote again to the *Evening Mail* in early February, achieving an even wider circulation when the *Freeman's Journal* published extracts from his letter.

> I do not know who were the individuals who rejected Dr Murray, and if I did I could not enter into their minds so as to assign a motive for that rejection: but, as far as I can form an opinion, I would say, that the period at which this reverend and respectable gentleman was balloted for was unfortunate. He had been engaged in active and exciting contention about some book of theology, and at this particular period also, he, for the first time, I believe, identified himself with the politics of Mr O'Connell and gave the very high and influential sanction of his authority to that gentleman's political career, by subscribing to the fund then being collected for him.[103]

Anti-O'Connell feelings had gripped large sections of the Dublin professional and middle classes in late-1835. Daniel O'Connell, and his running mate Edward Ruthven, had been elected MPs for Dublin earlier in the year. By that time O'Connell had lost the support of influential moderate unionists such as Arthur Guinness II. The legitimacy of the election was challenged, mostly on the grounds that many of the electors had not been entitled to vote, either for not meeting the property qualification, or for failure to pay arrears of taxes. Ruthven died, and O'Connell was unseated in 1836.[104] During November 1835 an election commission was in session, hearing evidence on the conduct of the election, which was extensively reported in the daily newspapers. The immediacy

99 RIA: Haliday collection, 1726/4, Anthony Meyler, *Irish tranquillity under Mr. O'Connell, my Lord Mulgrave, and the Romish priesthood* (Dublin, 1838). Hereafter, Meyler, *Irish tranquillity*. 100 White, *The story of the Royal Dublin Society*, p. 95. 101 *RDS Proc.*, var. dates; Elizabeth Malcolm, *Swift's hospital: a history of St Patrick's hospital, Dublin, 1746–1989* (Dublin, 1989), pp. 128–9. 102 *Freeman's Journal*, 26 Mar. 1836. 103 *Freeman's Journal*, 28 Jan., 5 Feb. 1836. 104 MacDonagh, *The emancipist*, pp. 143–5.

and the controversial nature of these events may have tipped some of the more conservative RDS members into the anti-Murray camp. Henry Joy, vice-president, and Thomas Ardill, a member of the house committee, were unable to attend the RDS meeting on 26 November 1835, being engaged in the work of the Dublin election commission.[105]

At the RDS general meeting on 25 February 1836 Richard Everard withdrew his motion to substitute open voting for the secret ballot. C.W. Hamilton gave notice of a motion repudiating Meyler's attack on the lord lieutenant, however, Henry Carey[106] gave notice of a counter-motion,

> That this Society cannot consider itself responsible for whatever any Member, in his individual capacity, may think it proper to publish, nor are they called on in any way to express any opinion thereon.[107]

William Harty gave notice of a nine-point motion in response to the government's propositions. Harty recommended the creation of a council with the same advisory powers as the general selected committee (but not the powers of a governing body), and that the election of members be by simple majority vote.[108]

A stated general meeting of the society was convened on 3 March 1836, with John Boyd in the chair, and 148 other members present. The government's propositions were discussed at length, but only propositions IX and X, on the appointment of auditors and the presentation of the annual accounts, were accepted without quibble. C.W. Hamilton, and J.E. Portlock,[109] moved for the adoption of simple majority voting, but were defeated by a counter-motion to retain the existing system. A subsequent attempt by Hamilton and Portlock to adopt the principle of an elected council as governing body was defeated by seventy-six votes to seventeen. All the remaining government proposals either fell with the defeat of number IV, or were rejected as presented. Hamilton, perhaps recognizing that the mood of the meeting was against him, withdrew his motion condemning Meyler's letter to the *Evening Mail.*[110] At the next ordinary meeting a special committee was appointed to prepare a memorial to the lord lieutenant on the subject of the propositions and the society's response to them. This was abandoned when a pre-emptive letter arrived from Thomas Drummond, on 17 March 1836.[111]

Drummond asserted that the government's propositions were designed to rid the society of the taint of religious or political bias. In a defence of his own decision to terminate the meeting on 2 February, he inferred that the RDS deputation had been inept in explaining the limitations on their powers, and that

---

105 *Freeman's Journal,* 17 Nov. 1835.   106 Henry Carey, barrister, was a member of the RDS 1834–72. (Source: *RDS Proc.,* var. dates.)   107 *RDS Proc.,* lxxii, minutes, 25 Feb. 1836.   108 Ibid. 109 Captain Joseph Ellison Portlock (1794–1864) was president of the Dublin zoological society, and a newly elected member of the RDS in February 1836. (Sources: *RDS Proc.,* var. dates; *DNB,* Foster, *Nature in Ireland.*)   110 *RDS Proc.,* lxxii, minutes, 3 Mar. 1836.   111 Ibid., 10, 17 Mar. 1836.

they could have arranged a resumption of discussions at a later date. He accused the society of looking for definitive proposals without preliminary discussion, and of then 'rejecting the most important of them, without assigning any reason beyond the mere expression of the will of the Society'. He went on to state that, under the two-third majority balloting system,

> opportunity is given to the few, who may be so disposed, to prevent the admission of individuals from political or religious considerations, not participated in by the majority of the Society, and wholly at variance with the legitimate principles by which the introduction of members to such an Institution ought to be regulated ...[112]

Drummond admitted to a clerical error in the presentation of the propositions, which had appeared to urge a reduction of £1 in the life membership fee, and added that C.W. Hamilton had been authorized to, and had pointed out this error to the meeting. He further added that the government had urged that annual membership be offered as an option to candidates who could not afford life membership, and not as a replacement for life membership. On the subject of a governing council, Drummond appealed to the widespread practice of similar bodies such as the Royal Irish Academy. He deprecated, in the case of the RDS, 'The cumbersome machinery by which trifling matters are referred to the whole body, and only confirmed at a subsequent meeting; and the endless and unprofitable discussions which are the natural consequence of such an arrangement'. Drummond reminded the society that, in deference to the recommendations of Lord Leveson Gower in 1829, it had ceased for a time to purchase newspapers out of public funds, and treated them as a charge on private funds. Finally he added that if the attraction of new members was dependent on the provision of newspapers the RDS might justifiably be viewed by the government as having the character of a club. 'It will now be for his Majesty's Government to determine whether, after what has occurred, they shall consider it their duty to apply to Parliament to renew the annual grant.'[113]

The society responded to Drummond's letter, on 24 March 1836, in the form of a memorial to the lord lieutenant. It expressed a willingness to resume discussions with the government, and denied being influenced in its actions by 'political feeling'. While evincing a willingness to introduce amendments to the system of election, it defended the existing system on the grounds that it served to admit only members willing to give a long-term commitment to the work of the society. Referring to the notion of a governing council, it expressed the fear that such a body could be prone to an improvident approach to the allocation of funds, if not accountable to the general body of members. It defended the purchase of newspapers on the grounds that 'It can scarcely be denied that a

112 *RDS Proc.*, lxxii, minutes, 17 Mar. 1836.   113 Ibid.

knowledge of passing occurrences is of importance to those engaged in the promotion and encouragement of arts, manufactures, agriculture, and various literary and scientific pursuits'. The use of a separate private fund to purchase newspapers had been introduced on an experimental basis in 1831 and had not proved successful. It had been tried as part of an attempt by the society to increase its private funds following the reduction of the grant and was not, as far as the memorialists were aware, a specific requirement of the treasury at that time. The memorial asserted, that

> this Society is not invested with the character of a Club, nor has the existence of the News Room been ever known to lead to the introduction of any political or religious discussion within the walls of the Society; such topics, owing to the mixed and opposite views of the Members, being, by common assent, sedulously avoided; – and in this respect, the Society affords a most gratifying and useful example, of the practicability of effecting a union of individuals, holding different and opposite political and religious opinions, for one common and patriotic purpose.[114]

Four days later the *Freeman's Journal* carried a report that the house of commons had voted to appoint a select committee to inquire into the affairs of the Royal Dublin Society.[115] The society responded with a resolution inviting 'the strictest scrutiny' of its affairs.[116]

Parliament ordered the inquiry on 28 March 1836, appointing fifteen members to the select committee. The committee consisted mostly of Irish MPs and was reasonably balanced as between liberal and conservative viewpoints. Two MPs, Thomas Wyse and Richard More O'Ferrall, were catholics, and a further two, William Sharman Crawford and George Evans, were members of the RDS, and liberals. A third RDS member, Joseph Devonsher Jackson, a conservative, was added as a substitute on 6 May 1836. William Smith O'Brien chaired the meetings, held between 29 March and 14 July 1836.[117] By 1835 select committees had become popular devices for investigating issues of public concern. They suffered the disadvantage of being for one session only, and therefore ran the risk of having their business rushed to a completion deadline. Quite often their composition was rather haphazard, and their meetings were confined to London, which tended to limit the number of witnesses who could be expected to attend.[118] In this instance some care seems to have been taken to achieve a reasonable balance in the composition of the committee, the decision to add Jackson giving a voice for the extremes of Irish protestant conservative views.[119]

114 Ibid., 24 Mar. 1836.   115 *Freeman's Journal*, 28 Mar. 1836.   116 *RDS Proc.*, lxxii, resolution, 31 Mar. 1836.   117 *Report on Royal Dublin Society*, 1836.   118 Sir Norman Chester, *The English administrative system, 1780–1870* (Oxford, 1981), pp. 102–3. Hereafter, Chester, *The English administrative system.*   119 *Freeman's Journal*, 23 July 1835, Jackson was authorized to speak for

William Smith O'Brien was MP for Ennis 1828–31 and a conservative unionist of moderate leanings, supporting catholic emancipation and parliamentary reforms, while also supporting the Wellington administration in its declining months, and defending the monopoly position of the East India Company.[120] By 1834 he had distanced himself from the conservative political and religious values of his family, and his ambition was to promote a united Irish representation in parliament, seeking a fairer distribution of revenue, and municipal and poor law reform. He wrote to Daniel O'Connell in late 1834 seeking membership of the anti-tory association. O'Brien supported the liberals and O'Connell in the formation of a government in April 1835. Despite this, he differed strongly from O'Connell on the need for an Irish poor law, which O'Connell opposed, and refused to acquiesce with him in the passage of an Irish coercion bill. O'Brien's strongest allies were William Sharman Crawford and Thomas Wyse, and he found himself in 1835 increasingly adopting radical positions and becoming more aligned with Crawford than with O'Connell.[121]

While the committee inquired into the running of all the society's institutions, most of its interest focused on the black-beaning of Dr Murray, the existence of political or religious cliques within the society, the procedure for electing members and conducting business, and the policy on purchasing newspapers. The chief witnesses examined were Isaac Weld (honorary secretary 1828–49), Robert Hutton (chemistry committee, 1812–30), Charles William Hamilton (agriculture committee, 1835–7), Dr William Harty (botany committee, 1829–37), and Dr Samuel Litton (botany professor 1826–47). Letters from James Naper, and Sir William Rowan Hamilton were also published in the report.[122] Terence de Vere White, in *The story of the Royal Dublin Society*, referred to earlier letters of C.W. Hamilton to W.S. O'Brien, in which Hamilton stated that he and Naper had joined the society to promote its involvement in agriculture. It had become apparent to them that the RDS was in need of constitutional reform. Also, they believed that Dublin-based members were over-represented at meetings and tended to treat the society as a Dublin-oriented club. Hamilton had discussions with Lord Mulgrave, long preceding the Murray affair, in which he had, he believed, received assurances that the government would pro-actively seek reforms. He was, nevertheless, appalled when the government used the rejection of Murray as a pretext, thus turning an internal domestic issue into a public political issue. Hamilton urged O'Brien to call R.B. Bryan, honorary secretary, as a witness, as he believed him to be pro-reform, rather than Isaac Weld who professed to be a reformer but could not be trusted since he had a 'narrow winding mind'.[123] O'Brien also received a letter from Sir William Rowan Hamilton, an honorary member of the RDS, dated 20

the duke of Cumberland on the subject of orange lodges in the army. 120 Davis, *Revolutionary imperialist*, pp. 23–43. 121 Ibid., pp. 78–83. 122 *Report on Royal Dublin Society*, 1836. 123 White, *The story of the Royal Dublin Society*, pp. 96–103.

April 1836. Sir William supported the concept of a governing council for the society, but disagreed with the government on the issue of charging for lecture admissions. On the nature of the Royal Dublin Society he wrote,

> The present plan of an almost unmixed republic appears ill-suited to the nature and efficiency of a scientific society: yet much indulgence ought perhaps to be shown to a body so unique, or at least so different in its object from societies exclusively scientific.

Sir William believed that the society made a valuable contribution in practical science, and in the popularisation of science, and that its lecture courses should be provided free to the public.[124]

Isaac Weld gave evidence to the parliamentary committee between 20 and 29 April 1836. His opinion was that although liberal supporters were numerous within the society, they had seemed indifferent to the impending ballot on 26 November 1835 and in failing to attend had given scope to a conservative element to out-maneouvre them. He said that he had heard reports that notices had been posted in some clubs, specifically the Sackville Street Club,[125] encouraging an anti-Murray vote.[126] The rejection of Murray had done positive injury to the society; its consequences were foreseen and attempts had been made to avert them. Weld had heard that an extremist protestant faction within the membership had combined against Murray. Prior to the meeting Weld, Boyd, and Naper, had met with some influential members of known orange views. John Boyd, himself a conservative, had urged them to respect the neutrality of the RDS, and expressed the hope that Murray would not be rejected. While ultimately the liberal members had failed, nevertheless the strength of liberal opinion within the society was such that a majority of members present had supported Murray's candidacy.[127]

Robert Hutton had also heard reports of notices in certain clubs intended to recruit support for an anti-Murray vote. He believed that Murray was rejected on political grounds, and not on religious grounds, although he had heard that the controversy over Dens' theological work was a factor. Taxed by W.S. O'Brien, Hutton, an O'Connellite, declared that he had never heard that Murray's recent support for O'Connell had been a factor in his rejection.[128] On the other hand, C.W. Hamilton believed that Murray's support for O'Connell was the sole

---

124 *Report on Royal Dublin Society*, 1836, appendix 12.   125 The Sackville Street Club, founded in 1795, drew its membership mostly from conservative landowners. (Source: Smith and Share, *Whigs on the Green*.)   126 William Harty claimed that one young man, acting on his own, and not a member of the RDS, had posted a notice in the Sackville Street Club. See [William Harty] *Analysis of the report and epitome of the evidence taken before a select committee of the house of commons in the session of 1836, on the Royal Dublin Society: together with notes and illustrations by a member of the society* (Dublin, 1836), p. 40.   127 *Parliamentary select committee report on Royal Dublin Society*, 1836, pp. 4–5, 99–103.   128 Ibid., evidence of Robert Hutton, 2 May 1836, p. 67.

reason for his rejection. He believed that Dr Murray was rejected on political, and not on religious grounds. In the past, Murray had opposed the use of his churches to make collections for O'Connell, but shortly before his rejection he had made a personal contribution of £10 to the O'Connell fund, and written in praise of O'Connell. Apart from his sudden reversal of position, the fact of a clerical participation in party politics had aroused strong feelings of hostility towards him. Hamilton did not believe the Dens controversy had played a significant role in Murray's rejection, and while he had heard that an anti-Murray placard had been displayed in one club, he had dismissed it as hearsay. He had also heard that resentment against a government threat to withdraw the annual grant if Murray was not elected had provoked an anti-Murray vote, but he had been unable to trace the source of the supposed government threat.[129] Dr William Harty also dismissed the notion that Dr Murray was rejected on religious grounds. 'I should scarcely believe it possible, but that I know it as a fact, that a society like the Dublin Society could exist in Ireland so totally devoid of all political and religious bias as a society.' Harty gave three reasons for Murray's rejection: firstly, his public commitment to O'Connell in November 1835; secondly, the intimation of threats from the government if he was rejected, and thirdly the perceived use of his candidacy as a political experiment.[130] Dr Samuel Litton also asserted that the RDS, in his experience, had always maintained a neutral stance on matters of politics and religion.

> As a philanthropist and a patriot, I would say the society, in that point of view, is a great blessing to the country. It is one of the points for which I have always valued the society: that I thought it a sacred ground on which, when people entered, they left all their political and religious animosities outside.[131]

Robert Hutton considered that the rejection of Murray, although not an expression of anti-catholicism, was certainly an expression of strong political feeling. C.W. Hamilton also did not believe that Murray's catholicism was the cause of his exclusion. On the other hand, Dr William Harty believed that Murray was the focus of strong religious and political feelings, and that the balance was tipped against him by the 'injudicious' interference of Dublin Castle. Harty blamed J.R. Corballis and James Naper for this development, as they had purported to speak for the lord lieutenant, and had inferred that the annual grant would be withdrawn if the society rejected Murray. Harty claimed that Naper had earlier expressed this threat to John Boyd, and strongly condemned both Naper and Hamilton for lobbying the government to change the constitution of the RDS, a body about which, he said, they knew little and

129 Ibid., pp. 144–7.   130 Ibid., pp. 227–35.   131 Ibid., pp. 294–5.

were not qualified to speak.[132] As regarded the religious and political composition of the RDS membership, Harty believed the majority 'has been, and
probably ever will be, Protestant'. He also believed them to be 'loyal' and
'constitutional' in outlook, and 'warmly attached to British connexion'.[133]

Unable to attend the select committee hearings in person, James Naper wrote
to W.S. O'Brien rebutting Harty's allegations against him. He said that at a
meeting prior to the 26 November 1835 he had taken an opportunity to speak
privately to John Boyd, Sir Edward Stanley, and other influential members on
the subject of the up-coming ballot for Dr Murray. He had not expressed
threats, and had he believed the government intended any coercive threats he
would in such circumstances himself have rejected Murray. His own and
Hamilton's early contacts with the government were in relation to the affairs of
the Agricultural Society of Ireland.[134] The new agricultural society to which he
referred (and which would ultimately merge with the RDS in 1888–9), was
founded in 1833 to act as a central co-ordinating body for local agricultural
societies. It held two annual meetings, at Ballinasloe fair in October, and at
the RDS Spring Cattle Show in April.[135] It was not well funded, and C.W.
Hamilton, as secretary, was in correspondence with the government seeking
permission to use the freepost facilities of Dublin Castle to circularise the
membership.[136]

The practice of electing new members by ballot was generally defended by
the RDS witnesses. Isaac Weld said that nothing in the charter precluded the
RDS from varying the rules for the admission of members in any way it wished.
He added that he would support a return to a simple majority vote, but did not
think that this of itself would eliminate the possibility of the exclusion of
candidates. Harty also argued that the ballot system was intrinsically unobjec-
tionable. Robert Hutton favoured a continuance of balloting, accepting that the
reason for retaining a power of exclusion was the difficulty of removing a
member once elected. He instanced the example of the Royal Irish Academy,
which also admitted members by a two-thirds majority vote. C.W. Hamilton
approved of the balloting system, and in general he did not think it likely to be
used to exclude suitable candidates.[137] Isaac Weld denied that the society
resembled a club. Pressed on the high cost of admission, he said that if it was
significantly reduced 'it would bring in an inferior class of persons, and lower
the consequence of the society'.[138] Weld defended the practice of taking
newspapers, and listed those taken regularly. He named them as *The Globe, The*

132 *Report on Royal Dublin Society*, 1836, pp. 67, 144–7, 229.   133 Ibid., pp. 226–35, 251.
134 Ibid., appendix 13.   135 Christopher Ryan (ed.), *Lewis' Dublin: a topographical dictionary of
the parishes, towns and villages of Dublin city and county* (Cork, 2001), p. 99. Hereafter, Ryan, *Lewis'
Dublin*.   136 NAI: CSORP 1835, 4101/29, Hamilton to Morpeth, 30 Dec. 1835.   137 *Report on
Royal Dublin Society, 1836*, pp. 66–9, 106–9, 146, 229.   138 Ibid., pp. 6–7, evidence of Isaac Weld,
20 Apr. 1836.

Times, The Sun, The Standard, The Observer, The Examiner, the *Dublin Evening Post, Evening Mail, Freeman's Journal, Morning Register,* and *Saunders' News Letter*; a selection of London and Dublin newspapers which mirrored a wide spread of political viewpoints. The absence of *The Pilot* indicates that a line was drawn at overt O'Connellite partisanship. Weld added that the majority of members did not take an active role in the society's affairs, and that the newspaper room provided for them a point of contact, which prompted W.S. O'Brien to comment 'Then, in short, the majority of the members use the society as little else than a club?'.[139]

Robert Hutton believed that the RDS was badly in need of constitutional reform. In his opinion, its inefficiency, and perceived political bias, inhibited many worthy men from joining. He was opposed to the recent development of a role in practical agriculture, and supported the suggestion of creating an executive council although worried about its probable composition. Hutton believed the withdrawal of newspapers and journals would rapidly diminish any political character attached to the society, and restore it to a sober pursuit of its stated objects. He agreed that the national interest in the society should be given appropriate acknowledgement and expression, since a large amount of public money was spent on its property and collections.[140] Hutton argued that the holding of weekly general meetings tended to make the RDS a debating society. While he had never heard politics discussed at these meetings he felt that of its nature the general meeting could move in that direction. Issues were adopted and as quickly dropped, and the machinery of decision making was cumbersome, although perhaps necessary to prevent jobbery.[141]

William Smith O'Brien was reaching conclusions of his own on the nature of the society. In his notes for the preparation of the select committee report is one headed 'Explain nature of Institution'. He thought the society was 'Too sluggish in action' and bearing 'too much of a club character', to make it attractive to 'Scientific men'. He objected particularly to the seemingly capricious use of its powers of exclusion. In a note headed 'Origins of the Society' he set down questions 'Whether Society not Trustees for Public', 'whether subscriptions not too high to allow Poor scientific men to join society', and 'whether affairs would not be better managed by a council'. In a second note headed 'General Questions' he again raised the subject of 'Legal questions as to Property'.[142]

When the report was published the deliberations of the select committee had reached conclusions which can be summarized as follows.

1. The society should be treated as the trustee of public funds.
2. The by-laws should be revised so as to make rejection difficult, and provide for annual membership.

139 Ibid., pp. 88–91. 140 Ibid., pp. 60–1, 66–9. 141 Ibid., p. 121. 142 NLI: William Smith O'Brien papers, 22, 389, mf 8401.

3. The management of the society should be entrusted to a council.
4. The council's membership should be drawn from the standing committees and from the general meeting of members.
5. Budgets should be prepared early each year, and made subject to the sanction of the council.
6. The RDS should become the central body for the diffusion of knowledge on practical science, art, and agriculture in Ireland.
7. The provincial lecture scheme should be further developed.
8. A school for gardeners should be developed in the botanic garden.
9. The museum, botanic garden, and Leinster Lawn should be generally opened to the public.
10. No books should be loaned out from the library.
11. Free lectures should be provided.
12. All standing committees should make regular reports.
13. Newspapers and periodicals should not be purchased.
14. The art schools should focus on technical rather than classical subjects.
15. A national museum should be built on the society's premises.[143]

The treasury quickly looked for an RDS response to the first resolution. A holding reply was sent by P.T. Wilson, registrar, which resulted in a second treasury letter, threatening that 'no further issue will be made upon account of the sum voted in the last session of Parliament' pending a response from the society to resolution number one.[144] When regular general meetings of the society were resumed in November 1836 a report on the resolutions of the parliamentary select committee was tabled. The special committee of the RDS, appointed the previous March, recommended compliance with the resolutions, but evaded that on newspapers by recommending that they be purchased out of private funds, and balked at what they interpreted as the terms of resolution number one. They believed that the society's property, under the terms of its charter, was 'possessed by them in absolute right', and 'it cannot, and ought not, to consent to any surrender of its property'. The general meeting on 10 November 1836 agreed with the recommendations of its special committee and, on the same occasion, replaced the earl of Meath with J.D. Jackson as a vice-president.[145]

The treasury had a difficulty with the society's response to resolution number one. The state had paid out grants amounting to £276,154 to the society since 1800, and,

> They cannot, therefore, feel justified in proposing any further vote to Parliament, without an unequivocal admission that the property of the Society is held for the public use of the institution only, and that no

143 *Report on Royal Dublin Society*, 1836, parliamentary select committee's resolutions. 144 *RDS Proc.*, lxxiii, minutes, 24, 30 Aug., 20 Sept. 1836. 145 Ibid., 3, 10 Nov. 1836.

absolute right of proprietorship is claimed, and that such property cannot be sold, or in any way alienated, without the consent of my Lords; but that the public shall be entitled to the full and entire use thereof.

The society went as far as it believed it could safely go in meeting this requirement. It adopted a resolution stating 'that they hold their property subject to a public trust, and for the public benefit, with a view to the objects of the Charter, and for the public use of the Institution only'.[146] In the aftermath of the parliamentary inquiry, the society expressed itself pleased that 'after an unusually full and laborious examination of four months' continuance, [the parliamentary committee] have seen no reason to accredit any of the statements or insinuations, so long and so industriously circulated to injure the Society'.[147]

The main issues arising from the rejection of Archbishop Murray were its impact on the ability of the society to attract public support, and the suitability of the society as an instrument of government policy. The rejection of Murray did no credit to the society, and brought about an immediate, if short-lived, fall-out in the form of the withdrawal of candidates, and adverse publicity. More important in the long run was the impetus that it gave towards government thinking on remodeling the society, and on bringing it clearly into the public domain. The main defect revealed by the affair was the society's archaic and cumbersome method of government by general meeting. Whatever its democratic merits, this system was crying-out for reform. On the evidence of the Murray case, corroborated by witnesses before the parliamentary select committee, it was a system too easily manipulable by emotive rhetoric. The balloting system, although not condemned, could clearly be used to express political, if not religious stances, inappropriate to a body priding itself on its strict neutrality. The issue of politics and religion within the society's membership could not, after all, be disregarded, and could manifest itself given the right set of circumstances.

In the aftermath of 26 November 1835 'a feeling of disgust at the society for having rejected Dr Murray' persisted and led to the withdrawal of a number of candidates for membership.[148] No current members resigned. However, four candidates for membership were withdrawn by their proposers (Benjamin Bowen Johnson[149] and Thomas Purdon)[150] on 18 February 1836. While the reasons for these and subsequent withdrawals were not specified, it seems probable that the spectacle of the RDS in a public scrimmage with its

146 Ibid., 15, 22 Dec. 1836.   147 Ibid., special committee report, 3 Nov. 1836.   148 *Report on Royal Dublin Society*, 1836, pp. 144–7.   149 B.B. Johnson, attorney, was a member of the RDS 1808–56. In 1835 he was active on both the house and the manufactures committees. (Source: *RDS Proc.*, var. dates.)   150 Thomas Rodney Purdon, Lisnabin, Co. Westmeath, was a member of the RDS, 1815–65, and a member of the manufactures committee, 1835–44. He was also the reform minded governor of the Richmond prison, where O'Connell would be incarcerated in 1844. (Sources: *RDS Proc.*, var. dates; MacDonagh, *The Emancipist*.)

paymaster, the government, was sufficient deterrent for many. Some candidates were believed to have withdrawn out of a sense of solidarity with Murray or in disgust at his rejection. Others may have been deterred at the prospect of the closure of the newspaper room arising from the government's propositions. At the RDS general meeting on 25 February 1836 three further names of candidates were withdrawn by Sir Robert Shaw, and Daniel McKay.[151] Subsequently Thomas Gresham, hotelier, withdrew his name on 28 April 1836,[152] and at a later date Archbishop Richard Whately refused to join an organisation which had rejected his friend Archbishop Daniel Murray.[153] Surprisingly, newspaper comment was muted, perhaps in deference to the wish expressed in Dr Murray's letter to J.R. Corballis, and published by the society. Apart from lending their columns to the occasional letter on the subject, the *Freeman's Journal* and the *Evening Mail* were remarkable at this period for a minimalist approach to the subject. There were no public boycotts of the RDS, or any pointed withdrawals of public support for its activities.

A structural problem exposed in the balloting system was the long, and, as it proved, fateful delay caused by the absence of all the vice-presidents at the society's general meeting on 9 July 1835. The poor attendance records of vice-presidents had for long been a sensitive issue for the society, especially as the third clause of the charter required their presence at meetings to elect new members, fill offices, or appoint staff.[154] In 1835 the society's seven vice-presidents in order of seniority were the earl of Meath, Sir Robert Shaw, John Leslie Foster, Henry Joy, John Boyd, the marquess of Downshire, and James Naper. In the decade 1825–34 fifty-four per cent of general meetings were chaired by vice-presidents. Superficially this seemed a respectable level of attendance, but it concealed the fact that just three people, Sir Robert Shaw, John Boyd, and Lord Harberton (who died in 1833), carried the burden of the work, chairing between them 157 meetings out of 325 held. Even the enthusiastic reformers, James Naper and Lord Downshire, recently elected vice-presidents, chaired only three meetings in all during 1833–4.[155] This problem was noted as far back as 1816, and efforts were made at that time to encourage the attendance of vice-presidents, especially when balloting was scheduled.[156] In 1822 John Burne attempted to move a resolution to replace any vice-presidents who failed to attend meetings during the preceding year. Baron Oriel, J.L. Foster, and the earl of Charleville, met this criterion, but only Charleville was replaced. When Henry Joy was elected a vice-president on 14 November 1822, he took care to record that 'I regret extremely that my other avocations will not

151 Daniel McKay, attorney, was a member of the RDS, 1815–41, and served on the fine arts committee, 1835–40. [Source: *RDS Proc.*, var. dates.]   152 *RDS Proc.*, lxxii; Gresham was later elected a member, in 1842.   153 Bowen, *The protestant crusade in Ireland*, p. 291.   154 *The charters and statutes of the Royal Dublin Society* (1989 ed., RDS, Dublin).   155 Author's analysis of attendances.   156 *RDS Proc.*, liii, minutes, 21 Nov. 1816.

permit me to give that constant attention, which it is my wish to bestow on the duties of the office'.[157] Subsequently, no amount of cajolery served to alter the behaviour of the frequently absent vice-presidents, and despite this the absentees were continued in office year after year.

The opportunity missed in 1832 to return to simple majority voting, was an example of the capriciousness of government by general meeting, and a factor in the embarrassing outcome of the Murray ballot. In the early years of the Dublin Society balloting for membership was by simple majority, only changed to a two-thirds majority in 1767.[158] Lord Leveson Gower had advised the society in 1829 of the Wellington government's opinion that election of members by ballot was inappropriate in an institution supported out of public funds, but the society had counter-argued that proceeding by election was an express term of its charter (see chapter three). An attempt by John Boyd to return to simple majority voting received considerable support in 1832, but was ultimately rejected.[159] In defending the balloting system in 1829 the RDS had argued that rejection had been used very sparingly, with only four instances occurring between 1800 and 1829, and that it was a necessary filter since no mechanism existed for the expulsion of a member once elected.[160] Isaac Weld, honorary secretary, in evidence given in 1836, said that the total of candidates rejected since 1800 was four, including Dr Murray in 1835.[161] This discrepancy in numbers is understandable when allowance is made for the errors, omissions, and sometimes light regard for its own standing orders to which the society seemed particularly prone in the opening years of the nineteenth century. Between 1801 and 1815, more than a score of candidates appeared to have been elected without any records of a proposer and seconder, or of having gone through the normal balloting procedure.[162] Only three candidates were incontrovertibly rejected during this period, and they were, as confirmed by Weld; Daniel O'Connell, Anthony Browne, and Peter Brophy. All three rejections occurred during 1811–12.[163]

O'Connell and Brophy were both catholics, but politics in the shape of a revived campaign for catholic emancipation,[164] rather than religion *per se*, appear to have caused their exclusion, since non-controversial catholics such as John Grainger and Thomas Farrell were elected during the same period. Anthony Browne, attorney, was proposed for membership by Christopher Abbott and James Walkinshaw Bell, and rejected on 30 May 1811. Browne may also have been the victim of political bias. According to Weld, whose informant was Cloncurry, Anthony Browne was a relative of Wogan Browne's.[165] The latter's

---

157 *RDS Proc.*, lix, minutes, 7, 14 Nov. 1822.   158 *RDS Proc.*, iv, resolution of 12 Nov. 1767.
159 *RDS Proc.*, lxviii–lxix, minutes, 5 Jan., 1 Mar., 8 Nov. 1832.   160 *RDS Proc.*, lxvi, letter to Lord Leveson Gower, 10 Dec. 1829.   161 *Report from the select committee on Royal Dublin Society*, HC (445), xvi, 1836, pp. 4–7, evidence of Isaac Weld, 20 Apr. 1836.   162 Author's database.
163 *RDS Proc.*, xlvii–xlviii, minutes, 28 Feb., 30 May 1811, 10 Dec. 1812.   164 Boyce, *Nineteenth-century Ireland*, pp. 34–6.   165 *Report on Royal Dublin Society*, 1836, evidence of Isaac Weld, 14 July 1836.

shadowy connections with the 1798 rebellion had placed him under a constant cloud of government mistrust, and he was dismissed the magistracy, for the second time, in 1810.[166]

Speculative though these reflections must be, it is possible to make some guess as to the breakdown of the 79:65 division of votes on 26 November 1835. Appendix VIII lists those members present, with some attempt at categorisation by occupation. Probably the twelve identifiable catholics present: Richard Corballis, John Richard Corballis, James Anthony Corballis, Patrick Curtis, Sir Thomas Esmonde, Thomas Farrell, Gonville Ffrench, Dr J.F. O'Neill Lentaigne, Michael O'Loghlen (attorney general), Andrew Christopher Palles, Walter Sweetman, and William Sweetman, supported Murray. Isaac Weld disclosed in a letter to the *Freeman's Journal* that he had voted for Murray,[167] and from the evidence of contemporary statements and positions taken, so did Reverend S.C. Sandes, John Boyd, C.W. Hamilton, Robert Butler Bryan, and the Reverend E.G. Hudson. The ardent O'Connellites present at the meeting, Leland Crosthwaite junior, James Haughton, William Haughton, and Robert Hutton, presumably voted for Murray. At least twice as many O'Connellites failed to attend the meeting, including Lord Cloncurry and Pierce Mahony, but their absence was made up to some extent by the presence of a strong liberal contingent. Amongst the committed supporters of Mulgrave's administration present, and therefore likely to have voted for Murray, were Maziere Brady, William Henry Curran, George Evans, MP, Baron de Robeck, Thomas Hutton, solicitor general John Richards, and Lord Talbot de Malahide.[168] A further fifty votes also went in Murray's favour.

The opponents of Dr Murray were more shadowy. Attempts by some members of the parliamentary select committee to implicate John Leslie Foster (who was not present at the meeting on 26 November 1835), were not borne out by the evidence. Isaac Weld said that Foster's period of greatest influence in the society was some twenty years in the past.[169] With greater justification, the *Freeman's Journal* hinted at the involvement of Henry Stanley Monck (1785–1848), created earl of Rathdown in 1822. Monck was a man of limited interests beyond the running of his Co. Wicklow estate, and meetings of the Orange Order. He was also a keen amateur actor and musician, and president of the Beefsteak Club, a musical society founded by the playwright Thomas Sheridan.[170] He used the club as a platform for his ultra-conservative political and religious views.[171] The treasurer of the Beefsteak Club was a minor customs official, James McAskey. Lord Rathdown and James McAskey were both

166 Des O'Leary, 'Wogan Browne', in Cullen and Geissel, *Fugitive warfare*, pp. 78–85.
167 *Freeman's Journal*, 18 Dec. 1835.   168 Hoppen, *Elections, politics and society*; MacDonagh, *The emancipist*, Walker, *Parliamentary election results*.   169 *Report on Royal Dublin Society*, 1836, pp. 6, 20.   170 Elisabeth Batt, *The Moncks and Charleville House: a Wicklow family in the nineteenth century* (Dublin, 1979), pp. 16–17, 33–5.   171 Anglesey, *One-leg*, p. 192.

members of the RDS, and while they hardly ever attended meetings of the society, and did not take an active role in its affairs, both were present at the meeting on 26 November 1835. The *Freeman's Journal* carried a report that stated,

> the Orangemen were present in force, assembled under the leadership of my Lord Rathdown, and flushed with the wine of a political dinner upon the preceding evening, where this gross outrage was concerted, amidst party tunes, and bumpers to the Duke of Cumberland.[172]

Apart from Rathdown, and McAskey, two other prominent Orange Order spokesmen were present at the meeting, namely Joseph Devonsher Jackson, and Thomas Young Prior,[173] secretary of the Co. Dublin grand lodge. Some prominent members of protestant conservative societies were also present; Theobald Billing, Drury Jones Dickenson, and Richard John Orpen. It seems likely the foregoing members might have opposed Murray's candidacy, and some may have provided a focus for a more general sectarian opposition. However, they were of themselves too few in number and too unfamiliar to the general body to have swayed the votes of forty-five per cent of the members present. The more vociferous amongst the Trinity College conservatives were absent from the meeting and TCD was represented by the minority liberals, Sandes, and the Reverend Richard MacDonnell.[174] Anti-O'Connellites were undoubtedly present, and conservatives of an earlier generation whose resentment at political change might have provoked a demonstrative rejection of anything perceived as government interference. Sir Edward Stanley might for personal reasons (he was D'Esterre's second in the 1815 duel with O'Connell), have found it difficult to support an O'Connell supporter. Nevertheless he was, twenty years on, a mature and conscientious senior committee member, and might simply have abstained. Conversely, there were others present such as Edward Croker, whose business was saved from a punitive confiscation by the intervention of Daniel O'Connell in 1833.[175] Also present was Dr William O'Brien Bellingham, a protestant whose appointment as a surgeon to St Vincent's hospital in 1835 was made on the personal recommendation of Archbishop Murray.[176] It is difficult to pinpoint a single source for the opposition to Murray. The anti-Murray faction was to a large extent an anti-government faction. They were apprehensive at an impending loss of power, office, and social prestige as the Whig-liberals relentlessly pursued reforms in the Irish church, public offices, municipal corporations, and the administration of justice, and positively discriminated in the advancement of catholic professionals. R.B. McDowell has described the Irish conservatives of this period as the embodiment of militant protestantism

172 *Freeman's Journal*, 9 Dec. 1835.   173 Ibid., 8 Apr. 1836.   174 McDowell, *Public opinion*, p. 113, and McDowell and Webb, *Trinity College Dublin*, pp. 79, 157.   175 O'Connell, *Correspondence*, v, index.   176 Cameron, *RCSI*.

tied to a privileged establishment. Their emergence in the late 1820s was a reaction to the prospect and implications of catholic emancipation.

In 1864, at another parliamentary inquiry, Laurence Waldron, MP, a catholic member of the RDS, and later an honorary secretary, asked Dr William Steele if he had ever heard that the anti-Murray faction was an extremist clique of 'the old corporation'.[177] Waldron's question, to which Steele could not provide an answer, was probably prompted by the regular presence at RDS meetings in the 1830s of members connected with Dublin Corporation, but who could not be said to represent a solid conservative bloc. C.W. Hamilton blamed the merchants,[178] although as a group they were so permeated by O'Connellites and liberals as to render their general culpability improbable. The wine trade was the most conservative element in the Dublin mercantile class[179] but its influence was no longer well represented in the RDS by 1835. The business world was pragmatic, and even the Bank of Ireland, with a charter which technically excluded catholic directors before 1845, had ignored such restrictions following catholic emancipation and appointed its first catholic director, Stephen Grehan, in 1830.[180] The disaffected were more likely to be found amongst the office holders in central and local government, apprehensive of change, and to them might be added lawyers dependent on government patronage to advance their careers in the legal profession. A generation later Sir Dominic Corrigan would say of the RDS that it was 'in its essence a great popular society, and therefore in its very constitution more likely to be led by prejudices than by calm consideration'.[181] Corrigan's identification of government by general meeting as an inherent structural problem was probably correct.

By the end of 1836 the society had been cowed by government threats of the withdrawal of its annual grant. The next few years would witness not only the extent of its willingness to adapt to changing circumstances, but an internal debate centred around its determination to preserve its independence. The rejection of Archbishop Murray precipitated immediate problems for the Royal Dublin Society and it is reasonable to ask how such an unwelcome occurrence was allowed to happen. J.R. Corballis presumably took soundings in the summer of 1835 and believed he would have an adequate level of support to secure Murray's election. His strategy might have worked in late June, before O'Connell's election began to receive serious public scrutiny, and when anticipation of the BAAS conference in August produced a temporary lull in partisan bickering. The June strategy failed because no vice-president was available to attend the meeting. Corballis and his supporters apparently

177 *Report from the select committee on scientific institutions* (Dublin), HC (495), 1864, p. 74.
178 *Report on Royal Dublin Society*, 1836.   179 Cullen, *Princes and pirates*, pp. 23–4.   180 F.G. Hall, *The Bank of Ireland, 1783–1946* (Dublin, 1949), pp. 140–44, 192. Hereafter, Hall, *Bank of Ireland*.   181 *Report from the select committee on scientific institutions* (Dublin), HC (495), 1864, pp. 41–2.

neglected to guard against this possibility, or to prevail upon allies such as RDS vice-president James Naper to attend. Having missed the first and probably best opportunity the question which arises is why they persisted with Murray's candidacy in November? The BAAS conference, the ostensible reason for Murray's interest in becoming a member, was over. By November the Dens controversy, and the questions surrounding O'Connell's election as MP, were simmering in the public press, and Murray had given a mark of approval to O'Connell. It might have been judicious to defer Murray's candidacy.

Nevertheless the lobbyists decided to press ahead. While there is no overt evidence of a Dublin Castle plot, it is just possible that the suspicions of Dr William Harty were well grounded. The statements of C.W. Hamilton do seem to indicate some influence of the Mulgrave administration behind that decision. It is possible that the government had covertly decided to make the archbishop's election a test case, from which a positive outcome would show the success of integrationist policies, and a negative outcome would provide an opportunity to insist upon a radical reform of the society. However, as the drama unfolded a new issue emerged; the right of the society to defend itself against government manipulation and interference in its internal affairs. In particular, older members such as Harty, who otherwise might have approved of Murray's candidacy, were alienated rather than persuaded by the threats of the withdrawal of government support. The pro-Murray lobby failed to keep such potential allies on side, or to prevail on their most influential supporters such as Cloncurry and Naper to attend the meeting, and seem to have suffered a last-minute loss of nerve. Their misjudgement of the mood of the society resulted in an appalling shambles, which did no great good to either side of the argument, and delivered a serious blow to the society's reputation for non-partisanship.

CHAPTER SIX

'An almost unmixed republic'
1837–9

The years immediately following the publication of the report of the parliamentary committee of inquiry were notable within the RDS as a period of internal debate as the society attempted to comply with the report's recommendations. The most profound administrative change effected during this period was the creation of an executive council with delegated powers for the day-to-day management of the society. The period was also notable for the further development of agricultural and industrial exhibitions, and for the increasingly dominant role of science in the society's activities. The government remained dissatisfied with aspects of the society's provision of membership facilities, particularly the continuance of the newspaper room, and by the end of 1839 a new crisis was looming on this unresolved issue.

This chapter examines the progress made by the society in implementing the recommendations of the parliamentary report, in developing exhibitions, and in responding to the public appetite for scientific knowledge. It will be argued that, despite financial constraints and uncertainties, much progress was made, especially in the development of the botanic garden, agricultural and industrial exhibitions, and public science lectures. The adverse publicity surrounding the Murray affair died away following the publication of the parliamentary select committee report, and the society's role as a national institution could be viewed once more in a positive light.

On 2 March 1837, Fenton Hort[1] presented a report to the general meeting of the society, on behalf of the special (by-law review and evidence) committee. He advised the meeting that no reply had been received from the government to the resolutions passed by the society during the previous November and December. These resolutions were a broad acceptance of the recommendations of the parliamentary committee, with only two unresolved issues – the right to purchase newspapers, and the state's interest in the properties held by the RDS

---

1 Fenton Hort (1794–1873), owner of a 500-acre demesne at Leopardstown, and a commissioner of the poor law inquiry, was a member of the RDS agriculture committee, 1830–7. On 31 Mar. 1836 he was appointed to the special committee to prepare evidence for the parliamentary committee of inquiry. (Sources: *RDS Proc.*, var. dates; *Burke*, Ryan, *Lewis' Dublin*.)

The latter had been the subject of a separate resolution of the society in December 1836, conceding that these properties were held 'subject to a public trust, and for the public benefit, with a view to the objects of the Charter, and for the public use of the Institution only'. In the absence of an official response, Hort recommended that no action be taken on revising the by-laws.[2]

Not knowing if the resolution of December 1836 had satisfied the treasury, the society requested the release of funds in February 1837. The request was met with a prevaricating reply from Under Secretary Drummond.[3] The terms of the 1836 parliamentary inquiry had been sufficiently broad to allow for the re-direction of a portion of the society's annual grant to other existing or purpose-formed institutions. Fortunately for the RDS, the parliamentary committee had concluded that its grant should remain intact. Lord Morpeth apparently did not share this view (as evidenced by his later attempt to break-up the grant in 1839–41), but he was constrained by the parliamentary committee's recommendation.[4]

The 1836–7 session ended in April with no further communication from Dublin Castle to the RDS, and no release of funds from the treasury. Sir Robert Shaw reported to the general meeting in May that after taking soundings through sympathetic MPs the special committee recommended to the society a further resolution on the subject of its property,

> That whilst the Society doubt their legal authority to make a by-law to the effect of the guarantee required by the minute of the Treasury, they are for themselves willing to admit, that in consideration of the Parliamentary Grants made to the Society, it is but just and reasonable that they should not alienate their property without the approval of the Lords of the Treasury.[5]

This additional resolution apparently placated the treasury, as the balance of the 1836–7 grant was released to the society at the end of June 1837, three months in arrears.[6] The society's position as a supplicant for government bounty had once again been exposed, and the government could at any time adduce arguments, from minute analyses of RDS expenditure, proving that stricter government supervision, or even a take-over of the society's affairs, was warranted.[7] Apart from a maximum £200 contribution towards the expenses of the provincial lecture scheme, the government refused to make any official increase to the RDS grant during 1837–9.[8] The general trend in RDS income and expenditure is shown in table 6.1 below. The account for 1819 is the earliest baseline available containing all the major analytical features of later accounts. While table 6.1 provides a good analogue, it is not an accurate comparison of

2 RDS Proc., lxxiii, minutes, 2 Mar. 1837.   3 Ibid., 9 Mar. 1837.   4 Meenan and Clarke, The Royal Dublin Society, 1731–1981, p. 33.   5 RDS Proc., lxxiii, special committee report, 11 May 1837. 6 Ibid., 29 June 1837.   7 Meenan and Clarke, The Royal Dublin Society, 1731–1981, p. 33.   8 RDS Proc., lxxiv, minutes, 31 May 1838.

year-to-year change in the modern accounting sense, for the technical reasons explained below.

Table 6.1 Abstract of RDS accounts, 1819–39

	1819 £	1834 £	1837 £	1838 £	1839 £
botany and botanic garden	1570	932	1169	1179	1636
library	693	630	1127	727	918
fine arts	506	467	395	408	454
science, geology, museum	1576	530	875	922	1181
agriculture	0	296	130	336	209
manufactures	0	113	0	521	8
rent, tax, insurance (Kildare-st)	1677	687	521	510	505
rent, tax, repairs (Hawkins-st)	907	0	0	0	0
salaries, wages (establishment)	1156	469	652	639	719
printing, stationery, advertising	236	171	348	336	316
repairs, furniture (Kildare-st)	336	168	428	311	444
heating and light (Kildare-st)	122	112	163	163	213
PAYMENTS	**8779**	**4575**	**5808**	**6052**	**6603**
parliamentary grant	9170	5300	5300	5300	5300
other receipts	497	1365	624	1049	949
RECEIPTS	**9666**	**6665**	**5924**	**6349**	**6249**

Notes on sources: **1819** *RDS Proc.*, lvi, appendix, receipts and payments for calendar year 1819. **1834** *Report on Royal Dublin Society, 1836*, appendix. **1837–9** *RDS Proc.*, lxxiv–lxxvi, appendices. The money values are expressed in British £s. For convenience, the 1819 values have been converted from Irish to British currency at the rate of £1 Irish = £0.92 British.

Up to the 1830s the society's accounts were presented on a receipts and payments basis, roughly equivalent to a cash-flow statement, and useful for gauging credit requirements. The period used was the calendar year, January through December (in practice the year was started and ended around Little Christmas, 5–6 January). The government decided in 1831 to introduce double-entry bookkeeping methods for all receipts and payments falling under its remit. First applied to the navy's accounts in 1832 the system was rapidly extended to the accounting of all government departments and government supported institutions.[9] Since the government's principal object was to facilitate the comparison of spending with estimates, the accrual concept (allocating receipts

9 Chester, *The English administrative system*, pp. 213–14.

and expenditure of a period to the period, irrespective of when received or paid) was gradually adopted. This was not yet the case in the 1830s when a mixed system prevailed and trailers continued to abound, for example routine painting in the botanic garden in 1837 was charged to the 1838–9 account. A further impediment to accurate comparison is a change from a calendar to a fiscal year (April through March) basis for annual accounting in 1837–8. The inclusion in table 6.1 of accounts for 1834 is important as typifying the period 1831–5 and this account was printed in the report of the parliamentary select committee. The account headings adopted in that report were followed fairly consistently in later accounts. The expenditure shown for 1834 seems low by comparison with 1837–9, and was probably understated by the netting-off of items such as exhibition receipts to show only the net expenditures incurred.

Even a cursory glance at table 6.1 reveals (i) the impact of the grant reductions made in 1820–1 and 1830–3; (ii) the society's dependence on the annual parliamentary grant, and (iii) the shifting emphasis in RDS activities during 1819–39. The Hawkins Street incubus had been quickly ditched (see pages 37–9), veterinary services and geological field-work were abandoned, and payroll costs were reduced. Despite the savings effected the remaining core activities were generally so tightly constrained as to put natural growth beyond their reach. New activities in agriculture and manufactures were only possible since they were to a large extent self-financing. A hidden cost was the almost total lack of capital investment during the 1830s. Dependence on the parliamentary grant, ninety-five per cent of income in 1819, remained high. Even following the substantial reductions of the intervening period the annual grant represented eighty-five per cent of the society's total income in 1839. Clearly the RDS was in no condition financially to contemplate severing its connection with the state.

An abstract of expenditure in the botanic garden[10] for the decade 1829–38 shows that spending in that department for that period was to all intents and purposes static. A significant increase in 1839 was almost entirely attributable to emergency repair work following the great storm of 6 January 1839. A comparable increase was also recorded in the Leinster House repairs account. Storm damage insurance, except for shipping, was not usual in 1839 and victims had to cope with such disasters from their own resources.[11] The RDS executive council received a report on 10 January 1839 that 'considerable damage has been done to the glass and slating of these premises by the Hurricane of Sunday night'. On the recommendation of John Papworth, master of the school of architecture since 1838, the council ordered emergency repairs to proceed immediately in Kildare Street, except on the stabling halls, which required more extensive

10 RDS Proc., lxxv, registrar's report on botanic garden accounts, 25 Apr. 1839. 11 Peter Carr, The night of the Big Wind (2nd ed., Belfast, 1994), p. 38. Hereafter, Carr, The night of the Big Wind.

treatment.[12] Maintaining a scientific detachment in the chaotic aftermath of the storm, the botany committee obtained the approval of the council to advertise for information on the species of trees observed to have sustained the most wind damage.[13] A large part of the boundary wall of the botanic garden had collapsed during the storm, and an estimate of £80 for repairs was accepted.[14] A subsequent petition from police constable Morrison for compensation for injuries sustained (he was standing nearby when the wall collapsed), was refused on the grounds that there was no compensation fund available.[15] The council reported to the general meeting on 28 February 1839 that the worst of the storm damage had consisted of the collapse of the boundary wall at Glasnevin, and severe damage to the roof of the stables in Kildare Street. The cost of repairs to the latter was estimated at £331 10s. for slates and £50 for timber.[16]

Developments at the botanic garden during 1834–8, despite a chronic lack of funds, owed much to the energy and vision of the curator Ninian Niven. He remodeled the gardens, and revived the training program for young gardeners during his period in office.[17] He persuaded the society to release £300 from its private reserves to refurbish the octagon house and make it suitable for the expanding collection of delicate tropical plants, much to the satisfaction of the botany committee.[18] During August 1836 he traveled on foot through Connemara, collecting examples of native flora from remote locations such as the summit of Mweelrea, and building a *hortus siccus* of shrubs, herbs, wild flowers, mosses, and lichens.[19]

In a report to the botany committee, dated 1 April 1837, Niven reviewed developments over the previous eighteen months. He was particularly proud of the tropical collection, and especially the South American species, the expansion of which was aided by regular acquisitions from John Tweedie, a botanical agent based in Buenos Aires. Niven continued his experiments in potato cultivation, unable to fathom the cause of sporadic outbreaks of blight that he attributed primarily to atmospheric conditions. He recommended the semi-annual sale by public auction of surplus plants to raise additional funds, arguing that it would not interfere unduly with the business of commercial nurseries, or be driven by market demands.[20] The botany committee supported Niven's recommendation to hold occasional auctions of surplus plants, and also supported his agency arrangements, pointing out that he had been able to exchange one example of a plant sent to him by Tweedie, for £50 value in nursery plants. Apart from accumulating a scarce and valuable orchid collection since early 1836, Niven had been responsible for adding over 2,000 species to the general collection since his

---

12 RDS Archive: Council minute book, 1838–44, 10 Jan. 1839.   13 Ibid., 24 Jan. 1839.   14 Ibid., 14 Feb. 1839.   15 Ibid., 16 May 1839.   16 *RDS Proc.*, lxxv, minutes, 28 Feb. 1839.   17 Phyllis Clinch, 'Botany and the botanic gardens', in Meenan and Clarke, *The Royal Dublin Society, 1731–1981*, pp. 193–4.   18 *RDS Proc.*, lxxii, botany committee report, 11 Feb. 1836.   19 *RDS Proc.*, lxxiii, curator's report, 3 Nov. 1836.   20 Ibid., botany committee report, 13 Apr. 1837.

appointment. The committee further recommended that Niven be encouraged to prepare a catalogue of the garden, and acquire a reference library, and that his salary of £100 per annum be reviewed.[21] One dissenting voice emerged from the committee when Dr William Harty resigned, questioning the propriety of holding auctions, and the position of the professor of botany *vis-à-vis* that of the very active curator.[22] Samuel Litton, the professor of botany, had been critical of Niven's plans for the garden as too unorthodox and draconian.[23] Harty tabled motions on these subjects on 1 June 1837, but, evidently perceived by the general meeting as petty and tiresome, they were defeated *seriatim*.[24] A subsequent report defined the professor's role in the botanic garden as advisory, and that of the curator as operations manager, implying that there was no conflict between them.[25]

Late in 1837 an opportunity arose to acquire additional land for the botanic garden. Lands adjoining the garden, the property of Alexander Carroll, a member of the RDS fine arts committee, had become available for lease or purchase. The lands were strategically positioned between the botanic garden and the proposed Glasnevin cemetery.[26] The botany committee recommended that a one-acre site, forming a triangular salient adjoining the botanic garden on two sides, should be leased from Carroll for ten guineas per annum. The committee was apprehensive that the cost of acquiring an additional four acres fronting the river, although its acquisition would be desirable, might be beyond their means.[27] However, the entire field consisted of nine acres, and Alexander Carroll was reluctant to dispose of it piece-meal.[28] Negotiations followed, and in March 1838 Carroll agreed to lease half the field, about four-and-a-half acres, to the society.[29] Carroll attended two meetings of the botany committee and offered a sub-letting arrangement that would ultimately allow the society to secure possession of the entire site.[30] Later that year an agreement was reached with the newly established Prospect Cemetery Company to share the costs of building a ten-foot high boundary wall where the two properties adjoined.[31]

In presenting the annual report on the garden for 1837, the botany committee again took the opportunity to press for a substantial increase in salary for Ninian Niven. Niven's own report contained an explanation of his connection with Tweedie, to whom he had been introduced in 1834 by the earl of Arran. Tweedie had supplied him with rare South American plants for the botanic garden, one of which, a verbena which he had acclimatized successfully, had become so popular as a garden flower that he was able to exchange a single specimen for the equivalent of fifty guineas in other plants. He argued the advantages of

21 Ibid., 4 May 1837.   22 Ibid., minutes, 25 May 1837.   23 RDS Archive: Committee of Botany minute book, 1834–45, report, 13 Mar. 1837.   24 Ibid., minutes, 1 June 1837.   25 Ibid., joint report with general selected committee, 19 June 1837.   26 *RDS Proc.*, lxxix, botany committee report, 16 Nov. 1837.   27 Ibid., 30 Nov. 1837.   28 Ibid., 14 Dec. 1837.   29 Ibid., 29 Mar. 1838. 30 RDS Archive: Committee of Botany minute book, 1834–45, 15, 26 Mar. 1838.   31 *RDS Proc.*, lxxv, botany committee report, 1 Nov. 1838.

exchanges with other botanic gardens and with nurseries, pointing out that during the four-year period 1834–7 the society had received 3,625 plants in exchange for 1,810. Tweedie made some donations of seeds to the garden, but sought a carriage charge for bulkier items.[32] The council later reported that Tweedie had been paid £23 5s. for seeds and bulbs. The sale of a single plant raised by Niven in the garden had realized fifty guineas, half of which was paid in exchange plants, and the cash balance of £26 5s. lodged in the society's account.[33] On 5 July 1838 Niven presented to the society a copy of his completed guide, *The visitors companion to the botanic gardens, Glasnevin: a general outline of the principles of botanical science*. A comprehensive work, it was never improved upon or emulated.[34]

In late 1838 Niven resigned to set up his own nursery business.[35] He advised the botany committee on 4 August 1838 of his intention to leave in November.[36] His departure was well signaled and he left on amicable terms with the society, which, at his request ten years later, provided him with a fulsome reference.[37] Niven's replacement was David Moore, who took office on 8 November 1838.[38] In his final report, dated 10 November 1838, Niven congratulated the botany committee on its choice of a successor.[39] His request for a botanical reference library was met fortuitously during the following year, when a bequest of over 400 volumes of botanical works was received from the estate of John Robertson (a Co. Kilkenny member of the society), through the good offices of Dr William Harty.[40] David Moore presented his first annual report as curator, on 9 November 1839. The effects of the great storm of 6 January had set back developments in the garden for the remainder of the year, but not without some compensation.

> This awful storm, I am happy to inform you, has, in my opinion, in some respects improved the picturesque appearance of this beautiful Garden, as several of the large trees which fell, obstructed some of the finest views capable of being obtained, particularly on the north side; and as most of those trees were common kinds, their places can be supplied by rarer and better sorts. It is, however, to be regretted, that so many fell in the direction of Glasnevin, which exposed that village to view, as well as the Garden to the cold north-east winds.

Moore continued Niven's policies, and made trips to northeast Ireland, Scotland and England, arranging exchanges and acquisitions and adding 1,800 species to the Glasnevin collection.[41]

32 *RDS Proc.*, lxxiv, botany committee report, 25 Jan. 1838.   33 *RDS Proc.*, lxxvii, council minutes, 12 Dec. 1839.   34 Phyllis Clinch, 'Botany and the botanic gardens', in Meenan and Clarke, *The Royal Dublin Society, 1731–1981*, p. 193.   35 ibid.   36 *RDS Proc.*, lxxv, minutes, 1 Nov. 1838.   37 *RDS Proc.*, lxxxv, council minutes, 17 Aug. 1848.   38 *RDS Proc.*, lxxv, minutes, 8 Nov. 1838.   39 Ibid., 6 Dec. 1838.   40 *RDS Proc.*, lxxvi–lxxvii, council minutes, 26 Sept., 7 Nov. 1839.   41 *RDS Proc.*, lxxvi, appendix IV.

Like the botanic garden, the RDS library received a favourable report from the parliamentary select committee of 1836, which saw it as having the potential to be developed into a national library operated on similar lines to the library of the British Museum.[42] As early as December 1836 the library committee reported that work was in progress to up-date the catalogue, and distinguish works of reference from those available for lending out to members. The committee also requested a separate reading room for researchers.[43] More than 160 works were purchased in 1837–8, and a further thirty or so were received as donations.[44] In addition, 182 volumes, principally on divinity, were bequeathed to the society by the Reverend William Tew, Ballysax, Co. Kildare, life member of the RDS from 1813 until his death in 1837. That there were some apprehensions about the appropriateness of accepting such a bequest is evident from the remarks of the then chairman of the library committee, Brindley Hone. He noted that the library could not purchase works on divinity, they being outside the scope of the society's objects, but there was nothing to prevent them from accepting a gift of such works.[45]

By comparison with the library, the art school continued to be in a relatively neglected state, and also suffered disruption following the deaths of two of its four masters, Baker and Brocas. This was reflected in the annual intake of pupils, which fell from 122 in 1836 to ninety-nine in 1837, and forty-three in 1838; rising to 105 in 1839.[46] Henry Aaron Baker, master of the architecture school in succession to Thomas Ivory for almost fifty years, died on 4 June 1836.[47] Supervision of the architecture school was temporarily placed in the hands of John Duckett, a former pupil.[48] Duckett remained in temporary charge of the school for almost two years.[49] On 31 May 1838 he was replaced by John Papworth.

The death of Henry Brocas, master of the ornament and landscape school since 1800, was reported to the general meeting on 2 November 1837.[50] The fine arts committee was unhappy with the state of the school under Brocas' supervision, and was anxious to avoid any accusation of a nepotistic succession. However, Henry Brocas junior had substituted for his father on a temporary basis, with the committee's agreement, during the latter's last illness in the summer of 1837. The committee ignored the claims of the younger Brocas and recommended that Andrew Nicholl be appointed to the vacant post. The recommendation was over-ruled by the general meeting, and Henry Brocas junior was elected master of the ornament and landscape school on 31 May 1838. On this occasion the collective wisdom of the general meeting was sound, and the younger Brocas effected immediate improvements in the running of the school.

42 Desmond Clarke, 'The library', in Meenan and Clarke, *The Royal Dublin Society, 1731–1981*, p. 80.   43 *RDS Proc.*, lxxii, library committee report, 15 Dec. 1836.   44 *RDS Proc.*, lxxiv, appendix X, library acquisitions.   45 Ibid., library committee report, 26 Apr. 1838.   46 Willemson, *Students and award winners, 1746–1876*.   47 *Freeman's Journal*, 7 June 1836.   48 *RDS Proc.*, lxxiii, fine arts committee report, 10 Nov. 1836.   49 *RDS Proc.*, lxxiv, fine arts committee report, 1 Mar. 1838.   50 Ibid., 2 Nov. 1837.

Under Brocas junior's supervision the quarterly submission of students' specimen work was replaced by an annual exhibition in 1838, and the custom of holding exhibitions in November, when natural light was poor, was replaced by a late-Spring exhibition from 1839.[51] Despite an improvement in teaching methods the art school still suffered from poor controls and lack of discipline. The underpaid masters continued to supplement their incomes with outside work, to the detriment of their school duties. R.L. West was admonished for poor attendance in 1839, the committee complaining that it could not 'expect punctuality of attendance in the Pupils, when the Master of the Schools [sic] furnishes such an example to them'.[52] Brocas, although attentive to his duties, was a victim of unruly behaviour. Two of his students were cautioned by the committee, following his complaint that they had 'quarrelled, and in exchanging blows, injured a drawing of his by running one of their hands thro it'.[53]

Turning to the fortunes of the agricultural and industrial shows, even the hitherto-steady progression of these public exhibitions faltered at times during 1837-9, but not for any reasons that could be connected to the Archbishop Murray affair. The 1837 Spring Cattle Show[54] was almost cancelled because of a shortage of winter feed for finishing cattle.[55] Over the Christmas recess the agriculture committee corresponded with exhibitors and cattle traders, and, on the strength of the information obtained from these sources, reversed their position early in 1837.[56] As a result of the late start in preparing for the show, cattle numbers were down, although the animals exhibited were of superior quality.[57] The *Freeman's Journal* in its opening day report made the same observation, noting also a dearth of new agricultural implements on display.[58]

Since 1831 the Spring Cattle Show had become a widely recognized venue for trade in breeding stock. The problem of feeding animals through the winter months, and of bringing them forward in good condition for the April show, deeply exercised the society. It may have been for this reason that hay classes were introduced at the 1839 show.[59] A further reason may have been John Classon's letter of 22 March 1838 on preparing hay for market. Classon (a member of the RDS, 1809-60), was an iron and timber merchant, and a general merchant in Smithfield market. Based on his experience in the market he argued that better merchantable quality, and a better price, could be achieved by

51 Turpin, *A school of art in Dublin*, pp. 103-6, 114-15.   52 RDS Archive: Fine Arts committee rough book, 1833-9, 25 Sept. 1839.   53 Ibid., 5 June 1839.   54 The show did not have an official title in its early years and was referred to as the 'annual cattle show', or the 'Spring cattle show'. By 1849 its banner title was 'Spring Cattle Shew', by 1860 'Great Spring Show', and by 1870 'Spring Show'. For clarity and consistency, 'Spring Cattle Show' is probably the most appropriate title, at least from 1837, when autumn, and winter shows of cattle and farm produce were introduced. 55 Denis Purdon, 'History of the society's shows', in Meenan and Clarke, *The Royal Dublin Society, 1731-1981*, p. 103.   56 *RDS Proc.*, lxxiii, agriculture committee report, 26 Jan. 1837.   57 Ibid., 13 Apr. 1837.   58 *Freeman's Journal*, 22 Mar. 1837.   59 Denis Purdon, 'History of the society's shows', in Meenan and Clarke, *The Royal Dublin Society, 1731-1981*, pp. 103-4.

bringing hay to market in tied trusses, rather than in the traditional mixed loose loads.[60] At the 1838 show cattle entries were almost double those of the previous year, but the display of agricultural implements was disappointingly small, as already noted by the *Freeman's Journal* in 1837. In a sign of official interest Chief Secretary Morpeth visited the show.

Encouraged by the general improvement in cattle entries, the agriculture committee decided to run an additional autumn show and sale of cattle and agricultural implements in September.[61] This was not a success, as the quality of animals exhibited was indifferent, and the auction sale was not well supported although anecdotal evidence suggested that private sales were brisk.[62] The 1839 Spring Cattle Show was the occasion for the introduction of many innovations tending to increase the show's attraction and prestige. Age classes were introduced for pedigree bulls, and the coverage of cash prizes was extended. Perhaps most importantly, as a guarantee of the integrity of the judging process, the use of overseas judges for the main cattle classes was introduced.[63] Probably reflecting as much as anything else the slow pace of railroad development in the 1830s, a report on the counties from which cattle were sent to the Spring Cattle Show indicated that few exhibitors were attracted from outside Leinster. Eleven of the twelve Leinster counties (the exception being Kilkenny) were represented, but no non-Leinster counties except Galway.[64]

Rather more than the Spring Cattle Show, the annual industrial exhibition, commenced in 1834, suffered a temporary decline of support in the late 1830s due to economic recession. The organizing committee was revived early in 1836 'to make the necessary arrangements for the third annual exhibition of manufactures'.[65] Discouraged by the feed-back of information it received from local manufacturers, the committee, after long deliberation, formed the opinion that the exhibition should be held triennially, and that there was insufficient time to organise a show in 1837.[66] The society resolved to hold the third exhibition in 1838.[67] The committee selected May 1838 as a suitable date, and took the opportunity to declare,

> That the object of the society is to show what Ireland is capable of affording from her native production, and talent, in the hope that, encouragement may be set out to develope [sic] the treasures which she proffers from her natural and internal resources.[68]

After an absence of four years the exhibition was well received by exhibitors and public, and the committee decided to augment its income and control

---

60 *RDS Proc.*, lxxiv, minutes, 22 Mar. 1838.   61 Ibid., report on Spring Show 1838, 5 Apr. 1838. 62 *RDS Proc.*, lxxv, report on autumn livestock show, 1 Nov. 1838.   63 Ibid., agriculture committee report, 28 Mar. 1839.   64 Ibid., assistant secretary's report, 25 Apr. 1839.   65 *RDS Proc.*, lxxii, minutes, 21 Jan. 1836.   66 Ibid., manufactures committee report, 23 Feb. 1837.   67 Ibid., minutes, 6 July 1837.   68 RDS Archive: Manufactures Committee minute book, 1829–38, 1 Sept. 1837.

numbers by charging an admission price of sixpence.[69] Sixpence was the third class fare for daily commuters from Kingstown to Westland Row in 1837.[70] In June 1838, Sir Edward Stanley presented the manufactures committee report on the exhibition, which was little short of jubilant. The four-year gap between shows had proved sufficient to manifest a repressed demand, and significant improvements in the numbers and quality of the products available for display. The flood of applications for exhibition space had far exceeded the capacity of the areas allocated initially. It had proved necessary to add two large temporary buildings to accommodate the increase in numbers of exhibits.[71] The decision to abandon the free admission policy and charge sixpence to visitors had not adversely affected public attendance. The committee estimated that 20,000 members of the public had visited the show, and an additional 2,000 'artisans and workmen' who were admitted gratuitously. Meenan and Clarke recorded the public admissions as 1,000,[72] but this cannot be correct, as the committee paid a gratuity of £50 to Robert Kane, which they could easily have afforded from visitor receipts of £500 but not from receipts of £25.[73] That the committee had a surplus is certain, because in the following year they jealously protected it against a scheme of Edward Clibborn's to disburse it in extra prizes and medals.[74] Kane's voluntary participation in the exhibition had contributed greatly to its success.

> Doctor Kane promptly undertook, at short notice, to prepare a course of Lectures, quite independent of his two regular courses, but suitable to this occasion. On each day during the Exhibition, he delivered a Lecture in the Theatre, to a crowded auditory, on some one branch of Manufacture or Art, illustrated, on each occasion, by an actual exhibition of the process of Manufacture, conducted by some individual engaged in the business.[75]

A gold medal was awarded to Thomas Grubb for his 'transit instrument'.[76] Seven silver medals were awarded to manufacturers of textiles, machinery and decorative plasterwork.[77] A total of 132 medals were awarded to 115 Dublin-based exhibitors, and one each to exhibitors from counties Meath, Wicklow, Kildare, Down, Armagh, Antrim, and Waterford.[78]

Robert Kane's contribution to the success of the manufactures exhibition typified the man, the remarkable growth in self-confidence of the society's scientific committees and staff, and the growing popular interest in science

69 RDSArchive: Council minute book 1838–44, 3 May 1838.   70 Ryan, *Lewis' Dublin*, p. 200. 71 *RDS Proc.*, lxxiv, manufactures committee report, 14 June 1838.   72 Meenan and Clarke, *The Royal Dublin Society, 1731–1981*, p. 36.   73 *RDS Proc.*, lxxiv, manufactures committee report, 14 June 1838.   74 *RDSProc.*, lxxv, minutes, 28 Mar. 1839.   75 Ibid.   76 C. Mollan, W. Davis, B. Finucane (eds), *People and places in Irish science and technology* (Dublin, 1985), pp. 18–19. Hereafter, Mollan, Davis, Finucane, *People and places.*   77 *RDS Proc.*, lxxiv, manufactures committee report, 14 June 1838.   78 Ibid., appendix VI.

during this period. Prior to the 1830s the public lectures provided by the RDS on scientific matters had been confined to six-week spring and summer courses, supplemented from 1824 with evening lectures for artisans and mechanics. In 1833 Edmund Davy was given permission to deliver lectures to the mechanics' institutes in Clonmel and Limerick, but this successful experiment was not followed through at that time.[79] Encouraged by the public interest aroused by the BAAS conference in 1835, and the support given to the embryonic provincial (extra mural) lecture courses by the parliamentary committee of inquiry in 1836, the RDS renewed its attention to practical science education. Initially, the society was inhibited by lack of funds from developing a formal program for provincial lectures. For instance, a request from a body calling itself the Wicklow Association in 1837 to send a visiting lecturer was affirmed, but conditionally on the association meeting all the lecturer's fees and expenses.[80] After much foot-dragging the government agreed in 1838 to provide additional funds annually, up to a limit of £200, to meet the expenses of provincial lectures by the society's professors and lecturers.[81] Lecture courses by Robert Kane, and Edmund Davy, were given in Portarlington, Wicklow, and Galway. An application from Dundalk was received too late for the 1838 season.[82] At year-end the society had devised a program whereby up to twelve provincial centres could apply for RDS lecture courses every year, the costs to be met in part from local subscriptions, supplemented by the additional government funding.[83]

More rapid progress was made by the society in expanding its science lectures in Leinster House. Early in 1836 evening scientific meetings were introduced at which papers were read on a wide range of topics of current scientific interest. The first to be held was on 26 January 1836 at which Edmund Davy communicated his discovery of acetylene.[84] Davy's discovery, a by-product of his researches on potassium, was not developed until the French scientist Berthelot rediscovered the gas in 1857. However, the original discovery has subsequently and correctly been attributed to Davy.[85] Interest in the evening scientific meetings was considerable, and the society decided to continue the series, and ordered in November 1836

> That these Meetings be open to all individuals who have improvements or inventions in the arts or manufactures, models of machines to exhibit, or papers and communications to make on all subjects relating to the objects of the Society.[86]

---

79 Denis Crowley, 'Chemistry', in Meenan and Clarke, *The Royal Dublin Society, 1731–1981*, pp. 171–3. 80 *RDS Proc.*, lxxiv, minutes, 30 Nov. 1837. 81 Ibid., 31 May 1838. 82 *RDS Proc.*, lxxv, council report, 8 Nov. 1838. 83 Denis Crowley, 'Chemistry', in Meenan and Clarke, *The Royal Dublin Society, 1731–1981*, pp. 171–3. 84 Ibid., and *RDS Proc.*, lxxv, appendices III, V. 85 Eva M. Philbin, 'Chemistry', in O Raifeartaigh, *The Royal Irish Academy*, p. 281. 86 *RDS Proc.*, lxxiii, minutes, 10 Nov. 1836.

The objects of the society being of considerable latitude, they could accommodate such diverse topics as Isaac Weld's personal reminiscences on early steamship voyages, and Edward Clibborn's lecture on the American banking system. At the first meeting of the second series, in November 1836, Robert Kane demonstrated an electromagnet built by the Reverend Nicholas Callan of Maynooth, and based on Faraday's principles.[87] Kane's lectures on electricity, mechanics, and the industrial applications of physics, became so popular that the police were engaged to control the entrance gate at Leinster House. Information coming from the evening and provincial lectures suggested modifications were desirable to the standard lecture syllabi, and by 1836–7 Edmund Davy was adapting his lectures to deal with the interests of farmers and artisans, taking in subjects such as 'vegetable chemistry', and the chemical aspects of natural phenomena.[88] Pressure of accommodation in the lecture theatre in Leinster House, which had capacity to seat 500, became so great that a motion was made, and rejected, to reserve a 'competent space' for RDS members.[89] Another problem high lighted by the success of the science lectures was a lack of funds for demonstration equipment.[90] The council sub-committee on finance recommended that the RDS members be levied five shillings each towards the costs of evening lectures, and that income from the trees felled in Leinster Lawn by the great storm of 1839 be applied to the same purpose. In the event neither recommendation was adopted.[91] However, something had to be done by way of response to the increased demand for space. The council decided in February 1839 that the evening lectures held at 3 p.m. should be repeated at 8 p.m. for the benefit of those, especially the artisans, who could not attend at the earlier hour. In addition, seating accommodation was increased to 550 by extending seating through the side passage formerly used for access to ladies seating.[92] The contributions of lecturers from other institutions were welcomed and Robert Ball was given permission to conduct lectures on behalf of the zoological society, while Hugh Ferguson was given access to the contents of the museum, and facilities to run a lecture course on the veterinary care of horses.[93]

The demand for scientific lecturers fell most heavily on Davy, Kane, and Scouler, and sometimes produced tensions between them and the committees. The science officers were relatively poorly paid, especially Kane, whose talents were widely acknowledged, and whose salary, despite representations made to the government by the society, remained at £100 per annum.[94] As happened earlier with the art school masters the scientists took on outside work to supplement their incomes. Samuel Litton, the botany professor, presented the

87 Berry, *A history of the Royal Dublin Society*, p. 269.   88 Denis Crowley, 'Chemistry', in Meenan and Clarke, *The Royal Dublin Society, 1731–1981*, pp. 171–3.   89 *RDS Proc.*, lxxiv, minutes, 5, 26 Apr. 1838.   90 *RDS Proc.*, lxxv, natural philosophy committee report, 6 Dec. 1838.   91 RDS Archive: Council minute book 1838–44, 7 Feb. 1839.   92 Ibid., 21 Feb. 1839.   93 Ibid., 14 Nov., 12, 19 Dec. 1839.   94 *RDS Proc.*, lxxiii, report, 15 Dec. 1836.

society with a *fait accompli* in 1837. During the Easter recess he accepted the post of professor to the Apothecaries Hall, assuring the RDS that this post would not interfere with his duties as their botanical lecturer.[95] Edmund Davy annoyed the chemistry committee in 1838 when, without reference to them, he accepted the invitation of the national education board to give lectures in agricultural chemistry to school superintendents in Marlborough Street. Davy compounded his offence by subsequently seeking the committee's permission to borrow laboratory equipment for these lectures.[96] Fearing loss of the control of a key employee, a motion of censure was passed against Davy at the society's general meeting on 22 February 1838. Its terms were as follows,

> That it appears irregular, and contrary to the usage of this Society, that any Professor thereof should engage himself to give public lectures, without, in the first instance, obtaining permission from the Society, and that the Society consider such a proceeding highly to be censured.

Nevertheless, Davy was directed to give a course of lectures in the RDS theatre, on agricultural chemistry, 'for the benefit of the public, and especially of the Inspectors of the National Schools'.[97] A week later, Dr Robert Harrison moved to rescind the censure. Harrison's motion was opposed by Henry Carey but the commissioners of education agreed that Davy's lectures for school inspectors could be held in the RDS and, since this met the committee's original objection, the censure of Davy was lifted.[98]

The national education board had inherited the school inspection system of the Kildare Place Society, and had overseen growth in schools from 789 to 1,384 and in pupil numbers from 107,042 in 1833 to 169,548 in 1838.[99] The controversy over Davy's acceptance of the lecture engagement without reference to the society rumbled on for a few more weeks. Henry Carey's counter-motion, a thinly disguised reproof of Davy for failure to consult the society, was passed despite a vigorous attempt by Dr James Macartney to replace it with a rule requiring consultation in future cases only.[100] That similar situations were likely to arise was a reasonable assumption, given that John Scouler had recently requested and been given permission to give a course of lectures on geology to the Liverpool mechanics' institute.[101] Scouler was rewarded for observing the hierarchical niceties, the museum committee even agreeing to his borrowing specimens and drawings to illustrate his lectures.[102] No one, it seemed, thought to challenge the constitutionality of extending the lecture scheme outside of Ireland.

At the same time that the chemistry committee was asserting its authority over Davy, the natural philosophy committee was under attack for apparently

95 Ibid., minutes, 20 Apr. 1837.   96 *RDS Proc.*, lxxiv, minutes, 8, 15 Feb. 1838.   97 Ibid., 22 Feb. 1838.   98 Ibid., 1, 8 Mar. 1838.   99 Akenson, *The Irish education experiment*, pp. 140–7.   100 *RDS Proc.*, lxxiv, minutes, 15 Mar. 1838.   101 Ibid., 22 Feb. 1838.   102 Ibid., 1 Mar. 1838.

dictating the minutiae of Robert Kane's public lecture course. The committee's overly detailed draft syllabus for 1838 was not accepted by the general meeting and was returned to the committee for further consideration. After consultations with Kane the committee agreed that a course designed to stimulate popular interest in science was their real object, rather than a detailed academic study of the various branches of physics.[103] The brilliant and tactful Kane was held in great esteem by the society. He had gained a Europe-wide reputation for his research on the compounds of ammonia with metallic salts. In 1837 he had achieved a scientific break-through when he prepared mesitylene from acetone, the first example of the derivation of a ring-structured compound from a straight-chained compound.[104] Kane's salary of £100 per annum was clearly inadequate, and the RDS made repeated representations to the government to have it increased to £150 in parity with Davy and the other professor's. Probably in a move to eliminate treasury excuses, the society decided on 28 February 1839 to formally appoint Kane as their professor of natural philosophy, a post which he had effectively discharged for several years although his initial engagement in 1834 was as natural philosophy lecturer.[105]

The increased utilization of the premises for lectures and exhibitions, and particularly their night-time use, brought with it an increased risk of fire hazards from the lighting and heating systems of the time, and almost inevitably an accidental outbreak of fire did occur in Leinster House. While closing up the house after the evening lecture on 18 January 1838, Peter Wilson, the registrar, detected an outbreak of fire in a small second-storey room. He raised the alarm, and the outbreak was extinguished within an hour, having caused little damage. On subsequent examination it was discovered that the source of the fire was in the chimney of the hypocaust heating system at the southern end of the house (installed under the supervision of Dr Anthony Meyler in 1822). A claim for damages was lodged with the National Insurance Company, and estimates sought for the demolition of the hypocaust chimney, and the erection of a replacement to be detached from the main building.[106] The general selected committee (of which Meyler was a member), together with the economy, and house, committees decided that an unacceptable risk was posed by holding evening lectures 'with fires and lights through the house to a late hour'. Their joint recommendation urged that no evening lectures be held between October and May. Apparently no blame was imputed to design defects in, or lack of maintenance of the central heating system. Despite its powerful backing, the general meeting of members did not accept this one-sided reasoning, and agreed only to the postponement of the evening lectures for a few weeks in February 1838.[107]

103 Ibid.   104 Denis Crowley, 'Chemistry', in Meenan and Clarke, *The Royal Dublin Society, 1731–1981*, pp. 172–3.   105 *R.D.S Proc.*, lxxv, minutes, 28 Feb. 1839.   106 *RDS Proc.*, lxxiv, house committee report, 1 Feb. 1838.   107 Ibid., minutes, 25 Jan., 1 Feb. 1838.

Lack of funds for reinvestment in the society's buildings led to deterioration in these heavily used assets during the 1830s. When evening scientific meetings resumed, on 27 February 1838, Edward Colles (a member of the general selected committee at that time) read a paper on Dublin street architecture. Colles asserted the reasonableness of the society's case for public funds for the construction of new museum and exhibition buildings, and for general parity of treatment with the British Museum. He condemned 'the unsightly schools, and statue gallery, which now deform the Royal Dublin Society House', describing them as 'mere temporary erections, which the Society preferred making with limited means, rather than delay the education of, perhaps, many generations of pupils, by waiting for funds sufficient for suitable buildings'.[108] Maurice Craig describes the RDS building programs of the 1830s and 1840s as obscure, seeming to have been confined to internal alterations or the adaptation of existing buildings.[109] A good deal of attention was given by the house committee to making more efficient use of the existing rooms in Leinster House to make extra space available, particularly for the display of museum exhibits.[110] However, no amount of teeming and ladling could solve these problems, and on 30 May 1839 the council submitted a special report on accommodation to the general meeting of members. The council concluded that the demand for additional space came mostly from the activities of the agriculture, manufactures, and museum departments, and could only be met by 'the erection of additional buildings, or the alteration or extension of those existing'. The opinion of the council was that this demand could best be met by developing the long range of stable buildings in the cattle yard, to a plan designed by the master of the architecture school, John Papworth.

> That by raising the walls of this building, and lighting it from the roof, a suite of rooms will be obtained of 220 feet in length, applicable to such purposes as the Society may hereafter think proper, whether for Museum, for exhibitions of Manufactures, or for Statue Gallery and Schools; besides ample rooms underneath for Agricultural Implements and Produce, and for other purposes, and furnishing accommodation for some of the servants of the Establishment, necessary for the care of the Premises – large additional sheds for cattle are also contemplated in this plan.

The council estimated the cost of this proposed development at £1,800.[111] Nine builders' estimates were obtained, ranging between £1,900 and £2,860 (even the lowest being £100 above the initial council estimate), and the general meeting agreed to lift the target cost to £2,200 on the recommendation of the council. The revised estimate made allowance for further improvements recommended

108 Ibid., appendix V.   109 Maurice Craig, 'The society's buildings', in Meenan and Clarke, *The Royal Dublin Society, 1731–1981*, pp. 62–3.   110 RDS *Proc.*, lxxiii, house committee report, 18 May 1837.   111 RDS *Proc.*, lxxv, council report, 30 May 1839.

by the architects John Papworth and Frederick Darley.[112] Henry Carey moved to over-rule the council and order it to revert to the original plan and estimate.[113] This represented the first direct challenge to the council, and it is appropriate at this point to trace the development of that body, and other changes introduced in the administration of the society after 1836.

On 2 November 1837, Henry Kemmis, vice-president, presented to the general meeting a set of proposed by-law changes, based on the recommendations of the parliamentary committee of inquiry, and on the resolutions passed by the society on 10 November 1836. The most significant change proposed was to rescind the existing by-laws on the society's committee system and create a superordinate executive council.

> That the management of the business of the Society be confided to a Council, the powers of such Council to be strictly as hereafter defined and limited, and subject to the direct control over its proceedings, upon the part of the Society at large[114]

The council was to consist of the honorary officers (the seven vice-presidents and two honorary secretaries); the chairman and one other member of each of the nine standing committees, and nine other members elected directly by the general body of members. In theory at any rate the thirty-six-member executive council was subject to annual election or re-election. An elaborate system was devised for rotating a quarter of the council membership every year, the annual sacrifice falling effectively on the standing committees' representatives. The powers and duties of the council were outlined as follows.

> That the business of the Society be in future committed to the management of the Council, who shall exercise a general superintendence over the affairs, officers, and servants of the Society, and over every branch of its establishment; and shall have power to make such orders and regulations for the management thereof, as it shall deem necessary or expedient (the same not being contrary to the existing laws of the Society), with such restrictions as are herein-after mentioned; such orders and regulations to be subject to the control of the Society as herein-after more particularly stated.[115]

The council was to exercise supervision over the standing committees, with the right to see all committee minutes, investigate committee decisions, and refer items back for specific reports. However, the issuing of new orders or regulations affecting the running of activities under standing committee supervision would require the joint agreement of both the council and the standing committee

112 *RDS Proc.*, lxxvi, minutes, 14 Nov. 1839.   113 Ibid., 5 Dec. 1839.   114 *RDS Proc.*, lxxiv, report, 2 Nov. 1837.   115 Ibid.

concerned. In the event of a failure to agree, the matter in contention was to be referred to the general meeting of the society, whose decision would be binding on both parties. The subordinate position of the council in relation to the general meeting of the society was further emphasised in proposed rules asserting the ultimate governing authority of the general meeting, including the power to rescind decisions of the council. The council would also be required to make its minute book accessible to members of the society, and to submit a regular report of its current work to the general meeting. Delegation of authority to the council was to be limited to the regulation of its own weekly meetings, to supervise and report on the work of the standing committees, and in emergencies to authorise spending up to a limit of £50. The quorum for a council meeting was fixed at seven.[116] The new by-laws establishing an executive council were confirmed by the general meeting of the society on 1 March 1838. One noticeable and imme-diate effect was a substantial reduction in the number of general meetings held, from an average of almost thirty-three per annum (1800–37),[117] to twenty in 1838, and twelve (the minimum under the new by-laws) in 1839.[118] Appendix II synopsises the number of general meetings held, and the numbers of members attending, between January 1800 and December 1839. A first glance at sections (a) and (b) would appear to indicate that only a small proportion of the mem-bership, generally less than ten per cent, attended meetings. However, section (c) shows that at any rate during the 1830s (and this probably held true for earlier decades), quite a high proportion of the total membership, exceeding one half in 1834, attended at least one meeting in any given year.

In chapter two (pages 54–5) the standing committee structure was outlined, as it stood following the Kilmaine reforms of 1816. At this point it may be useful to the reader to have an up-date of the structure as it stood following the reforms introduced in 1838. Nine standing committees were constituted on 1 March 1838, *viz*. botany and horticulture, chemistry, natural philosophy and mechanics, fine arts, library, agriculture and husbandry, manufactures, statistics, and the catch-all and ponderously named 'natural history, geology, mineralogy, and charge of the museum committee' (see appendix IV).[119] In practice the last-named was usually referred to as the natural history and museum committee. The changes introduced to the committee system in 1838 were the most radical since the reforms of 1816.

In the years between 1816 and 1838, six additional standing committees were created, bringing the total to twelve. A house committee was established in 1817, to administer Leinster House and its staff, and to conduct day-to-day business during the board's summer recess. No member of the economy committee was permitted to serve on the house committee.[120] In 1830, following the collapse of

116 Ibid.   117 *RDS Proc.*, xxxvi–lxxiv. A total of 1,243 general meetings or board meetings were held between January 1800 and December 1837 (author's analysis).   118 RDS Proc., lxxiv, minutes, 1 Mar. 1838.   119 Ibid., special committee report, 2 Nov. 1837.   120 *RDS Proc.*, liv,

the Farming Society of Ireland in 1828–9, the RDS agreed to establish a standing committee of agriculture and planting, separate from the botany committee. It consisted of fifteen annually elected members (plus the honorary officers *ex-officio*).[121] In 1831 the agriculture committee was increased to twenty-one elected members. A ninth standing committee, styled natural history and museum, was established in 1832.[122] Its function was to supervise the museum collection, which had grown in size and educational importance since the end of the Napoleonic wars in 1815. In 1834 a tenth standing committee, the general selected committee, was added.[123] First appointed as a sub-committee of the general meeting in 1829, the function of the general selected committee was to review the policies and activities of the society in the light of declining government financial support. As re-organized in 1834 it consisted of the vice-presidents and honorary secretaries, and two members appointed from each of the other eight standing committees, following the annual elections. Although it had a brief existence (1834–8), the general selected committee set a pattern for managerial reform that the society would re-visit in the future. It was, in many respects, the precursor of the executive council.

Two new standing committees were added in 1837–8: the manufactures committee and the statistics committee. The manufactures committee's function was to organize exhibitions of Irish industry and manufactures, and it was derived from a sub-committee formed for that purpose in 1833. The statistics committee had the single function of promoting the rationalization of the collection and presentation of county statistics for use by the county grand juries.[124] The statistics committee was established at the end of 1836, mainly at the instigation of a Co. Tipperary engineer and statistician, Jefferys Kingsley.[125] Kingsley had earlier attempted to interest a number of county grand juries in adopting his methods of presenting grand jury accounts and statistics. He had been received with suspicion as a possible harbinger of increased central government interference in local government. Frustrated, Kingsley turned to the RDS, and the society appointed a sub-committee to evaluate his system. The sub-committee was favourably impressed by Kingsley's method, and recommended it to the grand juries, noting that their presentation of annual accounts was seriously lacking in uniformity, and in easy comparability, and in some instances gave very sparse information on important items of expenditure.[126] There is a commendable impartiality about the decision of the RDS, itself the object of government mistrust, and having many grand juror members, to promote a system that would have the certain effect of facilitating more centralized government. Mistrust and misunderstanding, between the government and the

minutes, 20 Nov. 1817.   **121** *RDS Proc.*, lxvi, minutes, 12 May 1830.   **122** *RDS Proc.*, lxix, minutes, 8 Nov. 1832.   **123** *RDS Proc.*, lxx, minutes, 5 June 1834.   **124** *RDS Proc.*, lxxiv, minutes, 29 Mar. 1838.   **125** *RDSProc.*, lxxii–lxxiii, minutes, 5, 7 May 1836, 17 Nov. 22 Dec. 1836, and appendix II.   **126** *Dublin University Magazine*, xiii (1839), pp. 60–8.

grand juror class, had reached a peak at this time. The latter found themselves ousted from local law enforcement in the late 1830s, their powers eroded, their conduct the object of close scrutiny, and their concerns for the safety of their lives and properties dismissed.[127] By the end of 1841 the statistics committee had ceased to have a useful role (see next chapter) and was dissolved. The new standing committees introduced in 1838 consisted of nine in all, reduced to eight in 1841-2 by the deletion of the statistics committee. The economy, house, and general selected, committees were dissolved in April 1838, and their functions transferred to the executive council.

Balloting for membership of the first council took place on 26 April 1838,[128] and the first meeting was convened on 3 May. Twenty-one of the twenty-seven elected members attended, as did the two honorary secretaries, and one vice-president, Henry Kemmis. As the first half-dozen members arrived, uncertain how to proceed with the first meeting of a new body, they decided to invite the seventh person to enter the room to act as chairman (seven being the number for a quorum). The honour of chairing the first meeting fell to Dr Isaac M. D'Olier, at that time chairman of the botany and horticulture committee.[129] At the end of the year the society resolved 'That the Meeting of the Council be open to the Members of the Society, but without power of speaking or voting'.[130] The council met on eighteen occasions during 1838, reporting to the general meeting in November that most of its time had been taken up in organising the provincial lecture program, and in advertising for a new curator for the botanic garden. It drew the society's attention to the over-crowded state of the museum and recommended that additional rooms be erected to accommodate museum displays.[131]

By the end of 1837 the museum committee had become convinced that only the acquisition of additional rooms, or a new building, could meet their continuing demand for increased space. On the same day that Thomas Wall resigned as museum porter, after twenty years service, the committee resolved

> That a report be made to the Society of the insufficient state of the Museum, even for its present contents, from the want of space, and of proper light, and to suggest to the Society the expediency of having additional buildings at the end of the Schools and Statue Gallery, recommending that this Committee be empowered to call for Plans and Estimates for the same.[132]

In the slightly refined form in which this resolution reached the society's general meeting three days later, the committee suggested that such a building could also be used as accommodation for the agriculture and manufactures exhibitions.[133]

127 Crossman, *Politics, law and order*, p. 76.   128 *RDS Proc.*, lxxiv, minutes, 26 Apr. 1838.
129 RDS Archive: Council minute book 1838-44, 3 May 1838.   130 *RDS Proc.*, lxxv, minutes, 8 Nov. 1838.   131 Ibid., council report.   132 RDS Archive: Committee of Natural History and Museum minute book 1831-54, 4 Dec. 1837.   133 *RDS Proc.*, lxxiv, natural history and museum

The museum collection continued to be augmented by significant donations. James Reilly, engineer on the steamboat *Crescent*, donated artefacts on behalf of the 1837 Euphrates river expedition.[134] Richard Griffith donated a copy of his completed geological map of Ireland.[135] At its own request, the committee was authorized to purchase the natural history collection of Dr Andrew Gogarty.[136] Gogarty was elected a member of the society on 6 December 1838. He went to Brazil in 1839, and sent many specimens of South American plants to the RDS botanic garden during 1839–42.[137] Henry Joy (1763–1838), senior judge of the exchequer court since 1831, and a vice-president of the RDS since 1822, died on 7 June 1838. A wealthy bachelor, he maintained a private museum at his residence, Woodtown House, Rathfarnham,[138] and bequeathed his geological collection to the RDS.[139] Because of the size of the donation, and the conditions attached to it by Joy's sister, the society decided to keep the collection distinct from the general collection, and denominate it as the 'Chief Baron Joy cabinet'.[140] However, the demand for display space had become ever more pressing, and the committee later concluded that a radical re-organization of the collections was required, amalgamating collections, where relevant, to produce a coherent display. The committee also pressed for the appointment of an assistant to the professor, as the requirements of the museum were 'too extensive' to be fulfilled by one officer.[141] The society allocated additional funds for this purpose, but deferred any decision on accommodation, pending further developments on Papworth's scheme to refurbish the stables. Meanwhile the society directed the natural history and museum committee to focus its efforts on the creation of a comprehensive Irish natural history collection. Watching the slow progress of Papworth's plans (see p. 195), and its concentration on the needs of agriculture and manufactures, the museum committee became sufficiently apprehensive as to make a particular representation to the council not to ignore the museum's needs. The pressure on the museum to enlarge the display space available to it was undeniable, and it was coming from the general public, some 33,738 of whom visited the museum during its limited opening periods (two days per week) in 1838.[142]

Returning to the subject of institutional reform, on 24 October 1839 Henry Carey[143] presented a review sub-committee report to the council on the progress made by the society in implementing the recommendations of the parliamentary committee of inquiry, and the follow-up inquiries pursued by the treasury. The development of a national museum remained a problem, as the society had no funds available for investment in the requisite new buildings. The treasury had

committee report, 7 Dec. 1837.   134 Ibid., minutes, 8 Mar. 1838.   135 Ibid., 14 June 1838. 136 *RDS Proc.*, lxxv, minutes, 8 Nov. 1838.   137 *RDS Proc.*, lxxv–lxxviii, var. dates, index. 138 Ball, *The judges in Ireland.*   139 *RDS Proc.*, lxxv, minutes, 6 Dec. 1838.   140 Ibid., 31 Jan. 1839.   141 Ibid., natural history and museum committee report, 28 Feb. 1839.   142 RDS Archive: Committee of Natural History and Museum minute book 1831–54, 12 Mar. 1839.   143 *RDS Proc.*,

been satisfied by the two resolutions adopted by the society on the state's interest in its assets. A scheme of annual membership and of associate membership had been introduced, the standing committees were re-organized, and an executive council placed in charge of the day-to-day management of the society. Arrangements for public access to the society's institutions had been improved, and an enlarged program for the diffusion of practical scientific knowledge through public lectures in Dublin and the provinces had been successfully undertaken. It had not been found expedient to discontinue the lending of library books (other than reference works) to the members, or to stop the taking of newspapers. However, Carey added that the newspapers were being paid for out of the society's private funds.[144]

The admission that the newspaper room continued to operate re-ignited Dublin Castle's hostility towards the society, and led to the temporary withdrawal of the annual grant which will form the main theme of the next chapter. The government, not without some grounds, apparently took the view that the press was a prime fomenter of partisan agitation in the community. Newspapers of the time were certainly prone to embrace political and social issues, with an exuberance that frequently took them beyond the bounds of balanced comment. Brian Inglis concluded that the liberals, champions of a free press while out of office, very quickly adopted conservative attitudes towards the newspapers once in power. Irish newspapers, expecting continued liberal support for press freedom of comment, and a circulation enhancing reduction in newspaper tax, were disappointed. Prosecutions of newspapers actually increased during 1830–3, and the practice of giving government subsidies to compliant newspapers was revived. While the subsidies were for the most part removed by the late 1830s, government antipathy towards the press was, if anything, strengthened.[145]

The Whig-liberal government had made a sincere attempt to introduce reforms in Ireland, with mixed and in some cases disappointing results which the press, of all shades of political opinion, was not slow in pointing out. The best results were in Drummond's reforms of the justice system, particularly the passage of the Irish constabulary act of 1836, and the Dublin police act of 1838. Drummond insisted on the recruitment of catholics to the new police forces, and under his direction Maziere Brady developed rules for the empanelling of juries which put an end to the discriminatory practice of challenging the appointment of liberals or catholics.[146] Drummond's legal reforms also caused much anguish and misgivings to supporters of the *ancien regime* when in 1838 over a third of the old justices of the peace were dismissed, mostly clergymen of the established church, minor gentry, and land agents. Drummond's appointment of an Irish railway commission in 1836, chaired by Richard Griffith, and

lxxv, minutes, 27 June 1839.   **144** Henry Carey, barrister, and filazor of the exchequer court, was a member of the RDS, 1834–72. (Source: *RDS Proc.*, var. dates.)   **145** Inglis, *Freedom of the press*, pp. 197, 203, 226.   **146** M'Lennan, *Memoir of Thomas Drummond*, pp. 267–83.

its subsequent reports in 1837–8, was hailed as an example of progressive planning, but failed to translate into effective legislation as the government's majority became eroded. A more successful example of the collectivist and centralized approach of the liberals to the provision of Irish services was the steady expansion of local dispensaries for medical services to the poor.[147] The tithe act of 1838, while unexceptional in its terms, did put a temporary end to anti-church agitation. However, the Irish poor law act of the same year was an unwieldy graft of English legislation onto dissimilar Irish conditions.[148] The act was opposed in Ireland, not on party lines, but by those sensitive to local conditions who resented the importation of an English-based scheme which took little account of the opinions and recommendations of the Irish poor law commissioners. Under the Whig-liberals, the 1830s in Ireland were notable for the integration of catholics into politics and civil administration. In a sense it marked the growth of democratisation and reform, but it also marked the growth of confessionalism.[149]

O'Connell's shelving of repeal in 1834 arrested that movement and led to a slow decline of repeal MPs and an increase in conservative representation in 1835 which remained largely unchanged after the 1837 elections.[150] Out of the 105 Irish MPs elected in 1837, twenty-nine were catholics, forty-four were protestant liberals or nationalists, and thirty-two were protestant conservatives or unionists.[151] In England, the radical wing of liberalism lost heavily in 1837,[152] and Melbourne's government was returned to office with a slender majority in the house of commons. Melbourne was dependent on O'Connell's support in the commons for continuing his administration.[153] Concluding that the Whig-liberal government was no longer secure, O'Connell revived the repeal movement in 1838, thereby unsettling Irish protestants. His concept of repeal did not entail disloyalty to the monarchy, but was imbued with seventeenth century confederate and jacobite thinking, and based on Irish catholic majoritarianism.[154] As the position of Melbourne's government weakened in late–1838, O'Connell once again deleted repeal from his program. In May 1839 the government's majority fell to five on the issue of the Jamaican constitution, and Melbourne resigned. Peel tried to form a Tory-conservative government but withdrew when his attempt to have Queen Victoria's ladies-in-waiting replaced provoked a minor constitutional crisis.[155] Melbourne continued to lead a weakened Whig-liberal administration until mid-1841.

RDS members with seats in parliament increased in number during 1836–9, but most of the newer intake were supporters of the government and unlikely to champion the society against Morpeth and Drummond. In 1835, nine peers and

147 MacDonagh, *Early Victorian government*, pp. 183–6.   148 Ó Tuathaigh, *Thomas Drummond*, pp. 4–5.   149 Boyce, *Nineteenth-century Ireland*, pp. 58–9, 71–2.   150 McDowell, *Public opinion*, p. 135.   151 Hoppen, *Elections, politics and society*, table 2, p. 264.   152 Webb, *Modern England*, p. 250.   153 MacDonagh, *The emancipist*, pp. 160–1.   154 Boyce, *Nineteenth-century Ireland*, pp. 74–5.   155 MacDonagh, *The emancipist*, pp. 176–82.

seventeen MPs were members of the RDS. Two of the peers were liberals, the remainder being conservatives. By the end of 1839 the numbers of RDS peers had increased to thirteen, but conservative peers had fallen to six and liberals had increased to seven. While much of this change was attributable to natural causes, government intervention in 1837–8 ensured the promotion of the liberal aristocrats Charlemont, Carew, and Talbot de Malahide, to United Kingdom peerages, and so to hereditary seats in the house of lords. The cut and thrust of local politics itself explains the changes in the number of Whig-liberal MPs who were also members of the RDS. The seventeen members who were MPs in 1835 comprised seven Tory-conservatives, eight Whig-liberals, and two Repealers. O'Connell's dropping of the repeal agitation resulted in the merging of the last two categories by 1837. After the August 1837 elections twenty MPs were members of the RDS, of whom thirteen were Whig-liberals. Pierce Mahony, elected MP for Kinsale, was unseated on petition. Sir Michael O'Loghlen, and Stephen Woulfe, both of whom held liberal seats from earlier elections, resigned on appointment to senior judicial offices in 1837–8. The liberal Thomas Wallace lost his Co. Carlow seat in 1837, and the conservative Henry Maxwell resigned his on succeeding to the title of 4th earl of Farnham in 1839. By the end of 1839 there were sixteen RDS members with seats in the house of commons; six Tory-conservatives and ten Whig-liberals.[156]

Robert Hutton, a witness at the parliamentary committee of inquiry in 1836, was Daniel O'Connell's running mate in the 1837 election and took a Dublin city seat for the liberals. Hutton was trenchantly critical of the pace of reform at the RDS, and, as will be seen in the next chapter, expressed the view in parliament that the society was blatantly challenging the recommendations of the parliamentary committee, by its retention of the newspaper room.

By the end of 1839, four years had elapsed since the rejection of Archbishop Murray. The 1836 parliamentary committee of inquiry offered no conclusions as to why the incident had occurred. However, the internal evidence strongly suggested that the primary motivation had been political, and that the structures of the society's administration had been manipulated for political ends. In the aftermath of the inquiry the society had moved positively and fairly rapidly to address its internal problems, and to implement the inquiry's recommendations. There were limitations under the society's constitution to the degree of change that could be effected in its government, and the creation of an executive council was probably the best compromise that could be achieved. The society suffered very little directly adverse effects by way of public reaction to the Murray affair, and its activities drew increasing public support during the period 1837–9. Perhaps this was because its activities had become increasingly popularized by the new professionals heading its departments, and by the spectacle provided by its shows.

156 Author's analysis, and Walker, *Parliamentary election results.*

CHAPTER SEVEN

The newspaper crisis, 1840–2: origins and effects

This entire study has been in some sense an account of repeated crises in the relationship between the Royal Dublin Society and the government. The present chapter considers a further breakdown in that relationship, in the dying days of the Whig-liberal government of 1835–41. The breakdown, though of short duration, was of a total nature, and much more dangerous for the society than earlier crises. Precipitated by the society's failure to close the newspaper room in Leinster House, its primary result was the temporary withdrawal of the government grant; but a secondary result was the emergence of the society as an incidental symbol of nationalist aspirations. The withdrawal of the grant was the end of a process commenced by a second government inquiry into the society's structures. That inquiry might, had its underlying assumptions been fully implemented, have resulted in the dismemberment of the society. This second attack by Dublin Castle had a detrimental effect on the society's activities and building programs, much of which came to a temporary halt, and on the recruitment of new members. Political divisions within the RDS membership were expressed in the public statements of Robert Hutton, a Whig-liberal MP, and Dr Anthony Meyler, by that time a spokesman for protestant conservatism, and were an embarrassment to the society and beyond its control. A further external threat, but one which the society managed to cope with graciously, was the formation of a revived agricultural development movement, the Agricultural Improvement Society of Ireland, which will also be considered below.

In mid-1841 Melbourne's administration collapsed, the grant was restored, and Peel's paternalistic Tory-conservative administration (1841–6) gave the RDS a brief respite from overt government interference in its internal affairs. The newspaper crisis, which had been smoldering since the closure of the newspaper room was first mooted in 1836 (see page 128), and the appointment of a vice-regal commission of inquiry into the society, proved a further chastening experience for the RDS. The wisdom gained from this bruising encounter was reflected in a new maturity and detachment in the society's relations with government. The political context within which these events occurred was the temporary eclipse of Whig-liberalism, the revitalisation of Tory-conservatism, and the revival of the repeal movement in Ireland. I propose, therefore, to commence this chapter with a brief review of political developments in 1840–1.

Thomas Drummond, under secretary, died in Dublin on 15 April 1840. He was interred in Mount Jerome cemetery on 21 April.[1] On the same date Daniel O'Connell announced the formation of the National (Repeal) Association of Ireland, later the Loyal National Repeal Association of Ireland.[2] O'Connell's participation in imperial politics had helped to raise the political consciousness of the mass of the Irish people. His new repeal movement stressed loyalty to the crown, non-sectarianism, and constitutional methods.[3] Nevertheless he quickly reverted to the vague aspirations and ambiguous posturing of his earlier campaign, calling for unity amongst all Irishmen, but positing an identity between Irishness and catholicism. His close relationship with the Roman Catholic church strengthened the apparent confessionalism of the repeal movement.[4] Oliver MacDonagh has argued that by early 1840 O'Connell was attempting to create a popular movement which would have, in particular, the support of Archbishop MacHale of Tuam, and therefore he gave priority to an attack on the privileges of the established church.[5] In his correspondence with MacHale, O'Connell speculated that a restored Irish parliament would not only abolish tithes, but 'The law would of course sanction in the fullest measure the spiritual authority of the episcopal order over religious discipline amongst Catholics including Catholic education'.[6] MacHale publicly supported repeal, at a banquet held in Tuam on 13 August 1840.[7]

Initially, O'Connell failed to enthuse the public on the repeal issue, and his early efforts met with a response that could almost be described as public apathy.[8] While O'Connell remained the leader of popular and catholic opinion, a distinctive Irish conservatism, with considerable protestant support across the spectrum of social classes, was emerging to oppose him.[9] Even before the formal re-launch of repeal, conservatives were hitting back. In March 1839 Frederick Shaw, MP for Dublin University, complained to the house of commons that in Ireland 'the functions of justice [were] usurped by self-constituted and irresponsible associations'. He believed the government was complicit in this state of affairs by its courtship of O'Connell, and its failure to support law and order.[10] A year later, presenting a petition to the house of lords against the municipal corporations (Ireland) bill, on behalf of 7,000 Dublin electors, the marquess of Westmeath rhetorically asked,

> Had the noble Viscount [Melbourne] informed his Protestant Sovereign, that before she came to the throne a compact was entered into at Lichfield-house by which the Protestant church was to be despoiled of its

1 M'Lennan, *Memoir of Thomas Drummond*, pp. 425–9.   2 O'Connell, *Correspondence*, vi, 2704.
3 Macartney, *The dawning of democracy*, pp. 149–51; see also Nowlan, *The politics of repeal*.
4 Hoppen, *Ireland since 1800*, pp. 30–2.   5 MacDonagh, *The emancipist*, p. 185.   6 O'Connell, *Correspondence*, vi, 2730, O'Connell to MacHale, 16 July 1840.   7 Hilary Andrews, *The lion of the west: a biography of John MacHale* (Dublin, 2001), p. 87. Hereafter, Andrews, *The lion of the west*.
8 MacDonagh, *The emancipist*, p. 188.   9 Hoppen, *Ireland since 1800*, p. 26.

property, and that every effort should be made until that spoliation was accomplished?[11]

Amongst the peerage, English as well as Irish, opposition to municipal reform was based on fears of its eventual wider application to British county administrations, with consequent loss of personal power and prestige.[12] Isaac Butt was chosen to argue to the house of lords the case for maintaining the old privileges and restricted franchise of Dublin Corporation, which effectively excluded catholics. He did so with a combination of legal brilliance, protestant bias, and Irish patriotism. His core doctrine was a belief in an imperial partnership of the two islands with a joint mission to advance civilization, and a conservative patriotism that challenged the insular orthodoxies of O'Connell.[13] Butt was representative of a newly emerging and articulate protestant conservatism and unionism which increasingly attracted many former protestant supporters of O'Connell. Overshadowed and frequently ignored by O'Connell and his multiple associations and movements after 1832, many Dublin protestant whigs were unnerved by his attacks on the established church, Dublin Corporation, and the act of union. Gradually their views polarised, and numerous former whigs slowly drifted towards the conservative camp, the most notable defector being Arthur Guinness II in 1835. On the issue of municipal reform the conservatives were divided. A pragmatic wing, led by Frederick Shaw in the house of commons, was willing to compromise. Butt continued to voice the opinions of the intransigents. J.D. Jackson attempted to bridge their differences by proposing a power-sharing distribution of seats in Dublin Corporation, but his proposals were not acceptable to any party. The municipal reform act, which became law on 10 August 1840, abolished most of the fifty-eight Irish corporations, and introduced a property-based franchise for the remaining ten.[14] Once again protestant conservatives felt they had lost out to a conspiracy against their interests engineered by O'Connell and the Whig-liberal government.

O'Connell had an influential working relationship with the Whig-liberal administration, and their concerns frequently converged. However, that this amounted to a conspiracy is doubtful. O'Connell attempted to influence government appointments, but was often disappointed by the decisions made, which, from a government point of view, had to take into account the *real politik* of the availability and qualification of candidates.[15] On the issue of repeal, the government could offer no support to O'Connell, and even took the step of announcing on 30 September 1840 that supporters of repeal would not be

10 Crossman, *Politics, law and order*, p. 75.   11 *Hansard, parliamentary debates*, 3rd series, liii, 3, 7 Apr. 1840.   12 Webb, *Modern England*, p. 227.   13 David Thornley, *Isaac Butt and home rule* (London, 1964), pp. 15–17. Hereafter, Thornley, *Isaac Butt*.   14 Hill, *From patriots to unionists*, pp. 371–8.   15 Ó Tuathaigh, *Thomas Drummond*, pp. 7–11.

considered for government patronage.[16] O'Connell acknowledged that he was the principal target of this directive.[17]

The Whig-liberal government, in decline since 1839, finally left office on 6 June 1841 following the loss of a motion of no confidence.[18] In Ireland, Drummond had died, and been replaced as under secretary by Norman H. MacDonald. Lord Mulgrave had left office as lord lieutenant in 1839, and had been replaced by Hugh Fortescue, Viscount Ebrington. By late-1840 only Lord Morpeth, the chief secretary, remained of the 1835 team which had formed the Dublin Castle administration. Morpeth shared with Russell, Althorp, and others, a quasi-religious belief in the power of legislation to bring about improvements in human behaviour.[19] The attitude of the Whig-liberal government towards the RDS remained unchanged. De Vere White concluded that from a government viewpoint the existence of the RDS as a long-established educational institution meant that it could not be overlooked as a potential platform for the extension of higher education in Ireland. Assuming that to be the case, a question arose as to the suitability of the society to handle an enlarged remit. In this context, the continued existence of a newspaper room, with its club-like connotations, seemed at variance with what was expected of a public institution.[20]

The RDS became aware, through newspaper reports in June 1840, that one of its members, Robert Hutton, MP, had made statements to a sub-committee of the house of commons that placed the society in a bad light. Hutton had implied, or so it seemed, that its accounts were improperly kept, that part of its annual grant was used for political purposes, and that its professors were implicated in the misappropriation of funds.[21] Robert Hutton had been elected a life member of the society in 1811.[22] He gave evidence to the parliamentary committee of inquiry on the Royal Dublin Society in 1836, in the course of which he gave his opinion that the RDS suffered from 'political bias' and required constitutional change (see above, pages 135–7). A presbyterian and a liberal, but not a repealer, he nevertheless acted as Daniel O'Connell's running-mate in Dublin in 1837, taking a parliamentary seat which he held until the fall of the Whig-liberal government in 1841. Hutton's brother, Thomas, was also a prominent member of the RDS at that time, having been involved in the arrangements for the 1835 BAAS conference, and later becoming a member of the manufactures committee (1842–4). Thomas Hutton's politics were also liberal, and he supported the federalist formula for Irish independence

16 MacDonagh, The emancipist, p. 189.   17 O'Connell, Correspondence, vi, 2761, O'Connell to Lynch, 5 Nov. 1840.   18 MacDonagh, The emancipist, p. 194.   19 Jonathan Parry, The rise and fall of Liberal government in Victorian Britain (New Haven, 1993), p. 113.   20 White, The story of the Royal Dublin Society, pp. 107–11.   21 RDS Proc., lxxvi, report, 2 July 1840.   22 Robert Hutton served on the chemistry committee, 1812–30, and on the natural philosophy committee, 1816–20. He was not re-elected to the chemistry committee in 1831, having failed to attend any meetings in the previous year. (Source: RDS Proc., var. dates.)

advocated by William Sharman Crawford.[23] His daughter was the 'beloved Annie' Hutton of Thomas Davis' romantic attachment.[24]

The RDS decided on 2 July 1840, at a general meeting at which Thomas Hutton was present, to write to Robert Hutton, asking him to retract his recent allegations against the society and its professors.[25] The latter replied by letter of 6 July.

> I am this day honoured with your letter of 3rd July, containing a statement of certain remarks which I did not make in the House of Commons, and enclosing certain resolutions, which having been adopted under the supposition that what I did say was accurately reported, I need not further allude to. I did say, when the House was in Committee on the Irish Estimates, that I had two objections to make to the Royal Dublin Society; one was, that the Society continued to appropriate one of its rooms, and a portion of its funds, to political newspapers and such publications, in opposition to a distinct recommendation of a Committee of the House of Commons, which sat in 1836, and which was most anxious to disconnect the Society from all political objects. My other objection was, that the Estimate of the Royal Dublin Society was not drawn in the same manner as the Estimates of other bodies obtaining Parliamentary assistance. I instanced the Hibernian Academy, Royal Irish Academy, &c., &c. I said that if the Estimate had been so drawn as to exhibit the entire receipts and entire expenditure of the Society, it must have shewn the payment for newspapers, but that owing to the delusive manner in which it was drawn, the expenditure of which I complained was kept out of view.
>
> I said that the newspapers were nominally paid out of private funds, but (inasmuch as Parliament was called upon to contribute the difference between what the funds of the Society produced, and what is necessary to accomplish its objects) I considered that it was about to make an appropriation of money to purchase political newspapers for the Royal Dublin Society, in opposition to the recommendation of its own Committee, and to the practice of Scientific Societies in England. I did not say one word about the Professors, or allude to them in any way: and the above is, I believe, an exact report of what I did say. If you can shew that I have stated any thing as fact which is inconsistent with it, I shall of course be ready to withdraw it.[26]

Hutton's letter was read to an extraordinary meeting of the RDS, held on 30 July 1840. The meeting resolved that 'as he disavowed using the observations

23 Richard Davis, *The Young Ireland movement* (Dublin, 1987), p. 63. Hereafter, Davis, *The Young Ireland movement*.   24 John Neylon Molony, *A soul came into Ireland: Thomas Davis, 1814–1845, a biography* (Dublin, 1995), p. 228. Hereafter, Molony, *A soul came into Ireland*.   25 *RDS Proc.*, lxxvi, minutes, 2 July 1840.   26 Ibid., 23, 30 July 1840.

complained of, the Royal Dublin Society do not require any further explanation'. This apparently referred to a mistaken belief that he had accused the RDS professors of misuse of funds. As regards 'Mr. Hutton's remarks respecting the Newspapers, the Royal Dublin Society did not conceive they required any observation'.[27]

Hutton's condemnation of the society's taking of newspapers, however petty it might have appeared, was consistent with his views as expressed to the parliamentary committee of inquiry in 1836. He did not specify which newspapers were 'political', and therefore it must be assumed that he regarded all newspapers as falling into this category. His position was also consistent with the recommendations of the O'Brien committee in 1836, which, in this instance, the society had decided to ignore. Added to this the society's defence of the newspaper room, coupled with intemperate attacks on Lord Mulgrave made by Dr Anthony Meyler, and it is conceivable that the government may have construed the continued purchase of newspapers as a deliberate act of defiance by the Royal Dublin Society. Meyler, whose role was noted above (see page 128), was elected a member of the society in 1810, and from 1811 until 1844 served on several of the standing committees. During 1838–44 he was a member of the chemistry committee, the natural history and museum committee, and the executive council. He was, in effect, one of the most prominent, influential, and active members of the society during the period analysed by this and the preceding chapter. Meyler, as mentioned above, was born and educated as a Roman Catholic, the son of a Co. Wexford sympathizer with the United Irish movement. Following the 1798 rebellion he accompanied his father into exile in America.

According to his own account, Meyler had continued for many years to adhere to catholicism out of a sense of family loyalty. He regarded himself as a liberal and tolerant man but felt increasingly repelled by the tenets of catholicism, which he came to regard as superstitious, and by its association with the populist politics of Daniel O'Connell. By 1838 he had broken completely with catholicism and with Whig-liberal politics, and adopted a protestant conservative stance. Nevertheless in 1836 he had referred publicly to Archbishop Daniel Murray as a 'reverend and respectable gentleman' whose rejection by the RDS was 'unfortunate'. His opinion of Lord Mulgrave, the lord lieutenant, was far less restrained in expression (see page 128). By 1838 he had abandoned all semblance of civility towards either party and attacked Mulgrave as a cat's-paw for O'Connell, and Murray as a co-conspirator in a grand design to take over the privileges of the established church and overthrow the union. He also appeared to identify the hard-pressed RDS with the fortunes of conservative protestantism.

27 Ibid.

Nothing can shew in a stranger point of view the degrading subserviency to which Lord Mulgrave was obliged to submit, than his rude and arrogant communications to the Royal Dublin Society, ... because that in the exercise of the privileges entrusted to it by the charter, it did not choose to enroll among its members, a Romish priest, who had identified his church with the radical party in Ireland, and in his 'apostolic' character, sanctioned the system of agitation pursued by Mr. O'Connell, and even subscribed money to reward him for disturbing the country, and who also exhibited the grossest and most disgusting shuffling, respecting an infamous work of theology, in which the Maynooth priests are educated.[28]

Meyler had a brother who was a Roman Catholic priest (probably the Reverend Walter Meyler, parish priest of Westland Row, dean of the Dublin chapter, and a strong supporter of Archbishop Murray).[29] In a speech delivered to the Metropolitan Conservative Society of Ireland on 8 April 1839, Anthony Meyler claimed to esteem and respect the catholic clergy of his acquaintance. However, he doubted that their professed beliefs were sincerely held, and described them 'as the priesthood of an intolerant and apostate Church, who vow allegiance to a foreign despot'.[30] In a speech delivered to the same body on 20 July 1840 he continued to attack the former lord lieutenant, Lord Mulgrave.

He [Mulgrave] rudely and officiously obtruded himself on an institution of the highest station in the country, and over which he had no juris-diction, and in no measured tone presumed to censure the noblemen and gentlemen of the Royal Dublin Society, because in the exercise of their corporate privileges they rejected an obnoxious priest.[31]

Specifically, in his published correspondence in 1836, Meyler had defended the independence of the Royal Dublin Society, and condemned government inter-ference in its internal affairs. In his later publications (1838–40) he conflated the position of the RDS and that of conservative Irish protestantism under a Whig-liberal government seen by him as hostile to both. On an emotional level his arguments probably touched a chord with some RDS members. As a corporate body, however, the society did not involve itself in a public debate that would certainly have had divisive results amongst the general body of members.

28 RIA: Haliday collection, H.P. 1726/4, Anthony Meyler, MD, MRIA, *Irish tranquillity under Mr. O'Connell, my lord Mulgrave, and the Romish priesthood* (Dublin, 1838).   29 Kerr, *A nation of beggars*, p. 284.   30 RIA: Haliday collection, H.P. 7, 1752/3, *Speech delivered by Doctor Meyler, at the great meeting of the Irish Metropolitan Conservative Society, assembled in Dawson Street, April 8th, 1839, on a petition to the House of Commons, praying that the annual grant hitherto voted to the Roman Catholic College at Maynooth be discontinued* (Dublin, 1839).   31 RIA: Haliday collection, H.P. 1783/5, *The address of the Metropolitan Conservative Society of Ireland to the Protestants of Great Britain, along with the speech delivered by Doctor Meyler, on submitting it for their adoption.* (Dublin,

Whether prompted by Hutton, irritated by Meyler, or simply pursuing a broader design for reform of Irish educational institutions, Dublin Castle again turned its attentions to the affairs of the Royal Dublin Society, in late-1840. The RDS council received, with 'regret and surprise', a letter from Chief Secretary Morpeth on 17 December 1840.[32] The tone and content of the letter amounted to a severe censure of the society for failing to introduce all the reforms recommended by the government.

> I am directed by the Lord Lieutenant [Viscount Ebrington] to acquaint you, that the earnest attention of the Irish Government has been repeatedly called, both in and out of Parliament, to the imperfect fulfilment which has hitherto been given to several of the more important recommendations respecting the future constitution and management of the Dublin Society, made by the Parliamentary Committee of the year 1829 and 1836. His Excellency has had more particularly in view the two very decided recommendations of the former Committee, 'that the purchase of books and periodicals should be strictly limited to those species of publications which are suited to an establishment, scientific and literary'; and 'that in addition to the sum now fixed, or which may hereafter be fixed, for admission, an annual subscription may be settled, to such an amount as may be considered expedient'.[33]

Morpeth regretted to find that the society continued to operate a newspaper room, and that annual membership had not been re-introduced. On the latter point he was mistaken (and subsequently apologized).[34]

> His Excellency also regrets to observe the prevalence of a very general feeling, that the Society does not tend to the attainment of its professed objects, in a degree commensurate with its large annual grant, and that its constitution is not of a nature to insure the vigorous co-operation of the principal men of science in Ireland.[35]

Consequently, the lord lieutenant had been in communication with a number of prominent Irish scientists, and had formed the conviction that a more efficient organisation of the society's resources could be achieved.

> Under this impression – with the assurance that Parliament will not be disposed to renew the grant without the adoption of material alterations in the frame and procedure of the Society – and with a sincere desire both

1840). 32 RDS Archive: Council minute book 1838–44, 7 Jan. 1841. 33 RDS Proc., lxxvii, minutes of extraordinary general meeting, 14 Jan. 1841. 34 Ibid., minutes, 28 Jan. 1841. 35 Ibid., 14 Jan. 1841.

to obviate the causes of the feeling alluded to above, and to limit, as much as possible, the risk of future collision between the Executive and the Society, His Excellency feels himself called upon to recommend the adoption of the Propositions of which a copy is enclosed, before he allows the Estimate for the usual Grant to be submitted to Parliament.[36]

However delicately put, Dublin Castle had presented the society with a new set of rules to be observed (see Appendix XI) under threat of withdrawal of the annual grant. Morpeth reasoned that splitting the society into two autonomous sections under a joint council would allow members to be selective and focused in their commitment to the society's work, and thereby achieve a more efficient use of the society's resources. One section would be devoted to science in all its aspects, the second to agriculture and all other activities, including the art school. He intimated that the government would support appropriate modifications to the charter to give effect to the re-organisation of the society. The ninth proposition stated baldly, 'No News-room or Newspaper to be permitted in the House of the Society'.[37]

The RDS honorary secretaries, Isaac Weld and R.B. Bryan, replied to Lord Morpeth on 23 December 1840, on behalf of the council. They pointed out that the terms of the charter required that alterations of such a fundamental nature would have to be put to two successive stated general meetings of the society, and that this could not be completed under the rules earlier than June 1841. They also pointed out 'That engagements have been contracted, liabilities incurred, and expectations held out to the public, for the next year, upon the faith of the usual Parliamentary grant'. Not unreasonably, they asked that the society be given an adequate period of time to consider the propositions before such a drastic step as the withdrawal of the parliamentary grant was invoked. Lord Morpeth replied on 5 January 1841 that there was nothing to prevent the society from reaching a preliminary decision earlier than June. He undertook, but only if the preliminary decision should prove favourable to the propositions, to include the first moiety of the RDS grant in the government's annual estimates.

But His Excellency cannot allow any part of the usual Grant to be included in the Estimates in favour of the Dublin Society, until he sees a reasonable prospect of the adoption of those Propositions – which he deems essential to the due efficiency of that Institution – as soon as the provisions of the Charter will permit.[38]

The council presented a background statement to an extraordinary general meeting of the society on 14 January 1841. The statement regretted that 'the

36 Ibid.   37 Ibid.   38 Ibid.

public investigation by a Select Committee of the House of Commons, in the year 1836', 'and the subsequent cordial adoption by the Society of practical measures founded on the recommendations of that Committee (with the exception hereafter referred to); should all now appear insufficient to have obtained for your labours, the confidence of her Majesty's Government in Ireland'. The society believed it had just cause for complaint, in that, less than three years after its broad compliance with the wishes of parliament the Irish executive had decided to present it with a further set of propositions, 'tendering the Society the alternative of their adoption, or the withdrawal of the Grant'. Unlike the recommendations of the parliamentary select committee, whose business had been conducted in public, these fresh propositions were founded

> on evidence, to which the Society, as a body, has not been a party; the nature of which has not been communicated, and the authors of which are unknown: to which it may be added, that while the adoption of the recommendations of the Select Committee of the House of Commons left your Charter intact, the Propositions of His Excellency render necessary, and indeed contemplate, a surrender of that Charter.[39]

The council went on to state that the failures specifically attributed to the society in Lord Morpeth's letter were identified as the lack of an annual membership scheme, an over-generalized policy on library acquisitions, and the continued taking of newspapers. Lord Morpeth's letter also asserted that the high cost of admission to the society was a deterrent to interested parties of moderate means.[40] The council pointed out that an annual membership scheme had been put in place in 1838.

> If one gentleman only (as is the case) has yet been found to take advantage of an annual payment throwing open all the privileges of the Society,[41] while many are admitted monthly upon payment of the life composition, and some few on an annual payment of two guineas, as Associate Subscribers; the fact only serves to mark the preference of the Public in the option afforded them, and the suitableness of a life composition to that class of Gentry constituting our most desirable members.[42]

The last part of this observation was unfortunate, revealing an attitude of exclusivity of which the society had been accused, and running counter to the

---

39 Ibid., statement of the council, 14 Jan. 1841.   40 N.A.I.: C.S.O.R.P., 1837, 229/3/612, box 5, Henry Barnard to Morpeth, 19 Jan. 1837.   41 The single annual member was Robert Scallan, architect and builder, North Frederick Street, and Abbey View, Lusk, who was elected on 31 May 1838. Scallan remained a member for thirty-five years, until he was deleted for failure to pay his annual subscription, on 24 Apr. 1873. (Source: *RDS Proc.*, var. dates.)   42 *RDS Proc.*, lxxvii, statement of the council, 14 Jan. 1841.

government's object of making membership of the society accessible to a wider pool of candidates. That there was such a view held by a significant number of members is attested to by Isaac Weld's evidence to the parliamentary committee of inquiry.[43] Nevertheless, and however reluctantly, an annual membership scheme had been put in place in 1838.

The society's acquisitions policy for the library conformed to government requirements, except that some bequests of theological works had been accepted, at no charge to the exchequer. However, the continued purchase of newspapers, while not expressly prohibited by the parliamentary select committee, was clearly in defiance of the Irish executive's order of 1836. The council stood by the decision taken by the society at that time, 'that in the present state of the diffusion of knowledge the exclusion of Newspapers from your Reading-room would be hardly reconcileable with a desire to be informed of the daily accruing improvements, and discoveries in almost every branch of Science, Arts, and Manufactures, as well as Agriculture'.

> The Society never having been favoured by Government with any opinion upon the change of system which had been assented to [by the society], in deference to the high authority of Parliament, other than a letter from the Treasury, acquainting the Society, that directions had been given to issue the balance of the Grant then due; and no objections having been then or since raised by Government, on the subject of the Reading-room, and the usual annual Grants continuing to be recommended to Parliament until the present period; the Society naturally inferred an acquiescence on the part of Government in the justice of their reasoning on the question of the Newspapers, and indulged the hope that the objection was deemed too trivial, to be allowed any weight in estimating the general utility of the Institution, and the character of its Members.[44]

Finally, the council argued that the RDS was never intended to concentrate its resources on theoretical or abstract science. While it numbered many eminent scientists amongst its membership, it did not estimate their contribution more highly than that of its landed, professional, or mercantile members. The council respectfully pointed out,

> the unreasonableness of expecting an Institution like this, to extend its objects and usefulness, in proportion as the liberality of Parliament is withdrawn; the Grant having been gradually diminished from £10,000, Irish, to £5,300 of the present currency; and more particularly when it is considered, that the allocation of the Parliamentary funds to the different

43 *Report on Royal Dublin Society, 1836*, pp. 6–7.   44 *RDS Proc.*, lxxvii, statement of the council, 14 Jan. 1841.

departments of the Society is specially dictated by the Government itself.[45]

In a letter responding to the statement, Under Secretary MacDonald admitted that the Castle had been mistaken in claiming that the society had failed to make provision for an annual membership scheme. He rather lamely argued that the annual subscription was set too high in actuarial terms (as argued by Henry Barnard in a letter to Lord Morpeth in 1837, see p. 179). MacDonald's suggested solution was that a lower rate be applied to sectional membership. The lord lieutenant, according to MacDonald, was adamant in opposing the continuance of the newspaper room.

> On the subject of the News Room, His Excellency agrees in the opinion which the Parliamentary Committee of 1829, as well as that of 1836, have given upon it. He thinks (to use the words of the latter), 'that the admission of newspapers has a tendency to lower the character of the Society, as an association for the advancement of science, to make it degenerate into a second-rate club, and that the class of persons who join it merely from such motives of convenience, is not the class best fitted to administer the Parliamentary Grant in the manner contemplated by Parliament'. With these impressions, His Excellency feels bound to enforce to the utmost of his power, a compliance with the recommendations of these two Committees, as further embodied in the Resolution of the latter, 'that newspapers and political periodicals shall no longer be taken into the Society's Rooms, whether procured by special private subscription or paid for out of the general funds of the Society'.[46]

The treasury committee of 1829 had not required the society to cease taking newspapers. But that was hardly germane to the issue since Drummond's correspondence and the parliamentary committee of 1836 had repeatedly raised the subject, and MacDonald's quotation of the resolution of the parliamentary committee of inquiry was quite accurate. MacDonald went on to cast doubt on the society's compliance with the resolutions respecting the establishment of a council, and, in an unexpected interpretation, argued that the society and its professors had shown a lack of due diligence by failing to publish scientific works. On the issue of modifying the charter, he argued that this could be a means of settling the question of ownership of the society's property, by assigning that property to trustees. MacDonald did not accept that the society had no role in theoretical science. He pointed out that the society had 'been entrusted by the State with the cultivation of the sciences of Chemistry, of Geology, Zoology, of Botany, each of which bears so much upon agriculture and

45 Ibid.   46 *RDS Proc.*, lxxvii, minutes, 28 Jan. 1841.

the useful arts', and 'that its province is not really separated even from the highest branches of those important sciences'.[47]

The society considered MacDonald's letter at an extraordinary general meeting convened on 11 February 1841. The chair was taken by Sir Robert Shaw, and the large attendance of 209 members included the duke of Leinster, Dr Anthony Meyler, James Haughton, Arthur Guinness II, James McCullagh, FTCD, F.W. Conway, P.R. Webb, Dr William Harty, Dr John Lentaigne, Sir Thomas Esmonde, and the lord mayor of Dublin, Sir John Kingston James. A letter drafted by the council was adopted by the society and ordered to be transmitted to the under secretary. It expressed the frustration, and the barely suppressed anger of the society, at the demands of the Irish executive.

> surely if in obeying Parliament in this particular [the scheme of annual membership], the Society has the misfortune to dissatisfy the Executive of Ireland, it may respectfully be asked, where can any guiding principle be found, on which the Society can safely rely? when here, as throughout other parts of this case, the views of His Excellency, respecting the proper organisation of the Society, are so much at variance with those recommended by Parliament.[48]

The letter challenged the validity of the lord lieutenant's sources of information on the society. It added that the seven hundred or so members of the society were also, as individuals, members of the general public, and as such 'may be entitled to as much weight in regulating the balance of public opinion, as the few unknown persons from whom His Excellency has derived his information'. In trenchant terms, the society requested that it be heard in its own defence, if necessary by another public inquiry. The inference drawn by the society, from the continued payment of the parliamentary grant, was that it had satisfied the recommendations of the 1836 parliamentary committee. This 'was, under the circumstances, a perfectly fair and legitimate inference; founded on facts, such as in ordinary judicial proceedings, would have amounted to evidence in proof of acquiescence, both admissible, and difficult, if not impossible to rebut'. In further support of its case the society pointed out that Frederick Shaw,[49] MP, had raised the question of the grant in the house of commons in 1837. Shaw had been assured by the chancellor of the exchequer that the outstanding issues between the treasury and the society had been satisfactorily settled and that the grant would be included in the supplementary estimates. As for the variations adopted in the implementation of those reforms, 'The Society did not consider

---

47 Ibid.   48 Ibid., 11 Feb. 1841.   49 Frederick Shaw (1799–1876), baronet, was a son of Sir Robert Shaw's and was MP for Dublin University, 1832–48. He held the office of recorder of Dublin, 1828–76, and succeeded to his father's title on the death of his older brother in 1869: Source: Alfred Webb, *A compendium of Irish biography* (Dublin, 1878).

the Report of the Select Committee of the House of Commons, so mandatory, as necessarily to exclude all exercise of judgement on the part of the Society in matters of detail'.[50]

A second report of the council, on the letters of Morpeth and MacDonald, was also read to the meeting. The council objected to the first eight of the Castle's propositions, on the grounds that they were in conflict with the charter, and would have the effect of creating two societies. In particular they objected to the lack of any provision for general meetings of the society, whereas a minimum of three per annum was required under the charter.

> From the general purport of the Propositions, especially No. 8, and the entire omission therein, of any provision for a meeting of the Society at large, for general purposes, it may be inferred, that each Section might entertain a proposition for a change in its constitution, and consequently, it might reduce the subscription on the admission of Members into that Section, whether annual or for life – it might annul the ballot – it might vest the management of its affairs exclusively in a President or other person, and allow him to nominate its officers and servants – in short, it might, without consulting the other Section, make any conceivable alteration in its management, and thus influence the general affairs of the Society.[51]

The council foresaw manipulative competition between the sections for the limited parliamentary grant, with the result that neither section would be able to rely on a consistent level of funding from year to year. The council believed that the funds allocated by government to the society had been 'economically and judiciously employed', and that 'greater advantages would be gained to the public, by an increased grant to the Society, than by any alteration in its present system'. Regarding the ninth proposition, on newspapers, the council stated 'They will abstain from making any comment on the terms in which this proposition is conveyed, or on the menaces accompanying it', but would consider it on its merits. The society from its earliest days had found newspapers to be an essential tool in advertising its services and publicising its activities. The expense of taking newspapers was less than £60 per annum and was borne in effect out of the society's private funds since it was not provided for in the government grant. The operation of the newspaper room did not give rise to political debate within the society, but was a source of immediate information on developments and discoveries in science and art.

> In conclusion, the Council are of opinion, that the Society, as proprietors of a large property, and contributing to the maintenance of its great

---

50 *RDS Proc.*, lxxvii, minutes, 28 Jan. 1841.   51 Ibid., council report.

establishment, partly from their own means, while it honourably applies the Parliamentary Grant to the purposes to which it is allocated, are entitled to a voice in the mode in which their own funds are to be disbursed. For these reasons, the Council recommend to the Society, not to yield to the command of excluding Newspapers from its Conversation Room, not being sustained by any solid grounds, being arbitrary in its nature, and derogatory to the character of the Society as an independent body.[52]

Dr William Harty, seconded by Thomas Quinton[53] moved that the council's report be adopted and confirmed. A counter-motion by the honorary secretaries, Isaac Weld and L.E. Foot (Foot succeeded R.B. Bryan in 1841) called for the discontinuance of the newspaper room in deference to the wishes of the lord lieutenant. This was defeated by a margin of seventy votes (129:59). A second motion, to defer consideration of the report for a week, was put by Pierce Mahony[54] and William Smith.[55] This counter-motion was defeated by a margin of fifty-five votes (112:57). An attempt to adjourn the meeting, or to have the original motion put to a ballot, was disallowed by the chairman, Sir Robert Shaw, and the report was adopted by default on the defeat of both counter-motions.[56]

The relationship between the society and Dublin Castle had reached breaking point, and Under Secretary MacDonald rejected the society's case by letter of 22 February 1841.

Finding, therefore, that the Society have rejected the Propositions contained in my letter of the 25th ultimo, based as they were, on the Resolutions of two Parliamentary Committees, His Excellency has directed me to express his regret, that he cannot recommend to Parliament any further continuance of the Annual Grant to the Society.[57]

On the motion of Pierce Mahony, seconded by James Perry,[58] MacDonald's letter was referred to the council. That body had produced a supplementary report that was read to the meeting, recapitulating the arguments for an increased grant. The Castle's decision made its arguments redundant, except that against the proposed division of the society's functions.

52 Ibid.   53 Thomas James Quinton, Dublin city sheriff 1837–8, was a member of the RDS, 1838–77. He moved to London in 1864. (Sources: *RDS Proc., Thom's*, var. dates.)   54 Pierce Mahony (1792–1853), Priory House, Stillorgan, and Kilmorna, Co. Kerry, was Daniel O'Connell's family lawyer and parliamentary agent to the Catholic Association in the 1820s. He had an extensive practice as solicitor to various banks and insurance companies. At O'Connell's urging he contested Kinsale as a Whig-liberal candidate in 1837. Pierce Mahony was elected a life member of the RDS in 1815. (Sources: *RDS Proc.*, var. dates; *Burke's landed gentry*, O'Ferrall, *Catholic emancipation*, Smith and Share, *Whigs on the Green*, O'Connell, *Correspondence*.)   55 William Smith, Merrion Square, was a member of the society 1835–79 and served on the executive council, 1838–9. He left Dublin in 1866 to reside in Torquay, Devon. (Source: *RDS Proc.*, var. dates.)   56 *RDS Proc.*, lxxvii, minutes of extraordinary meeting, 11 Feb. 1841.   57 *RDS Proc.*, lxxvii, minutes, 25 Feb.

It is a Society *sui generis*, differing, in the nature of its establishment, from any Society that ever has existed in these, or any other countries; and as such, its self government, may, and does require to be materially different from that of any society which has but one single professed object to attend to.[59]

The society met again, on 4 March 1841. The council advised the meeting 'that in the present position of their affairs, they have judged it necessary, to recommend to the several Committees, not to incur any liabilities, engagements, or expenditure in their respective departments, without being previously sanctioned by the Council'. As a gesture of goodwill towards Dublin Castle the meeting unanimously agreed to reduce the admission fine for candidates for annual membership from five guineas to three guineas, subject to ratification at the June meeting.[60] At the end of March, Henry Kemmis, vice-president, gave notice of a motion calling on the council to prepare a memorial to parliament requesting the restoration of the annual grant, and inviting a parliamentary inquiry into the administration of the society.[61]

The reaction of the Dublin press to the withdrawal of the society's grant was less supportive than the Castle might have hoped. Liberal and reformist opinion, led by F.W. Conway's *Dublin Evening Post*, did endorse the government's action. However, Thomas Davis, the future Young Irelander, defended the society in the *Morning Register* as a national institution, and, while acknowledging the society's defects, condemned the action of government in denying the right of Irish people to run their own institutions in the manner which they saw as most appropriate.[62] Dublin Castle and the *Dublin Evening Post* were baffled by this identification of the RDS with Irish nationalism, and F.W. Conway thought it preposterous. But Davis had wider support than the official establishment suspected. John Blake Dillon, another future Young Irelander, reiterated Davis' arguments in the *Morning Register*: 'Whatever party be in office – Whig, Tory, or Radical – if we see it acting arbitrarily or using unjustly its Imperial strength against an Irish institution, we shall oppose it independently and decisively'.[63]

Davis' most recent biographer, J.N. Molony, understandably, but incorrectly, describes him as a member of the RDS.[64] Davis' interest in and sympathy for the society was almost certainly the result of his friendship with Patrick Robert Webb. Molony stresses the importance of this friendship throughout Davis'

1841.   **58** James Perry (1795–1858) was a successful businessman, with investments in the Hibernian Gaslight Company, The Royal Bank of Ireland, and the Hibernian mine in the Rhuhr valley of Germany. He was a member of the RDS, 1835–58, and served on the chemistry committee, 1841–4. (Sources: *RDS Proc.*, var. dates; Richard S. Harrison, *A biographical dictionary of Irish Quakers* (Dublin, 1997).)   **59** *RDS Proc.*, lxxvii, minutes, 25 Feb. 1841.   **60** Ibid., 4 Mar. 1841.   **61** Ibid., 25 Mar. 1841.   **62** Molony, *A soul came into Ireland*, pp. 62–4.   **63** Ibid., cited, p. 64.   **64** Ibid., p. 296. No membership lists were published between 1829 and 1845, but the present author has thoroughly researched all elections of members between those dates, and can confirm that Davis was not a member.

brief life. Webb was a contemporary of Davis', and had befriended the latter at school; a friendship which continued through their student days in Trinity College, and afterwards. In their adult years, Webb was the confidant and sharer of Davis' developing liberal and nationalist views.[65] Patrick Robert Webb was a life member of the RDS 1838–76, and a member of the library committee 1839–52. He was present at the general meetings of the society during January–March 1841 when the Castle's letters and propositions were discussed, and, as indicated by Molony, acted as a sounding board for Davis' opinions on the national character of the RDS.[66]

The position adopted by the *Freeman's Journal*, which was broadly liberal-repealer in its sentiments at that time, was not altogether dissimilar to Davis' and perhaps was influenced to some extent by his arguments. The paper condemned both parties to the dispute, unable to completely set aside its hostility towards the RDS since the Murray affair.

> We have seen one after another of these lingering lineaments of life, and health, and dignity, and self-respect, swindled from us, under the sham plea of assimilation. And the Dublin Society, one of the last left, is in danger now. In danger from whom? From those without and those within. Nothing can be worse than the conduct of the government, except the conduct of the Society. To read the correspondence that has recently passed between the Englishmen of the Castle and the Orangemen of Leinster House, one would really suppose that the whole affair was a squabble between an overbearing landlord and an ill-conditioned tenant, as to whether the latter was breaking the covenants in his lease or no.[67]

The *Freeman's Journal* could not at first resist the opportunity to revel a little in the society's predicament, and to take a swipe also at Doctor Meyler. The black-beaning of Archbishop Murray was past history for Davis. However, it was not forgotten by the *Freeman's Journal*, which lamented that 'The Society, – alas, that we should have to write it, – the Society did perpetrate that disgraceful act, an act that years of usefulness and public service will not, in the minds of the nation, suffice to expiate'. The paper did draw its readers' attentions' to the impartiality displayed by the society in appointing the catholic Robert Kane as its natural philosophy professor.

---

65 Ibid. pp. 13, 37, 64.   66 Ibid., and *RDS Proc.*, var. dates. Molony also mentions (p. 82, fn) that the society removed Davis' statue in 1849 to avoid embarrassing the visiting Queen Victoria. He cites Terence de Vere White (*The story of the Royal Dublin Society*, p. 111) in support. I cannot trace this allegation, either in White's book, or in the society's proceedings, and conclude that Molony must have been mistaken.   67 *Freeman's Journal*, 8 Mar. 1841.

Now let it be remembered, that up to the present moment, there is not a single Catholic professor in the University, or a Catholic member of the Board of Works. What will the public think then, of the furious and unrestrainable liberality of a government who having failed to dragoon the Dublin Society into a compliance with their flippant field orders, and finding that they could not assimilate this institution also into a subsidiary branch of the British Museum, come to the resolution of offering to leave the arbitration of the quarrel to – reader, who do you think? – Lord Oxmantown, – two English engineer officers, – and three professors of Trinity College![68]

The government had indeed decided to appoint a vice-regal commission of inquiry into the functions and organisation of the RDS. The members of the commission as finally selected were the duke of Leinster, the earl of Rosse, Viscount Adare, General J.F. Burgoyne, Sir William Rowan Hamilton, Humphrey Lloyd, James MacCullagh, and Thomas Larcom.[69] Two of the eight members, the duke of Leinster and James MacCullagh, were also members of the RDS. Sir W.R. Hamilton was an honorary member of the society, but his appointment to the commission was in his capacity as president of the Royal Irish Academy.[70] The society was not notified officially, and first learned of the establishment of the commission through reports in the press. The lord lieutenant's directions to the commissioners, a copy of which, dated 29 March 1841, came into the society's hands (probably through MacCullagh), contained what was regarded by the council as a serious error of fact.[71] The council convened an extraordinary general meeting of the society on 15 April 1841 to consider what steps should be taken to redress the society's position. Amongst those present was James MacCullagh (1809–47), TCD professor of mathematics, and recently appointed chairman of the vice-regal commission. MacCullagh had been elected a life member of the RDS in 1839. The meeting heard, through the report of the council, that no effort had been made by the Castle to advise the RDS of its intention to appoint a commission of inquiry. The directions to the commissioners were to recommend alternative applications of the society's grant, and contained the following statement:

in consequence of the refusal of the Dublin Society to make, at the instance of Government, certain changes in its constitution and management, which were strongly recommended by Parliamentary Committees, His Excellency has felt it his duty to intimate to that Society, his intention of declining to propose to Parliament a continuance of their Grant.[72]

68 *Freeman's Journal*, 15 Mar. 1841.   69 *RDS Proc.*, lxxvii, report of vice-regal commission, 3 June 1841.   70 O'Donnell, *William Rowan Hamilton*, p. 134.   71 RDS Archive: Council minute book 1838–44, 8 Apr. 1841.   72 *RDS Proc.*, lxxvii, minutes, 15 Apr. 1841.

The council objected strongly to the first part of this statement on the grounds that it was factually incorrect, and injurious to the public reputation of the society. On behalf of the society the council had written to the under secretary on 13 April 1841, refuting the allegation that the society had refused to implement the recommendations of the 1836 committee of inquiry, while admitting to one derogation – the continued taking of newspapers.

> In the Propositions accompanying Lord Morpeth's letter to the Society, of the 17th December, are to be found embodied, the 'changes in its constitution and management', which the Royal Dublin Society has refused to make, 'at the instance of Government', but it is respectfully submitted, that so far from those Propositions (with one admitted exception) having been 'strongly recommended by Parliamentary Committees', they, on the contrary, were directly at variance with such recommendations; and contemplated fundamental changes in 'the constitution and management' of the Society, superceding [sic] altogether the recommendations of the Parliamentary Committee of the year 1836, upon which the existing organisation of the Society is expressly based.[73]

The only resolution agreed at this meeting was to open a communication with the commissioners, and this was reciprocated two days later by James MacCullagh, in his capacity as chairman of the commissioners, enclosing a resolution to hold discussions with the society.[74] More good news followed three days later, when MacCullagh forwarded a resolution of the commissioners. It stated 'That this Commission do not consider themselves entitled to inquire into any thing which has already passed between the Government and the Royal Dublin Society; but, that they do consider themselves at liberty to receive any information from the Society, bearing upon the prospective application of the Grant'.[75] It was clear that the commission was not going to sit in judgement on the fine detail of the quarrel between the government and the RDS.

The commission reported to the Castle on 26 May 1841, the society receiving a copy of their report on 3 June. Far from recommending the break-up of the RDS, the report recommended that its grant be continued, and that some of the smaller scientific bodies in Dublin should be assimilated into it. The report refrained from any comment on the issue of the newspaper room, but did recommend that 'the distribution of the entire fund [the annual grant] be left by Government to the Society itself'.[76] The commission did put forward seventeen propositions of its own, being careful to offer them as points for discussion, and not as binding regulations.

73 Ibid.   74 RDS Archive: Council minute book 1838–44, 17 Apr. 1841.   75 Ibid., 22 Apr. 1841.
76 *RDS Proc.*, lxxvii, report of the commission, 3 June 1841.

Propositions 1–2 recommended the appointment of a supervisory court of visitors, with power to arbitrate on issues arising between the government and the society. Propositions 3–8 and 12 suggested the creation of separate sections within the society, but differed from the government's propositions by including agriculture in the science group. They further suggested that full members of the society should be members of all sections, and that avenues should be open to sectional members to permit them to become full members. Proposition 8 recommended that both full and sectional members should be represented on a general council. Propositions 9–10 suggested slightly reduced subscription rates for each category of membership, and proposition 11 recommended the absorption of the Dublin geological and zoological societies within the RDS. Propositions 13–15 recommended that the society should have complete control over the allocation of its funds, whether publicly or privately sourced, and strongly recommended an increase in the salaries of the professors. Proposition 16 recommended that the society be encouraged to establish a school of mechanical drawing, and that the fine arts schools should be transferred to the control of the Royal Hibernian Academy. Finally, proposition 17 recommended that the society should publish a journal.[77]

While generally welcoming the propositions outlined in the commission's report, the RDS council had reservations about the future arrangements for arts and manufactures, the future of the drawing schools, and the absence of a recommendation for increased funding to defray the extra costs of the proposed new management structure.[78] The council entered discussions with the commission on 9 June 1841 and outlined suggested modifications to the commission's propositions. These were, principally, that a sixth section for arts and manufactures be added; that sectional members be admitted on the same terms as associate members (i.e, without the right to vote at general meetings), and that the art schools be left under the control of the RDS. The commission replied to the RDS council on 11 June. They agreed that the annual grant of £5,300 was inadequate to meet the expanded responsibilities of the re-organized society, but believed it was not a part of their remit to recommend an increase in the grant. To meet the objection expressed by the council, they were willing to modify the title of the first section to 'Natural Philosophy and Chemistry, with their application to Arts and Manufactures'. The commission was unwilling to withdraw its recommendation that the art schools should be transferred to the RHA, 'but the proposed arrangement being altogether prospective, and dependent on a future contingency [the agreement and capacity of the RHA], it does not appear necessary to call for any immediate decision respecting it on the part of the Society'. The council met on 14 June, and held fast on the issue of the art schools, recommending to the society,

77 Ibid. 78 RDS Archive: Council minute book 1838–44, 7, 4 June 1841.

That as the Drawing and Modelling Schools form one of the oldest departments of the Society's establishment, and have been productive, beyond all doubt, of great public advantage to all the useful as well as ornamental Arts, so, in the opinion of the Council, the Society ought, under no circumstances, to consent to abandon them.[79]

Despite their differences and sticking points the negotiations between the RDS council and the vice-regal commission appeared to be approaching an acceptable compromise. The Castle's interventions, however, were less than helpful. Under Secretary MacDonald wrote to the society on 16 June 1841, praising its positive approach to the commission's propositions, and adding ominously that 'Those Propositions, coupled with the original condition, respecting the abolition of the Newsroom, form the whole extent of the alterations which the Government desire to recommend'.[80] On 14 July the commission wrote again in reference to the society's objections, conceding the inclusion of a separate section for arts and manufactures.[81] The last communication between the society and Lord Ebrington's administration on the subject of the grant was on 19 July 1841 when MacDonald advised P.T. Wilson, the society's registrar, 'that Parliament has not voted any sum for the Dublin Society for the current year'.[82]

Even as MacDonald wrote, voting in the general election that would turn his government out of office had just concluded.[83] The Whig-liberals lost heavily, and in Ireland the O'Connellite *bloc* slipped from thirty-one MPs in 1837, to eighteen in 1841.[84] When he failed to achieve adequate electoral support O'Connell began to look to extra-parliamentary means, the moral force of public opinion, to pursue his repeal campaign.[85] Robert Hutton refused to contest Dublin as a repeal candidate, as did Lord Kildare, forcing O'Connell to contest the seat himself. He lost Dublin, but was returned to parliament as an MP for Co. Cork.[86] At Westminster, a Tory-conservative administration under Sir Robert Peel took office with a majority of seventy-six seats. Peel had changed voter perceptions of the Tories, beginning with his 'Tamworth manifesto' of 1834. He accepted the reforms of 1832, and advocated a moderate conservatism, willing to undertake further reforms while taking into account traditional interests.[87]

In the 1841 general election Irish Tory-conservatives won forty seats, Irish Whig-liberals forty-seven seats, and Repealers, as already mentioned, eighteen seats. The big loser was O'Connell, with the gains going to mainstream

79 *RDS Proc.*, lxxvii, minutes, 24 June 1841.   80 Ibid.   81 RDS Archive: Council minute book 1838–44, 15 July 1841.   82 Ibid., 19 Aug. 1841.   83 Walker, *Parliamentary election results*, balloting took place 1–17 July 1841.   84 Hoppen, *Ireland since 1800*, p. 25.   85 Macartney, *The dawning of democracy*, p. 151.   86 MacDonagh, *The emancipist*, pp. 195–7.   87 Webb, *Modern England*, pp. 250–9.

conservatives and liberals. However, Peel failed to capitalize on this opportunity for harmony, and appointed Earl de Grey as lord lieutenant. De Grey was an elderly, self-confident, conservative peer, of only moderate ability, related by marriage to the arch-tory Lord Enniskillen.[88] The numbers of RDS members with parliamentary seats in the commons declined from sixteen to fourteen. Tory-conservative numbers remained unchanged at six, but included the new Irish under secretary, Edward Lucas, chief adviser to Earl de Grey. Of the remaining eight, five were liberals, including Sir Thomas Esmonde; two, Colonel Henry White and Henry Grattan, were repealers, and C.A. Walker fitted the hybrid description of liberal-repealer.[89]

Encouraged by the change in the political climate, the RDS council decided to send a memorial to the new lord lieutenant, requesting a restoration of the parliamentary grant. However, the lord lieutenant had been detained on business in London, and the memorial was presented instead to the chancellor of the exchequer, through the good offices of Frederick Shaw.[90] Government response was slow, and the council reported to the general meeting on 4 November 1841 that it had obtained the agreement of the professors and senior staff to continue operations on the understanding that funds might not be available to meet their salaries in full.[91] In the meantime the lord lieutenant, earl de Grey, had returned to Dublin and had received a deputation from the society on 23 October 1841. This was followed by a personal visit by de Grey to Leinster House, during which he showed a particular interest in the work of the art school. Subsequent to this a communication had been received from his private secretary, 'expressive of his expectation of receiving from the Society a statement of the future changes and regulations which they propose to adopt'.[92]

To meet this request, the council submitted fourteen resolutions to the society. The first was that the purchase of newspapers, despite its usefulness, should be discontinued. The second was that the society should in future have seven sections, two more than the five recommended by the vice-regal commission. The sixth and seventh were to cover fine arts, and 'manufactures, products, and inventions' respectively. The remaining recommendations dealt with the establishment of sectional memberships, and the placing of the sections under the control of the council and the general meeting rather than their autonomous working as envisaged by Lord Morpeth and by the commission. The twelfth recommendation was 'That the Society will adopt measures for increasing the salaries of the Professors, and will also establish a School of Mechanical Drawing at the earliest period that the funds of the Society will permit'. The thirteenth recommendation proposed to discontinue printing the proceedings, and replace them with a monthly journal of general reports. The final

88 McDowell, *Public opinion*, pp. 135, 204. 89 Walker, *Parliamentary election results*; and author's database. 90 Ibid., 23, 27 Sept., 7 Oct. 1841. 91 *RDS Proc.*, lxxviii, minutes, 4 Nov. 1841. 92 Ibid., council report, 11 Nov. 1841.

recommendation was that the president, vice-presidents, and honorary secretaries, be *ex-officio* members of all sections.[93]

The general meeting was adjourned, and reconvened on 18 November 1841; Sir Robert Shaw in the chair. The first recommendation, on discontinuing newspapers, was formally put to the meeting. James Naper and Lord Downshire, vice-presidents, moved an amendment.

> That induced by circumstances, over which the Society have no control, they deem it expedient that the establishment of the present Newspaper Room be discontinued from the 1st day of January next.[94]

The motion was passed by the slenderest of majorities, with forty-four for and forty-three against, and the meeting was adjourned for the second time. When the meeting reconvened on 22 November the second and third recommendations, dealing with the creation of sections was put to it. Dr Anthony Meyler, supported by Dr Howard Cooke, attempted to have these recommendations set aside pending further discussions with the new administration, but their counter-motion was defeated by thirty-six votes to eighteen votes, and the recommendations were agreed as presented by the council.[95] The meeting was adjourned again to 24 November, and then adjourned to the following day, to allow the honorary secretaries to meet with the lord lieutenant. On 25 November the honorary secretaries reported that Lord de Grey had informed them that it was his intention to apply to the lords of the treasury for the restoration of the society's annual grant.[96] A letter from Lord Eliot, chief secretary, of the same date, confirmed the lord lieutenant's decision. A deputation from the society met the lord lieutenant at the vice-regal lodge in the Phoenix Park on 30 November. They invited him to accept the office of president of the society, and, in his formal acceptance, Lord de Grey set forth his attitude and aspirations.

> Our Gracious Sovereign has been pleased to appoint, as her Representative here, a man who has hitherto been little mixed up with public or political life, with a view, no doubt, to demonstrate her anxiety to encourage those pursuits, which may promote harmony and good-will amongst Her subjects in Ireland: and which, by fostering scientific knowledge, and extending practical improvement, may assist in withdrawing their minds from those topics, which have a tendency to excite hostility and keep up dissension.[97]

A letter from Under Secretary Lucas, dated 8 January 1842, advised the society that Sir Robert Peel had authorized the Irish executive to apply for a

93 Ibid.   94 *RDS Proc.*, lxxviii, minutes, 18 Nov. 1841.   95 Ibid., 22 Nov. 1841.   96 Ibid., 24, 25 Nov. 1841.   97 Ibid., 2 Dec. 1841.

17 Isaac Weld by Martin Cregan, 1843 (*courtesy* Royal Dublin Society).
Weld was an RDS honorary secretary, 1828–49.

18 RDS President's chair, by James Mannin, 1767 (*courtesy* Royal Dublin Society).
In use for over two centuries, and still in use in 2004. Ballots were recorded
beside this chair, in which the presiding member was seated.

19 Giesecke medal, by W.S. Mossop, 1817 (*courtesy* Royal Dublin Society).
Giesecke presented his Greenland collection of minerals to the RDS museum in 1816.

20 Sir William Rowan Hamilton, scientist and mathematician, by Thomas Kirk, 1830 (*courtesy* National Gallery of Ireland). Hamilton was elected an honorary member of the RDS in 1834.

21 Daniel O'Connell, silhouette by Edouart, 1835. In 1835 O'Connell made an informal coalition that kept the whigs in government until 1841 (*courtesy* National Gallery of Ireland).

22 Humphrey Lloyd, artist unknown (*courtesy* Royal Dublin Society). A leading supporter of the BAAS Dublin conference in 1835, he was RDS Vice-President, 1868–81.

23 Daniel O'Connell by David Wilkie, 1837 (*courtesy* Ulster Bank Ireland Limited, Royal Bank of Scotland Group). His successful general election campaign of 1837 left Melbourne's government in absolute dependence on his support.

24 Sir Maziere Brady by Thomas Alfred Jones (*courtesy* National Gallery of Ireland).
A member of the RDS, 1822–71, Judge Brady assisted Under Secretary
Drummond in reforming the Irish legal system, 1836–40.

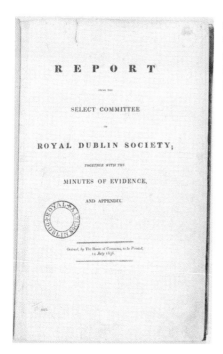

25 Parliamentary report 1836, title page (*courtesy* Royal Dublin Society). The report's recommendations set the agenda for change in the RDS over the ensuing forty years.

26 Niven's guide to the Botanic Garden, title page, 1838 (*courtesy* Royal Dublin Society). Niven remodeled the garden and revived apprentice gardener courses during his term as head gardener, 1834–8.

27 Hothouse, Botanic Garden 1838, engraving by J. Kirkwood (*courtesy* Royal Dublin Society).
Picturesque, but dilapidated, the early buildings were largely replaced in the 1840s.

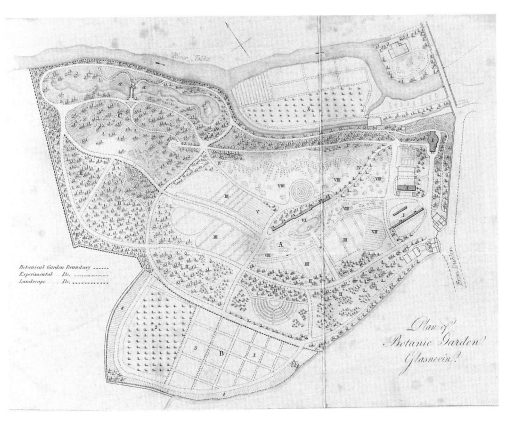

28 Plan of Botanic Garden 1838 (*courtesy* Royal Dublin Society).
Niven's layout gave the garden its familiar modern shape.

29 Richard Whately by William Brocas. Anglican archbishop of Dublin, 1831–63.
Whately's liberal positions on education and church reform disappointed conservatives.

30 Lord Mulgrave by Daniel Maclise, 1835 (*courtesy* National Portrait Gallery, London).
Lord Lieutenant Mulgrave seemed tyrannical and capricious in the view
of many RDS members during 1835–8.

31 Earl de Grey, lord lieutenant, by Thomas Farrell, 1844
(*courtesy* Royal Dublin Society). More benign towards the RDS
than his predecessors, de Grey's active support boosted
the prestige of the art school.

32 Royal Agricultural Society of Ireland medal (*courtesy* Royal Dublin Society).
Despite the potential for rivalry, relations between the RASI and the RDS
were good and the two bodies merged in 1888.

33 Sir Michael O'Loghlen by George Francis Mulvany, 1843
(*courtesy* National Gallery of Ireland). A member of the RDS,
1834–42, O'Loghlen was Irish attorney general, 1835–6.

34 Tickets for Dargan's Great Industrial Exhibition 1853 held on
Leinster Lawn (*courtesy* Royal Dublin Society). It was organised
with facilities and expertise provided by the RDS.

35 Francis Blackburne by Shakesper Wood, 1865 (*courtesy* Royal Dublin Society).
Judge Blackburne, an RDS Vice-President, 1856–67, threw down legal challenges
to government attempts to exercise control of the RDS institutions in the 1860s.

restoration of the RDS grant. The council proposed that the mechanics of adopting sectional arrangements could best be handled by attaching the sections to the existing standing committees.[98] Lucas followed up his first letter with a second, dated 29 January, offering an interim payment to the society 'to obviate, as far as in their power, any inconvenience arising to the Society, from the withholding of the accustomed Grant from Parliament, during the past Session'. Dr William Harty and Sir Edward Stanley attempted to have the council's recommendations on the provision of sectional membership arrangements rejected, but were defeated by forty-four votes to eleven. The government was advised that all the council's recommendations, and in effect the government's propositions, had been adopted with modifications, with the exception of the establishment of a journal, which was deferred for further consideration.[99]

Pursuing the proposal that the geological and zoological societies should merge with the RDS, the council met a deputation from the Geological Society of Dublin on 17 March 1842. Charles William Hamilton led the geologists' deputation, acting in his capacity as secretary to the geological society.[100] Similar meetings, or correspondence, took place with the zoological society, and with the about to be formed Agricultural Improvement Society of Ireland (AIS). Robert Ball, secretary of the zoological society; Peter Purcell, founder secretary of the AIS, and Charles William Hamilton, were all members of the RDS. The AIS replied on 24 March that they could see no advantage to a merger of the two bodies. They acknowledged that almost one hundred of their members (including C.W. Hamilton, and James Naper) were also members of the RDS. However, they could not contemplate a merger unless it contained provisions allowing them to continue the independent pursuit of their own objects. C.W. Hamilton replied on behalf of the geological society on 7 April 1842. That body was reluctant to submerge its identity and objects in a larger grouping in which it would have a very restricted voice. Robert Ball replied on behalf of the Royal Zoological Society on 16 April, to the effect that the discussion of a merger was a matter for the general body of his members, and they had shown no inclination to act upon it. In sum, none of the target bodies for merger was willing to sacrifice its independence.[101]

Meanwhile, further mutually conciliatory gestures between the RDS and Dublin Castle were continuing to take place. The society reduced the admission fine for annual members from five guineas to three guineas on 3 March 1842. On the same date the society also acknowledged the right of the government to appoint a court of visitors (never implemented). Chief Secretary Eliot advised the society on 25 March that an additional £300 per annum would be granted to extend the duration and the geographical spread of the RDS provincial

98 *RDS Proc.*, lxxviii, minutes, 27 Jan. 1842.   99 Ibid., 10 Feb. 1842.   100 RDS Archive: Council minute book 1838–44, 17 Mar. 1842.   101 *RDS Proc.*, lxxviii, minutes, 28 Apr. 1842.

lectures.[102] A nervous RDS inquired if the government wished to give directions on the manner in which the additional grant was to be applied, and was assured by Under Secretary Lucas,

> It is placed at the disposal of the Royal Dublin Society, as the most prominent and distinguished body of scientific and practical gentlemen of the country; and His Excellency has most perfect reliance upon their judgement and discretion in the distribution, and would feel very reluctant to hamper them with too much restriction.[103]

The crisis was over, and a semblance of normality was restored. The council reported in November 1842 that the main effects of the suspension of the grant had been to delay the building programs, and to discourage the recruitment of new members. The numbers of new members elected fell from fifty-one in 1839 to twenty-five in 1842, with a corresponding fall of about fifty per cent in subscription income. The council attributed this decline 'as well to the unhappy differences which existed between the Government and the Society, as to the Resolution of withdrawing Newspapers from the Reading Room, which had always been a means of considerable attraction to new Members'.[104]

Terence de Vere White concluded that rather than a quarrel between the RDS and a dictatorial Whig-liberal government, the RDS newspaper crisis of 1840–2 should be seen as part of a much broader problem occupying all governments of the period. That wider problem was the integration of Irish catholics into the British body politic.[105] Probably this object did motivate to some degree the government's reform program in Ireland, but the RDS, with its growing catholic membership, was hardly a compelling test case. The disagreements between the government and the society are just as likely to have been influenced by personal and subjective assessments of the society's role as a national institution. Lord Morpeth's arguments that the society had failed to implement the recommendations of the 1836 parliamentary committee were mendacious in most respects. His real grievance appeared to be that his radical new proposals were rejected, and his position was undermined when his own commission reported largely in favour of the society. Nevertheless there were those, both within and without the RDS, who agreed with his policy of getting rid of the newspaper room on the grounds that its existence threatened the political neutrality of the society.

Turning to the fate of the building program, hard-hit by the suspension of the grant, this is well illustrated by the story of the largest RDS building project under consideration in 1840, the construction of a museum and general

---

102 Ibid., 3, 31 Mar. 1842.   103 RDS Archive: Council minute book 1838–44, 16 June 1842.
104 *RDS Proc.*, lxxix, council report, 10 Nov. 1842.   105 White, *The story of the Royal Dublin Society*, pp. 107–11.

purposes building in an upper storey of the Leinster House stables. The society allocated £2,200 for this purpose, but doubts were expressed about the load-bearing capabilities of the first storey structural walls.[106] Despite the assurances of a team of architects, William Farrell, Frederick Darley, and John Papworth, the society withdrew its initial allocation of funds and asked the council to review the project.[107] The council reported back that a new building could not be afforded from the funding contemplated, but that a suitable extension and alteration of the existing statue gallery above the art school could be achieved for an expenditure of about £2,500.[108] The society considered what was essentially Papworth's plan, and agreed to allocate £1,500, but only for its part execution.[109] Tenders were received from five builders, all of which exceeded the amount budgeted, and the council recommended that an additional £400 should be allocated.[110] While this heavy demand on the society's reserves was still under consideration, all work was suspended on the withdrawal of the parliamentary grant, and Papworth, who was granted sick leave at the end of August, died in Paris on 6 October 1841.[111]

The development of a national museum, based on the RDS collection, and the provision of an appropriate building to house it, had been a key recommendation of the 1836 parliamentary committee. Visitors to the existing museum fell slightly, from a peak of 43,656 in 1840, to 41,872 in 1841.[112] Pressure on space was further increased with the donation of Richard Griffith's geological collection of over 2,000 specimens, in early 1840.[113] In 1841 Henry Charles Sirr, former Dublin town major, died, and his family offered his fossil and conchology collection to the society.[114] The council agreed to store Sirr's collection, until it became clear (through a letter sent by Colonel George Colomb on 27 April 1842), that Reverend Joseph D'Arcy Sirr wished to sell rather than donate his father's collection to the society.[115] Relations worsened when it was discovered that Reverend Sirr had hung his father's paintings in the statue gallery, and billed the costs to the society. The assistant secretary was ordered to advise him that his unauthorized action had embarrassed the council.[116] Motivated by want of room, and probably by disappointment at the behaviour of the Sirr family, the council refused to purchase Sirr's collection, despite the strong advocacy of George Colomb.[117] The collection was subsequently removed from the RDS, sold to the Royal Irish Academy, and later transferred to the National Museum of Ireland.[118]

---

106 *RDS Proc.*, lxxvi, council report, 27 Feb. 1840.   107 Ibid., minutes, 5 Mar. 1840.   108 Ibid., council report, 30 Apr. 1840.   109 Ibid., minutes, 7, 28 May, 4 June 1840.   110 Ibid., council report, 23 July 1840.   111 RDS Archive: Council minute book 1838–44, 14 Oct. 1841.   112 *RDS Proc.*, lxxviii, museum report, 27 Jan. 1842.   113 RDS Archive: Council minute book 1838–44, 2 April 1840.   114 Ibid., 9 Sept. 1841.   115 *RDS Proc.*, lxxviii, minutes, 28 Apr. 1842.   116 RDS Archive: Council minute book 1838–44, 24 Mar. 1842.   117 RDS Archive: Council minute book 1838–44, 12 May 1842.   118 Joseph W. Hammond, 'Town Major Henry Charles Sirr', in *Dublin Historical Record*, iv (1941–2).

On 24 November 1842 William Elliott Hudson[119] gave notice of a motion to the general meeting,

> That the Council be requested to take into their immediate and serious consideration, the best means of meeting the declared wishes of the successive Parliamentary Committees, appointed to inquire into the affairs of the Society, with a view to the wider extension of the advantages of the Annual Parliamentary Grants to this Institution, and especially to consider the specified recommendations of the Committee of 1836, for supplying the defects of its Museum by exchanges between it and the British Museum; their recommendation of a considerable extension of accommodation, in point of room, for the reception of Mr. Griffith's collections, the Collections made in the progress of the Ordnance Survey of Ireland, and other objects, so as to form in the metropolis of Ireland a great National Museum, to be placed under this body; and to extend the buildings of Leinster House, in such a manner as to provide ample room for the reception, arrangement, and exhibition of the objects, as desired by the Committee; and generally to place the Library, and other Establishments of the Society, on a footing equivalent, for Ireland, with the station accorded to the British Museum and other public Institutions, fostered by Parliamentary Grants in the metropolis of Great Britain.[120]

Hudson's motion was discussed by the society on 1 December 1842. Whether through timidity, or battle weariness, or caution at the nationalistic challenge implicit in Hudson's wording, the society decided to refer only the first part of his motion to the council, requesting them to report only on the society's general compliance with the recommendations of the 1836 committee of inquiry.[121]

Meanwhile, the building stock in the Glasnevin botanic garden was, if anything, in a more parlous state than the Kildare Street premises, and in greater need of refurbishment or replacement. The damage done on the 'Night of the Big Wind' in 1839 continued to entail emergency expenditures on glass, structures, and roadways in 1840.[122] The premises allocated for the establishment of a botanic library were too damp to house the Robertson bequest (see p. 96).[123] The professor's house, and the gate lodge, also suffered severely from damp, and were a threat to the health of staff accommodated there.[124]

---

119 William Elliott Hudson (1796–1853) was a member of the RDS, 1840–53. An early Irish nationalist and supporter of Gaelic literature and music, he published *The Citizen* magazine, to which Thomas Davis was a frequent contributor. (Sources: *RDS Proc.*, var. dates; Molony, *A soul came into Ireland*; Smith and Share, *Whigs on the green*.) 120 *RDS Proc.*, lxxix, minutes, 24 Nov. 1842. 121 Ibid., minutes, 1 Dec. 1842. 122 RDS Archive: Council minute book 1838–44, botany committee report, 23 Jan. 1840. 123 *RDS Proc.*, lxxvi, botany committee report, 26 Mar. 1840. 124 Ibid., 28 May 1840.

David Moore submitted his annual report on the state of the garden on 1 November 1840. He drew the attention of the society to 'the decayed and tottering state of the lower range of hot-houses, which both architect and builders have stated to be quite unworthy of more extensive repair'. He also complained that in the absence of pipes to take water to the hot-houses 'All that is accomplished at present by this machine [Oldham's hydraulic ram], is simply raising the water to the pond in front of the Conservatory', from which it had to be conveyed in a barrel on a two-wheeled carriage.[125] The burden of this work, and the additional task of developing the extra land acquired for the garden, placed an impossible strain on his limited and ageing labour force. Moore had drawn attention to his staff problem in an earlier report to the botany committee. He had pointed out that he had only three general labourers out of a staff of fifteen, which included eight students and apprentices, and that all three labourers were in their seventies, having been employed in the gardens for between thirty-six and forty years.[126] Meanwhile visitor numbers to the botanic garden had grown, from 18,067 in 1839, to 22,283 in 1840 and to 31,661 in 1841.[127]

Professor Samuel Litton supported Moore's recommendation for a substantial investment in replacement conservatories.[128] The hidden aftermath of the 1839 storm added again to the woes of the botany committee when a seventeen-foot-long section of the boundary wall suddenly collapsed on the night of Monday, 21 June 1841. The adjoining stretch, also seventeen feet in length, was so damaged as to necessitate its dismantling, and 'the garden is, in the meantime, without sufficient protection against cattle or plunder'.[129] Another storm, on 25–6 December 1841, brought down more of the boundary wall, and the council allocated funds to carry out emergency repairs. The same storm also damaged roofs and glass in the conservatories. The committee obtained a report from Jacob Owen, architect to the board of works, in which he stated that only the octagon house was in sound condition. The upper and lower ranges of glass houses were in such a dilapidated state as to be beyond repair and in need of total replacement.[130] The botany committee, supported by the council, recommended that a subscription fund be opened to raise £2,500, which they hoped would be partially financed by the treasury, to replace the old buildings.[131]

The fund-raising efforts proved disappointing, and by the end of the year only £254 had been subscribed.[132] The prospect of implementing a major building program in the near future having receded, temporary repairs were carried out to the glass houses, including the insertion of timber props to prevent the walls from collapsing.[133] However, the general condition of the

125 *RDS Proc.*, lxxvii, appendix I, 5 Nov. 1840.   126 RDS Archive: Committee of Botany minute book 1834–45, 13 Apr. 1840.   127 *RDS Proc.*, lxxvi–lxxviii, curator's reports, 1840–2.   128 *RDS Proc.*, lxxvii, appendix II, 12 Nov. 1840.   129 RDS Archive: Council minute book 1838–44, 1 July 1841.   130 *RDS Proc.*, lxxviii, minutes, 10 Feb. 1842.   131 RDS Archive: Council minute book 1838–44, 14 Apr. 1842.   132 *RDS Proc.*, lxxix, minutes, 10 Nov. 1842.   133 Ibid., appendix I, 24

buildings was so bad that the council decided at the end of 1842 to renew its efforts to raise a reconstruction fund by private subscription.[134]

The society's art school survived the dispute with Dublin Castle in reasonably good shape, although it suffered a further loss of key staff during 1840–2, and the government proposal, endorsed by the vice-regal commission, to transfer its management to the Royal Hibernian Academy, placed a question mark over its future. Student enrollments fell to eighty-eight in 1840, but, remarkably, rose to 110 in 1841, and to 125 in 1842.[135] John Smyth, master of the sculpture and modeling school since 1811, died in 1840. His son, William Smyth, replaced him on a temporary basis, and was a candidate for the vacant post.[136] However, he was not on the short-list of candidates, and Constantine Panormo, a former prize-winning pupil, was appointed master in June 1840.[137] John Papworth, master of the architecture school, died in 1841 (as mentioned above), and pending the restoration of the government grant his replacement was deferred.[138] To avoid disruption to the pupils' studies, Joseph George O'Brien, an architectural draughtsman, was seconded from Frederick Darley's practice to take temporary charge for the remainder of the academic year 1841–2.[139] Thirteen candidates, including O'Brien, applied for the vacant post when it was advertised in 1842. O'Brien made the short-list, but the society's eventual choice was Duncan Campbell Ferguson, a former pupil, elected on 9 June 1842.[140]

In 1841 the council recommended that the art school students' exhibition be held in conjunction with the manufactures exhibition. The fine arts committee seized the opportunity to recommend that a retrospective exhibition of the works of distinguished former pupils be held at the same time. They supplied a list of seventy former pupils, mostly painters, whose work was of particular merit. The list included Martin Cregan, president of the Royal Hibernian Academy (and a member of the RDS fine arts committee 1834–54), and Sir Martin Archer Shee, president of the Royal Academy, London.[141] The ostensible reason for the exhibition was the centenary of the first distribution of art premiums in 1741, but Turpin points out that it was also a useful exercise in public relations at a time when the future of the school was under threat.[142] The joint exhibition took place with what appears to have been only moderate success, and the fine arts committee recommended that in future student prizes should consist of medals and books, and that money prizes should be discontinued.[143] The fine arts committee also wanted to revert to the former practice of publicising prize-winners names in the newspapers. The prize

Nov. 1842.   134 RDS Archive: Council minute book 1838–44, 15 Dec. 1842.   135 Willemson, *Students and award winners.*   136 *RDS Proc.*, lxxvi, minutes, 28 May 1840.   137 Ibid., 4 June 1840. 138 *RDS Proc.*, lxxviii, minutes, 4 Nov. 1841.   139 Turpin, *A school of art in Dublin*, p. 106. 140 *RDS Proc.*, lxxviii, minutes, 2, 9 June 1842.   141 *RDS Proc.*, lxxvii, minutes, 27 May 1841. 142 Turpin, *A school of art in Dublin*, pp. 118–19.   143 *RDS Proc.*, lxxviii, fine arts committee

categories showed that little change had taken place in the school curriculum since the early nineteenth century. The book prizes offered also showed that the society had not advanced much in artistic taste beyond Regency neo-classicism.[144] However, there were some straws in the wind indicative of a fresh approach towards the administration of the schools, and a wider acknowledgement of their importance to the community. During 1842 the zoological society, and the RHA, offered visitor privileges to prize-winning pupils. In November 1842 selected categories of pupils in the art school were admitted as readers to the RDS library, and the fine arts committee recommended that a formal prize-giving day be held at the end of the school-year.[145] A deputation from the council met with Lord de Grey, and secured his agreement to preside at the prize-giving meeting on 8 December 1842.[146]

Lord Morpeth's proposal to divide the RDS into distinct sections appealed especially to the scientists. Meenan and Clarke have noted an under-lying tension between the competing claims of science and agriculture at this period.[147] Committee rivalries aside, the prestige of science in the RDS rested to a great extent on the individual work of the professors, especially Kane and Davy, neither of whom seemed to have any problem in directing research towards the needs both of agriculture and of industry when required. During 1841 Kane published his *Elements of chemistry*, in three parts,[148] a work which rapidly became a best-selling standard textbook.[149] Kane was interested in the chemistry of plant products, and in 1841 he was awarded the gold medal of the Royal Society for his research on the colouring matters found in lichens. Meanwhile Davy was developing an interest in agricultural chemistry, and by 1840 was conducting regular analyses of soil types, and manures.[150] Kane replied to the congratulations of the society on his receiving the gold medal,

> It has always been my highest object to elevate the scientific character of the Society and of our country, by the cultivation of original research, calculated to extend our abstract knowledge by the discovery of new principles or laws, and to improve the practical Arts by perfecting the theories of the processes which they involve.[151]

Nevertheless, 1841 was the last year in which Kane devoted himself to pure research.[152] On 3 December 1840 the society introduced a requirement that each professor deliver two courses of lectures during each session, extending this to

report, 24 June 1841.   144 Turpin, *A school of art in Dublin*, pp. 118–20.   145 *RDS Proc.*, lxxix, fine arts committee report, 3 Nov. 1842.   146 RDS Archive: Council minute book 1838–44, 24 Nov. 1842.   147 Meenan and Clarke, *The Royal, Dublin Society 1731–1981*, p. 33.   148 *RDS Proc.*, lxxvii–lxxviii, appendix II, and minutes, 25 Feb., 11 Nov. 1841.   149 Mollan, Davis and Finucane, *Some people and places*, p. 25.   150 Denis Crowley, 'Chemistry', in Meenan and Clarke, *The Royal Dublin Society, 1731–1981*, pp. 172–4.   151 RDS Archive: Council minute book 1838–44, 16 Dec. 1841.   152 Mollan, Davis, Finucane, *Some people and places*, p. 25.

include attendance at, and the delivery of lectures to scientific meetings from 1842.[153] In the latter year the government granted an additional £300 per annum towards the costs of provincial lectures. The reason given by the treasury secretary E.C. Trevelyan was that 'the sums issued in each of the last three years to that Society, in furtherance of this object, have been productive of beneficial effects, and have given satisfaction so far as they have extended'.[154] Only one aspect of the society's science program, the work of the statistics committee, suffered directly from the withdrawal of the government grant in 1841. While discussions continued on the best means of introducing sections into the society, the statistics committee was allowed quietly to lapse at the end of 1841, no place having been found for it in the reorganized structures of sections and committees. Its work on local taxation had, in any event, been largely overtaken by the development of regular sources of statistical information reporting directly to the government.[155]

On the agriculture scene, the 1840 Spring Cattle Show was the most successful in the nine years since it had been established. Cattle, pig, and poultry exhibits reached record numbers, and cattle numbers in particular exceeded by a third the capacity of the shedding available, leading the agriculture committee to once more look for additional stabling. Only in the quality of working horses was disappointment expressed.[156] The allocation made by the society for agricultural purposes was £150, but the gate receipts at the 1840 Spring Cattle Show added a further £131 to total income. Expenses amounted to £256, leaving a surplus available to the committee of £25. 'The receipts, however, are at all times very fluctuating, and depend much on the weather at the time, and on the state of fullness or emptiness of the city'.[157] Realistically, the society subsidised the Spring Cattle Show to the amount of £125 in 1840. The agriculture committee was adamant that it did not wish to continue organising an autumn cattle show, which could only detract from the Spring Cattle Show, and which had shown a loss of £53 in 1839. The committee mustered the support of leading exhibitor/members, such as Robert Latouche, Arthur Pollock, William Filgate, and Thomas Lee-Norman, all agreed that it would be wiser for the society to concentrate its resources on developing the Spring Cattle Show.[158] The prize list for the 1841 Spring Cattle Show included additional premiums for butter classes, poultry breeding, and Scotch (probably Ayrshire) cattle.[159] An outbreak of pleuro-pneumonia ravaged cattle stocks in early 1841, and serious consideration was given to canceling the show because of the risk of cross-infection in the cattle-yard.[160] This epidemic was first reported in Ireland in

153 RDS Proc., lxxviii–lxxix, minutes, 30 June, 3 Dec. 1842.   154 RDS Proc., lxxviii, minutes, 28 Apr. 1842.   155 Webb, Modern England, pp. 260–1.   156 RDS Proc., lxxvi, agriculture committee report, 30 Apr. 1840.   157 RDS Archive: Council minute book 1838–44, agriculture committee report, 2 July 1840.   158 Ibid.   159 RDS Proc., lxxvii, appendix III, Spring Show prize list. 160 Denis Purdon, 'History of the society's shows', in Meenan and Clarke, The Royal Dublin

1839, having earlier been reported in Holland and Germany, and it continued to recur up to 1851. The newly introduced breeds, especially Devon cattle, were particularly susceptible, whereas native and acclimatized breeds (such as the ubiquitous Kerry cow) seemed to enjoy a comparative immunity.[161] In the event, the committee decided to proceed with the show, and noted that the standard of cattle exhibited, particularly the numerous native 'Black Cattle', seemed little affected by the disease. All other livestock categories, with the exception of horses, showed considerable improvement on the previous year. Agricultural implements, up to that point poorly represented at the Spring Cattle Show, showed an unexpected increase in numbers and quality in 1841.[162] The agriculture committee followed up this development with a request, agreed by the council in early 1842, to offer silver medal awards for inventions or improvements to agricultural implements;[163] a policy which was to be continued up to 1992.[164] About the same time the society agreed, on the motion of Dr Robert Collins, to allocate £265 for the erection of a double row of cattle sheds in the courtyard of Leinster House, to provide shelter for cattle exhibits.[165] As a result, all cattle exhibited at the 1842 show were sheltered from the weather.[166]

Adding to the survival problems of the RDS in 1841 was the establishment of a rival body in agricultural development work, the Agricultural Improvement Society of Ireland (later the Royal Agricultural Society of Ireland). The objects of the new body were to hold an annual provincial show, aid local agricultural societies, establish an agricultural museum, library, and college, disseminate information on good farming practices, and improve the standards of farm labourers' housing. None of these objects threatened the viability of the Spring Cattle Show, but they did have implications for the broader work of the RDS in agriculture. In practice, the RDS conceded some of its agricultural work to the AIS, thereby freeing more resources for science.[167] Simon Curran points out that for over forty years the AIS relieved the RDS of much of the burden of agricultural development work. It employed itinerant instructors, encouraged drainage and reclamation, stimulated improvements to farm homesteads and labourers' cottages, and assisted the development of agricultural shows. Albeit uneven and limited in effectiveness, these projects had formerly been preoccupations of the RDS.[168]

The AIS could trace its lineage from the Farming Society of Ireland, through the exhibitors' committees formed at the early Spring Cattle Shows, and an earlier, unsuccessful, agricultural improvement society which was the brain-

Society, 1731–1981, p. 104.   **161** John O'Donovan, *The economic history of livestock in Ireland* (Dublin, 1940), pp. 168–9. Hereafter, O'Donovan, *The economic history of livestock*.   **162** *RDS Proc.*, lxxvii, agriculture committee report, 29 Apr. 1841.   **163** RDS Archive: Council minute book 1838–44, 13 Jan. 1842.   **164** *RDS Spring Show Catalogue 1992* (Dublin, 1992). This was the last general Spring Show and industries fair held on the Ballsbridge premises.   **165** *RDS Proc.*, lxxviii, minutes, 27 Jan., 24 Feb. 1842.   **166** Ibid., 28 Apr. 1842.   **167** Meenan and Clarke, *The Royal Dublin Society, 1731–1981*, pp. 33–4.   **168** Simon Curran, 'The society's role in agriculture since

child of James Naper and C.W. Hamilton in 1833. The scheme for the creation of a new agricultural improvement society was launched at a public meeting at the Royal Exchange, Dublin, in February 1841. It had the support of many prominent RDS members and exhibitors, including Sir Percy Nugent, Thomas Lee-Norman, Arthur Pollock, and David Sherrard.[169] A prime mover in the establishment of the new body was Peter Purcell, of Halverston, Co. Kildare, appointed its first honorary secretary. Parliamentary supporters included John O'Connell and Robert Hutton.[170] The lord lieutenant, Lord Ebrington, also supported the new society with a personal donation of £200.[171]

Peter Purcell had been elected a member of the RDS on 5 November 1840.[172] A landowner, he was also the publisher of a Dublin liberal journal, *The Monitor*, which he founded in 1838. In the same year he joined Daniel O'Connell's Precursor Society (predecessor of the Loyal National Repeal Association). He was expelled in January 1839 for disclosing in an acrimonious and public debate that O'Connell had lodged the funds of the Precursor Society to his personal account in the National Bank, Tralee, instead of appointing public treasurers as Purcell had urged. No evidence of misuse of funds was discovered, O'Connell looked for an apology, and the incident strained relations between Purcell and O'Connell to the breaking point.[173] Subsequently, O'Connell and his partisans saw no merit in the AIS. The pages of *The Pilot* were used to call on the AIS to advocate rent reductions during the agricultural depression of 1842, and condemned it for failing to do so. O'Connell appears also to have toyed with the notion of embarrassing the catholic Purcell with accusations of AIS sectarianism. In a letter to Richard Barrett, dated 5 December 1842, O'Connell asked 'Have you observed how exactly suited Peter Purcell's Agricultural Society is to enable the landlords to combine together for the exclusion of Catholic tenants?'.[174]

Despite its critics (the *Freeman's Journal* also had reservations about its membership and objects), the AIS was formally established on 5 April 1841. Peter Purcell was asked to continue as honorary secretary; discussion of political matters was prohibited, and a considerable cross-membership with the RDS was noted.[175] The RDS showed considerable wisdom in its dealings with the nascent AIS and later managed to avoid conflicts between the two bodies. As early as March 1841 it passed a resolution, 'That this Society is ready and willing to give such aid and cooperation, as its means and premises afford, to the New Agricultural Improvement Society, should the same be required'.[176] In June 1841 the AIS appointed Edward Bullen as a paid secretary, and decided to defer its first show until 1842.[177] A meeting between representatives of the two bodies

1800', in Meenan and Clarke, *The Royal Dublin Society, 1731-1981*, p. 91. **169** *Freeman's Journal*, 16 Feb. 1841. **170** Ibid., 19 Feb. 1841. **171** Ibid., 19 Mar. 1841. **172** *RDS Proc.*, lxxvii, minutes, 5 Nov. 1840. **173** O'Connell, *Correspondence*, vi, 2582. **174** O'Connell, *Correspondence*, vii, 2988. **175** RDS Archive: R.A.S.I. council minute book 1841-46, 5, 8 Apr. 1841. **176** *RDS Proc.*, lxxvii, minutes, 25 Mar. 1841. **177** RDS Archive: R.A.S.I. council minute book 1841-46, 3 June 1841.

took place on 30 October 1841.[178] Following a second meeting, the AIS requested the RDS to give them facilities in 1842 to mount a cattle show in the court-yard of Leinster House, and install agricultural exhibits and an agricultural museum in the long gallery above the stable range. The RDS agriculture committee responded by recommending April as the best month to hold a cattle show, and offering to cancel the Spring Cattle Show to facilitate the AIS. The society agreed to these arrangements, including the cancellation of the Spring Cattle Show.[179] The AIS must have been taken by surprise at this generous gesture, especially the cancellation of an established national show of proven benefit to many of its own members, for the sake of an untested project. On 22 November 1841 it resolved that it had, after all, no desire to compete with the Spring Cattle Show.[180] The RDS was informed that the AIS had decided to hold its show in the autumn.[181] In the event it held its first show at the Cornmarket in Cork on 20–2 July 1842.[182]

From its foundation, the AIS seems to have been considered, at least by the RDS as one of those smaller bodies which might usefully merge with the RDS. The AIS could see no advantage to a merger, but suggested the RDS might offer them administrative accommodation, and a share of the subscriptions of its agricultural associate members. The RDS found this suggestion too one-sided and outside the scope of the government's recommendations. James Naper moved that the RDS should enter into discussions with the AIS on this topic, but was defeated 22:20, and there the matter rested for the time being.[183] In October 1842 the RDS council issued a prospectus for the formation of an agricultural museum, thus pre-empting an early object of its would-be junior partner.[184]

By the end of 1842 the RDS was well on the way to recovery from the disruptions of 1841, and was showing signs of renewed confidence about its place in the educational and economic life of the country. The abolition of the newspaper room may have had some impact on the recruitment of new members, which did not recover to 1839 levels until the 1850s, but it seems probable that uncertainty about the intentions of the government were of far greater import. The society might have been wound up, or broken up, if the Whig-liberals had continued in office, and was fortunate to be given a respite from government interference during the Tory-conservative administration of 1841–6. In the meantime it was able to develop a more confident view of itself as a genuinely national institution, a perception of its place in the life of the community which was also slowly gaining a measure of public support.

---

178 RDS Archive: Council minute book 1838–44, 28 Oct. 1841.   179 *RDS Proc.*, lxxviii, minutes, 11, 18 Nov. 1841.   180 RDS Archive: R.A.S.I. council minute book 1841–46, 22 Nov. 1841. 181 *RDS Proc.*, lxxviii, minutes, 2 Dec. 1841.   182 RDS Archive: R.A.S.I. council minute book 1841–46, 20 July 1842.   183 *RDS Proc.* Lxxviii, minutes, 28 Apr. 1842.   184 RDS Archive: Council minute book 1838–44, 20 Oct. 1842.

As to the winners and losers in the newspaper crisis, it could be argued that the RDS had gained a tactical victory. It was forced to concede the abolition of the newspaper room, and its building projects were brought to a temporary halt. Nevertheless the principal government proposals, the appointment of a court of visitors, the transfer of the art school to the RHA, and the division of the society into autonomous sections, were all quietly dropped. Over and above this the annual grant for science was increased and government control of the minutiae of expenditure was relaxed. Nevertheless the thrust of government strategy, to make the RDS more accountable to the Irish executive, continued.

CHAPTER EIGHT

Epilogue: 1843–5 and after

At the beginning of 1843 the RDS had reason to hope that its building program would receive parliamentary support. Dublin Castle informed the society that the society's memorial to the treasury had been forwarded to London by the lord lieutenant, with his strong recommendation that it be viewed favourably.[1] The memorial requested that the treasury treat the society with 'the same judicious and increasing liberality which has characterized its recent Grants to the British Museum'. It referred to the recommendation of the parliamentary committee of 1836 that £3,000 be allocated to the building of a museum. Since 1839 the RDS had entered into contracts totaling £4,000 to build a museum, and to extend the library, intending to draw on a reserve fund created from its members subscriptions. However,

> the fiscal resources applicable to this object had been seriously deranged, by the steps taken against the Society, by Her Majesty's Government in Ireland, in the year 1840, followed up by the severe and extreme measure, of totally withdrawing the Parliamentary Grant in the following year.
> … added to which, the Society have been coerced by the Report of the Parliamentary Committee, to abandon a very important inducement to public favour and support in the advantages hitherto offered by its Newspaper Room.[2]

In less than a fortnight the lord lieutenant dashed the society's hopes. In a letter of 17 January 1843 he wrote 'I feel it my duty to apprize you, that the answer I received the night before last, is not favourable'.

> I was aware, when I forwarded the Memorial, that the present state of the National Finances might interpose an obstacle, but I should delude the Society, if I were to assign that, as the only motive which appears to influence the Government.[3]

---

1 *RDS Proc.*, lxxix, council minutes, 5 Jan. 1843.   2 Ibid., minutes, 26 Jan. 1843.   3 Ibid.

The lord lieutenant's letter was followed on 20 January by a letter from Sir George Clark, secretary to the treasury, confirming that the request for a capital grant had been rejected. Sir George wrote 'my Lords feel themselves bound to have reference to the state and prospects of the Society, and their probable means, if so large an outlay of public money be authorized, of rendering it beneficial to the public'. A further consideration was the inability of the treasury to meet the demands that might be placed upon it by similar bodies throughout the United Kingdom. Regarding the fall in RDS membership subscriptions, he ignored the society's complaint of government culpability, and identified the cause as lack of public interest.

> My Lords cannot but view this as an indication of the little interest which the educated portion of Society in Dublin, compared with that of other great towns, take in the support of the objects of such an Institution.[4]

Sir George concluded his letter of refusal with what he may have regarded as two compelling arguments. The first, which is necessarily a consideration for the state in a situation of public-private partnership, was that the society would be unable to fund the on-going maintenance costs of such a large-scale investment and responsibility would therefore fall back on the government. The second was that the society had acted unilaterally in engaging in building contracts, and had never received the sanction of the treasury.[5]

The society replied to Sir George Clark by letter of 9 February 1843. It rejected the claims of supposed competitors for government support, unless, like the RDS, 'they can point to a Parliamentary origin, for the objects requiring support, and can rest their claims upon the Report of a Select Committee of the House of Commons'.[6] The society insisted that the decline in its recruitment of members

> [was] properly referable to the proceedings taken against the Society by Her Majesty's late Government in Ireland, whereby public confidence in the stability of the Institution was weakened, and which confidence could not be expected to revive, until the restoration of the Grant, towards the close of the Session of 1842.[7]

The society pointed out that during the early years of its existence it had relied entirely on its own resources, 'accommodating its pursuits to its means'. From 1761 onwards the Irish parliament had 'adopted the Society as a suitable instrument for promoting the national improvement'. From that point

---

4 Ibid.   5 Ibid.   6 *RDS Proc.*, lxxix, minutes, 9 Feb. 1843.   7 Ibid.

The foundation of the Society's Parliamentary support was now laid; and henceforward we find new duties, new obligations, and with them, new establishments, superinduced upon the original and limited objects of the Society, by the Irish Parliament, which supplied liberal funds for their support.[8]

By the end of the eighteenth-century the society had taken on its familiar role as the trustee and manager of a cluster of educational institutions, 'and thus the Society was moulded by the very hand of the Legislature, into that form it now retains'. These joint foundations were entrusted to the care of the RDS, 'but the state retained the obligation of maintaining what it had created'. Finally, the society argued,

> The contributions of Members and private individuals, though liberal, were merely auxiliary; unimportant as a source of permanent support; formed no element in the estimated expenses annually laid before Parliament; and, although they have always been, and continue to be, expended in subservience to the main objects of the Institution, it is remarkable, that they have been ever found to fluctuate in proportion to the confidence entertained in the continuance of Government support.[9]

At the end of March, the new treasury secretary, E.C. Trevelyan, wrote advising the society that the treasury had not changed its mind, and that the RDS request for a supplementary grant was rejected.[10] The *Freeman's Journal* attacked the government for its niggardly treatment of the RDS, seeing in it an expression of a general attitude of neglect of Irish institutions. Contrasting the government's treatment of the British Museum with its treatment of the Royal Dublin Society, the newspaper claimed that over the previous two years the former had been given £173,000 in public funds, while the latter had received only £11,000. The newspaper was particularly annoyed at the government's refusal to support developments in the RDS botanic garden, 'the finest botanic garden in Europe'.[11]

Accepting that no additional funds would be forthcoming in 1843, the RDS cast about for plans to reduce current spending. A suggestion by Joshua Abell that the society's proceedings be printed in a new journal he was launching was politely declined.[12] Nevertheless, the honorary secretaries were asked to consider means of shortening the minutes to effect economies in printing.[13] A rates demand from Dublin Corporation was held in abeyance, to give time to consider whether or not the new borough rate was applicable to the society's headquarters.[14]

8 Ibid   9 Ibid.   10 *RDS Proc.*, lxxix, minutes, 30 Mar. 1843.   11 *Freeman's Journal*, 21 Mar. 1843.   12 *RDS Proc.*, lxxix, council minutes, 28 Feb., 9 Mar. 1843.   13 Ibid., 16 Mar. 1843. 14 Ibid., 9 Mar. 1843.   15 Ibid., minutes, 22 Dec. 1842.   16 Ibid., council minutes, 12, 19 Jan.

While these attempts to curtail spending were going on the society was alarmed by a grandiose scheme to circumvent government parsimony in the development of the Kildare Street premises. The scheme was first signaled at the end of 1842 in newspaper advertisements, giving notice 'respecting the intended application to Parliament, for an Act enabling the Royal Dublin Society, and other parties, to sell certain part of these Premises, and for other purposes'. Knowing nothing about the origin of these advertisements, or the identities or intentions of the 'other parties', a furious RDS resolved 'That the answer to be given to the notices in question be – the Dissent of the Society'.[15] The identity of the 'other parties' was disclosed when William Eliot Hudson asked for and was accorded two lengthy meetings with the council in January 1843, at which he explained the purposes of the proposed bill. In essence, Hudson was proposing to obtain private investor capital to erect a large concert hall on part of Leinster Lawn, with facilities for a national museum attached.[16] Hudson, a scholar of Irish music and antiquities, and a friend of Thomas Davis', was elected a life member of the society in 1840. At the time the newspaper advertisements appeared, he had placed a motion before the RDS general meeting (see p. 196) urging the society to develop a national museum and library modeled on the British Museum. The council gave Hudson's scheme a courteous hearing, but recommended that it be opposed, as it would 'have the effect of depriving the Society of a portion of its property, and applying it to purposes [music concerts] distinct from those for which the Society was instituted'.[17] As mentioned previously, the council may have been apprehensive not just of the scale of the plan, but of its inherent potential for further conflict with the government, since it required what the society had long sought and been denied, that is, parity of treatment with the British Museum. By that stage, however, the bill was already believed to be in course of preparation. At a general meeting of the society on 2 March 1843 a petition was prepared opposing the bill. Edward Grogan, MP for Dublin city and a member of the society, was asked to present the petition to the house of commons. G.A. Hamilton, Thomas Edward Taylor, and W.H. Gregory, all Tory-conservative MPs, and none at that time members of the RDS, attended the general meeting by invitation, and offered to support the petition.[18] Grogan and his allies wrote to the council later in March to report that the 'Leinster Lawn Improvement Bill' had not been properly prepared and had been rejected on those grounds, and there the matter ended.[19]

Prompting Hudson's solo scheme was the patent inability of the RDS to finance the expansion of its activities, or to develop its assets from its own resources. The society's reliance on patient lobbying of the government was not to the taste of enthusiastic and impatient members such as Hudson. A second

1843.   17 Ibid., 28 Feb. 1843.   18 Ibid., minutes, 2 Mar. 1843.   19 Ibid., 30 Mar. 1843.

instance of this type of problem occurred early in 1843, leading to a rift between some of the chief exponents of agricultural development, and causing public embarrassment to the society. By January 1843 the agriculture museum had been readied to receive exhibits, and required only a curator to take charge of its operation.[20] Invited to suggest means to raise funds to pay a curator's salary, the agriculture committee recommended placing a levy on exhibits. The council opposed the notion of a levy, and recommended instead the payment of a salary of £50 per annum, but without offering an opinion as to how this sum might be raised.[21] While the agriculture museum continued to lie idle, the agriculture committee held its most successful Spring Cattle Show to date.

The agriculture committee reported that the show took place during 18–20 April 1843, and presented a marked improvement in livestock exhibits. Robert Archbold, MP, a member of the society, acted as chief cattle judge for cattle classes totaling 125 animals. The pig classes attracted considerable attention as the main exhibits featured a successful new variety of Irish pig derived from a cross of the old variety with Berkshire, Yorkshire, and Chinese Brawn types. A decided improvement was also noted in the working horses exhibited, and in the display of agricultural implements.[22] Agricultural draught horses were not in general use in Ireland at this period; a multi-purpose animal being preferred for economic reasons.[23] An increase in the numbers of visitors attending the show was noted, and is included in the ten-year table 8.1 below.[24]

Table 8.1 Spring Cattle Show visitor numbers, 1836–45

1836	1,760	1841	4,063
1837	1,195	1842	3,643
1838	1,963	1843	4,227
1839	2,353	1844	4,760
1840	2,633	1845	7,094

The committee's report concluded with a condemnation of 'the injurious imputation lately made by a Member of this Society, in the newspapers, to the effect, that they [the agriculture committee] did not sufficiently exert themselves in disseminating the knowledge of Husbandry'. This was followed up at the meeting by a notice of motion from Henry Carey,

> That this Society have witnessed, with great concern, the recent attempt made by a Vice-President and a noble Member, to injure and disparage the Society, through the medium of the public press.[25]

20 Ibid., 26 Jan. 1843.   21 Ibid., council report, 2 Mar. 1843.   22 *Freeman's Journal*, 21 Apr. 1843.
23 O'Donovan, *The economic history of livestock in Ireland*, pp. 199–200.   24 *RDS Proc.*, lxxix, agriculture committee report, 27 Apr. 1843 and later reports.   25 Ibid., minutes.

The cause of this public row was a letter written to the *Dublin Evening Mail* and published on 14 April 1843. It was signed by the duke of Leinster, and by James Naper, a vice-president, and was copied in the columns of the *Freeman's Journal* of the following morning. Written by Naper, and dated 29 March 1843, the letter was addressed to the council and the members of the Royal Dublin Society, and endorsed a criticism of the society made in the treasury letter of 20 January 1843 (see above). In particular, it accused the society of failing to engage the interest of the educated classes. It argued that the reason for this was the poor judgement displayed by the society in the application of its annual grant. The bulk of its funds were directed towards the maintenance of its longer established activities, and very little funding was made available for newer programs. As a result many potential members of the RDS had found other avenues to explore their interests. Taking the example of agriculture, Naper estimated that the net amount of the government grant applied to agricultural purposes, after allowing for Spring Show receipts, was £90 per annum. This was paltry in the context of the relative importance of agriculture in the Irish economy,

> And it is owing to this apathy on the part of the Royal Dublin Society towards that which was the leading object of its original establishment, that we have seen the rise of an agricultural society [the Agricultural Improvement Society of Ireland], which within two years of its formation already numbers 562 members, including donors and subscribers, eighty-five of whom are also members of the Royal Dublin Society.

Naper observed that he, and the duke of Leinster, had been deterred by the rigidity of the rules from putting a case directly to the general meeting of the society, and in frustration had decided to use a more public forum. Their object was to stimulate discussion amongst the membership, and obtain the support of like-minded members.[26] There must have been some broader support or sympathy for Naper's action, as Henry Carey was persuaded to withdraw his motion of censure.[27] Naper was not re-elected a vice-president in November 1843, but remained a regular exhibitor of cattle at RDS agricultural shows during the 1840s and 1850s. Over twenty years after this incident, he was elected a member of the agriculture committee on 1 December 1864.[28]

Internal wrangling amongst the RDS membership did nothing to alleviate the pressing problems of inadequate or dilapidated accommodation. In its memorial to the treasury the society had drawn particular attention to the plight of the botanic garden. Under the management of David Moore, the gardens had reached a peak of attractiveness and popularity, with 31,661 public visitors in

26 *Freeman's Journal*, 15 Apr. 1843.   27 *RDS Proc.*, lxxix, minutes, 25 May 1843.   28 *RDS Proc.*, ci, minutes, 1 Dec. 1864.

1842. However, the conservatories and other original buildings were in such bad state of repair as to require complete replacement. In his report of 21 January 1842, Jacob Owen, architect to the board of works, had concluded that the professor's house, the lecture room, the labourers' accommodation, and the conservatories, were in such an advanced state of decay as to be largely beyond recovery.[29] To add to the woes of the botany committee, the best maintained of the newer buildings, the octagon house, caught fire in May 1843, and was only saved from serious damage by the prompt action of the staff.[30] The condition of the lecture room was so dangerous that the botany committee was given permission to transfer Samuel Litton's lecture courses temporarily to the theatre in Kildare Street.[31] At the beginning of June 1843 the botany committee submitted plans and elevations prepared by Duncan Ferguson for a new 'wrought iron curvilinear Conservatory, to be heated by Hippocaust', which for the time being would remain a pipedream.[32]

The art school was experiencing a different type of accommodation problem. The fine arts committee complained that 'the Schools of the Society have never been so full at any former period, and that the applications for admission are far more numerous than the vacancies, or than the accommodation in the Schools will admit of'.[33] Despite the capacity constraint, the schools admitted 162 students in 1843.[34]

The manufactures committee, with no exhibition in hand in early 1843, took a new direction by honouring an individual Irish *entrepreneur*. The RDS general meeting agreed on 30 March 1843 that the manufactures committee should award a silver medal to James Fagan, for 'establishing a dock-yard at Kingstown, and in building a new ship to be called the *Duchess of Leinster*'.[35] This was a retrospective approval, as the committee had, on its own initiative, already presented the medal on 21 March. Such a breach of procedures required an explanation, which was supplied to the council by Sir Edward Stanley. Sir Edward reported that the committee had acted in the belief that had time been available, the approval of the council and the general meeting would have been forthcoming. However, with only four days to go before the ship launch, the committee had decided,

> being perfectly convinced of the very important advantage which it must be to this country, and particularly to Dublin, to encourage here ship-building in all its branches, we unanimously resolve, that the large Silver Medal of the Society, with an honorary certificate, be presented to Mr Fagan, in testimony of our approbation of his work ...[36]

---

29 *RDS Proc.*, lxxix, minutes, 26 Jan. 1843.   **30** Ibid., council minutes, 4 May 1843.   **31** Ibid., 11, 24 May 1843.   **32** Ibid., botany committee report, 1 June 1843.   **33** Ibid., fine arts committee report, 23 Feb. 1843.   **34** Willemson, *Students and award winners, 1746-1876.*   **35** *RDS Proc.*, lxxix, minutes, 30 Mar. 1843.   **36** Ibid., council minutes, 23, 28 Mar. 1843.

Sir Edward Stanley's judgement was sound. Not only did the society approve of his committee's initiative, the publicity surrounding the ship launch also reflected favourably on the society. The launching of a new ship from a Dublin yard, something that had not occurred for many years, aroused considerable public interest. A large crowd gathered in the harbour area several hours before the launch time of two o'clock in the afternoon of 21 March. The band of the 5th dragoon guards provided music from the deck of a new trawler anchored nearby. The guests of honour at the ceremony were the duke and duchess of Leinster, and other notable figures attending included Daniel O'Connell, MP, Lord Kildare, Baron de Robeck, and General Sir John Burgoyne. Shortly before the launch took place Sir Edward Stanley and a deputation from the RDS manufactures committee moved to the front of the platform and presented the society's silver medal to James Fagan. Sir Edward offered the congratulations of the society to Fagan, and read the resolution passed by the manufactures committee on 17 March. Shortly afterwards the launching of the brig took place,

> The bands struck up the national anthem – every hat waved in the air – the billows opened to receive their mistress, and, amidst the roar of cannon and the enthusiastic shouts of the assemblage, echoed back in softened accents from the tens of thousands assembled on the opposite pier, the noble creation of human genius, waving her banners in the breeze, plunged into the world of waters, henceforth to be her home.[37]

That Daniel O'Connell could find the time in early 1843 to attend the launch was as sure an indication of its perceived national significance as the awarding of an RDS medal. O'Connell had decided that 1843 would be the repeal year. As in the past, he seemed unable to set out clearly what repeal meant, and his unrealistic pronouncements alienated public opinion in Britain, as also amongst the majority of Irish protestants and large numbers of middle-class Irish catholics. His new campaign rapidly assumed a confessional hue, with its main support coming from the mass of Irish catholics and clergy.[38] Influenced by the success of Fr Mathew's temperance rallies, O'Connell expressed the strength of the repeal movement through the convening of 'monster' public meetings. The first of these was held in Trim, Co. Meath, in March 1843. Between March and October about forty meetings were held around the regions. The largest was the Tara meeting, which was believed to have attracted an attendance of three-quarters of a million people, on 15 August 1843. As his support grew, O'Connell's speeches became more militant and menacing. His intention appeared to be to force Peel's government into granting concessions through the force of massed public opinion, and in order, as in 1829, to avoid the prospect of civil war.[39]

37 *Freeman's Journal*, 22 Mar. 1843.   38 Hoppen, *Ireland since 1800*, pp. 30–2.   39 McCartney, *The dawning of democracy*, pp. 152–7.

O'Connell almost invariably used the network of Roman Catholic parish priests as his local organizers for the reconstituted repeal movement. Perhaps as a result, the monster meetings were held in a disciplined and sober manner, which served only to frighten opponents. By May 1843 the lord lieutenant, de Grey, was panicking, alarmed at the growing adhesion of clerical support for repeal.[40] In 1843–4, twelve of the twenty-seven member Roman Catholic hierarchy in Ireland, led by Archbishop John MacHale of Tuam, publicly supported O'Connell's repeal campaign. Only Archbishop Murray of Dublin stood out as an opponent of the movement.[41] Murray's opposition was low-key, but he managed adroitly to avoid being inveigled by O'Connell into authorising a novena of prayer for repeal in September 1843.[42]

Earl de Grey removed known repealers from the magistracy in mid-May 1843. This led to protest resignations by prominent liberals such as Lord Cloncurry, and Henry Grattan junior.[43] William Smith O'Brien, who had held himself aloof from the repeal movement in 1840–2, moved closer to O'Connell when he resigned the magistracy in protest at de Grey's policy.[44] Sir Colman O'Loghlen, a moderate liberal (son of Sir Michael O'Loghlen), was so outraged by the government's decision that he joined the repeal association,[45] a step also taken by W.S. O'Brien in October 1843.[46]

An incidental casualty of the public excitement caused by the repeal agitation was an exhibition of George Catlin's paintings, scheduled to be held in the RDS art school gallery in the autumn of 1843. Catlin travelled the North American plains in the 1830s and 1840s, producing remarkable contemporary portraits of frontiersmen and indigenous tribes, and depicting in faithful detail the tribal way of life.[47] He toured Europe with his collection, and on 29 June 1843 was given permission by the RDS to hold an exhibition for up to three months, commencing in the autumn. His permission was conditional on his reimbursing the society for any direct costs incurred, and allowing free access for the society's members and students.[48] By September the repeal agitation had reached a peak, with preparations and counter-preparations in train for a monster meeting in Clontarf. Catlin prudently made alternative arrangements, and decided, with some regrets, to cancel his exhibition, by letter of 20 October.

> Since I acknowledged the receipt of your letter, and the very kind offer of the use of the new Gallery, by the officers of your noble institution, I have been constantly in doubt as to the propriety of bringing my collection to Dublin, under the alarming appearances of the Repeal excitement, and

40 MacDonagh, *The emancipist*, pp. 223–32.   41 Kerr, *Peel, priests and politics*, pp. 7–27.
42 MacDonagh, *The emancipist*, p. 237.   43 Ibid., p. 233.   44 Davis, *Revolutionary imperialist*, pp. 145–9.   45 Nowlan, *The politics of repeal*, p. 46.   46 Davis, *Revolutionary imperialist*, pp. 157–8.
47 See for example, Geoffrey C. Ward, *The west: an illustrated history* (London, 1996), pp. 70, 79.
48 *RDS Proc.*, lxxix, minutes, 29 June 1843.

have consequently made such other arrangements for its exhibition, as will now prevent me from occupying the rooms thus offered to me. From the turn that the Repeal business has now taken, I am led very much to regret, that I am not on the ground, for I am led to believe that Dublin will be very full of strangers and of fashion at this time. This I cannot now help, and at the same time please to inform the Board, and tender to them the continuance of my thanks for their very kind offer made to me.[49]

The RDS was otherwise uninvolved in the political skirmishes of 1843. When the help of parliamentarians was needed to block Hudson's Leinster Lawn bill, the society turned to conservative supporters of the incumbent administration. The choice was limited, as of only ten MPs who were also members of the RDS in early 1843 seven were liberals or liberal-repealers.[50] In practice the society's choice of a champion was limited to Edward Grogan, as the two other conservatives were based in Ulster and not readily accessible for consultation. Grogan was an MP for Dublin city from 1841 to 1865, and a dull man, lacking in charisma, who did little to inspire support for conservatism in Dublin.[51] He had been elected a life member of the RDS on 23 February 1843. During the course of 1843 three more conservative MPs joined the society, bringing the total to thirteen, and the conservative component to six. The three were T.E. Taylor of Ardgillan Castle, C.P. Leslie of Glaslough, and Thomas Vesey, later Lord de Vesci.[52]

At the beginning of 1843 total ordinary membership of the RDS amounted to 679, and had remained relatively static since 1840. During 1840–2 sixty-seven new members had been elected, and sixty-one old members deleted. In the course of 1843 twenty-seven new members joined, giving a net increase for that year of fifteen members. Approximately one-half of the 1843 intake was from the substantial landowning class.[53] By early 1843, only one candidate, Henry Chinnery Justice, a barrister, had applied for election in the non-voting associate sectional category of membership. Described as having an interest in both arts and agriculture, HC Justice was admitted as a sectional member in 1843, but opted to become a full life member in 1844.[54]

The sectional membership scheme did not to have the public appeal that Dublin Castle had presumed. The chemistry, and natural philosophy committees recommended in early 1844 that occasional sectional meetings should be convened, at which the professors should be present in an *ex officio* capacity, and 'where subjects connected with the business of each Section should be brought forward, and discussion thereon invited'.[55] By early 1844, only two sectional

49 Ibid., council minutes, 26 Oct. 1843.   50 Walker, *Parliamentary election results*; and author's database.   51 Hoppen, *Elections, politics, and society*, pp. 80, 304.   52 Walker, *Parliamentary election results*; and author's database.   53 Author's database.   54 *RDS Proc.*, lxxix–lxxx, May 1843, February 1844.   55 *RDS Proc.*, lxxx, council minutes, 11 Jan. 1844.

members had been elected and the joint committees could see no sensible way of organising meetings for such small numbers.[56] Once again Dr Robert Kane came to the rescue, and at his suggestion so-called 'sectional' meetings, open to the wider interested public, were held at regular intervals during May-June 1844. They amounted, in practice, to an additional series of public science lectures, and were an outstanding success. Lecturers included John Duffy, Thomas Grubb, Edward Clibborn, and Thomas Antisell. Antisell's paper on rock and soil analysis proved particularly popular, and was published as an appendix to the proceedings.[57]

So satisfactory were the lecture programs generally that the council had been encouraged into an analysis of their popularity, as a guide to future planning. The door porters were ordered to keep an exact account of the numbers attending each lecture, and provide regular returns to the registrar.[58] Letters were received from the Limerick philosophical and literary institution, and from the Royal Cork Institution, thanking the society for sending lecturers to those cities.[59] In Dublin, Robert Kane's lectures on the industrial resources of Ireland were attracting so much public interest that the society considered publishing them in book form.[60] Kane had become a celebrity, and a source of pride to the society. There was some public disquiet, reflected in the pages of the *Freeman's Journal*, when Kane was excluded, because of his catholicism, for consideration by Dublin University as a replacement professor of chemistry. Due to Kane's apparent indifference the controversy did not develop further, but it was a temporary source of embarrassment to TCD, and of plaudits for the RDS.[61] Kane attended the BAAS conference at Cork in August 1843, and afterwards delivered a lecture course in Limerick.[62] Back in Dublin, he delivered an expanded course of lectures on the subject of Irish industrial resources, in early 1844, and the society decided to proceed with publication.[63] Kane wished to retain copyright on his work, and, showing an equal confidence in its likely popularity, Hodges and Smith agreed to publish in consideration for a minimum guarantee from the RDS.[64] Around the same time the treasury finally authorized an increase in Kane's salary to £150 per annum, and at the general meeting on 30 May 1844 Henry Kemmis and Isaac Weld proposed Kane for honorary membership of the society.[65] Kane presented a copy of the *Industrial resources of Ireland* to the society on 6 June 1844, acknowledging that 'This work has been in great part called into existence by the desire expressed by the Society that the lectures recently delivered by me in their Theatre, should be published'.[66] The book was well received by the reading public, and was given enthusiastic support by Thomas Davis and his allies.[67]

---

56 Ibid., report, 25 Jan. 1844.   57 Ibid., 6 June 1844.   58 *RDS Proc.*, lxxix, council minutes, 5 Jan. 1843.   59 Ibid., minutes, 26 Jan. 1843.   60 Ibid., 29 June 1843.   61 *Freeman's Journal*, 20 Mar. 1843.   62 *RDS Proc.*, lxxix, council minutes, 10 Aug. 1843.   63 *RDS Proc.*, lxxx, council minutes, 14 Mar. 1844.   64 Ibid., natural philosophy committee report, 21 Mar. 1844.   65 Ibid., minutes, 28 Mar., 30 May 1844.   66 Ibid., 6 June 1844.   67 Molony, *A soul came into Ireland*, p. 244.

The RDS was proud of Kane's achievements, and in its support for him might well have been accused of displaying some insensitivity towards the feelings of its other science professors. The agriculture committee invited Kane to lecture on agricultural science at the 1844 Spring Cattle Show. The committee also urged the society to focus more attention on this subject, and to appoint an agricultural chemist.[68] Acting on this report, the council recommended that Dr Kane be requested to take on the additional duties of agricultural chemist.[69] Dr Edmund Davy, the incumbent professor of chemistry, protested this recommendation. Davy claimed, not unreasonably, that he had been carrying out the work of an agricultural chemist as a routine part of his duties.

> Those services, though humble, and not at any time brought prominently before you, have not failed, I trust, to produce beneficial effects; and will serve at least to shew, that I have not been unmindful of the duties of Agricultural Chemist, which has ever been attached to your Professorship of Chemistry.

Dr William Harty supported Davy, and gave notice of a motion that it would be inexpedient to separate the duties of agricultural chemist from those of professor of chemistry.[70] The resulting impasse, which might have developed into a major row, was resolved by the prompt action of Kane himself. On 6 May 1844 he wrote to the council declining the post.[71] His letter amounted to a direct support of Davy's position.

> If the performance of new duties regarded only an increase of my personal exertions for the benefit of the Society, I should gladly undertake them, but it would appear, on considering the extensive range of important subjects which the functions of Agricultural Chemist, if properly discharged, should embrace, that it would be impossible for me to enter upon their performance without trespassing upon the scientific territories of certain of my colleagues, the sacredness of possession of which I have no desire to violate.[72]

While Davy battled to protect his position Dr John Scouler, in charge of the museum, seized the opportunity to look for an increase in salary. His case was that he was really doing two jobs, that of curator of the museum, and that of professor of mineralogy, and all for a salary of £150 per annum. He complained also that an increasing burden of work prevented him from supplementing his salary.

68 RDS Proc., lxxx, agriculture committee report, 7 Mar. 1844.   69 Ibid., council minutes, 4 Apr. 1844.   70 Ibid., minutes, 25 Apr. 1844.   71 Ibid., council minutes, 9 May 1844.   72 Ibid., minutes, 30 May 1844.

Under these circumstances I need only add, that the small sum which I
receive from the Royal Dublin Society has always been inadequate to the
indispensable exigencies of my situation, the deficiency being supplied
from my own personal resources. Even these considerations should not
have induced me to trouble the Council, but recent arrangements on the
part of the Royal Dublin Society induce me to submit my claims, especially as in my capacity of Professor, the usual amount of labour devolves
on me, while in addition, the charge of the Museum excludes me from
occupying my time in a more profitable manner.[73]

When the treasury refused, in early 1843, to grant aid a new museum
building, C.W. Hamilton initiated a move to take stock of the current collection
and its suitability for visitors and students.[74] Sir Edward Stanley, chairman of
the museum and natural history committee, reported to the society's general
meeting on 1 June 1843. Stanley informed the general meeting that the natural
history collection had quadrupled within the space of a few years. Scouler had
managed to cope with the classification of the higher orders of vertebrates, but
had been unable to keep up with the expansion of the conchology and entomology collections. The geology display was based on the Leskean, Giesecke, and
Joy collections. It was fully classified, and comprehensive for basic minerals. A
separate Irish collection was in course of compilation. Regarding the museum's
suitability for students, Stanley's committee had concluded that it was unsuit-
able, having inadequate display space. The collections were only partially
catalogued, and this defect the committee attributed to the excessive demands
placed upon Scouler's time.[75] Visitor numbers in 1842 amounted to 46,370.[76]

In November 1843 the council reported that building work on the museum
extension was continuing, funded from the society's private resources. The
contractor had been paid £3,200 for certified work, and the building, when
complete, would 'present the appearance of a splendid Gallery for any purpose'.[77]
Visitor numbers increased by over twenty per cent in 1843 to 56,238 and
donations continued to arrive, including, curiously, 'Five live Rattlesnakes, from
North America' donated by Dr Scouler himself.[78] A perhaps more curious
donation was 'an Indian chieftain's quiver and arrows' which came with the
assurances of Sir Edward Stanley that the arrows were poison-tipped.[79] Scouler
received a letter from Richard Griffith, dated 19 March 1844, offering his large
fossil collection to the society.

I look upon the Royal Dublin Society as the parent of the Geology of
Ireland, and hence it is my wish that their Collection should be enriched

---

73 Ibid., 28 Mar. 1844.   74 *RDS Proc.*, lxxix, minutes, 2, 30 Mar. 1843.   75 Ibid., museum and
natural history committee report, 1 June 1843.   76 Ibid., appendix IV.   77 *RDS Proc.*, lxxx,
council report, 9 Nov. 1843.   78 Ibid., appendix VII.   79 Ibid., minutes, 30 May 1844.

by the best of every thing I have been able to collect. I should think the Collection will contain about 2000 specimens of Fossils, all from the carboniferous limestone. I have also a Collection of Fossils from the Silurian series, which I hope to present soon.[80]

This donation was followed by a large collection of Irish mineral samples, presented by Richard Purdy of the Mining Company of Ireland, and prompted by the entrepreneurial inspiration which Purdy had taken from Griffith's lectures on mining in 1822–3.[81] The council entrusted the selection and classification of samples from Griffith's collection to Frederick McCoy (1817–99), who had worked under Griffith, and was later professor of natural history in Melbourne university.[82] Although these accessions made the society's Irish geological collection the most comprehensive available to students, they also added to the pressure on display and storage space, and to Scouler's work. In his report on the first part of Griffith's donation, Scouler acknowledged the work done by Frederick McCoy, and that the acquisitions had doubled the size and filled in the gaps in the society's collection of Irish limestone fossils, but pointed out the continuing lack of display space.[83] His earlier request for a salary increase brought no response from the society.

The necessity to reduce operating expenditure, and allow a build-up of reserves, was so pressing that the executive council was given full authority to exercise direct control over spending for 1844–5.[84] Table 6.1 (page 148) shows the general trend in the society's finances for the fiscal years 1819–39. Table 8.2 below gives the same information for the fiscal years 1839–41 and 1843–5. These abstracts are taken from the published accounts in the RDS Proceedings, disregarding capital grants, and funds raised privately for capital development. The government's operating grant was suspended in 1841, and no accounts were published for that year, the society getting by through dipping into its reserve funds. The parliamentary grant for 1842–3 included the balance of grants deferred from 1841, less an interim payment of £2,000 given in early 1842.

In April 1844 the council formed a sub-committee to liaise with the standing committees on the control of expenditure.[85] A tight grip was kept on all day-to-day spending, with some exceptions being made for botany, science, agriculture, and manufactures, the reasons for which are as set out below.

The botany committee submitted to the general meeting on 1 June 1843, plans and elevations, prepared by Duncan Ferguson, master of the architecture school, for a wrought-iron curvilinear conservatory.[86] Private donations played a significant part in developing the botanic garden's collection of exotic flora,

80 Ibid., 28 Mar. 1844.   81 Ibid., 25 Apr. 1844.   82 Foster, *Nature in Ireland*, p. 320.   83 *RDS Proc.*, lxxx, report, 30 May 1844.   84 Ibid., minutes, 7 Dec. 1843, 25 Jan. 1844.   85 *RDS Proc.*, lxxx, council minutes, 4, 11 Apr. 1844.   86 *RDS Proc.*, lxxix, botany committee report, 1 June 1843.

Table 8.2 Abstract of RDS accounts, 1839–45

	1839–40 £	1840–1 £	1841–2 £	1842–3 £	1843–4 £	1844–5 £
botany and botanic garden	1636	1183	Grant	1340	1609	1770
library	918	766	suspended.	1185	705	704
fine arts	454	471	No accounts	531	480	478
science, geology, museum	1181	1227	published.	1282	1094	1256
agriculture	209	268		424	630	637
manufactures	8	140		0	10	757
rent, taxes, insurance (Kildare-st)	505	552		560	425	318
salaries and wages (establishment)	719	708		713	711	719
printing, stationery, advertising	316	496		218	314	322
repairs and furniture (Kildare-st)	444	272		499	227	280
coals, candles, oil, gas (Kildare-st)	213	176		194	138	139
PAYMENTS	**6603**	**6259**		**6946**	**6343**	**7380**
parliamentary grant	5300	5300		9026	5600	5908
other operating receipts	949	1800		1211	781	1800
RECEIPTS	**6249**	**6800**		**10237**	**6381**	**7708**

and the year 1842 had witnessed a continuing flow of plants and specimens from around the world, including more Amazonian epiphytes from Dr Gogarty, by that time based in Rio de Janeiro. Numbers of visitors to the botanic garden in 1842 amounted to 20,012.[87] Visitor numbers increased to 25,662 in 1843, and donations continued to arrive, including a large collection of seeds from the Swan River settlement, Australia, which was considered to be the most valuable single presentation for some time.[88] Keeping a close eye on running costs, the council questioned the value of maintaining Oldham's hydraulic ram in working order, at an annual expense of £12. However, it agreed to spend £6. 10s on emergency repairs to the professor's house.[89] The council reported to the general meeting in early November 1843 that it had proceeded with the 'building of a new Conservatory at the Botanic Garden, as the commencement of an entire range', and had by that date paid £400 to the contractor, out of private subscriptions.[90] David Moore, the curator, reported in December that one hundred linear feet of the old houses had been repaired, painted, had a new heating system installed, and were being used to house the more valuable and delicate plants.[91] The following month the society received a letter from Under Secretary Lucas, stating that the treasury had agreed to increase the curator's salary by £50 (to £150 per annum) added to the annual grant.[92] Samuel Litton,

87 Ibid., appendix V. 88 *RDS Proc.*, lxxx, appendix VI. 89 *RDS Proc.*, lxxix, council minutes, 26 Oct. 1843. 90 *RDS Proc.*, lxxx, report, 9 Nov. 1843. 91 Ibid., appendix III. 92 Ibid., minutes, 29 Feb. 1844.

the professor of botany, complained to the botany committee that no steps had been taken to provide him with a lecture room for the public lecture course scheduled for summer 1844.

> I have indeed heard, casually, that a back room in the new Conservatory has been appropriated by you for a Lecture-Room, but I trust that I have been misinformed. Should, however, this be the case, I would most respectfully entreat you to reconsider the subject. I myself have no doubt that the public will feel great dissatisfaction at the very inadequate means of accommodation which would be thus afforded, when so frequent remonstrances were made in the newspapers, of the insufficiency even of the former Lecture-Room in this respect.[93]

Litton followed up this letter with another, couched almost in the tones of a disinterested observer, complaining about the condition of his official residence.

> When so much expense has been incurred, and I admit properly incurred, every where around him, he cannot be considered unreasonable, if he also requests some share of your attention. I need not say, what is only too striking, that the whole appearance of every thing in and about the house, has an aspect of slovenliness, and this is, I assure you, as disagreeable to myself, as it must be to every one who visits the Garden, and has been a frequent subject of public complaint.

Perhaps irritated by these letters, the council questioned the policy of providing a professor's residence in the garden, and recommended, given the poor description of their reported condition, that the lecture room and Litton's house be demolished. A startled Litton protested in a further letter.

> My letter was, I believe, hastily written, but I cannot conceive how it could be so understood, as to convey the impression that I asked for an expenditure beyond what might be required for giving to the exterior of my residence, at Glasnevin, a decency of character in harmony with the rest of the Garden. With its internal condition I did not express any dissatisfaction. I was, therefore, much surprized that so simple a request should have given rise to the resolution of destroying both the Lecture Room and the House.[94]

The entire business was referred to the general meeting, and that body, having discussed possible compensation to Litton for loss of a perquisite, decided, on the motion of Dr William Harty, to repair the house and demolish the lecture room.[95] The old lecture room was taken down and removed in December 1844.[96]

93 Ibid., 28 Mar. 1844.   94 Ibid., 27 June 1844.   95 Ibid., 4 July 1844.   96 *RDS Proc.*, lxxxii,

Meanwhile, a correspondence had been taking place between Dublin Castle and the society on the subject of a government capital grant for the botanic garden. Lord Eliot, chief secretary, requested a report on the state of the conservatories, which was provided by L.E. Foot on behalf of the society. Foot explained that the general condition of the old conservatories was so poor that the society had decided to replace them with a new suite. The centre-piece would be a curvilinear glass-house on which construction had already commenced. The contract price for this element was £800, towards which the society had already raised over £600 by private subscription. The estimated additional cost of completion of a full replacement range of conservatories was £4,000.[97] The treasury was sufficiently impressed by the importance of the collection, and the private fund raising efforts of the society, to agree to ask parliament for a vote of £2,000 towards the project.[98] Frederick Darley's plans for the new conservatory range were approved on 13 June 1844.[99] The botany committee reported to the council in October 1844 that it intended to apply the £2,000, by then sanctioned by parliament, to the construction of the right-hand range of conservatories. They recommended acceptance of an estimate of £47 16s. 6d. for cisterns and pipes to supply water to the plant-houses, and asked for £6 5s. to build a fire arch above the hypocaust heating system then being installed by Dr Anthony Meyler.[100] In January 1845 the committee recommended that Richard Turner, Ballsbridge, be commissioned to erect the central conservatory for which he had given an estimate of £1,695.[101] Construction work on the left-hand range of new conservatories was completed in November 1844 at a cost of £969, met entirely from private subscriptions and the society's reserve funds. The treasury agreed that the £2,000 of capital grant be used to construct the right-hand range and to install central heating in all the new conservatories.[102] There were much heavier costs still to be met for construction of the central conservatory, estimated at £3,150 including Turner's costs, and for general refurbishments, estimated at over £4,000.

A modest increase in spending on the science program occurred when the government, conscious of the growing popularity of the RDS provincial lecture series, increased the grant for that purpose to £300 in 1843, and to £500 in 1844.[103] The last increase barely anticipated a move by the mechanics' institutes of Clonmel, and Waterford, notified to the society in March 1844, to petition parliament to increase the grant to £500.[104] There was much interest in and enthusiasm for the science lecture courses offered by the society in 1843–4. William Nunan, on behalf of Clonmel mechanics' institute, thanked the society for the course on geology and astronomy delivered by Reverend Dr D.W.

report, 6 Nov. 1845.   97 *RDS Proc.*, lxxx, council minutes, 11 Apr. 1844.   98 Ibid., minutes, 30 May 1844.   99 Ibid., council minutes, 13 June 1844.   100 Ibid., 24 Oct. 1844.   101 *RDS Proc.*, lxxxi, council minutes, 23 Jan. 1845.   102 Ibid., minutes, 7 Nov. 1844.   103 *RDS Proc.*, lxxx, minutes, 9 Nov. 1843, 7 Mar. 1844.   104 Ibid., council minutes, 14 Mar. 1844.

Cahill.[105] Kane's lectures on physics, given in Limerick, were well attended, and 'the most respectable and influential inhabitants' of Enniskillen petitioned the society to send Dr Meyler to them to provide a course on health and ventilation.[106] Shortage of funds prevented the society from sending a lecturer to Cork city in November 1843, resulting in a heated correspondence with a local representative.[107] In January 1844 the Waterford mechanics' institute sent a formal resolution of thanks to the society, signed by Thomas Meagher, then mayor of Waterford (and father of the future Young Irelander). The accompanying report said that Reverend Dr Cahill had delivered twelve lectures on astronomy and optics, and one on geology, 'shown to be in accordance with the Mosaic account of the Creation'. Cahill's lectures had been well received by a packed audience and, according to Meagher's report, demonstrated the harmony amongst all classes and denominations when gathered 'for the purpose of advancing the interests of Science, and assisting in the uninterrupted progress of general improvement and civilization'.[108] With this level of public support the way was smoothed for an additional treasury grant.

The society's spending on agriculture showed an apparent increase of almost fifty per cent between 1842-3 and 1843-4. This was due in part to an increase in the scale of the Spring Cattle Show, and in part to the opening of the new agricultural museum. Facilities for the museum had been readied in January 1843 but had lain idle since then. In September 1843, in the aftermath of the Naper controversy, the agriculture committee requested that immediate steps be taken to open the museum to the public.[109] Over the ensuing six weeks, work on the museum area was completed, and the agriculture committee pronounced it ready to receive exhibits in November 1843.[110] Leaving the issue of operating costs still unsettled, the agriculture committee proceeded with the commissioning of the museum. A curator, James Duffus, had been appointed in March 1843, and a subcommittee to superintend the museum had been appointed in May. The subcommittee laid claim to Richard Purdy's donation of Irish minerals, and issued a circular inviting agriculturists and manufacturers to send in exhibits. By April 1844 over 200 cereal varieties and a similar number of forage grass varieties were on display. Specimens of turnips, mangel-wurzels, carrots, potatoes, and other root crops, prize-winning exhibits at the agricultural shows, were available for display in season. Eighty full sized agricultural implement exhibits, and a range of gardening tools, were placed on permanent display by their manufacturers. The chief contributors of implements and tools were Courtney and Stephens, Ringsend, and Loftus A. Bryan, Bride Street, both firms headed by prominent members of the society.[111] L.E. Foot, honorary secretary, moved that the agricultural museum be allocated £150 annual running costs from the society's private funds.[112]

105 Ibid., 5 Oct. 1843.   106 Ibid., 26 Oct. 1843.   107 Ibid., 16 Nov. 1843.   108 Ibid., minutes, 25 Jan. 1844.   109 RDS Proc., lxxix, council minutes, 21 Sept. 1843.   110 RDS Proc., lxxx, minutes, 2, 9 Nov. 1843.   111 Ibid., 25 Apr. 1844.   112 Ibid., 30 May 1844.

The 1844 Spring Show continued the increase in size and popularity evident from 1843. In November 1843 the agriculture committee recommended the addition in 1844 of extra classes for commercial cattle, and the holding of an auction sale of breeding stock on the final day of the show.[113] Paying visitors to the 1844 show (excluding members, exhibitors, and guests) numbered 4,760. This was an increase of more than twelve per cent on the previous record set in 1843. The committee reported a great improvement in the quality of the poultry classes, and its only serious criticism was of the tendency of exhibitors to present over-weight bulls in the cattle classes.[114] Silver medals were awarded to seven implement exhibitors.[115]

The exhibition organized triennially by the manufactures committee also experienced an increase in size and popularity in 1844. Temporary use of the art school gallery was once again agreed for the duration of the manufactures exhibition, and led to a complaint by the manufactures committee that Reverend Sirr had failed to remove several cases containing his late father's fossil collection, despite repeated requests. The council resolved, 'That the Committee of Manufactures be requested to take such steps as they themselves may think fit, consistent with their preservation, for the removal of Mr Sirr's Collection remaining in the Statue Gallery'.[116] The art school was ordered closed for seven weeks to facilitate the exhibition. Temporary wooden buildings were erected on the lawn adjoining the statue gallery to house additional smaller exhibits, while 'the more massive and rougher articles were accommodated in the Court-yard, and under the sheds'. In most categories, the numbers of exhibitors and of articles exhibited exceeded all earlier shows. The lord lieutenant spent several hours visiting the exhibition and addressed the exhibitors on the importance to Ireland of developing its own industrial enterprises. Pleased with the success of the exhibition, the manufactures committee attributed this to the 'collateral interest' generated by the agricultural museum, and the lectures on manufacturing resources delivered by Dr Kane.[117] The judges awarded four gold medals, seventy-five large silver medals, fifty-nine small silver medals, and eighty certificates of merit to exhibitors. A gold medal was awarded to Thomas Kennan and Son for examples of lathes. Michael H. Gill, University Press, received a large silver medal for specimen printing. J. and H. Rathborne were awarded a small silver medal for specimens of wax and spermaceti candles. The governor of the Richmond Bridewell, Thomas Purdon, received a certificate for 'Linsey-woolsey, made by prisoners'.[118] The cost of mounting the exhibition was £757, offset by admission receipts of £539, and leaving a net cost to the society of £218.[119]

113 Ibid., agriculture committee report, 9 Nov. 1843.   114 Ibid., 25 Apr. 1844.   115 Ibid., appendix VIII, adjudication of premiums.   116 Ibid., council minutes, 21 Mar. 1844.   117 Ibid., manufactures committee report, 27 June 1844.   118 Ibid., appendix XIII, Fifth exhibition of Irish manufactures.   119 RDS Proc., lxxxi, appendix X, accounts 1844–5.

Earl de Grey, the lord lieutenant, who had been a generous supporter of the RDS since his appointment in September 1841, left office in July 1844. The society commissioned a former pupil, Thomas Farrell, RHA, to execute a marble bust of him, still in the RDS collection.[120] Lord de Grey's interest in the cultivation of arts and industry won him the respect of the upper and middle classes, but made little impression on the mass of Irish people.[121] His faithful adherence to Peel's policies on patronage and education annoyed many Irish Tories, whose displeasure was expressed in the election of an extreme conservative, George Alexander Hamilton (1802–71), as MP for Dublin University in 1843.[122] Hamilton was elected a life member of the RDS on 4 December 1845, and was a vice-president, 1847–71. He held a deep-seated prejudice against the Roman Catholic church as exemplified in his letter to Father John Smyth, Balbriggan, in 1834. In that letter he had refused the priest a site for a chapel, requested by Hamilton's own catholic tenants. His stated grounds were that 'the Roman Catholic Church is a corrupt and degenerate church', and that he would be less than honest 'if I made myself an instrument in advancing or extending what I believe to be an erroneous system of religion'.[123]

In the spring and summer of 1843 de Grey was terrified by the revolutionary undertones of O'Connell's mass movement for repeal. However, under Peel's guidance, the government kept its head as the scale and minatory tone of O'Connell's monster meetings escalated. The militant wording of O'Connell's advertisement for a climactic monster meeting at Clontarf, in October 1843, finally provided an excuse for the government to shut the campaign down.[124] By banning the Clontarf meeting the government called O'Connell's bluff. O'Connell cancelled the meeting, but was subsequently tried for conspiracy to foment disloyalty, and received a prison sentence of four months. Peel followed up with conciliatory measures, aimed at placating the catholic middle class and clergy. In 1844, his administration established the board of charitable bequests and in the following year increased the Maynooth grant and established non-denominational third-level colleges. The repeal movement slowly collapsed in disillusionment.[125]

In O'Connell's absence, William Smith O'Brien, MP, first took the chair at a repeal meeting on 22 January 1844. Thereafter he became the movement's temporary leader for most of the period February–September 1844.[126] At about the same time O'Brien decided to apply for membership of the RDS. His grandfather Sir Lucius, his uncle Donough, and his brother Edward, had all been members but were long deceased. He might have called on his wide circle

120 White and Bright, *Treasures of the Royal Dublin Society*, p. 53.   121 Joseph Robins, *Champagne and silver buckles: the viceregal court at Dublin Castle, 1700–1922* (Dublin, 2001), pp. 118–20. 122 Boyce, *Nineteenth-century Ireland*, pp. 86–7.   123 D.D.A., Murray papers, AB3/31/3–4, G. A. Hamilton to Reverend John Smyth, 18 Nov. 1834.   124 MacDonagh, *The emancipist*, p. 239. 125 McCartney, *The dawning of democracy*, pp. 152–9.   126 Davis, *Revolutionary imperialist*, pp.

of acquaintances amongst the membership, especially those with nationalist sympathies, to support his application, but choose not to do so. Instead, from his Co. Limerick residence, Cahirmoyle, on 26 December 1843, he addressed a letter to the honorary secretaries.

> Mr William S. O'Brien presents his compliments to the Honorary Secretaries of the Royal Dublin Society, and will feel much obliged if they will cause him to be proposed for admission as a Member of the Dublin Society. Being unacquainted with the personal influences which predominate in the Society, he thinks it better to leave the nomination of his proposer and seconder to the Honorary Secretaries, trusting that they will forgive the liberty which he takes in asking them to undertake this office.[127]

O'Brien was proposed for membership by the two honorary secretaries, Isaac Weld, and Lundy Edward Foot, and duly elected an annual member on 29 February 1844. On the same occasion on which O'Brien's letter was read to the general meeting the society also received, through Thomas Wyse, MP, a copy of his own, and William Smith O'Brien's, speeches on the condition of Ireland, and of Irish education.[128] O'Brien attended two out of twelve monthly general meetings of the society in 1844 and several meetings in the early part of 1845. His main interest appeared to lie in the arts and the manufactures programs. He supported the opinion of the RDS fine arts committee that design studies should be promoted in the art school by the appointment of a master of design (a post eventually created in 1936). The treasury refused an additional grant for this purpose, an outcome which Turpin describes as in marked contrast to the supportive attitude of the old Irish parliament, and a demonstration of the negative effects of the act of union on Irish art and technical education.[129] O'Brien also actively supported an RDS scheme to mount an exhibition of 'old masters' paintings on the premises, a precursor of the national gallery.[130]

On 13 February 1845 a public meeting was convened at the Royal Exchange, Dublin, 'to devise measures to restore the Manufactures and revive the drooping trade of this country'. A committee was appointed consisting of Daniel O'Connell, MP, Edward Grogan, MP, W.H. Gregory, MP, William Smith O'Brien, MP, and John L. Arabin, lord mayor, to request the lord lieutenant, Lord Heytesbury, to appoint a commission of inquiry into the state of Irish manufactures. William Smith O'Brien was further asked to request the support of the Royal Dublin Society for the encouragement of Irish industry.

> It appeared to the Committee that there were two or three manifest causes for the decline of Irish Manufactures, to counteract which the Royal

165–73. **127** *RDS Proc.*, lxxx, minutes, 25 Jan. 1844. **128** Ibid., 25 Jan., 29 Feb. 1844.
129 Turpin, *A school of art in Dublin*, pp. 138–9. **130** *RDS Proc.*, lxxxi, minutes, 6 Mar. 1845.

Dublin Society might be brought into beneficial action, namely, first, want of industrial education, and secondly, prejudices on the part of the consumers against home-produced manufacture.[131]

O'Brien believed the society could assist in two ways; firstly by developing a polytechnic institute for industry, and secondly by establishing a permanent exhibition of manufactures with an associated course of evening lectures for artisans. He acknowledged that the implementation of these proposals would involve the society in considerable additional expense, and suggested that,

> an application might be successfully made to Government, founded on those increased appliances for the instruction of the people, and might be backed by special efforts, as well as by public opinion, for an increase of grant to the Royal Dublin Society.[132]

O'Brien asked the RDS to consider assisting in breaking down prejudice against Irish manufactures, and promoting technical education.

> Such a public service will render the Society a great National Institution, whose benefits would not be confined to the few, the wealthy, or the scientific, but would be a great and lasting benefit to the Irish people, tending to improve their social state, and to provide the means of subsistence to a large and necessarily unemployed population.[133]

The society agreed in principle with O'Brien's request, which it perceived as being entirely consistent with its own chartered objects and past endeavours. In particular the idea of creating a manufactures museum had much appeal, in the light of the experience provided by the newly established agricultural museum. The council was instructed to send the O'Brien appeal, together with a memorial on the topic, to the government, stressing 'that the absolute necessity of an additional Grant be strongly impressed on the Government' if the society was to carry out the suggested developments.[134] The council's memorial argued 'that capabilities do exist on their [the society's] extensive premises, and in their well-organized departments, for assisting the great industrial movement of the present day, if supported with adequate liberality'. The memorial encapsulated the proposal as 'the establishment of a Central School of Industrial Education in Ireland, with a view to the improvement of Agriculture and Manufactures'. Charles Trevelyan replied curtly on behalf of the treasury on 17 April 1845, 'I am commanded to acquaint you, that my Lords do not deem it advisable to make any addition to the Grant for the Dublin Society for the purpose of the proposed Establishment'.[135]

131 Ibid., letter signed Thomas MacNevin.   132 Ibid.   133 Ibid.   134 Ibid., minutes, 27 Mar. 1845.   135 Ibid., 24 Apr. 1845.

The matter rested for the time being, and W.S. O'Brien moved on to other issues. He had already founded the 82 Club, a repeal affiliate outside of O'Connellite control, on 2 January 1845.[136] The club, with its semi-military uniform designed by Thomas Davis and Sir Colman O'Loghlen, was intended to attract middle-class support. O'Connell could not control its operations, and eventually its independent character helped to facilitate a permanent split in the repeal movement. Early recruits included Thomas Francis Meagher, and Richard N. O'Gorman. O'Gorman, a *protégé* of William Smith O'Brien's, was more a rhetorician than a revolutionary.[137] Thomas Davis was a cultural rather than a political nationalist, and hoped to avert the replacement of protestant ascendancy with a catholic ascendancy.[138] When the repeal movement lost its impetus in October 1843 Davis toyed with the federalist solution espoused by Robert Hutton and William Sharman Crawford.[139] By the time of his death, on 9 September 1845, Davis was aligned with the O'Brien faction of the repeal movement, and it was from their differences with the O'Connellites, caused as much as anything else by divisions on educational policy,[140] that the Young Ireland movement later emerged. Several RDS members were associated with this development, especially William Smith O'Brien, and James Haughton. Amongst known seceders from repeal who later joined the Irish Confederation, the political wing of Young Ireland, were Dr Thomas Antisell (see p. 215), and Walter Thomas Meyler.[141] Meyler became a life member of the RDS in 1839, his proposers being George Roe, and Dr Anthony Meyler (at that time a politically active protestant conservative).[142] W.T. Meyler was, presumably, a close relative of Dr Anthony Meyler's. Interestingly, his entry in the Irish Confederation list for 23 April 1848 describes him as 'MRDS', an acronym commonly used at that time to indicate membership of the Royal Dublin Society.

In 1845 the government decided to set up a 'Museum of Irish industry and government school of science applied to mining and the arts'. Dr Kane was appointed its first director, and an unworkable arrangement was at first put in place whereby the teaching staff was under the joint control of the Royal Dublin Society and the government.[143] Initially welcomed by the society,[144] this development would prove to be the first in a long assimilative process, whereby the educational functions of the society were gradually transferred to the state. The society anticipated that the new museum would primarily benefit the work-in-progress of the ordnance survey of Ireland, which was, it believed, underfunded by the government. Commenced in 1824, under the direction of

136 Davis, *Revolutionary imperialist*, p. 181.   137 Davis, *The Young Ireland movement*, pp. 74–9. 138 Boyce, *Nineteenth-century Ireland*, pp. 78–9.   139 Molony, *A soul came into Ireland*, p. 275. 140 Hoppen, *Ireland since 1800*, p. 33.   141 Minute book of Irish Confederation 1847–8, RIA, MS 23/H/43.   142 *RDS Proc.*, lxxvi, minutes, 5 Dec. 1839.   143 G.F. Mitchell, 'Mineralogy and geology', in Meenan and Clarke, *The Royal Dublin Society, 1731–1981*, p. 163.   144 *RDS Proc.*, lxxxi, notice of motion by L.E. Foot, 8 May 1845.

Thomas Colby, the ordnance survey had at first also collected topographic and demographic information, geological specimens and observations.[145] This aspect of its work was discontinued in 1837 due to scarcity of funds.[146] In 1844 the RDS had petitioned the government to continue the ordnance survey 'memoirs', regarding them as a more professionally compiled and improved version of its own earlier county survey series.[147]

On the same occasion the society also petitioned the government to amend the laws in support of the Irish Art Union, a body formed to encourage through patronage aspiring artists, and art education.[148] Because of the manner in which some similar London bodies had been operated, all art unions offering prizes to exhibitors had been deemed in breach of the gaming and lotteries acts.[149] Since 1842 the RDS had taken a more confidently proactive role in the broader world of fine art education, and it may have been this attitudinal change which encouraged W.S. O'Brien to suggest that the society should organize a major fine art exhibition. While this was not immediately feasible, the society did decide to hold its art school prize giving ceremony in public. Dr John Turpin argues that the society's decision (in conscious imitation of a practice commenced by the London based Society of Arts since 1787), significantly enhanced the public status of the art school. The prestige and importance of this annual ceremony was such that it continued to be held in Leinster House, beyond the era of RDS control, until 1915. The RDS certificate presented to graduating pupils was the ancestor of all the subsequent Irish art and design certificates, diplomas, and degrees.[150] From the outset (and credit for this must be given to Lord de Grey) the ceremony had the support of Dublin Castle, and the educational, judicial, and religious establishment.[151] However, despite the steps taken to up-grade the school's image, it remained chronically under-funded and its masters underpaid. Robert Lucius West (c.1774–1850), master of the drawing school since 9 November 1809, asked permission to retire on 5 December 1844. His salary thirty years earlier had been £100 per annum, but was reduced to £80 per annum in 1833.[152] The treasury agreed to sanction a full pension of £60 per annum for West,[153] which he lived long enough to draw for five years.

The treasury's pursuit of accountability in all grant-aided institutions continued. Dublin Castle advised the society early in 1845 that in future the annual estimates should be accompanied by a report showing the society's progress in carrying-out its objects, and 'the circumstances under which the public Grant had been originally made, and continued to the Institution'.[154]

145 J.H. Andrews, *A paper landscape: the ordnance survey in nineteenth-century Ireland* (2nd ed., Dublin, 2002), pp. 31, 144–7.   146 Patrick Wyse Jackson, 'Fluctuations in fortune', in Foster, *Nature in Ireland*, pp. 97–100.   147 *RDS Proc.*, lxxx, council report, 30 May 1844.   148 Ibid., minutes, 30 May 1844.   149 *Freeman's Journal*, 1 Apr. 1843.   150 Turpin, *A school of art in Dublin*, pp. 120–1.   151 *RDS Proc.*, lxxix, appendix III, art school prize distribution, 8 Dec. 1842.   152 *RDS Proc.*, lxxxi, minutes, 5 Dec. 1844.   153 Ibid., 24 Apr. 1845.   154 Ibid., 30 Jan. 1845.

Taking this new requirement at face value, the society replied on 30 January 1845, listing its activities as follows:

1. The botanic garden, of twenty-eight acres.
2. A chemical laboratory.
3. A museum of natural history.
4. An agricultural museum.
5. An annual agricultural exhibition.
6. A triennial manufactures exhibition.
7. A library, open to students.
8. Lecture courses in botany, agriculture, and science, held in Dublin and in provincial centres.
9. A school of art.

The society believed that all these activities were progressing well, given that they had received the approbation of the lord lieutenant, and had grown in popularity to the point where they generally required additional space and funding. Finally, the society's letter drew attention to the decline in its annual grant since 1819, and the need for additional grants to complete the botanic garden conservatories, and the museum.[155] The treasury found this generalized statement of affairs unsatisfactory, and demanded a detailed accounting statement, and detailed returns of visitor numbers. The annual report of the British Museum was put forward as a model. The society agreed to comply, and called on the committees and the professors to prepare reports compatible with the treasury guidelines, the council being given over-all editorial responsibility.[156] The first such report was prepared and forwarded to the treasury in July 1845, and was the template for successive annual reports up to 1877.[157]

Reinforcing the society's confidence in the success of its current programs, the 1845 Spring Cattle Show set a new record for attendances, with visitor numbers recorded as 7,094 (an increase of forty-nine per cent on the previous record set in 1844). The Dublin–Drogheda Railway Company gave free passage to exhibitor's livestock, and fifteen counties were represented in the judging classes, including Cavan, Monaghan, and Roscommon. A celebrity amongst the exhibitors was Albert, prince consort, two of whose cattle were awarded prizes.[158] Prince Albert subsequently accepted the society's invitation to become its vice-patron.[159] He did not personally visit the society until 1849.

The provincial lecture series continued to grow in popularity, but not without problems. The Cork city mechanics' institute again applied for a lecturer, and despite the unavailability of their first preference, Dr Kane, the RDS managed

155 Ibid.   156 Ibid., 29 May 1845.   157 Ibid., 3 July 1845.   158 Ibid., agriculture committee report, 24 Apr. 1845.   159 Ibid., minutes, 29 May 1845.

to provide a lecture course in astronomy.[160] Dr Anthony Meyler resigned from the chemistry and natural history committees at the end of 1844, and was replaced by Thomas Antisell.[161] Antisell had engaged the notice of the society for his analyses of soil types and manures. However, when his services were offered to lecture on zoology, Clonmel mechanics' institute refused the nomination.[162] The Clonmel organizers, on their own initiative, engaged the services of George Allman,[163] to which the RDS council gave a reluctant, retrospective, agreement.[164]

In the botanic garden, David Moore's report for 1844 showed a continued flow of donations and acquisitions. A number of exotic conifers had been established in the arboretum, including Ponderosa pine, Noble fir, and Himalayan cedar (cedrus deodara).[165] Captain Edward Madden of the East India Company sent two large packets of seeds to the botanic garden in 1844. He followed these up with a letter written from Simla on 11 November 1844. Madden wrote, 'I trust your beautiful Garden is as flourishing as when I saw it. I know none in Europe or in Asia to rival it'. He advised the society that he was sending two further packets of seeds, including a large quantity of seeds of the Himalayan cedar, and asked the RDS to apportion both packets between the Glasnevin garden, TCD, and the Belfast botanical garden.[166] Major Madden's donations are nowadays thought to be one of the earliest Irish sources of the popular butterfly bush (buddleia davidii).[167]

As 1845 drew to a close the society could look back with some satisfaction on the progress it had made since the newspaper room crisis of 1841. However, the coming catastrophe of the prolonged potato famine was already beginning to impinge on its work. The committee of agriculture offered a gold medal and twenty sovereigns for the best essay on preserving the potato harvest from disease.[168] Edmund Davy was relieved of all other responsibilities to enable him to conduct laboratory research on the disease, and his winter lecture series was postponed indefinitely.[169]

This study ends in 1845, but would be incomplete without some reference to developments beyond that date. The RDS was no more effective than any other scientific or official body of the time in finding a solution to the horrendous effects of the potato crop failure. It loaned its premises and its professors for investigations into the potato disease and offered a platform for disseminating

160 Ibid., council minutes, 12 Dec. 1844.   161 Ibid., minutes, 7 Nov., 5 Dec. 1844.   162 RDS Proc., lxxx, council minutes, 17, 24 Oct. 1844.   163 George James Allman (1812–98), was a life member of the RDS, 1845–98, and a member of the natural history and museum committee 1845–55. He was professor of botany, TCD, 1844–55, and professor of natural history at Edinburgh University 1855–70. (Sources: RDS Proc., var. dates; D.N.B.)   164 Ibid., 31 Oct. 1844.   165 Ibid., appendix II, report on botanic garden, 27 Feb. 1845.   166 RDS Proc., lxxi, minutes, 30 Jan. 1845.   167 Sunday Independent, article by Joe Kennedy, 30 June 2002.   168 RDS Proc., lxxxii, minutes, 4 Dec. 1845.   169 Ibid., 13 Nov. 1845.

the results of scientific tests and observations. Extensive trials were carried out in the botanic garden during 1846–7, but with inconclusive results. David Moore continued the potato trials commenced by Niven in 1834. He was, at times, tantalizingly close to discovering the pathology of the blight, and its cure. However, it was probably an impossible task for one man, and he never managed to achieve the intuitive break-through that would have been required at that time.[170]

Robert Kane served on the government's scientific commission on the potato disease, and was knighted by the lord lieutenant in 1846. The circumstances of his conferring were unique in being the only instance of a knighthood conferred during a meeting of the Royal Dublin Society.[171] Kane formally tendered his resignation from the society's employment on 3 November 1847.[172] Since 1846 he had been a member of the central board of health, which supervised the work of 473 medical doctors in 373 temporary fever hospitals, attempting to cope with the epidemics associated with the great famine.[173] He was later appointed first president of the Queen's College, Cork.

The famine associated epidemics, or the debilitation that they caused amongst the elderly, swept away many of those members of the RDS prominent in the 1830s and early 1840s. Medical doctors treating or in contact with the victims were particularly at risk, and it is noteworthy that John Oliver Curran, and Thomas Taylor (both known to have contracted 'famine' disease), also Valentine Flood, and Anthony Meyler, all died within a short period in 1847–8.

In mid–1846 Peel's government was replaced by a Whig-liberal administration led by Lord John Russell. Russell reversed Peel's decision of 1843 by restoring the repeal magistrates to office, and adding to their numbers.[174] Meanwhile O'Connell's repeal movement became mired in internal arguments, and the O'Connellites expelled the Young Irelanders, ostensibly because of the latters' advocacy of physical force. Several RDS members involved in the repeal movement departed for the Young Ireland camp. These included W.S. O'Brien, Richard O'Gorman, and James Haughton. Haughton deserves some attention, since he was later an active RDS committee member, and played a part in effecting constitutional reform in the society in the 1860s. He withdrew from the repeal movement in 1846, in protest at what he regarded as the hypocrisy of the O'Connellites on the physical force issue. Along with the other Young Ireland dissidents, he helped form a new political grouping, the Irish Confederation, on 13 January 1847.[175] The Irish Confederation appointed James Haughton as treasurer. Haughton, described by John Mitchel as 'an amiable monomaniac',

170 See Phyllis Clinch, 'Botany and the botanic garden', in Meenan and Clarke, *The Royal Dublin Society, 1731–1981*, and Austin Bourke, 'The visitation of God?', in J. Hill and C. Ó Gráda (eds), *The potato and the great Irish famine* (Dublin, 1993).   171 Ibid., appendix IX, prize distribution, 16 Feb. 1846.   172 *RDS Proc.*, lxxxiv, minutes, 4 Nov. 1847.   173 Eoin O'Brien, *Conscience and conflict: a biography of Sir Dominic Corrigan, 1802–1880* (Dublin, 1983), pp. 192–3.   174 Kerr, *A nation of beggars*, pp. 25–6.   175 Haughton, *Memoir of James Haughton*, pp. 82–5.

espoused almost the entire gamut of liberal causes, including anti-slavery, temperance, land reform, and the abolition of capital punishment. His anti-slavery views led to clashes with a considerable element in the new movement, and especially with Father John Kenyon. In April 1847 Haughton chaired a meeting of the Irish Confederation, with W.S. O'Brien present, and was shouted down when he attempted to move resolutions condemning slavery. He thereupon resigned from the movement.[176]

Alarmed at the increasingly menacing statements of the Young Ireland leaders, the government increased the strength of the Irish garrison in an attempt to discourage an anticipated rebellion. Most of the RDS premises were placed in military occupation from 3 April 1848,[177] including the cattle yard. The Spring Cattle Show was transferred to Leinster Lawn, the lord lieutenant allocating £200 to provide temporary cattle shedding.[178] All evening meetings of the society were suspended.[179] As the military emergency eased in intensity, the art school was re-opened on 8 May, the daytime lecture courses were resumed on 15 May, and the gates of Leinster Lawn were re-opened to members on 8 June.[180] While the military authorities appeared to be at pains to ease the society's problems, the presence of a large body of soldiers on the premises was inevitably inconvenient and disruptive. The RDS council recorded a complaint from the officer of health of St Anne's parish regarding the stench from 'the soldiers' privy in the yard of Leinster House'.[181] The occupation continued for over eight months and the premises were not fully re-opened to the public until shortly before Christmas, 1848.[182]

W.S. O'Brien led a small and futile uprising in July 1848, for which he was sentenced to transportation to Tasmania. Two other RDS members, Richard O'Gorman and Thomas Antisell, both Young Irelanders, became fugitives at this time. O'Gorman escaped to America, where he practised law along with John Blake Dillon, and ultimately became a judge of the New York superior court.[183] Antisell also moved to America, where he became professor of chemistry at Georgetown University, and later chief chemist to the railroad surveys of California and Arizona.[184] The RDS discreetly deleted Antisell and O'Gorman from its membership list on 25 January 1849, for failure to renew their annual subscriptions. O'Brien presumably paid his 1848 subscription, as he was not stricken for arrears until 31 January 1850.[185] The government pardoned O'Brien in 1854 and he returned to Ireland in 1856. He did not rejoin the RDS but continued to show an interest in its affairs. In 1858 he corresponded with the

176 Davis, *The Young Ireland movement*, pp. 117–24.   177 RDS Proc., lxxxiv, council minutes, 3 Apr. 1848.   178 Ibid., minutes, 27 Apr. 1848.   179 Ibid., council minutes, 13 Apr. 1848. 180 Ibid., 4 May, 8 June 1848.   181 *RDS Proc.*, lxxxv, council minutes, 8 Nov. 1848.   182 Ibid., 14, 21 Dec. 1848.   183 Crone, *A dictionary of Irish biography*.   184 John Wilson Foster, *Out of Ireland: naturalists abroad, in Foster, Nature in Ireland*, p. 321.   185 *RDS Proc.*, lxxxv–lxxxvi, 25 Jan. 1849, 31 Jan. 1850.

society regarding the loan of paintings for an art exhibition in Limerick,[186] and on art bursaries to enable students to study abroad.[187] This was followed up, through O'Brien's contacts with 'Irish gentlemen settled in California', by an offer to provide funds for an annual bursary.[188] A sum of £50 for this purpose was sent in August 1860 to the society, from William McCann, San Francisco, to which W.S. O'Brien added a personal contribution of £5.[189] Further substantial donations were received from California when the fund-raising body was wound up a few years after the end of the civil war in the United States. O'Brien died on 18 June 1864, leaving two paintings to the RDS. His will contained a proviso that 'in case of the suppression of the Royal Dublin Society, or of the Royal Irish Academy, those objects [the paintings] shall not be sold, but shall be placed in the keeping of some other national institution of a permanent kind'.[190] The RDS later transferred both paintings to the National Gallery. The California Fund still exists under RDS trusteeship, and the California gold medal and the William Smith O'Brien cup, are still awarded at RDS arts and crafts competitions.[191]

The manufactures exhibition, in which W.S. O'Brien had also shown an interest, continued to be held at three year intervals. Visitor numbers reached 12,407 in 1847, and the exhibition produced a small surplus.[192] Sir Edward Stanley retired from the manufactures committee on 31 January 1850, and was replaced as chairman by Walter Sweetman.[193] The seventh manufactures exhibition was held over a six-week period in 1850, and attracted more than 30,000 visitors.[194] In 1852 William Dargan (1799–1867), industrialist, and a member of the society, offered £20,000 to fund the holding of the 1853 exhibition, subject to its being housed on Leinster Lawn, and thrown open to exhibitors from all parts of the United Kingdom.[195] The RDS agreed, as did Sydney Herbert, the ground landlord of Leinster Lawn, and Dargan increased his subvention to £26,000 and later to £40,000.[196] 'The Great Industrial Exhibition, 1853, in connection with the Royal Dublin Society', opened on 12 May, in an iron and glass structure erected on Leinster Lawn. Queen Victoria visited the exhibition on four occasions between 30 August and 2 September.[197] The exhibition's success provided the inspiration for the subsequent construction of the Natural History Museum on the south side of the Lawn, and the National Gallery on the north side.[198]

In 1856 the manufactures exhibition was discontinued and its agricultural machinery and implements exhibits were transferred to the Spring Cattle

186 RDS Proc., xciv, minutes, 24 June 1858.   187 RDS Proc., xcv, council minutes, 1 July 1858.   188 Ibid., 18 Nov. 1858.   189 RDS Proc., xcvii, council minutes, 2 Aug. 1860.   190 RDS Proc., c, council minutes, 21 Sept. 1864.   191 RDS annual report, 2001.   192 RDS Proc., lxxxiv, minutes, 11 Nov. 1847, and appendix I.   193 RDS Proc., lxxxvi, minutes, 31 Jan. 1850.   194 RDS Proc., lxxxvii, council report, 5 Dec. 1850.   195 RDS Proc., lxxxviii, minutes, 24 June 1852.   196 RDS Proc., lxxxix, council minutes, 29 June, 15 July, 21 Oct. 1852, 3 Feb. 1853.   197 Berry, A history of the Royal Dublin Society, pp. 280–3.   198 RDS Proc., xci, council minutes, 14 July, 8 Dec. 1853.

Show.[199] Meanwhile the manufactures committee had become involved in promoting Irish manufactures at overseas events. They arranged and supervised the Irish exhibits at the Paris International Exhibition in 1855. The following year, in a joint project with the Royal Agricultural Improvement Society of Ireland (RAIS), the manufactures committee chartered the steamship *Windsor* to provide a direct Dublin-Le Havre passage for exhibitors, machinery and livestock. During the 1856 Paris show a delegation from the RDS were given an audience by Napoleon III at the Tuileries, and subsequently the society elected the emperor an honorary member.[200] Andrew Corrigan (*c.*1820–75), who replaced James Duffus as curator of the RDS agricultural museum in 1847, played a key role as general superintendent of the Irish cattle exhibits in Paris in 1856.[201] Corrigan was frequently seconded to the RAIS in the 1850s and 1860s, to run their provincial shows. In 1864 his services were routinely seconded to the RAIS to organize an experimental horse show in Kildare Street, one of the most momentous decisions made by the RDS in the second half of the nineteenth century.[202] In 1866 the government withdrew the society's agricultural grant.[203] This had the ultimately beneficial effect of freeing the RDS to concentrate its private resources on the development of agricultural shows and projects. The society resolved to hold an annual horse show, which continues to the present day.[204] John O'Donovan commented that it was only post-1864 that the society spent significant sums on developing the livestock shows and the horse show.[205]

On 21 March 1849, the RDS organized a public meeting to gather support and raise local subscriptions for a school of design in Dublin. The board of trade responded with an outline proposal for a government-supported scheme. It stressed that the government would have the right of nomination of a head-master. Henry MacManus, RHA, was designated headmaster in June 1849.[206] 'The government school of design, in connection with the Royal Dublin Society' was opened on 1 October 1849. All the RDS art school-masters were retained, and their salaries increased by £20, to £100 per annum. The annual elections of art school masters by the RDS general meeting was discontinued.[207] The RDS was at first reluctant to participate in the earlier government scheme, launched in 1836, to create a central school of design in London, setting a uniform syllabus for locally managed schools. The society's opposition was based on the belief that fine arts studies should not be abandoned for a purely utilitarian industrial design course, and, just as importantly, that Irish art students should not be charged tuition fees. The society was persuaded to

199 RDS Proc., xciii, minutes, 13 Nov. 1856.   200 *RDS Proc.*, xcii, minutes, 6 Mar., 1 May, 19 June 1856.   201 Ibid., council minutes, 25 Oct. 1855, 24 Apr. 1856.   202 *RDS Proc.*, c., council minutes, 18 Feb. 1864.   203 *RDS Proc.*, cii, minutes, 5 Apr. 1866.   204 *RDS Proc.*, ciii, council minutes, 10, 31 Oct. 1866; general meeting, 8 Nov. 1866.   205 O'Donovan, *The economic history of livestock in Ireland*, p. 252.   206 *RDS Proc.*, lxxxv, minutes, 29 Mar., 31 May, 28 June 1849.   207 *RDS Proc.*, lxxxvi, minutes, 8 Nov. 1849.

participate in 1849 by the strong representations of the Dublin manufacturers, and by the government's expressed willingness to allow fine arts studies to continue.[208] Early in 1854, control of the RDS grant was transferred to the newly created government department of science and art. In April of that year, the new department announced its intention of taking over control of the RDS teaching staff, previously shared with the government museum of Irish industry. It further proposed that all RDS departments be kept open for six days of every week, and reverted to the 1836 issue of government dissatisfaction with the delineation of public and private interests in the society's property. The RDS protested vigorously that the departments' proposals 'would largely and prejudicially interfere with the original constitution and objects and the most useful functions of the Royal Dublin Society'.[209] This produced a visit from Henry Cole, who threatened to withdraw the art school grant and substitute a performance related payment if the society wished to continue in sole charge of the school. The society protested to the lord lieutenant.[210] However, the government was unmoved, and control of the art school-masters, and also of the provincial lecture scheme, was removed from the RDS in 1854 and transferred to the government department of science and art.[211]

Encouraged by the suggestion of the department of science and art that the society should extend its opening hours, James Haughton, seconded by Charles Bianconi, moved to open the botanic garden to the public on Sundays. This first step in a lengthy saga was voted down by the general meeting on 7 December 1854.[212] Haughton returned to the subject in 1858 with a similar motion that was once again defeated.[213] In 1840 James Haughton and Robert Ball had persuaded the Royal Zoological Society to open its grounds to the public on Sundays. Haughton's view on Sunday opening was encapsulated in the following statement cited in his biography.

> I attach no particular holiness to the Sabbath day, as Sunday is erroneously called, for our lives should be devoted to God and man, every day; but I do value the Sunday as a season to be particularly devoted, in the first place to religious duties, and in the next place to rational and innocent enjoyment.[214]

Haughton revived his motion for Sunday opening, in 1859.[215] Finally, the council learned in 1861 from the department of science and art, that the government had also become persuaded that the botanic garden should open on

208 Turpin, *A school of art in Dublin*, pp. 131-45. 209 *RDS Proc.*, xci, council minutes, 19 Jan., 17, 24 Apr. 1854. 210 Ibid., minutes, 19 Oct., 2 Nov. 1854. 211 Ibid., council minutes, 21 Sept. 1854, 11 Jan. 1855; annual report 1854. 212 Ibid., 2 Nov., 7 Dec. 1854. 213 *RDS Proc.*, xciv, minutes, 1 Apr., 3 May, 6 June 1858. 214 Haughton, *Memoir of James Haughton*, pp. 6, 46. 215 *RDS Proc.*, xcv-xcvi, minutes, 9 June, 3 Nov. 1859.

Sundays.[216] The council recommended compliance, and the society responded to this development by convening a special general meeting on 27 May 1861. The subject of Sunday opening was discussed and rejected on the basis that the board of trade had given a commitment by minute of 11 April 1854 that 'beyond aiding the Society in giving the fullest publicity to its labours, their Lordships will not interfere in its general management'.[217]

The issue was debated in parliament, with little sympathy shown for the society's position by either house. The house of commons voted to make the issuing of the society's annual grant conditional on the Sunday opening of the botanic garden.[218] Opposition within the society collapsed and the general meeting rescinded its earlier decision, on 25 July 1861.[219] The bishop of Meath, and former TCD evangelical, Joseph Henderson Singer (1786–1866) resigned his life membership.[220] The botanic garden was opened to the public on Sunday's from 18 August 1861.[221]

This episode drew the attention of the treasury to the RDS council's lack of executive authority.[222] In 1862 the treasury appointed a small commission of inquiry into the management of the RDS. R.B. McDowell concludes that the decision to appoint a commission was triggered by the RDS request for major capital development grants (for the museum), and the ensuing parliamentary debates on its suitability for grant aid in the light of its resistance to change.[223] The treasury commissioners recommended *inter alia* that the government of the society should be transferred from the general meeting to an elected council, and the society expressed its willingness to adopt this change, appointing a sub-committee to review the charter and the by-laws.[224] Progress was slow, and was interrupted by a decision of the house of commons to appoint a select committee of inquiry into all the scientific institutions in Dublin. This fifteen member committee, which included RDS members Sir Colman O'Loghlen, and Sir Edward Grogan, reiterated the view that full executive authority within the RDS should be transferred from the general meeting to the council. The great defect of the RDS constitution, as perceived by the select committee, was that any decision of the council could be rescinded by the general meeting.

The supplemental charter, designed to remedy this situation, was accepted by the general meeting on 4 January 1866.[225] The first meeting of the council as governing body of the society took place on 31 January 1866.[226] In a symbolic move, the new council agreed to resume the purchasing of newspapers for the members' reading room, on 25 April 1866.[227]

---

216 *RDS Proc.*, xcvii, council minutes, 9 May 1861.   217 Ibid., special general meeting, 27 May 1861.
218 *RDS Proc.*, xcviii, council minutes, 4, 13, 23 July 1861.   219 Ibid., minutes, 25 July 1861.
220 Ibid., council minutes, 1 Aug. 1861.   221 Ibid., minutes, 5 Dec. 1861.   222 Ibid., council minutes, 12 June 1862.   223 R.B. McDowell, *The Irish administration*, pp. 257–63.   224 *RDS Proc.*, xcix, council minutes, 29 Aug. 1862, 11, 25, 29 June 1863.   225 *RDS Proc.*, cii, minutes, 4 Jan. 1866. 226 Ibid., council minutes, 31 Jan. 1866.   227 Ibid., 7 Mar., 11, 25 Apr. 1866.

CHAPTER NINE

Conclusion

Four key issues were identified at the beginning of this study. The first was an internal structural issue, the efficiency of the government of the RDS by the general body of its members – 'the almost unmixed republic'. This system was severely tested in the early nineteenth century, and its appropriateness for the changing times was challenged both internally and externally. The second key issue was the relationship between the society and the state, and its implications for the independence and viability of the society. In part arising from this was a third issue, namely, the ability of the society to fulfill its chartered role as a national development institution. The final issue that requires to be addressed is the imputation of sectarian bigotry arising from the rejection of Archbishop Murray.

Control of finance, of paid staff, and of the formulation of policy, was vested in the general meeting of members under the charter of 1750. This system became cumbersome and slow as total membership grew. As early as 1802 the need to delegate the financial control function to a smaller group was acknowledged. This led to the establishment of the economy committee. However, its role was confined to acting as an adviser on finance to the general meeting. The economy committee's advice was not always consulted, as was the case in 1815 when the general meeting decided, in an outburst of popular enthusiasm, to acquire Leinster House (see chapter 2). Moreover, the effectiveness of the economy committee was further diminished after 1817, when it had to share some functions with the newly established house committee. Substantial changes in the administrative structure of the RDS were introduced between 1815 and 1845. The earliest change effected was the re-organization of the standing committees in 1816. After the reforms of 1816 the numbers, and the functions, of the standing committees were more clearly defined and annual elections were introduced. Nevertheless, the standing committees had very limited discretionary control, even over their own budgets.

The next attempt by the general meeting to delegate effective managerial authority was the creation of a 'general selected committee' in 1829 (see chapter 3). Consisting of ex officio officers and representative members of the standing committees, the general selected committee might have been expected to exert a weighty influence on the policy decisions of the general meeting. It does not appear to have done so to any great extent, and it had hardly any role in negotiations with Dublin Castle during 1836–8. Perhaps this is what prompted

Meenan and Clarke[1] to conclude that the society lacked leadership in the 1830s. Nevertheless, the format of the general selected committee is interesting insofar as it provided a partial model for the executive council in 1838.

The creation of an executive council, formally proposed by Dublin Castle, and recommended by the parliamentary select committee in 1836, was championed within the society by Robert Hutton, Charles William Hamilton, and many others (see chapters 5 and 6). It took two years to accomplish, although this was not due to deliberate procrastination. The charter of 1750 had no provision for the delegation of executive authority from the general meeting to any other body. While accepting, however reluctantly, the need for change, the general meeting had to consider how far it could safely go without the risk of later legal challenge. The council established in 1838 was a compromise. Like the general selected committee, the vice-presidents and honorary secretaries were *ex officio* members, as honorary officers under the charter. Also like the general selected committee, representative members of the standing committees were elected annually to the council by the general meeting. In addition, the general meeting also directly elected representatives to the council. It is clear that the under-lying policy adopted by the general meeting was to tie the council as closely as possible to itself, and in that way to minimize the legal risks attendant on delegation.

Did this formula result in the dissolution of the 'almost unmixed republic'? The answer to that question must be a definite no. The council remained subordinate to the general meeting in all its activities. Although the council was given supervisory control of the standing committees, in any dispute arising between a committee and the council the general meeting exercised final authority. Some control over staff, over the supervision of budgets, and over emergency spending, was conceded to the council. However, accountability and ultimate authority in all these matters, and especially in the formulation of policy, remained with the general meeting. One feature of the 1838 reforms that did operate in the council's favour was the decision to reduce the number of general meetings held from over thirty per annum to twelve. This brought about some natural erosion of control by the general meeting. The council, meeting on a weekly basis, gradually developed an authoritative voice in handling the day-to-day business of the society. To a considerable extent the general meeting did give the council the latitude it needed to work effectively. However, quite early in its existence the council faced a challenge from the general meeting on capital spending. Having noted these inherent difficulties affecting the constitutional position of the council, it is only fair to add that for over twenty years the general meeting honoured the understanding entered into by the delegation of its authority to an executive council. In the end, it was the government of the

1 James Meenan and Desmond Clarke (eds), *The Royal Dublin Society, 1731–1981* (Dublin, 1981).

day that grasped the nettle in the 1860s, and offered the society a supplemental charter designed to remove the power of the general meeting (except in constitutional matters) and transfer the government of the society to an elected council. Government by 'an almost unmixed republic' was not invariably bad, the general meeting often showing surprising wisdom and flexibility in its deliberations. The main problems it exhibited were a tedious slowness in reaching decisions, and a tendency to be swayed by passing impulses.

The history of the Royal Dublin Society for much of the nineteenth century revolved around its relationship with the United Kingdom government, and its struggle for financial independence from that government. From the state's perspective the society was an unwieldy, and uncertain partner, which did not always enjoy the confidence of the Irish people. Unlike less independent bodies, which could be dissolved by cutting off grant aid, the society had too large a membership, and too great a presence in Irish science and art education, to be easily dismissed. Its private interest in its extensive Dublin properties and collections was so enmeshed with the public interest that the two could not readily be divorced. The society, for its part, saw itself as a victim of the act of union. By comparison with the esteem in which it had been held by the Irish parliament, the Westminster parliament, in between long bouts of neglect, appeared to show a gross insensitivity to the society's public position.

Meenan and Clarke[2] concluded that the society had in some measure lost its sense of purpose following the passage of the act of union. Certainly, its eighteenth century role as a dispenser of government subsidies, and a promoter of agricultural development, faded after the union. There is a sense in which the *Proceedings* for the first thirty years of the nineteenth century reflect an uneasiness with these changes, but loss of a sense of purpose seems too sweeping an explanation for the adjustment problems then being experienced. The United Kingdom government offered no substitute for the intimate relationship between the Irish parliament and the society, and this must have been disconcerting. John Turpin[3] argues that the society failed to adapt to the post-union world through an inability to make new political alliances. There are sound arguments for taking this view, and it is also in some respects an endorsement of the society's stated position as a neutral body. The corollary is that neither of the two major political groupings likely to form a government in Westminster had much empathy with the RDS. Although the Tory government, as represented in Dublin by Lord de Grey, did show some sympathy and generosity towards the society in the early 1840s, their predecessors in the 1820s were responsible for initiating the grant reductions. Moreover, the Wellington administration had taken the first steps, in 1829, towards demanding constitutional reforms in the society.

2 Ibid. 3 Turpin, *A school of art in Dublin*.

The Whig-liberal alliance with O'Connell in the 1830s seems retrospectively to have played the dominant and defining role in relations between the RDS and the state. However, in most respects the positions the Whigs adopted can be seen as part of a continuum of policy, inherited from the earlier Tory administrations, and picked up again, if a little more tactfully, by the Tories in succession to the Whigs. That the Whigs were more ideologically driven than the Tories in their approach to the RDS can hardly be doubted. Meenan and Clarke detected such undertones in the Morpeth proposals of 1840 (see chapter 7). There was certainly a Whig obsession with the issue of ownership of the society's property. Oddly, however, it was the Tories who put forward one of the most radical ideas (never implemented), that the society should open its membership to all applicants, without election. If there was a single uniting issue for both Whigs and Tories it was that the society should reform its internal structures, in particular the exercise of control by the general meeting, deemed slow and capricious. The creation of an executive council went some distance to meet this demand. The Whigs, as represented by Lord Morpeth, remained dissatisfied, but the Tories accepted in 1841 that the RDS had fully implemented all government requirements at that time. By 1845 the RDS had settled into an amicable relationship with the Tory administration and was apparently once again in good standing with the government.

Given its difficulties with the state, and diminishing income, how did the RDS measure up to its responsibilities as defined in the charter, during 1815–45? According to De Vere White, *pace* Thomas Davis, not only was the society's structure, but also the scope of its objects, too diffuse by nineteenth century standards. Be that as it may, it is arguable that the very diversity of its objects enabled it to cope remarkably well with its straitened circumstances. R.F. Foster[4] remarks that the society's reliance on state subsidies discouraged it from innovating, and this is probably true of the late eighteenth-century society. However, from the 1820s, when subsidies were diminishing, there is clear evidence of innovatory policies receiving widespread support within the society. This is illustrated in a minor way by the straw-hat project (chapter 2), and more clearly in the development of the agricultural and industrial exhibitions during the 1830s. The inauguration of the Spring Cattle Show, and the manufactures exhibition, appears to have owed little to government influence, and much to the vision of Isaac Weld that Dublin should have a general exhibition on the French model. Likewise, the development of practical science education, while its initial impetus came from the Irish parliament, was an outstanding example of the society's innovatory spirit.

The reduction of state subsidies impacted most strongly on elements of the society's eighteenth century heritage. The case for discontinuing geological

4 Foster, *Modern Ireland, 1660–1972.*

fieldwork was strengthened although not entirely met, by the establishment of the Irish ordnance survey under direct government control. However, the discontinuance of the veterinary establishment served no purpose other than cost savings, and left a gap in Irish agricultural services not filled until the late-nineteenth century. It was one bad decision, acknowledged as such by the society at the time, which could clearly be attributed to government parsimony. Surprisingly, most other of the society's eighteenth-century projects experienced growth during 1815–45, the short-fall in government support being made up from the private funds of the society, the donations of individual members, and the wider public. By 1845 the museum, the botanic garden, the library, and the art school, had developed the characteristics of national institutions, and to some extent the physical presence that they have retained under state control to the present day. The society was a popular body amongst the small but growing educated class. Its reach, through the broad scope of its activities, was country wide, and it was broadening its audience through its work in science and agriculture. While many commentators had reservations about its structure, or its efficiency, or its utility, or its Dublin orientation, few doubts were expressed about its philanthropic nature. Intellectual nationalism, as represented by Davis, seemed to view it with some pride as a uniquely Irish institution. At the same time its history and its traditions enabled it to serve as an intellectual bridge between all political persuasions. Its own view of its work was that it represented an example of practical patriotism.

Finally for consideration is the interesting issue of sectarianism; whether or not it existed within the society, and, if so, was it a part of the society's ethos? The answer to the first part of the question must surely be in the affirmative. Elements in Irish society during 1815–45 had become increasingly attached to an aggressive form of religious identification that viewed tolerance as weakness. As individuals, the members of the RDS could not be altogether immune from the religious animosities and controversies flowing all around them. Some, indeed, did not conceal zealousness in religious matters that needed as part of its sustenance the demonising of any and all opposite viewpoints. While acknowledging that some members held sectarian attitudes, a few notoriously so, it would be unreasonable to argue that such views predominated within the society. In early nineteenth century terms it was not very sectarian. Its admission and employment policies were not exclusivist and it took a genuine pride in being a body where people of conflicting religious, and political viewpoints could set aside their differences and work in harmony.[5] In particular, accusations of an anti-catholic bias hardly stand up to scrutiny when measured against the record of catholic participation rates in both voluntary and paid offices within the society (see chapters 1 and 5).

5 See p. 127, memorial to lord lieutenant, *RDS Proc.*, lxxii, 17 Mar. 1836.

How then can the rejection of Archbishop Murray be explained? While residual sectarian feeling cannot be ruled out as a factor, there is little evidence to suggest that it could have been sufficient to sway the decision. The parliamentary select committee report of 1836 reached no conclusion on the matter. While the evidence of witnesses conflicted, there was a near universal rejection of the notion that sectarianism had played any significant part in determining the decision of the meeting. Instead, the overwhelming body of evidence suggests that quasi-political motives prompted opposition to Murray's candidacy. It was, in effect, an expression of distaste for the politics of Daniel O'Connell. However, there is also a further possible motive that cannot be disregarded. This was a widespread perception that gained credence before the meeting that Dublin Castle was using Murray's candidacy as a test of the society's willingness to comply with its wishes, and therefore, in the view of many, as a threat to the society's independence. This perspective on the issue was addressed forcefully by Dr William Harty in his evidence, and its power acknowledged by the pro-Murray vice-president James Naper. Archbishop Murray was the unfortunate victim of this power struggle. While the society survived the outcome, the episode left the allegation of sectarian bias buried deep in public perceptions and liable to surface from time-to-time. Thus, even in the late twentieth century, Daniel Hoctor wrote of the RDS, 'It could be bigoted on occasions as when it rejected the Most Rev. Dr Murray, Catholic Archbishop of Dublin – a man who was popular with all classes – for membership'.[6]

The underlying feature of the society's history during 1815–45 is its struggle to maintain its institutional independence. The RDS had clearly over-extended itself financially with the acquisition of Leinster House, and its money problems became increasingly obvious as government subsidies were decreased. The contrastingly generous treatment of the British Museum became the yardstick by which the society measured its own decline. In the end, there was no path to sustainable growth in partnership with the state. The society needed, above all, independent sources of income, and it found these through its own efforts in the world of exhibitions and agricultural shows.

6 Daniel Hoctor, *The department's story: a history of the Department of Agriculture* (Dublin, 1971), p. 13.

Estimated RDS members at 1 January in selected years, 1815–45
(source: Appendix I)

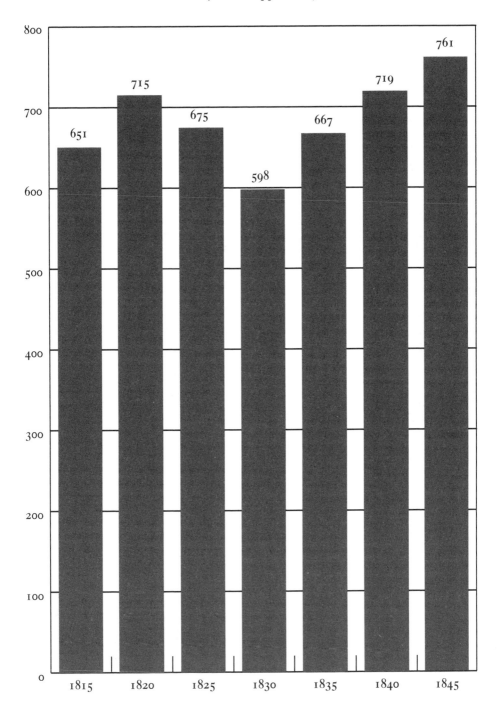

RDS members elected in selected years, 1815–45
(source: Appendix I)

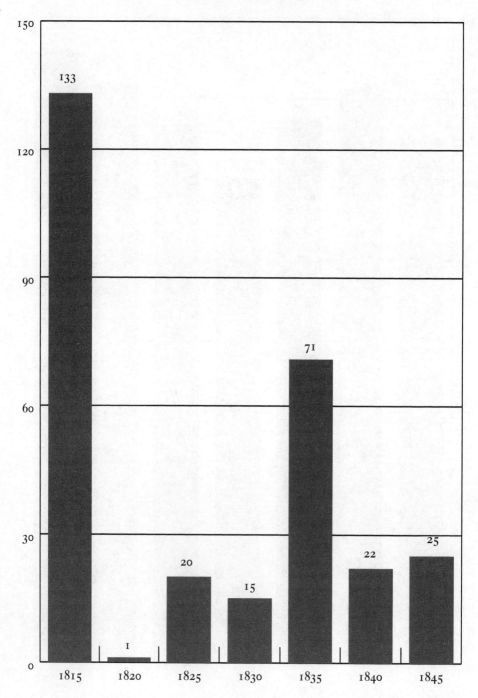

Ordinary members of the Dublin Society/RDS, at 1 January 1800–50

	1 January	Elected in year	Deleted in year		1 January	Elected in year	Deleted in year
1800	293	69	9	1826	674	10	26
1801	353	101	15	1827	658	5	36
1802	439	51	25	1828	627	7	9
1803	465	40	11	1829	625	7	34
1804	494	13	19	1830	598	15	22
1805	488	5	7	1831	591	4	21
1806	486	21	11	1832	574	7	13
1807	496	30	11	1833	568	54	15
1808	515	40	14	1834	607	84	24
1809	541	32	18	1835	667	71	32
1810	555	62	10	1836	706	12	24
1811	607	43	15	1837	694	12	18
1812	635	14	11	1838	688	33	13
1813	638	17	15	1839	708	51	40
1814	640	17	6	1840	719	22	33
1815	651	131	10	1841	708	20	15
1816	772	7	32	1842	713	25	14
1817	747	2	9	1843	724	26	12
1818	740	3	18	1844	738	39	16
1819	725	7	17	1845	761	25	15
1820	715	1	11	1846	771	46	38
1821	705	16	16	1847	779	34	22
1822	705	11	25	1848	791	37	23
1823	691	11	19	1849	805	26	22
1824	683	15	23	1850	809		
1825	675	20	21				

Source: Author's database at 26 March 2004. Non-voting members excluded. The membership lists published in the *Treble Almanack* up to 1830 were not wholly reliable and details of new members have been taken instead from the election reports published in the society's proceedings.

Deletion dates up to 1830 are based on comparisons of the annual published lists. More reliable information on death dates has been substituted where available from sources such as *Burke*, *DNB*, newspaper obituaries, and references in the society's proceedings. For the period 1830–45 numbers at 1 January, and numbers deleted during the year, are approximations, and subject to revision.

Attendances at RDS general meetings, 1800–39

1 Total meetings and average attendance each decade, 1800–39

decade	meetings	average attendance	% of membership
1800–09	337	22	4.8
1810–19	312	51	7.3
1820–29	334	43	6.3
1830–39	192	48	7.6

2 Total meetings and average attendance, 1830–39

	meetings	average attendance	% of membership
1830	33	32	5.3
1831	39	32	5.5
1832	35	29	5.1
1833	30	40	6.9
1834	30	63	10.0
1835	31	58	11.8
1836	33	63	9.0
1837	29	42	6.0
1838	20	59	8.5
1839	12	57	8.0

3 Members attending at least one general meeting, 1830–39

	members attending at least once	% of membership
1830	190	32.8
1831	196	34.8
1832	159	28.5
1833	272	45.6
1834	344	52.4
1835	320	46.1
1836	284	41.6
1837	232	34.3
1838	275	41.5
1839	226	33.6

Source: RDS *Proc.*, xxxvi–lxxiv, attendance lists analysed by the author. During 1802–54 a full list of names of all members present at general meetings was given in the minutes. Prior to, and post-1854, only the name of the chairman, any honorary officers present, and the number of ordinary members present, are given.

RDS vice-presidents and honorary secretaries, 1815–45

Vice-presidents

Up to seven vice-presidents were elected annually under the 1750 charter. They played a key constitutional role at general meetings, and were (from 1802) ex-officio members of all committees.

Vice-presidents	*served*
John Foster (1740–1828), 1st Baron Oriel	1775–1828
Lodge Morres (1747–1822), 1st Baron Frankfort de Montmorency	1776–1822
David Latouche (1729–1817), Bank of Ireland	1801–17
Charles Bury (1764–1835), earl of Charleville	1803–22
Robert Shaw (1774–1849), banker	1812–49
John Brabazon (1772–1851), 10th earl of Meath	1812–36
John Leslie Foster (1781–1842), MP Co. Louth	1813–42
Peter Digges Latouche, merchant banker	1817–20
George Knox, MP Dublin University	1820–27
John Pomeroy (1758–1833), Lord Harberton	1822–33
Henry Joy (1763–1838), chief baron of the exchequer court	1822–38
John Henry North, MP Dublin University	1827–31
John Boyd (1769–1836), Ballymacool, Letterkenny, Co. Donegal	1828–36
Arthur Hill (1788–1845), Lord Downshire	1831–45
James Naper (1791–1868), Loughcrew, Co. Meath	1833–43
Henry Kemmis, barrister, Kildare Street	1836–57
John Devonsher Jackson (1783–1857), MP Bandon	1836–57
Sir William Betham, Ulster king of arms	1838–53
William Trench (1803–72), Lord Clancarty	1842–72
John Butler, Lord Ormonde	1843–47
Charles Fitzgerald (1819–87), Lord Kildare	1845–74

Honorary secretaries

Two honorary secretaries were elected annually. Their function was to supervise the administration of the society, and arrange general meetings. From 1822 they were ex-officio members of all committees.

Honorary secretaries	
Jeremiah D'Olier, banker	1810–17
Henry Joy (1763–1838), barrister, later vice-president 1822–38	1813–22
John Beatty, physician	1822–31
John Boyd (1769–1836), barrister, later vice-president 1828–36	1817–28
Charles Stewart Hawthorne, excise commissioner	1831–4
Robert Butler Bryan, barrister	1834–41
Isaac Weld (1774–1856), later vice-president 1849–56	1828–49
Lundy Edward Foot (1791–1863), barrister, later vice-president 1857–63	1841–57

RDS standing committees, 1815–45

committee	established	function
fine arts	c.1750	Supervised drawing schools, 1750–1877. Masters of schools reported to this committee.
botany	1795	Supervised botanic garden, Glasnevin, 1795–1877. Professor, curator, head and under gardeners reported to this committee. Incorporated agriculture, 1815–30. Re-named committee of botany and horticulture in 1838.
chemistry	1802	Supervised laboratory and organised public lectures. Was also responsible for geological museum, and geological surveys, 1802–38. Professors, lecturers, and mining engineer reported to this committee. Amalgamated with natural philosophy committee to form science committee in 1867.
economy	1803	Supervised financial control and internal audit of the society until replaced by the executive council in 1838.
natural philosophy	1811	Supervised lectures on physics. Professors and lecturers reported to this committee. Re-named committee of natural philosophy and mechanics in 1838–67.
library	1812	Supervised library and librarian, 1812–77, and transition to national library, 1877–91.
house	1817	Supervised maintenance of Leinster House and grounds until its functions were taken over by the executive council in 1838.
agriculture and planting	1830	Supervised agricultural shows and dealings with agricultural societies. Re-named committee of agriculture and husbandry in 1838.
natural history and museum	1832	Supervised museum collections, and work of curator, 1832–77. The geological museum was transferred to its charge in 1838, when it was re-named the committee of natural history, geology, mineralogy, and museum. It was frequently referred to as the museum committee.
general selected	1834	Created as a sub-committee of the general meeting in 1829, its function was to monitor the activities of the society and report to the general meeting. It consisted of the vice-presidents, the honorary secretaries, and representatives of the standing committees appointed by the general meeting. It was the precursor of the executive council, and abolished on the establishment of that body in 1838.
manufactures	1838	Supervised the organisation and running of industrial exhibitions, 1838–67.
statistics	1838	Created to promote improvements in the presentation of official statistics, it was discontinued in 1841.

Occupations of RDS members, in selected years, 1800–50

Principal occupation	1800 %	1820 %	1829 %	1834 %	1841 %	1850 %
peers and baronets	20.1	9.7	8.4	9.3	7.9	6.8
politicians	8.5	4.1	4.6	1.6	2.1	1.8
landowners	31.7	22.4	21.7	19.8	18.1	18.0
clergy of the established church	6.8	7.6	8.3	8.1	7.2	5.9
miltary and naval officers	2.4	1.7	1.7	2.1	2.0	2.1
government and municipal officials	3.8	5.0	5.4	4.7	4.5	3.4
judiciary and lawyers	3.1	18.7	19.0	22.2	22.4	21.2
medicine and science	1.4	4.1	4.3	5.4	8.6	9.0
engineers and architects	1.7	1.9	2.4	2.8	2.7	2.1
banking and insurance	3.1	3.2	3.5	3.4	4.4	4.8
commerce and manufacturing	11.6	16.7	15.6	14.1	14.5	15.8
other	5.8	4.9	5.1	6.5	5.6	9.1
total	100.0	100.0	100.0	100.0	100.0	100.0
number of members, at 1 January	293	715	625	607	708	809

Source: Author's database at 10 Jan. 2001. These are point measurements, and occupation may vary from one decade to another.

RDS elected paid officials, 1815–45

ADMINISTRATION		
assistant secretary	Bucknall McCarthy (1774–1829)	1808–29
	Edward Hardman (1769–1854)	1829–50
registrar	Thomas Lysaght	1808–19
	Peter Theodore Wilson (1780–1853)	1819–53
housekeeper	Peter Theodore Wilson	1807–19

LIBRARY		
translator and corrector of the press	Reverend John Lanigan	1798–1828
assistant librarian	Reverend John Lanigan	1808–14
librarian	Samuel Litton (1795–1847)	1815–25
	Frederick Cradock	1826–33
	John Patten	1833–55

ART SCHOOL		
architecture master	Henry Aaron Baker	1786–1836
	John Papworth	1838–41
	Duncan Campbell Ferguson	1842–55
drawing and ornament master	Henry Brocas	1800–37
	Henry Brocas, junior	1838–55
figure drawing master	Robert Lucius West (1774–1850)	1809–45
sculpture and modeling master	John Smyth (1773–1840)	1811–40
	Constantine Panormo	1840–52

SCIENCE		
chemistry professor	William Higgins (1763–1825)	1795–1825
	Edmund Davy (1785–1857)	1826–57
chemistry assistant	Samuel Wharmby	1805–24
	Edward Bell Stephens	1824–31
mining engineer	Richard Griffith (1784–1878)	1812–29
mineralogy professor	Robert Jameson (resigned)	1812–13
	Sir Charles Ludwig Giesecke	1813–33
	John Scouler (1804–71)	1834–64
natural philosophy professor	Robert Kane	1839–47
natural philosophy lecturer	James Lynch	1800–33
	Robert Kane	1834–39

AGRICULTURE		
veterinary professor	Thomas Peall	1800–25
model maker	Adam Oliver	1803–24
agricultural museum curator	James Duffus	1843–45

BOTANY		
botany professor	Walter Wade (1760–1825)	1796–1825
	Samuel Litton	1825–46
curator	Ninian Niven	1834–38
	David Moore	1838–65
head gardener	John Underwood	1798–1834
under gardeners	John White	1800–35
	John Mackie	1815–21

Elected members of RDS standing committees, 1815–45

[Where breaks occurred, actual service is shown after members details.]

member	committee	served
	FINE ARTS	
Henry Hamilton (1760–1844), Ballymacoll, Dunboyne		1800–20
Alexander Carroll, barrister, [(1807–16, 1820–3, 1834–49)]		1807–49
Richard Fox (1760–1833), Foxhall, Co. Longford		1808–33
Henry Charles Sirr (1764–1841), Dublin town major		1808–35
Isaac Weld (1774–1856), Bray, [(1808–14, 1823–9)]		1808–29
James Gandon junior, architect, [(1809–20, 1837–40)]		1809–40
Francis Johnston (1760–1829), architect		1809–15
John Madden, junior		1809–15
Arthur Richards Neville, Dublin city surveyor		1809–18
John Crossley Seymour, clergyman		1809–31
William Cusack Smith (1766–1836), 2nd baronet		1809–15
Thomas Walker, chancery court judge		1809–15
Wilcocks Huband (1787–1834), barrister		1811–17
John Gage Davis, barrister, Booterstown		1813–34
Henry Maning [sic], Royal Irish Art Institution		1814–37
John Boyd (1769–1836), Ballymacool		1816–21
John Cash, alderman		1816–23
Samuel Guinness, barrister		1816–20
Reverend Henry Moore, Granby Row		1816–20
Charles Mulvany, glass merchant		1816–23
Reverend John Pomeroy (1758–1833), 4th Viscount Harberton		1816–22
Ralph Ward Reid, Clare Street		1816–19
George Cash, barrister [(1817–19, 1834–43)]		1817–43
Joseph P. Griffith, clergyman		1818–34
John Beatty, M.D.		1819–20
William Digges La Touche, junior		1819–20
John Crosbie Graves (1776–1835), Dublin police magistrate		1823–27
Matthew Weld Hartstonge, barrister		1823–34
Richard Dunne, Sackville Street		1828–39
Jonathan Rogers, Belvedere Place		1829–31
Arthur Percy Aylmer (1801–85), 11th baronet, Donadea Castle		1831–37
Isaac Matthew D'Olier, Bank of Ireland		1832–48
Martin Cregan (1788–1870), RHA		1834–54
William John Moore, attorney		1834–35
Frederick Darley junior, architect		1835–48
Daniel McKay, lawyer		1835–40
George Carr, Bank of Ireland		1837–39
William Hardman, Upper Mount Street		1839–44
Arthur Burgh Crofton		1839–41

member	served
William Vicars Griffith	1840–45
Henry Smith, William Street	1840–41
James Richard Cooke, barrister	1841–48
Edward Tighe, barrister	1841–52
Robert Callwell, Bank of Ireland	1842–56
George Colomb, army general, Dalkey	1842–54
William Longfield, surveyor and valuer	1843–49
John Hamilton, physician	1845–56

BOTANY

member	served
Edward Houghton, barrister	1806–33
Jeremiah D'Olier	1809–16
James Symes, clergyman, Co. Wicklow	1810–19
Isaac Matthew D'Olier, Booterstown	1811–49
John Dunne, lawyer	1812–16
Hugh Hamill, calico merchant	1812–16
Henry Moore, clergyman, Granby Row	1812–23
John Slacke, barrister	1812–19
Richard Cave, North Frederick Street	1813–17
Stephen Draper, postal official	1813–18
John Giffard, newspaper publisher	1814–19
Thomas Taylor, botanist	1814–20
Christopher Stone Williams, barrister	1814–23
John Boyd, Ballymacool	1816–20
James Browne, Lord Kilmaine	1816–20
Richard Cane, Dawson Street	1816–17
Richard Fox, Co. Longford	1816–20
Edward William Scott, barrister	1816–20
Thomas Townsend, barrister	1816–23
Reverend Dr Robert Handcock	1817–19
Nathaniel Hone, alderman	1818–19
Sir William Betham, Ulster king of arms	1819–30
Walter Glascock, attorney	1819–20
Robert Moore Peile, surgeon	1819–27
Simon Purdon, barrister	1819–24
Peter Digges Latouche, Barrow Navigation Company	1820–23
George Chamley, Upper Gardiner Street	1823–26
Joseph Clarke, master of Rotunda hospital	1823–34
Simon Foot, Grand Canal Company of Ireland	1823–73
Robert Rundel Guinness, merchant banker	1823–26
George Colley, Ferney, Stillorgan	1824–28
Isaac D'Olier, banker	1824–25
Robert Lanigan, barrister, Harcourt Street	1825–27
Brindley Hone, barrister	1826–28
Robert Shaw junior, 2nd baronet, Bushy Park, Terenure	1826–68
John Robertson, Kilkenny	1827–28
William West, physician, Gardiner Place	1827–37
Lundy Edward Foot, tobacconist	1828–29
Henry William Mulvany, barrister	1828–61
Haliday Bruce, insurance broker, Dame Street	1829–41
William Harty, physician	1829–37
Leland Crosthwaite junior, merchant, Fleet Street	1833–52

member	served
John George junior, judge, Leeson Street	1834–44
Edward Croker, merchant, Mountjoy Square	1835–39
Arthur Burgh Crofton [(1837–43, 1847–48)]	1837–48
Martin Brownly Rutherfoord, barrister	1839–41
Francis Whitla, solicitor	1841–43
Charles Perceval Croker, physician, Merrion Square	1842–62
Robert Wybrants, barrister, Rutland Square	1842–67
Sir Edward Borough	1843–44
George Roe, distiller	1843–61
Arthur B. Cane, Dawson Street	1844–57

CHEMISTRY

member	served
Henry Hamilton, Ballymacool, Dunboyne	1802–26
George Knox, MP	1802–20
Abraham Mills, Co. Wicklow	1802–25
Henry Joy, barrister	1808–21
Thomas Weaver, geologist [(1808–20, 1829–30)]	1808–30
Richard Griffith, 1st Baronet [(1809, 1830–37)]	1809–37
John Staunton Rochfort, Cloghgrennan, Co. Carlow	1809–20
Anthony Meyler, physician [(1811–14, 1828–44)]	1811–44
Richard Steele, baronet	1811–16
Robert Hutton, coach builder, Summerhill	1812–30
Thomas Staples, 9th Baronet	1812–23
John Slacke, barrister	1814–20
Charles Wye Williams, engineer	1814–16
James Cleghorn, physician	1816–23
Quin John Freeman, army general	1816–17
John Giffard, publisher	1816–19
Charles Mulvany, glass merchant	1816–17
Edward William Scott, barrister	1816–27
Henry Charles Sirr, town major	1816–20
Nicholas Philpot Leader, MP Kilkenny	1817–31
James Browne, 2nd Baron Kilmaine	1818–20
Morley Saunders, Co. Wicklow	1819–23
Robert Barnwall, 8th baronet	1821–22
Hugh Hamill, calico merchant	1821–35
John Duffy, textile manufacturer, Ballsbridge	1823–47
John Patten, wool merchant [(1823–29, 1832–33)]	1823–33
William Willans, woollen manufacturer	1823–29
Maziere Brady, barrister	1824–25
William Hargrave, surgeon	1824–56
Isaac D'Olier, secretary Board of First Fruits	1825–38
David Hastings McAdam, physician	1827–29
William Crofton Beatty, physician	1830–46
Alexander Read, surgeon	1833–58
Edward Clibborn, secretary Royal Irish Academy	1835–36
Joshua Abell	1837–46
William O'Brien Bellingham, surgeon	1838–40
Simeon Boileau, druggist	1837–41
Thomas Grace Geoghegan, surgeon [(1840–1, 1858–60)]	1840–60
James Perry, ironfounder	1841–44

member	*served*
Richard Purdy, Mining Company of Ireland	1842–44
Edward Irwin, merchant	1842–44
Thomas Antisell, surgeon	1844–46
William Vallancey Drury, physician	1844–47
John Moore Neligan, physician	1844–47
Joseph Hone junior, attorney	1844–45
John Oliver Curran, physician	1845–47

ECONOMY

Lundy Foot, tobacconist	1803–20
John Campbell, Eccles Street	1810–21
Thomas Browne, Baggot Street	1811–31
Thomas Goffe, clergyman, Eccles Street	1812–28
Stephen Draper, postal official	1814–17
John Giffard, newspaper publisher	1814–16
William Harty, physician	1814–16
Thomas Nowlan, lawyer, Westmoreland Street	1814–16
John Patten, wool merchant	1814–16
Charles Wye Williams, engineer	1814–20
Robert Butler Bryan, barrister	1816–34
Richard Darling, merchant	1816–20
John De Courcy, lawyer	1816–20
John Swift Emerson, attorney	1816–28
Walter Glascock, attorney	1816–17
Reverend Joseph P. Griffith	1816–18
Thomas Richard Needham, banker	1816–20
Thomas Edward Herbert Orpen, physician	1816–38
John Schoales, barrister	1816–29
George Tuthill, Fitzwilliam Square and Kilmore, Co. Limerick	1816–26
Peter Digges Latouche, Barrow Navigation Company	1817–20
Edward Tierney, barrister	1819–38
John Berrell, architect	1821–31
William Stewart, Major 30th regiment	1826–34
Joseph Thomas Kane, land agent	1829–35
Thomas McKenny, alderman	1829–37
Richard Palmer, lawyer	1829–31
Robert Rundel Guinness, Guinness and Mahon bank	1831–38
Henry Darley, physician, Kildare Street	1832–38
Hugh Ferguson, physician	1832–36
Percival Hunt, MD	1834–35
Robert Moore Peile, surgeon	1834–38
William Haughton, flour merchant	1835–38
George Pim, merchant	1835–38
Thomas Willans, woollen merchant	1836–38
Joseph Hone junior	1837–38

NATURAL PHILOSOPHY

Hugh Hamill, calico merchant [(1812–16, 1834–5)]	1812–35
Nicholas Philpot Leader, MP Kilkenny	1812–20
John Patten, wool merchant [(1812–16, 1830–33)]	1812–33

member	served
Stephen Draper, postal official	1815–22
Henry Adair, barrister	1816–40
Robert Bennett, barrister	1816–22
Josias Dunn, solicitor	1816–20
Reverend Robert Handcock	1816–20
William Harty, physician	1816–17
Edward Houghton, barrister	1816–20
Robert Hutton, coach builder	1816–20
William Digges Latouche, barrister	1816–23
Archibald Hamilton Rowan, Rathcoffey, Co. Kildare	1816–29
Reverend John Crossley Seymour	1816–17
Thomas Taylor, MD	1816–18
Thomas Weaver, geologist	1816–20
John Staunton Rochfort, Co. Carlow	1817–20
Robert Lanigan, barrister	1818–24
Arthur Richards Neville, surveyor	1818–23
Reverend Joseph P. Griffith	1819–20
Lundy Foot, tobacconist	1821–23
John Crosbie Graves, magistrate	1821–23
George Grierson, printer	1821–22
John Richard Corballis, barrister	1822–34
Fenton Hort, Leopardstown	1822–25
John Henry North, MP	1823–24
Charles Putland, Bray, Co. Wicklow	1824–38
Stephen Creagh Sandes, FTCD	1824–31
James Bulwer, clergyman	1825–27
Lundy Foot, clergyman	1825–28
Richard MacDonnell, FTCD	1825–32
John Goddard Richards, Co. Wexford	1825–26
John W. Hart, professor of surgery, RCSI	1826–49
John Charles Martin, FTCD	1826–32
Charles William Wall, FTCD	1826–32
John Oldham, engineer	1829–32
Francis Sadleir, FTCD	1830–35
H.H. Harte, FTCD	1830–33
Edward Stephens, soap merchant	1831–34
John Oliver, Co. Wicklow	1832–36
John Duffy, textile manufacturer, Ballsbridge	1834–47
William Cotter Kyle, lawyer	1833–34
Edward Clibborn, secretary Royal Irish Academy	1835–49
Howard Cooke, physician [(1835–36, 1846–47)]	1835–47
Michael Bernard Mullins, civil engineer [(1835–36, 1861–62)]	1835–62
Richard Townson Evanson, surgeon	1835–36
Crofton Moore Vandeleur, Co. Clare	1836–37
Joshua Abell, publisher	1838–44
Reverend Smith Whitelaw Fox	1838–41
Nathaniel Hone junior, banker	1838–39
William O'Brien Bellingham, surgeon	1838–40
William Longfield, surveyor and valuer	1839–54
John Francis O'Neill Lentaigne, physician	1840–49
James McCullagh, FTCD	1840–42
Michael Martin O'Grady, physician	1841–49

member	served
Reverend Hugh Edward Prior	1841–42
William Edward Bolton, solicitor [(1842–3, 1846–55, 1860–65)]	1842–65
Villiers Bussy Fowler, attorney	1842–43
Robert Walker Greer, attorney	1842–52
James Pim junior, Dublin-Kingstown railway	1844–45

LIBRARY

Henry William Arabin, barrister, Clare Street	1812–20
Robert Butler Bryan, barrister	1812–16
William Farran, solicitor, Eccles Street	1812–16
Richard Fox (1760–1833), Foxhall, Co. Longford	1812–16
Hugh Hamill, calico merchant	1812–16
George Knox, MP Dublin University	1812–16
Nicholas Philpot Leader, MP	1812–16
Henry Moore, clergyman, Granby Row	1812–16
Stephen Draper, postal official	1813–16
John Giffard, newspaper publisher	1813–16
William Harty, physician	1813–17
Henry Joy, barrister	1813–16
Thomas Nowlan, lawyer, Westmoreland Street	1813–17
Charles Wye Williams, engineer	1813–16
Robert Barnwall (1767–1836), 8th baronet	1815–16
John Boyd, barrister, Ballymacool, Co. Donegal	1815–16
Thomas Goffe, clergyman, Eccles Street	1815–16
John Madden junior, barrister, Mountjoy Square	1815–16
James Mahon, barrister, North Cumberland Street	1815–22
Anthony Meyler, physician [(1815–16, 1824–28)]	1815–28
John Gage Davis, barrister	1816–20
John Dunne, lawyer	1816–20
Molesworth Greene, town clerk	1816–20
Samuel Guinness, barrister	1816–22
Reverend Samuel Kyle, provost TCD	1816–19
Arthur Chichester Macartney, barrister	1816–27
Paul L. Patrick, MRIA [(1816–23, 1829–31)]	1816–31
Reverend John Middleton Scott, Co. Wicklow	1816–18
John Smyly, barrister	1816–20
Ambrose Smyth, governor of Foundling Hospital	1816–28
John White, Atlas Insurance Company	1816–23
Thomas Taylor, MD	1817–20
Edward Fitzsimons, Hibernian Journal	1818–20
Reverend Dr Robert Handcock	1819–28
Robert Smyth, St Stephen's Green	1819–28
John Smyth, Co. Wicklow	1821–26
Arthur Forbes, barrister	1822–23
Edward O'Grady, barrister, St Stephen's Green	1822–32
John Smith, barrister	1822–25
John McKay, merchant	1823–39
Lundy Edward Foot	1824–25
John Anster (1793–1867), [(1825–7, 1829–36, 1839–66)]	1825–66
Robert Moore Peile, surgeon	1827–33
Wilcocks Huband, barrister	1828–32

member	*served*
Richard Hemphill, attorney, Charlemont Street	1829–63
Thomas Henley, barrister	1829–34
Thomas Hewson, surgeon	1829–31
Eccles Cuthbert, barrister	1830–35
Brindley Hone (1796–1862), barrister, Monkstown	1830–43
John Hare, attorney, Baggot Street	1831–39
Robert Harrison, surgeon	1831–33
John George junior (1804–71), barrister	1833–48
Edwards Richards Purefoy Colles, barrister	1834–49
William West, physician	1835–37
James Richard Cooke, barrister, Blessington Street	1836–53
John Robert Boyd, barrister	1836–39
Edward Clibborn, secretary Royal Irish Academy	1838–57
William O'Bryen Bellingham (1805–57), surgeon, St Vincent's hospital	1839–54
Patrick Robert Webb, barrister, St Stephen's Green	1839–52
Mountifort Longfield, law professor TCD	1842–44
Edward Tighe, barrister, Hatch Street	1842–48
Robert Tighe, barrister	1843–44
John Smith Furlong, barrister, Leeson Street	1844–46

HOUSE

John Beatty, physician	1817–22
John Cash, alderman	1817–20
Stephen Draper, post office official	1817–21
John Giffard, publisher	1817–18
Walter Glascock, attorney	1817–24
Molesworth Greene, town clerk	1817–20
Henry Maning	1817–20
Charles Mulvany, glass merchant	1817–20
James Palmer, prison inspector	1817–27
Paul L. Patrick	1817–20
Reverend John Pomeroy	1817–20
Reverend John Crossley Seymour	1817–20
Henry Charles Sirr, town major	1817–18
Sir Edward Stanley, prison inspector	1817–38
Thomas Townsend, barrister	1817–20
Edward William Scott, barrister	1818–19
William Stamer, baronet	1818–30
William Cosby, army major	1819–26
John Creighton, surgeon	1820–26
Benjamin Bowen Johnson, attorney [(1820–34, 1835–38)]	1820–38
William Walsh, merchant	1820–38
Patrick Thomas Flood, merchant	1823–38
William Jones	1824–31
Reverend William Betty	1826–29
Edward Hardman	1826–29
Austin Cooper, antiquarian	1827–29
Leonard Thornhill, ordnance official	1827–38
George Connor, attorney	1828–38
Thomas Conolly, attorney	1829–38

member	served
Thomas Ardill, attorney, Aungier Street	1830–37
John Hughes, secretary to the Barrack Board	1831–38
Edward Richards Purefoy Colles, barrister	1834–38
Arthur Hill Griffith, attorney	1835–37
Alexander Boyle, stockbroker	1837–38
William Thomas Lloyd, barrister	1837–38

AGRICULTURE

member	served
Robert Butler Bryan	1830–34
George Hampden Evans, MP	1830–35
Richard Fox, Co. Longford	1830–33
John Payne Garnett, Arch Hall, Navan	1830–39
Francis Gore, barrister	1830–35
William Harty, physician	1830–35
Charles Stewart Hawthorne	1830–31
Arthur Hill, marquess of Downshire	1830–31
Fenton Hort, Leopardstown, Co. Dublin	1830–37
Valentine Browne Lawless, 2nd Baron Cloncurry	1830–35
James William Lennox Naper	1830–33
George Lucas Nugent, Castlericard	1830–35
Sir Samuel O'Malley, Castlebar	1830–35
Wray Palliser, Comeragh, Co. Waterford	1830–37
John Rorke, Jamestown, Co. Dublin	1830–35
Isaac D'Olier, Board of First Fruits	1831–35
William Filgate, Lisrenny, Co. Louth	1831–50
Joseph Hone, attorney, Harcourt Street	1831–54
Edward Houghton, barrister	1831–33
Robert Latouche, Harristown, Co. Kildare	1831–44
Arthur Hill Cornwallis Pollock, Mountainstown, Co. Meath	1831–43
John Staunton Rochfort, Cloghgrennan, Co. Carlow	1831–37
George Tuthill, Fitzwilliam Square and Kilmore, Co. Limerick	1831–42
James Anthony Corballis, Ratoath Manor, Co. Meath	1835–42
John Laurence Cornwall, Castle Park, Slane, Co. Meath	1835–37
Leland Crosthwaite junior, merchant, Fleet Street	1835–37
Simon Foot, Grand Canal Company of Ireland	1835–42
Richard Griffith, commissioner of valuations	1835–37
Charles William Hamilton, Hamwood, Dunboyne, Co. Meath	1835–37
Nathaniel Hone junior, St Doulough's Park, Co. Dublin	1835–37
Anthony Strong Hussey, Westown, Balbriggan, Co. Dublin	1835–37
Henry Hutton, barrister, Dundrum, Co. Dublin	1835–37
William Owen, Eskendale, Queen's Co.	1835–37
Robert Shaw junior, Bushy Park, Terenure	1835–37
William Sherrard, Dunleer, Co. Louth [(1835–7, 1839–46)]	1835–46
Robert Collins, physician, Ardsallagh, Co. Meath	1838–67
David Charles Latouche, Marley, Co. Dublin	1841–54
John Farrell, Moynalty, Co. Meath	1842–43
Joseph Kincaid, land agent [(1842–5, 1867–9)]	1842–69
Thomas Rutherfoord, Mooretown House, Ardee, Co. Louth	1842–62
Thomas Seymour, Ballymore Castle, Co. Galway	1842–57
Thomas Johnston Barton, Glendalough	1843–45
Edward Lawless, 3rd Baron Cloncurry [(1843–8, 1857–61)]	1843–61
Robert Archbold, MP Co. Kildare	1844–51

member	served

NATURAL HISTORY AND MUSEUM

member	served
William Crofton Beatty, physician	1830–45
John W. Hart, professor of surgery, RCSI	1830–53
Anthony Meyler, physician	1830–44
John Patten, wool merchant	1830–33
Henry Charles Sirr, town major	1830–35
Arthur Percy Aylmer (1801–85), 11th baronet, Donadea Castle	1831–37
Eccles Cuthbert, barrister	1831–35
John Oliver, Co. Wicklow	1833–36
Sir Edward Stanley, prison inspector	1833–49
Howard Cooke, physician	1834–48
R.T. Evanson, surgeon	1836–38
Arthur Hill Griffith, attorney	1836–38
Joseph Ellison Portlock, Dublin Zoo	1836–38
Reverend Smith Whitelaw Fox	1837–41
Robert Ball, Dublin Zoo [(1838–9, 1843–5)]	1838–45
James Macartney, professor of medicine	1838–39
William O'Bryen Bellingham (1805–57), surgeon	1839–49
Richard Weld Hartstonge, army officer	1839–45
Thomas Rutherfoord, barrister	1839–44
Robert Harrison, surgeon	1841–49
William Vicars Griffith	1842–43
Francis Whitla, solicitor	1842–55
Robert Callwell, Bank of Ireland [(1843–8, 1857–8, 1860–70)]	1843–70
Thomas Antisell, surgeon	1844–46
George J. Allman, botanist	1845–55
Philip Bevan, surgeon	1845–79
Hugh Carlisle, surgeon	1845–48

MANUFACTURES

member	served
Patrick Thomas Flood, merchant	1833–41
Benjamin Bowen Johnson, attorney	1833–42
Sir Edward Stanley, prison inspector	1833–50
John Francis O'Neill Lentaigne, physician	1835–49
Thomas Purdon, governor Richmond prison	1835–44
George Tuthill, Co. Limerick	1835–42
Thomas Conolly, attorney	1838–54
Lundy Edward Foot	1838–40
Walter Sweetman, barrister	1838–56
Robert Walker Greer, attorney	1840–49
William Thomas Lloyd, barrister	1841–58
John James Bagot, Rathcoole	1842–43
Henry Darley, physician, Kildare Street	1842–55
Thomas Hutton, coach builder	1842–44
William Henry Porter, surgeon, Meath hospital	1842–53
William Edward Bolton, solicitor	1843–46
Theobald Billing, attorney	1844–46
John Bonner, army major	1844–45
Peter Nugent Fitzgerald, Donore, Co. Westmeath	1845–50

member	*served*
STATISTICS	
Edward Cane, army agent	1838–41
Joseph Hone, solicitor	1838–39
Jefferys Kingsley, Co. Tipperary	1838–41
Anthony Meyler, physician	1838–40
Reverend Hugh Edward Prior	1838–41
James Henthorn Todd, librarian TCD	1838–41
Reverend Richard Wall, schoolmaster	1838–40
Thomas Wallace, MP	1838–40
Reverend James Wilson	1838–40
James Macartney, professor of medicine	1839–40
Henry Courtnay, engineer	1840–41
Villiers Bussy Fowler, secretary Law Society	1840–41
Robert Rundel Guinness, banker	1840–41
Garrett Wall, woollen manufacturer	1840–41
Thomas Willans, woollen manufacturer	1840–41

Members present at RDS general meeting, 26 November 1835 (rejection of Dr Murray)

CHAIR: Sir Robert Shaw, bart., vice-president

Peers and baronets (5)
Henry Stanley Monck, 1st earl of Rathdown
Richard Wogan Talbot, 2nd Baron Talbot de
    Malahide
Sir Thomas Esmonde, 8th baronet
Sir Matthew Barrington, 2nd baronet
Sir Thomas McKenny, baronet

Politicians (5)
Michael O'Loghlen, attorney general
John Richards, solicitor general
Maziere Brady, adviser to under secretary
George Hampden Evans, MP Dublin city
Joseph Devonsher Jackson, MP Bandon

Landowners (18)
Nathaniel Hone, junior, St Doulough's Park
Fenton Hort, Leopardstown
Thomas Young Prior, Mount Dillon, Roebuck
Hugh Barton, Straffan House
Baron de Robeck, Gowran, Naas
Edward Tickell, Carnolway, Co. Kildare
James Anthony Corballis, Ratoath Manor
Charles William Hamilton, Hamwood
Isaac Ambrose Eccles, Co. Wicklow
John Oliver, Co. Wicklow
Reverend William Wakely, Edenderry
Robert Clayton Browne, Co. Carlow
Francis Leigh, Rosegarland, New Ross
John Charles Lyons, Ledestown, Mullingar
George Marmaduke Forster, Carrickmacross
Gonville ffrench, Co. Roscommon
George Tuthill, Kilmore, Co. Limerick
John Boyd, Letterkenny, RDS vice-president

Academics (3)
Reverend Richard MacDonnell, FTCD
Reverend Stephen Creagh Sandes, FTCD
Reverend Edward Geoghegan, Hume Street
    school

Clergy (4)
Reverend William Handcock, Clontarf
Reverend E.G. Hudson, dean of Armagh
Reverend Edward George
Reverend James Duncan Longe

Army officers (3)
Captain Richard Dunne, Sackville Street
William Parsons Hoey, United Services Club
John Atkinson, army agent

Government and municipal officials (9)
Sir William Betham, Ulster king at arms
J.T. Kane, wide streets commission
Thomas Rodney Purdon, Richmond prison
Sir Edward Stanley, prisons inspector
John Hughes, secretary barrack board
Leonard Thornhill, ordnance office
Thomas Connolly, revenue comptroller
James McAskey, customs and excise
John Turner Cooper, stamp office

Dublin Corporation (6)
John Smith Fleming, lord mayor 1822–3
Thomas Abbott, lord mayor 1825–6
Ponsonby Shaw, city sheriff 1828–9
Patrick Thomas Flood, city sheriff 1828–9
Drury Jones Dickenson [*sic*], city sheriff
    1833–4
George Archer, town clerk

Medicine and science (15)
William O'Brien Bellingham, surgeon
John Hart, professor RCSI
Robert Moore Peile, surgeon
Alexander Read, surgeon
William Wilson, surgeon
Dr William Crofton Beatty
Dr Thomas Clarke
Dr Charles Percival Croker
Dr Henry Darley

Medicine and science (15) (cont.)
Dr Hugh Ferguson, Cow Pock institution
Dr William Harty, Finglas asylum
Dr John Francis O'Neill Lentaigne, Tallaght
Dr David Hastings McAdam, Killucan
Dr Michael Martin O'Grady, Malahide
Dr Thomas Herbert Orpen

Engineers and architects (2)
Frederick Darley, junior, architect
David Joseph Henry, canal engineer

Banking and insurance (2)
Patrick Curtis, Hibernian insurance
Charles Haliday, Bank of Ireland

Commerce and manufacturing (25)
Simeon Boileau, druggist
Robert Fannin, junior
Richard Corballis, timber merchant
Edward Croker, corn merchant
James Haughton, flour merchant
William Haughton, flour merchant
Leland Crosthwaite, junior, textiles
Garret Wall, woollen manufacturer
William Willans, woollen manufacturer
Thomas Farrell, brewer
William Sweetman, brewer
George Roe, distiller
Thomas Laffan Kelly, wine merchant
Joseph Pasley, wine merchant
Bartholomew Moliere Tabuteau
Simon Foot, Grand Canal Company
Henry Roe, railway company director
William Rotheram, soap manufacturer
Robert Hutton, coach bulder
Thomas Hutton, coach builder
George Howell, army clothier
Alexander Johnston, newspaper agent
James Callwell, general merchant
Thomas Long, general merchant
William Walsh, general merchant

Judiciary and lawyers (39)
John Anster, law professor, TCD
William Thomas Barlow, ecclesiastical courts
Edward Tierney, crown solicitor

Thomas Abbott, junior, barrister
Henry Adair, barrister
John Robert Boyd, barrister
George Bruce, barrister
Robert B. Bryan, RDS honorary secretary
Henry Carey, barrister
Edward R.P. Colles, barrister
John Richard Corballis, barrister
William Henry Curran, barrister
William Fletcher, barrister
Arthur French, barrister
George Blake Hickson, barrister
Brindley Hone, barrister
George Kelly, barrister
William Thomas Lloyd, barrister
William McKay, barrister
Henry William Mulvany, barrister
Richard John Orpen, barrister
Walter Sweetman, barrister
Theobald Billing, attorney
George Connor, attorney
Yelverton Dawson, attorney
John Swift Emerson, attorney
Joseph Farran, attorney
George Fearon, attorney
Arthur Hill Griffith, attorney
John Hare, attorney
Richard Hemphill, attorney
Joseph Hone, attorney
Joseph Hone, junior, attorney
William Houghton, attorney
Benjamin Bowen Johnson, attorney
William Todderick Kent, attorney
Andrew Christopher Palles, attorney
Charles M. Stack, attorney
Francis Barlow, solicitor

Other occupations (9)
George Baker, Dublin
Richard Weld Hartstonge, Molesworth Street
Henry Maning, Royal Irish Art Institution
William Morgan, Shanagolden
Samuel Morris, Fortview, Clontarf
James O'Farrell, Kingstown
Henry Smith, William Street
William Meade Smyth, Drogheda
Isaac Weld, RDS honorary secretary

RDS annual operating costs, 1818–21

payments (Irish £s)	1818 £	1819 £	1820 £	1821 £
rents, rates, taxes, and insurance				
Leinster House and Glasnevin	1562	1823	1811	1396
Hawkins Street	731	986	634	59
repairs and maintenance				
Leinster House and Glasnevin	840	729	495	328
Hawkins Street	34	13	0	0
light and heat	225	242	251	217
salaries, wages and labour costs				
salaries, gratuities and pensions	3293	3268	3192	3212
wages, apprentices, work clothes	933	1036	999	956
books, periodicals, and newspapers	524	480	439	425
general operating expenses				
printing, stationery, and advertising	194	257	283	229
botanic garden	99	40	31	107
natural philosophy and museum	33	57	28	69
chemistry and mineralogy	257	397	627	264
art school	46	115	108	96
legal fees, and sundry expenses	13	99	16	8
TOTAL	8784	9542	8914	7366

Source: Compiled from accounts published in *RDS Proc.*, lv–lviii, 1818–22. These accounts were presented on a receipts and payments (i.e. cash flow) basis and are not the same as modern accounts presented on an accruals basis. Nevertheless they do provide an analogue of spending trends at the point where the society's annual grant was cut. Later trends are shown in the text in tables 6.1 and 8.2.

New by-laws creating an RDS executive council

Confirmed by the general meeting on 1 March 1838

'That the management of the business of the Society be confided to a Council, the powers of such Council to be strictly, as hereafter, defined and limited, and subject to the direct control over its proceedings, upon the part of the Society at large, and that the Council and Committees of Management shall consist of, and be formed as follows:–

Standing Committees, each to consist of nine Members, to preside over the following departments, viz. :–

Botany and Horticulture.
Chemistry, with its application to the Useful Arts.
Natural Philosophy and Mechanics.
Natural History, Geology, Mineralogy, and charge of the Museum.
Fine Arts.
Library.
Agriculture and Husbandry.
Manufactures.
Statistics.

'That the powers and duties of the Council shall be as follows:–

1st. That the business of the Society be in future committed to the management of the Council, who shall exercise a general superintendence over the affairs, officers, and servants of the Society, and over every branch of its establishment; and shall have power to make such orders and regulations for the management thereof, as it shall deem necessary or expedient (the same not being contrary to the existing laws of the Society), with such restrictions as are herein-after mentioned, such orders and regulations to be subject to the control of the Society, as herein-after more particularly stated.

2nd. That the House Committee and the Committee of Economy do cease, from and after the appointment of a Council, and that the duties thereof thenceforth shall devolve on the Council. ; That the several other Committees do continue, and transact the business of their respective departments, as heretofore, with such modifications as may hereafter be provided.

3rd. That the several Committees do report their proceedings from time to time to the Council, which reports shall be laid before the Society, at its meetings, by the Council.

4th. That the Council shall have power, at its discretion, to require from each Committee, that the minutes of its proceedings be laid before it: and shall also be empowered to make such references as it shall think proper, to any Committee upon any matters within its department; and the Committee so referred to shall be bound to make a report on the subject of such reference to the Council, who shall be enabled to make such orders or regulations thereon, with the concurrence of the Committee, as it shall deem expedient, the same not being contrary to the existing laws of the Society; which order or regulation shall then be carried into effect; provided that the Council shall make no order or new regulation on any matter within the department of such Committee, without the concurrence of said Committee. Provided also, that if the Council and the Committee of any department shall not concur in any new regulation or order in such department, proposed by the Council, the same shall be referred to the Society, who shall make such order thereon as it shall think proper, which shall be carried into effect by the Council and Committee respectively.

5th. That the Society shall have power and authority to rescind or alter any order or regulation of the Council, of a prospective nature, at the Meeting of the Society next but one after such order or regulation shall have been made; but no order or regulation of the Council shall be altered or rescinded, unless notice of a motion to that effect be given at least seven days before the said Meeting of the Society, at which same may be altered or rescinded; such notice to be given in writing, and signed by the mover, to the Assistant Secretary, to be by him posted in a conspicuous part of the Society's Conversation Room.

6th. That the Council shall hold its meetings weekly, with power to adjourn on public holidays, and at any time in the summer recess, not exceeding three months; and that seven members do constitute a quorum.

7th. That the Council shall cause minutes of all its proceedings to be entered in a book – such book to be accessible to the Members of the Society; and that the Council shall specially report to the Society at each of its Stated General Meetings.

8th. That in case of any emergency requiring an expenditure which could not properly be delayed from one Meeting of the Society to another, the Council be empowered to expend a sum not exceeding £50 on any given object.

9th. That at each Meeting of the Society, the proceedings of the Council, since the preceding Meeting of the Society, be read.

10th. The Council shall have power to make By-laws for its own regulation, provided such By-laws be not opposed or repugnant to the Charter or By-laws, or any express regulation of the Society.

That the several Committees be chosen annually by ballot; the first election of whom shall be made at the first Monthly Meeting of the Society which shall take place next after the confirmation of this By-law; and every future election shall be made on the first Monthly Meeting of the Society in December in each year; that each Committee shall choose its Chairman, who, with one other Member thereof, to be also elected by each Committee respectively, within one week after the election of such Committee, shall be Members of the Council.

That the Council shall consist of the seven Vice-Presidents and two Honorary Secretaries, the Chairman and one other Member of each Committee, to be elected as before stated, and of nine Members (not being Members of any of the standing Committees) to be elected by ballot, by and from the Society at large; such last-mentioned election to be held at the Monthly Meeting which shall next ensue after the election of the Committees as afore-said, seven days previous to which each Committee shall return the names of their Chairman and other Members by them elected to the Council; such lists to be posted in the Society's public room.

That the Vice-Presidents and Honorary Secretaries are to be considered ex-officio Members of each Committee, provided that the Vice-Presidents and Secretaries shall not have the power of voting in the several and respective Committees for the Election of Members of the Council.

That in case any vacancy shall occur in the Council, or in any of the Committees, such vacancy shall be filled up by the same mode of election and by the same body who elected the individual who filled the office so vacant. Such election to be held at the next meeting of the body having such power of election, which shall be held after such vacancy.

That one-fourth of the Council go out annually. This rotation to be effected by requiring that the second Member to be nominated by each Committee shall be a different person from the Member so elected the preceding year.

That besides the Stated General Meetings prescribed by Charter, General Meetings of the Society shall be held on the first Thursday in November, the first Thursday in December, and on the last Thursday in each of the other months during the Society's sittings.

Lord Morpeth's propositions, presented to the RDS by letter of 17 December 1840

I.– The Society to consist in future of two Sections, having the House, Library, Theatre, Museums, &c. in common.

1. The object of the one Section to be the promotion of Chemistry, Natural Philosophy, Geology and Mineralogy, Zoology, together with any other kindred branches of useful knowledge.
2. The object of the other Section to be the promotion of Agriculture, Horticulture, and Botany, Manufactures, Fine Arts, Statistics, together with any other kindred branches of useful knowledge.

II.– The Members of each Section to be elected in the manner which is now observed in the Society. But instead of the present payment of £21, the admission fee to be £1, with an annual subscription of £1, or a life composition of £10.

III.–

1. Each Section to elect annually, by ballot, a Council of 23; of whom one to be President, five to be Vice-Presidents, two to be Secretaries, and one to be Treasurer of the Section.
2. Five members of each Council to go out every year, but to be re-eligible after one year.
3. The President to be eligible for two years in succession: but not to be re-eligible till after the interval of a year.
4. Two of the Vice-Presidents to go out of office every year, but to be re-eligible into the Council.
5. Each Council to furnish to its Section at the Annual Meeting a list of persons it would recommend to be elected as the Council for the ensuing year.

IV.–Each Council to manage the affairs of the Section, and appoint all paid officers and servants exclusively attached to the Section, subject to the approval of the Members of the Annual Meeting.

V.–Each Council to subdivide itself into as many Committees as it has distinct objects, and to have power to add three Members of the Section to each Committee, if deemed necessary.

VI– Each Council to contribute an equal number of its Members to form a General Committee for the management of the House, Library, &c., &c., and the appointment of all its paid officers and servants attached to the Society at large.

VII.–

1. The Parliamentary Grant to be divided between the Sections by the Treasury, in proportion to the amount of the subscriptions.
2. Each Council to apportion its share amongst its Committees.
3. Each Council to make an Annual Report of its proceedings, and to include in it a detailed statement of its expenditure.

VIII.–

1. Each Section to meet annually to receive the Report of its Council for the past year; to elect the Council for the ensuing year, and to transact any other general business.
2. No other meeting of the Section for general business to take place, except on the requisition of at least thirty Members.
3. Each Section to meet for scientific or other instructive purposes, and for the election of Members, as often as it may think advisable.
4. No motion affecting the constitution or general interests of the Section or Society to be made at the Annual or any Special General Meeting, except upon a month's previous notice in writing.
5. If the two Sections do not agree upon any matter of common interest, the question to be decided by the majority of voices upon a union of the Sections.

IX.– No News-room or Newspaper to be permitted in the House of the Society.

Bibliography

PRIMARY SOURCES

MANUSCRIPT SOURCES

Royal Dublin Society archive, Ballsbridge, Dublin
Council minute book 1838–44.
Economy committee minute book 1829–38.
House committee minute book 1820–37.
House committee rough book 1828–38.
Botany committee minute book 1816–34.
Botany committee minute book 1834–45.
Fine Arts committee rough book 1833–9.
Manufactures committee minute book 1829–38.
Natural Philosophy committee minute book 1816–59.
Chemistry committee minute book 1817–52.
General selected committee minute book 1832–8.
Royal Agricultural Society of Ireland council minute book, 1841–6.

National Archives of Ireland, Bishop Street, Dublin
Chief Secretary's Office, registered papers, MSS 1835 B23/3073/3/611, MSS 1835 B29/4101/
2/611, MSS 1836 B5/229/3/612, MSS 1838 288/07/3/614/41.

National Library of Ireland, Kildare Street, Dublin
William Smith O'Brien papers (MSS 22.389) POS 8401 read on micro-film.

Dublin Diocesan Archives, Clonliffe
Archbishop Daniel Murray papers, miscellaneous correspondence, MSS AB3/31/3–4.

Royal Irish Academy, Dawson Street
Irish Confederation minute book 1847–8, MS 23/H/43.

PRINTED SOURCES

Royal Dublin Society
Proceedings of the Royal Dublin Society, iv–ciii, 1767–1867.
The charters and statutes of the Royal Dublin Society (Dublin, 1989 ed.).

Newspapers and magazines
Dublin University Magazine, i–xv, 1833–45.
Freeman's Journal, 1829, 1831–2, 1834–9, 1841.
Freeman's Journal 1840–5 (read on micro-film in N.U.I.M.).

Parliamentary papers
Estimates of miscellaneous services, 1829, HC (read on micro-film in N.U.I.M.).
Report from the select committee on the state of Ireland, HC, 1830 (read on micro-film in N.U.I.M.).
Estimates of miscellaneous services, 1832, HC (read on micro-film in N.U.I.M.).
Report from the select committee on the state of Ireland, HC, 1832 (read on micro-film in N.U.I.M.).
Report from the select committee on the Royal Dublin Society, HC, 1836 (445), xli.
Report from the select committee on scientific institutions (Dublin), HC, 1864 (495).
The statutes at large passed in the parliament held in Ireland, xx, 1800.

Contemporary printed sources

Barrington, Sir Jonah, *Personal sketches of his own times*, ii (3rd ed.; London, 1869).

Cloncurry, Lord Valentine, *Personal recollections of the life and times with extracts from the correspondence, of Valentine Lord Cloncurry* (Dublin, 1849).

Drummond, William H. (ed.), *The autobiography of Archibald Hamilton Rowan* (Dublin, 1840; reprint 1972 with introduction by R.B. McDowell).

Fitzpatrick, W.J., *Irish wits and worthies: including Dr. Lanigan, his life and times* (Dublin, 1873).

Gilbert, John T., *Documents relating to Ireland, 1795–1804* (Dublin, 1893).

Grattan, Henry, *Memoirs of the life and times of the Rt. Hon. Henry Grattan*, v (London, 1846).

Gregory, Augusta (ed.), *Mr. Gregory's letter-box, 1813–1830* (London, 1898).

Hansard, parliamentary debates, 3rd series, 1836, 1840–2.

[Harty, William] *Analysis of the report and epitome of the evidence taken before a select committee of the house of commons in the session of 1836, on the Royal Dublin Society: together with notes and illustrations by a member of the society* (Dublin, 1836).

Haughton, Samuel, *Memoir of James Haughton* (Dublin, 1877).

Mant, Richard, *History of the Church of Ireland*, ii (London, 1840).

MacDermot, Brian (ed.), *The Irish catholic petition of 1805: the diary of Denys Scully* (Dublin, 1992).

McLennan, John F., *Memoir of Thomas Drummond* (Edinburgh, 1867).

Morgan, Sidney, *Lady Morgan's memoirs*, ii (London, 1862).

O'Connell, Maurice R. (ed.), *The correspondence of Daniel O'Connell*, v–vii, 1833–45 (Irish Manuscripts Commission, Dublin, 1978–82).

Porter, Frank Thorpe, *Twenty years recollections of an Irish police magistrate* (9th ed.; Dublin, 1880).

Wyse, Thomas, *Historical sketch of the late Catholic Association of Ireland* (London, 1829).

Contemporary pamphlets

Hamilton, W.H., *State of the Catholic cause, from the issuing of Mr. Pole's circular letter, to the present day* (Dublin, 1812).

Meagher, William, *Notices of the life and character of his grace, Most Rev. Daniel Murray, late archbishop of Dublin: as contained in 'The commemorative oration' pronounced in the Church of the Conception, Dublin, on occasion of his grace's month's mind: with historical and biographical notes* (Dublin, 1853).

Meyler, Anthony, *Irish tranquillity and Mr. O'Connell, my lord Mulgrave, and the Romish priesthood* (Dublin, 1838).

— *Speech delivered by Doctor Meyler, at the great meeting of the Irish Metropolitan Conservative Society, assembled in Dawson-street, April 8th, 1839, on a petition to the House of Commons, praying that the annual grant hitherto voted to the Roman Catholic College at Maynooth may be discontinued* (Dublin, 1839).

— *The address of the Metropolitan Conservative Society of Ireland to the Protestants of Great Britain, along with the speech delivered by Doctor Meyler, on submitting it for their adoption* (Dublin, 1840).

Reference works, directories

Bence-Jones, Mark, *A guide to Irish country houses* (2nd rev. ed., London, 1990).

Bennett, Douglas, *Encyclopedia of Dublin* (Dublin, 1991).

Burke, Sir Bernard *Dictionary of the landed gentry of Great Britain and Ireland* (London, 1858).

Burke, Sir Bernard (ed.), *History of the landed gentry of Great Britain and Ireland*, ii (8th ed., London, 1894).

— *History of the landed gentry of Great Britain and Ireland*, ii (9th ed., London, 1898).

Burke, Ashworth P. (ed.), *The landed gentry of Ireland* (10th ed., London, 1904).

Burke, Sir Bernard, and A.P. Burke (eds), *A genealogical and heraldic history of the peerage and baronetage, the privy council and knightage* (London, 1910).

— *A genealogical and heraldic history of the peerage and baronetage, the privy council and knightage* (85th ed., London, 1927).

Pine, L.G. (ed.), *Burke's genealogical and heraldic history of the landed gentry of Ireland* (London, 1958).

— *The new extinct peerage, 1884–1971* (London, 1972).

— *Burke's Irish family records* (London, 1976).

Connolly, S.J. (ed.), *The Oxford companion to Irish history* (Oxford, 1998).

Crone, John S., *A concise dictionary of Irish biography* (Dublin, 1928).

De Burgh, U.H. Hussey, *The landowners of Ireland* (Dublin, 1878).

Dictionary of national biography, i–xx (Oxford, 1921–2).

Ellis, Eilish, and P. Beryl Eustace (eds), *Registry of Deeds, Dublin, abstracts of wills*, iii, 1785–1832 (Irish Manuscripts Commission, Dublin, 1984).

Harrison, Richard S., *A biographical dictionary of Irish Quakers* (Dublin, 1997).

Keane, Edward, Phair, P. Beryl, and Sadleir, Thomas, *King's Inns admission papers, 1607–1867* (Irish Manuscripts Commission, Dublin, 1982).

McCready, C.T., *Dublin street names dated and explained* (Dublin, 1892; reprint 1987).

The formation of the Orange Order, 1795–1798, edited papers of William Blacker and Robert H. Wallace (Belfast, 1994).

Osborough, W.N. (ed.), *The Irish statutes 1310–1800* (London, 1885; reprint 1995).

Ryan, Christopher (ed.), *Lewis' Dublin: a topographical dictionary of the parishes, towns and villages of Dublin city and county* (Cork 2001).

Slater, I., *National commercial directory of Ireland* (Dublin, 1846).

Somerville-Large, Peter, *Irish eccentrics: a selection* (London, 1975).

— *The Irish country house: a social history* (London, 1995).

Walker, Brian M. (ed.), *Parliamentary election results in Ireland, 1801–1922* (Dublin, 1978).

Stewart, Watson, *The Treble Almanack* (Dublin, var. dates), 1799–1829.

Thom's Dublin directory, var. dates.

Webb, Alfred, *A compendium of Irish biography* (Dublin, 1878).

White, James, and Kevin Bright, *Treasures of the Royal Dublin Society: a summary catalogue of the works of art in the collection of the Royal Dublin Society* (Dublin, 1998).

Wills, James, *Lives of illustrious and distinguished Irishmen, from the earliest times to the present period, arranged in chronological order, and embodying a history of Ireland in the lives of Irishmen*, vi (Edinburgh, 1847).

Willemson, Gitta, *The Dublin Society drawing schools: students and award winners, 1746–1876* (Dublin, 2000).

SECONDARY SOURCES

General histories

Anderson, M.S., i (2nd ed.; New York, 1985).

Colley, Linda, *Britons: forging the nation, 1707–1837* (London, 1996 ed.).

Foster, R.F., *Modern Ireland, 1600–1972* (London, 1988).

Hobsbawm, E.J., *The age of revolution: Europe, 1789–1848* (London, 1962; reprint 1997).

— *The age of capital, 1848–1875* (London, 1975; reprint 1992).

— *Nations and nationalism since 1780: programme, myth, reality* (2nd ed., Cambridge, 1992).

Howe, Stephen, *Ireland and empire: colonial legacies in Irish history and culture* (Oxford, 2000).

Kennedy, Paul, *The rise and fall of British naval mastery* (London, 1976).

Stewart, A.T.Q. *The narrow ground: aspects of Ulster, 1609–1969* (Belfast, 1997 ed.).

Vaughan, W.E. (ed.), *A new history of Ireland*, v, *Ireland under the union, 1801–70* (Oxford, 1989).

British politics and administration

Anglesey, Marquess of, *One-leg: the life and letters of Henry William Paget, first marquess of Anglesey, K.G., 1768–1854* (London, 1961).

Chester, Sir Norman, *The English administrative system, 1780–1870* (Oxford, 1981).

Evans, Eric J., *The great reform act of 1832* (2nd ed., London, 1994).

Gash, Norman (ed.), *The age of Peel. documents of modern history* (London, 1968).

Hibbert, Christopher, *Wellington: a personal history* (London, 1997).

MacDonagh, Oliver, *Early Victorian government, 1830–1870* (London, 1977).
Parry, Jonathan, *The rise and fall of liberal government in Victorian Britain* (New Haven, 1993).
Thomson, David, *England in the nineteenth century, 1815–1914* (London, 1950).
Webb, R.K., *Modern England: from the eighteenth century to the present* (2nd ed., London, 1980).

Irish politics and society

Beames, Michael, *Peasants and power: the Whiteboy movements and their control in pre-Famine Ireland* (Brighton, 1983).
Blackstock, Allan, *An ascendancy army: the Irish yeomanry, 1796–1834* (Dublin, 1998).
Bolton, G.C., *The passing of the Irish act of union: a study in parliamentary politics* (Oxford, 1966).
Boyce, D. George, *Nineteenth-century Ireland: the search for stability* (Dublin, 1990).
Boyce, D. George, and Alan O'Day (eds), *The making of modern Irish history: revisionism and the revisionist controversy* (London, 1996).
Broeker, Galen, *Rural disorder and police reform in Ireland, 1812–36* (London, 1970).
Brynn, Edward, *Crown and Castle: British rule in Ireland, 1800–30* (Dublin, 1978).
Crossman, Virginia, *Local government in nineteenth-century Ireland* (Belfast, 1994).
— *Politics, law and order in nineteenth-entury Ireland* (Dublin, 1996).
Daly, Mary E., *The famine in Ireland* (Dundalk, 1986).
Davis, Richard, *The Young Ireland movement* (Dublin, 1987).
— *Revolutionary imperialist: William Smith O'Brien 1803–64* (Dublin, 1998).
Dickson, David, *New foundations: Ireland 1660–1800* (2nd ed., Dublin, 2000).
Dickson, David, Daire Keogh, and Kevin Whelan, (eds), *The United Irishmen: republicanism, radicalism and rebellion* (Dublin, 1993).
Elliott, Marianne, *The catholics of Ulster: a history* (London, 2000).
Fagan, Patrick, 'Infiltration of Dublin freemason lodges by united Irishmen and other republican groups', in *Eighteenth-century Ireland*, xiii, 1998.
Geoghegan, Patrick M., *The Irish act of union: a study in high politics, 1798–1801* (Dublin, 1999).
Graham, A.H., 'The Lichfield House compact, 1835', in *Irish Historical Studies*, xii, 1960–1.
Haddick-Flynn, Kevin, *Orangeism: the making of a tradition* (Dublin, 1999).
Hill, J. R., 'The politics of privilege: Dublin Corporation and the catholic question, 1792–1823', in *Maynooth Review*, vii, December 1982.
Hoppen, K. Theodore, *Elections, politics, and society in Ireland, 1832–1885* (Oxford, 1984).
— *Ireland since 1800: conflict and conformity* (2nd ed., London, 1999).
James, Francis G., *Lords of the ascendancy: the Irish house of lords and its members, 1600–1800* (Dublin, 1995).
Kerr, Donal A., *Peel, priests, and politics: Sir Robert Peel's administration and the Roman Catholic church in Ireland, 1841–1846* (New York, 1982).
— *A nation of beggars: priests, people, and politics in famine Ireland, 1846–1852* (Oxford, 1994).
Lynam, Shevawn, *Humanity Dick Martin 'King of Connemara' 1754–1834* (Dublin, 1989 ed.).
Lyons, F.S.L., and R.A.J. Hawkins (eds), *Ireland under the union: varieties of tension* (Oxford, 1980).
Magan, William, *Ummamore: the story of an Irish family* (2nd ed., London, 1985).
McCartney, Donal, *The dawning of democracy: Ireland, 1800–70* (Dublin, 1987).
Malcolm, Elizabeth, *'Ireland sober Ireland free': drink and temperance in nineteenth-century Ireland* (London, 1986).
McAnally, Sir Henry, *The Irish militia, 1793–1816: a social and military study* (London, 1949).
MacDonagh, Oliver, *The emancipist: Daniel O'Connell, 1830–1847* (London, 1989).
McDowell, R. B., *Public opinion and government policy in Ireland, 1801–1846* (London, 1957).
— (ed.), *Social life in Ireland, 1800–45* (Dublin, 1957).
Molony, John Neylon, *A soul came into Ireland: Thomas Davis, 1814–1845, a biography* (Dublin, 1995).
Nowlan, Kevin B., *The politics of repeal: a study in the relations between Great Britain and Ireland, 1841–50* (London, 1965).
O'Brien, Gerard (ed.), *Parliament, politics, and people: essays in eighteenth-century Irish history* (Dublin, 1989).
O'Brien, Grania, *These my friends and forebears: the O'Brien's of Dromoland* (Whitegate, 1991).

O Broin, Leon, *The unfortunate Mr Robert Emmet* (Dublin, 1958).
O'Donnell, Ruan, *Aftermath: post-rebellion insurgency in Wicklow, 1799–1803* (Dublin, 2000).
O'Faolain, Sean, *King of the beggars: a life of Daniel O'Connell* (Dublin, 1980 ed.).
O'Ferrall, Fergus, *Catholic emancipation: Daniel O'Connell and the birth of Irish democracy, 1820–30* (Dublin, 1985).
O Tuathaigh, Gearoid, *Ireland before the famine, 1798–1848* (Dublin, 1990).
— *Thomas Drummond and the government of Ireland, 1835–41* (Galway, 1977).
Pakenham, Thomas, *The year of liberty: the great Irish rebellion of 1798* (London, 1969).
Robins, Joseph, *Champagne and silver buckles: the viceregal court at Dublin Castle, 1700–1922* (Dublin, 2001).
Senior, Hereward, *Orangeism in Ireland and Britain, 1795–1836* (Toronto, 1966).
Thornley, David, *Isaac Butt and home rule* (London, 1964).
Tillyard, Stella, *Citizen lord: Edward Fitzgerald, 1763–1798* (London, 1998).
Trench, William Chenevix, *Grace's card: Irish catholic landlords, 1690–1800* (Cork, 1997).
Whelan, Kevin, *The tree of liberty: radicalism, catholicism and the construction of Irish identity, 1760–1830* (Cork, 1996).

Dublin
Brady, Joseph, and Anngret Simms (eds), *Dublin through space and time: c.900–1900* (Dublin, 2001).
Campion, Mary, 'Dublin textile industry', in *Dublin Historical Record*, xviii, 1962.
Craig, Maurice, *Dublin, 1660–1860* (rev. ed., London, 1992).
Cullen, L.M., *Princes and pirates: the Dublin Chamber of Commerce, 1783–1983* (Dublin, 1983).
Daly, Mary E., *Dublin the deposed capital: a social and economic history, 1860–1914* (Cork, 1985).
Dickson, David (ed.), *The gorgeous mask: Dublin, 1700–1850* (Dublin, 1987).
Hill, Jacqueline, *From patriots to unionists: Dublin civic politics and Irish protestant patriotism, 1660–1840* (Oxford, 1997).
Maxwell, Constantia, *Dublin under the Georges, 1714–1830* (London, rev. ed. 1956).
Smith, Cornelius F., and Bernard Share (eds), *Whigs on the green* (Dublin, 1990).

Irish economy
Barrow, G.L., *The emergence of the Irish banking system, 1820–45* (Dublin, 1975).
Bourke, Austin, *The visitation of God: the potato and the great Irish famine* (Dublin, 1993).
Carr, Peter, *The night of the big wind* (2nd ed., Belfast, 1994).
Clarke, Desmond, *Thomas Prior, 1681–1751: founder of the Royal Dublin Society* (Dublin, 1951).
Cullen, L.M., *An economic history of Ireland since 1660* (2nd ed.; London, 1987).
— *The emergence of modern Ireland, 1600–1900* (New York, 1981).
Curran, P.L., *Kerry and Dexter cattle and other ancient Irish breeds: a history* (Dublin, 1990).
Delany, Ruth, *The Grand Canal of Ireland* (Dublin, 1995).
Gill, Conrad, *The rise of the Irish linen industry* (Oxford, 1925).
Guinness, Michele, *The Guinness legend* (London, 1989).
Hall, F.G., *The Bank of Ireland, 1783–1946* (Dublin, 1949).
Harrison, Richard S., *Irish insurance: historical perspectives, 1650–1939* (Cork, 1992).
Inglis, Brian, *Freedom of the press in Ireland, 1784–1841* (London, 1954).
Jones, Winston Guthrie, *The Wynnes of Sligo and Leitrim* (Manorhamilton, 1994).
Kinane, Vincent, *A history of the Dublin University Press, 1734–1976* (Dublin, 1994).
Kinealy, Christine, *This great calamity: the Irish famine, 1845–52* (Dublin, 1994).
Leonard, Hugh, 'A reflection on the origin of the Irish horse' in *RDS Horse Show official programme 2000*.
Maguire, W.A., *The Downshire estates in Ireland, 1801–45: the management of Irish landed estates in the early nineteenth century* (Oxford, 1972).
Milne, Kenneth, *A history of the Royal Bank of Ireland* (Dublin, 1964).
O'Donovan, John, *The economic history of Irish livestock* (Dublin, 1940).
Wilson, Derek, *Dark and light: the story of the Guinness family* (London, 1998).

Religion

Akenson, Donald Harman, *The Church of Ireland: ecclesiastical reform and revolution, 1800–85* (New Haven, 1971).

— *A protestant in purgatory: Richard Whately, Archbishop of Dublin* (South Bend, 1981).

Andrews, Hilary, *Lion of the west: a biography of John MacHale* (Dublin, 2001).

Bland, F.E., *How the Church Missionary Society came to Ireland* (Dublin, 1935).

Bowen, Desmond, *The protestant crusade in Ireland, 1800–70: a study of protestant-catholic relations between the act of union and disestablishment* (Dublin, 1978).

Comerford, R.V., Mary Cullen, Jacqueline Hill, and Colm Leonard (eds), *Religion, conflict and coexistence in Ireland* (Dublin, 1990).

Connolly, S.J., *Priests and people in pre-famine Ireland, 1780–1845* (Dublin, 1982).

Leighton, C.D.A., *Catholicism in a Protestant kingdom: a study of the Irish ancien regime* (Dublin, 1994).

Phillips, Walter Alison, *History of the Church of Ireland: from the earliest times to the present day*, iii, *The modern church* (London, 1933).

Wigham, Maurice J., *The Irish Quakers: a short history of the Religious Society of Friends in Ireland* Dublin, 1992).

Law

Ball, F. Elrington, *The judges in Ireland, 1221–1921*, ii (Dublin, 1926).

Day, Ella B., *Mr. Justice Day of Kerry, 1745–1841: a discursive memoir* (Exeter, 1938).

Hammond, Joseph W., 'Town Major Henry Charles Sirr', in *Dublin Historical Record*, iv, 1941–2.

Hogan, Daire, *The legal profession in Ireland, 1789–1922* (Dublin, 1986).

Somerville, Edith, and Martin Ross, *An incorruptible Irishman: being an account of chief justice Charles Kendal Bushe, and of his wife, Nancy Crampton, and their times, 1767–1843* (London, 1932).

Education, science, and art

Akenson, Donald Harman, *The Irish education experiment: the national system of education in the nineteenth century* (London, 1970).

Andrews, J.H., *A paper landscape: the ordnance survey in nineteenth-century Ireland* (2nd ed., Dublin, 2001).

Berry, Henry Fitzpatrick, *A history of the Royal Dublin Society* (London, 1915).

Bowler, Peter J., and Whyte, Nicholas (eds), *Science and society in Ireland: the social context of science and technology in Ireland, 1800–1950* (Belfast, 1997).

Davies, G.L. Herries, and R.C. Mollan, (eds), *Richard Griffith, 1784–1878* (Dublin, 1980).

Foster, John Wilson (ed.), *Nature in Ireland: a scientific and cultural history* (Dublin, 1997).

Jarrell, R. A., 'The department of science and art and control of Irish science, 1853–1905' in *Irish Historical Studies*, xiii, 1983.

Maxwell, Constantia, *A history of Trinity College Dublin, 1591–1892* (Dublin, 1946).

McDowell, R.B., and D.A. Webb, *Trinity College Dublin, 1592–1952: an academic history* (Cork, 1982).

Meenan, James, and Desmond Clarke (eds), *The Royal Dublin Society, 1731–1981* (Dublin, 1981).

Mollan, R.C., W. Davis and B. Finucane, (eds), *Some people and places in Irish science and technology* (Dublin, 1985).

— *More people and places in Irish science and technology* (Dublin, 1990).

Morrell, J., and Thackray, A., *Gentlemen of science: early years of the British Association for the Advancement of Science* (Oxford, 1981).

Nelson, E.C., and E.M. McCracken, *The brightest jewel: a history of the National Botanic Gardens, Glasnevin* (Dublin, 1987).

Nevin, Monica, 'General Charles Vallancey, 1725–1812' in *Journal of the Royal Society of Antiquaries of Ireland*, cxxiii, 1993.

O Cairbre, Fiacre, 'William Rowan Hamilton (1805–1865): Ireland's greatest mathematician' in *Riocht na Midhe*, xi, 2000.

O'Donnell, Sean, *William Rowan Hamilton: portrait of a prodigy* (Dublin, 1983).

O Raifeartaigh, T. (ed.), *The Royal Irish Academy, 1785–1985* (Dublin, 1985).

Sobel, Dava, *Longitude* (London, 1996).
Turpin, John, *A school of art in Dublin in the eighteenth century: a history of the National College of Art and Design* (Dublin, 1995).
White, Henry Bantry, 'History of the science and art institutions, Dublin', in *Museum Bulletin*, i, 1911.
White, Terence de Vere, *The story of the Royal Dublin Society* (Tralee, 1955).

Medicine
Cameron, Sir Charles A., *History of the Royal College of Surgeons in Ireland, and of the Irish schools of medicine* (2nd ed., Dublin, 1916).
Coakley, Davis, *Irish masters of medicine* (Dublin, 1992).
Lyons, J.B., *The quality of Mercer's: the story of Mercer's hospital, 1734–1991* (Dublin, 1991).
Malcolm, Elizabeth, and Jones, Greta (eds), *Medicine, disease and the state in Ireland, 1650–1940* (Cork, 1999).
Malcolm, Elizabeth, *Swift's hospital: a history of St Patrick's hospital, Dublin, 1746–1989* (Dublin, 1989).
O'Brien, Eoin, *Conscience and conflict: a biography of Sir Dominic Corrigan, 1802–1880* (Dublin, 1983).
Robins, Joseph, *The miasma: epidemic and panic in nineteenth century Ireland* (Dublin, 1995).
Widdess, J.D.H., *A history of the Royal College of Physicians of Ireland, 1654–1963* (Edinburgh, 1963).

Local histories
Batt, Elisabeth, The *Moncks and Charleville House: a Wicklow family in the nineteenth century* (Dublin, 1979).
Carty, Mary-Rose, *History of Killeen castle* (Dunsany, 1991).
Cullen, Seamus, and Hermann Geissel, *Fugitive warfare: 1798 in north Kildare* (Kilcock, 1998).
Handcock, William Domville, *The history and antiquities of Tallaght* (2nd ed. 1899; reprint, Dun Laoghaire, 1991).
Jackson, Victor, *The monuments in St Patrick's Cathedral Dublin* (Dublin, 1987).
Joyce, Weston St John, *The neighbourhood of Dublin* (Dublin, 1912; reprint 1994).
Kavanagh, Art, and Rory Murphy, *The Wexford gentry*, i (Bunclody, 1994).
Lyons, John, *Louisburgh: a history* (Louisburgh, 1995).
Parkinson, D., 'Note on Corballis family', in *Dublin Historical Record*, xlv, 1992.
Rice, Gerard, *Norman Kilcloon, 1171–1700* (Dublin, 2001).
Rochfort, James, *The Rochforts* (Naas, 2000).
Steele, John Haughton, *Genealogy of the earls of Erne* (Edinburgh, 1910).
Whelan, Kevin (ed.), *Wexford: history and society* (Dublin, 1987).
Ball, Francis Elrington, and Everard Hamilton, *The parish of Taney: a history of Dundrum, near Dublin, and its neighbourhood* (Dublin, 1895).

Index